Through French Windows

Through French Windows

An Introduction to France in the Nineties

James Corbett

Ann Arbor

THE UNIVERSITY OF MICHIGAN PRESS

Published in the United States of America by
The University of Michigan Press
Manufactured in the United States of America

2000 1999 1998 1997 7 6 5 4

A CIP catalogue record for this book is available from the British Library.

Library of Congress Cataloging-in-Publication Data

Corbett, James, 1942–
Through French windows : an introduction to France in the nineties / James Corbett.
p. cm.
Includes bibliographical references and index.
ISBN 0-472-09469-6 (alk. paper). — ISBN 0-472-06469-X (pbk. : alk. paper)
1. France—Civilization—20th century. 2. France—Cultural policy—History—20th century. 3. France—Politics and government—1981– 4. France—Social conditions—1945– I. Title.
DC33.7.C597 1994
994.083′9—dc20 93-41808
CIP

For Georgette, Isabelle, and Yann

Acknowledgments

Grateful acknowledgment is made to the following:

Groupe Bouygues for permission to reproduce the photograph of L'Arche de la Défense (cover).

Mino Music, on behalf of Renaud Séchan, for permission to print my translation of the excerpt from Hexagone. Copyright. © Mino Music.

Editions Bernard Barrault et Eugénie S.A. on behalf of Michel Raby for permission to reproduce the drawing by Michel Raby (fig. 1) from Guy Nevers, *Les français vu par les Français* (Paris: Barrault, 1985). Copyright © 1985.

Les Editions Albert René for permission to reproduce the drawing of Astérix (fig. 3). Copyright © Les Editions Albert René.

Pancho, for permission to reproduce his drawings (figs. 5 and 17). Copyright © Pancho 1989 and 1988.

SNCF for permission to reproduce the map of the high-speed European rail network of the future (fig. 6). Copyright © SNCF.

JRG Editions on behalf of Jean-Jacques Goldman for permission to print my translation of Elle a fait un bébé toute seule. Copyright. © JRG Editions.

INSEE for permission to reproduce information on social security benefits (fig. 13). Copyright © INSEE 1990.

Pessin for permission to reproduce his drawing (fig. 14). Copyright © Pessin 1990.

Plantu for permission to reproduce his drawings (figs. 16, 21, and 27). Copyright © Plantu 1989, 1988, and 1990.

DATAR for permission to reproduce the figure on the axes of European development (fig. 23).

Editions Jean-Claude Lattès, on behalf of Alain Schifrès, for permission to translate and print excerpts from Alain Schifrès, *Les Parisiens* (Paris: J.C. Lattès, 1990), 36, 381.

The New York Times Syndication Sales Corporation for permission to reproduce the following illustrations: How social security is financed (fig. 15) from *Le Monde Dossiers et Documents,* February 1988; L'Hexagone nucléaire (fig. 26) from *Le Monde Dossiers et Documents,* June 1990; Japan, the United States and Europe from (fig. 28) *Le Monde: Bilan Economique et Social 1988* and the excerpt

"Hullo Trouble" by Claude Sarraute from *Le Monde,* 13 May 1989. Copyright © The New York Times Syndication Sales Corporation.

Les Editions du Seuil for permission to reproduce my translation of the excerpt "Peasants, Ruralists, and City People" from Annie Moulin, *Les Paysans dans la société française.* Copyright © Editions du Seuil, 1988.

Les Editions Flammarion for permission to reproduce my translation of the excerpt "Liberty versus reason" from Armand Frémont, *France: Géographie d'une société.* Copyright © Flammarion 1988.

Contents

Introduction

In an article in the *French Review* in 1988, Eugene F. Gray questioned "the teaching of French civilization in American schools and the image of France generated in the minds of the students as a result of that teaching."

> Civilization classes stress the cultural heritage of France, because this rich and varied heritage has contributed so much to Western culture. As a result many students derive a totally outmoded image of France. To be sure, France is filled with old churches, crenellated castles, country mansions, and other historical monuments; to be sure one encounters French people on bicycles. But not a few French people now live in modern housing in a suburb and commute to work by automobile. . . . The true France is much more complex, much more modern, than the impression transmitted by many of the illustrations in textbooks on French civilization, generating some surprise on the part of students visiting France for the first time.

After describing a number of French technological breakthroughs, Professor Gray concluded: "A new image of France is in the making. Let us hope that it will be reflected in classes of French civilization."[1]

A survey published in March 1991 by the French-American Foundation in New York would seem to confirm Professor Gray's estimate of the American view of France.[2] The poll showed that Americans rated France high for culture, fine wines, and fashion and low for technology. Only a quarter of the respondents perceived France as a leader in telecommunications, and even fewer saw it as occupying a prominent position

1. Eugene F. Gray, "Technology and the Teaching of French Civilization: La Télématique," *French Review* 61 (1988): 504–8.

2. Gallup-Harris poll published by the French-American Foundation (New York, 7 March 1991). See "Comment Français et Américains se voient," *Le Monde*, 9 March 1991.

in nuclear energy and aerospace. This survey also showed that the French rated the United States high for technology and low for culture. Jacques Portes, professor of American civilization at the University of Lille, noted that such opinions were commonplace one hundred years ago and wondered why they persist, since both French and American societies have changed enormously in the interval. "It is absurd," he said, "to be content with these global, simplifying views, even if there may be some slight truth in them." He concluded pessimistically that mentalities are slow to change and that "understanding between nations is often nothing more than a vain wish."[3]

The United States should not be singled out for the way in which France is portrayed in American classrooms; foreign language education in other parts of the world is not essentially different. Teachers can hardly be blamed for stressing a cultural heritage of France that is part of the image the country has always promoted. However, at a time when an increasing number of programs of study abroad in North America and Europe are addressing—or should be addressing—undergraduates and graduates in the social sciences, as well as those in history and literature, an awareness of issues in contemporary France would permit a better understanding of the French approach to economic, political, and social questions.

Few can deny the importance of familiarity with foreign languages and civilization to world trade today, even if many business schools, particularly in the United States, fail to provide cultural training. It is a commonplace to remark that you can buy in your own language, but you must sell in the language of the buyer. An incalculable number of business deals have been lost and political blunders committed because of a misunderstanding of cultural phenomena in the broad sense.[4]

It is no use proclaiming that the global village has done away with national differences. Even if symbols of American civilization such as blue jeans, fast food, and Coca-Cola can be found worldwide, the values attached to these products vary from one country to another in the same way that Perrier or a baguette has different connotations in New York and in Paris.

Statistical similarities in consumer habits and social trends (e.g., di-

3. Jacques Portes, "France-Etats-Unis: Les idées reçues," *Le Monde*, 22 March 1991.

4. See David A. Ricks, *Big Business Blunders: Mistakes in Multinational Marketing* (Homewood, Ill.: Dow Jones–Irwin, 1983).

vorce rates, contraception, attitudes toward education) often reveal subtle national differences in how issues are perceived, based on the history and shared values of each nation. Why, for example, is the level of environmental consciousness in France one of the lowest in Europe? Why do some countries feel that it is primarily up to the government and industry to concern themselves with environmental protection, while others feel that it is the duty of the average citizen?[5] France, like many countries in Europe, has a high rate of unemployment. Economic considerations apart, why is it so difficult to solve the problem of unemployment in France?[6] These and many other questions may be impossible to appreciate fully without some understanding of national cultural traits.

Further, while English has become something of a lingua franca, the renaissance of cultural and linguistic assertiveness that John Naisbitt predicted in the early 1980s—"The Swedes will become more Swedish, the Chinese more Chinese and the French, God help us, more French"[7]—is very real today (witness the breakup of the Soviet Union and Yugoslavia into ethnic enclaves or, less tragically, the continuing use of nine official languages by the European Community even though the member countries have never been closer to achieving political and monetary union).

Forty years ago Margaret Mead and Rhoda Metraux underlined "the extent to which, as ties become worldwide, local awareness is intensified."

> As our political forms and our technology become more uniform, the significance of national cultural styles becomes greater. The differences among the ways in which Frenchmen and Germans, Englishmen and Italians view human relationships in the family, the community, the nation and the world, become differences to be taken into account in predicting whether an international conference will fail or succeed or in gauging the chances which any international plan has for acceptance.[8]

---

5. See Rudolf Deitert, "How Green Is Europe?" *Europanel Marketing Bulletin*, 1990, 16-19.

6. See chap. 20.

7. John Naisbitt, *Megatrends* (London: Futura, 1984), 76.

8. Margaret Mead and Rhoda Metraux, *Themes in French Culture: A Preface to a Study of French Community* (Stanford: Stanford University Press, 1954), xi.

Whether you are a representative of a sister city, a corporate executive, a journalist, a student, or simply a traveler, it is hard to deny that an understanding of the language, mores, and behavior of foreign nations can help temper culture shock and create a positive impression of you or of the organization you represent. It enables you to pick subjects of conversation likely to interest your host, to steer clear of pitfalls, and to decode attitudes correctly. Apart from these practical considerations, a better appreciation of a country's attitudes and values may enhance the pleasure of reading its literature—and vice versa.

The study of national traits is an extremely hazardous undertaking. There is the constant threat of the oversimplification denounced by Jacques Portes as well as, in the case of France, the danger of overlooking the "anthropological diversity" brilliantly described by researchers Hervé le Bras and Emmanuel Todd.

> Each one of the *pays* (regions) of France represents in fact a culture, in the anthropological sense of the term, that is to say, a way of living and dying, a set of rules defining fundamental human relationships, between parents and children, between men and women, between friends and neighbors. . . . From an anthropological point of view, Brittany, Occitanie, Normandy, Lorraine, Picardy, Vendée, Savoy, and many other provinces are still alive.[9]

Although this book will attempt not to overlook diversity, its aim is something different: to describe objectively the functioning of French society today and to highlight some of the underlying values the people share wherever they live. These values, inherited from a long history of centralized administration, are the counterpoint to anthropological diversity. They help to make France unique. As le Bras and Todd remark, "France, which combines administrative unity and anthropological diversity is a historical exception in Europe, and probably in the world."[10]

The book begins with a description of the land and the people. Some knowledge of the geography of France, often neglected in school texts on French civilization, is absolutely essential for any understanding of the economic history and development of a nation whose identity is

9. Hervé le Bras and Emmanuel Todd, *L'invention de la France* (Paris: Librairie Générale Française, 1981), 7.

10. Le Bras and Todd, *L'invention de la France,* 8.

defined by geography rather than by ethnicity. The shift from an agricultural to a high-tech urban society is described along with the change in life-styles and values that reveal important differences from developments in other Western countries. French education, which plays such a vital role in inculcating the secular value system that is specific to France, is analyzed in detail. The burdensome revolutionary heritage of liberty, equality, and fraternity, which the French still cling to, is covered in the chapters devoted to incomes and wealth, health care, and social security. A description of community life as well as detailed study of the problems of immigration and integration help understand the pattern of social relations in France today. The nature of the institutions of the Fifth Republic and the current political scene are explained, as are the specificities of decentralization *à la française.* An overview of the economy illustrates some of the major changes that have taken place in the last decade and outlines the assets and liabilities of industry and the services today. Unemployment and the demise of worker organizations are shown to follow a pattern different from that in other countries. The plight of farmers and the threat to rural France and its values conclude the chapters devoted to the economy. Finally, the French contribution to the European Community and reaction to U.S. pressure, which is giving rise to a form of Europatriotism, show that the future of France for historical, economic, geographical, and cultural reasons lies in a united Europe. This may attenuate somewhat the famous Gallic singularity but is unlikely to wipe out completely a view of issues that is distinctively French.

The book was written with the needs of the nonspecialist in mind and is based on a seminar I have given for a number of years at the Université Pierre Mendès France in Grenoble to a group of U.S. students spending their Spring semester in France. There is nothing in this book about French literature, music, or the arts. These are admirably dealt with in more scholarly works. Indeed, at the risk of shocking the purists, I have made a deliberate attempt to refer to present-day popular culture, such as movies, television, comic strips, and songs. Though I have not been able to explore every aspect of contemporary culture in detail, I hope the wide range of topics covered will provide clues for understanding modern France and French thought processes.

My hope is to provide basic information that will help readers to prepare for and to profit from work, study, or travel in France. At the same time I have tried to avoid the pitfall of oversimplification that would give a distorted picture. One quickly learns that nothing is simple in France; *Oui, mais* (Yes, but) is a favorite expression.

Through French Windows was inspired by the desire to dispel stereotypes but as work progressed, it became clear to me that to be content with a description of modern France was to replace the old stereotypes with new ones—some of which the French are doing their best to encourage. High-tech France is as limited a description as "France, Mother of Arts." Both tell less than half the story. The traveler who arrives in France with glossy visions of the TGV, Airbus, and Ariane, the wonders of *télécarte,* the miracle of the "green revolution," the new dynamism of corporations, and so on is likely to be bewildered. Modernism and conservatism are the two faces of contemporary France.

While there is no denying the changes in or the achievements of France one has to admit that many things, some good, some bad, have not changed and may never change, so anchored are they in the collective psychology of the nation. Some knowledge of the *pourquoi,* the French questioning of things that are often accepted without discussion in other societies, is essential to an understanding of the country. Readers will find plenty of facts and figures in this book, but insofar as possible, I have also attempted to present objectively the questioning modern developments provoke.

In a beautiful article entitled "What Is a Frenchman?" the journalist Jean-Maurice de Montrémy suggests that perhaps what characterizes most this "odd, democratic, secular animal" is the tendency to have an opinion about everything.[11] The French intellectual, of course, is highly qualified for this task, but others are equally ready to speak—such as the *énarque* (technocrat) of popular anecdote—"I'm afraid I haven't understood your question, *monsieur,* but I shall answer it anyway!" Citizens of adamant conviction can be found in the *café du commerce* of the tiniest village "exposing admirable plans," as André Maurois ironically wrote.[12]

My bibiliographical sources, like my informants, are almost exclusively French for three reasons. The first is that despite the almost masochistic pleasure the French derive from reading foreigners' views of France,[13] there is hardly a more penetrating glance than their own. Few

11. Jean-Maurice de Montrémy, "Qu'est-ce qu'un Français?" *L'Histoire,* January 1987, 20–25.

12. André Maurois, *Un art de vivre* (Paris: Librairie Plon, 1939), 37.

13. See Yves Daudu, *Les Français à la une: La presse étrangère juge les Français* (Paris: Editions la Découverte, 1987) and Dominique Frischer, *La France*

nations are ready to bare their souls to the same degree. Of course this does not mean that the French are without chauvinism—after all, the word is of French origin—but it would be hard to find a country more inclined to self-mockery. If the views of foreigners sometimes carry more weight in France than elsewhere, it may be because the French put such a high price on objectivity—unless it is because they never listen to their compatriots!

My second reason is that some of the most interesting remarks on contemporary France are to be found in books, newspapers, periodicals, and specialized reviews that are unlikely to be familiar to nonspecialist readers in English. Last but not least, a nation is not only what outsiders perceive but what its population sees, the self-image derived from collective memory and cultural myths. Only by looking at France with French eyes—through French windows—can one appreciate this dimension of Frenchness.

A final feature of the book is frequent comparisons with U.S. society, with which the French maintain a love-hate relationship. To them, the United States symbolizes the modernity that they adore and detest; therefore, the United States is also seen here through French windows in an attempt to reveal more about France itself.

Unpretentious as the goal of *Through French Windows* is, it required extensive documentation. I am deeply indebted to the numerous writers, journalists, and researchers who helped me gain an understanding of the wide variety of themes that had to be covered. While I have taken pains to reproduce as faithfully as possible the views of these experts, this book necessarily gives a very partial view of their work, and I am entirely responsible for any unintentional misrepresentation of their opinions. Finally, I would particularly like to thank the journalists and staff writers of *Le Monde* (and its numerous supplements), whose in-depth coverage of current events has been a constant source of information for me. *L'Expansion, L'Evénement du Jeudi, Le Nouvel Observateur, L'Express, Le Point,* and *L'Histoire* have also been helpful. I am grateful to the generations of students at the Ecole supérieure des affaires and, especially, to my family and all my friends, from every walk of life, who have given me a more earthy and more intimate view of France with inimitable Gallic irony.

I would like to express thanks to Chantal Euzeby, an economic adviser

---

vue d'en face: L'image de la France analysée et jugée par des étrangers (Paris: Robert Laffont, 1990).

of the International Bureau of Labor and the European Communities Commission, as well as her husband Alain, both professors of economics at the Université Pierre Mendès France, for agreeing to review the chapters dealing with social security and the economy. Their generous help in explaining issues and their observations on these subjects were extremely useful. I am also deeply indebted to Professor Jean Tournon, a researcher at the Institute of Political Science in Grenoble, for his keen comments on the section dealing with politics. Special thanks are due to my friend Professor Jacques Joly, a specialist in urban questions, for reading the draft manuscript, and for his penetrating remarks concerning history, geography, and the urban and rural environment, as well as for his constant advice and stimulating conversation. Two other friends, Jean-Claude Gésior and René Doucet, are to be thanked for their help in solving a complex data problem. Jean-Claude's discreet *gentillesse* is unforgettable. Finally, I would like to thank the editorial staff of the University of Michigan Press for their invaluable assistance and L'Ecole supériure des affaires for material support with the manuscript. The title of part 7, "France, Inc.," has been shamelessly borrowed from Lothar Baier's admirable book, *Firma Frankreich,* which describes the new business spirit of France. It does not imply any agreement of the German writer and journalist with the judgments proffered here.

PART 1

From Soap to Smart Cards

They hug and kiss in January
To usher in the New Year
But France from all eternity
Has hardly changed I swear.

—Renaud Séchan, *Hexagone.* Copyright. © Mino Music.

FIG. 1. "Say, where's France?" (© 1985, Editions Bernard Barrault et Eugénie S.A.)

1

The Hexagon

> To know the geographical situation of a country is to infer a wealth of information about it. To know that France lies in the temperate latitudes of the Northern Hemisphere, that it is a chunk of the old European continent, that it is one of the four largest countries in the European Community, that it forms a bridge between the north of Europe and the south is to know what it is almost essential to know about France and the French.
>
> —Denise Pumain, Thérèse Saint-Julien, and Robert Ferras, *France–Europe du Sud*

In elementary school, French children draw a map using one of the plastic cutouts that form part of their mandatory school kit. As they carefully trace the outlines of their country they learn that it forms a hexagon. Indeed the term *l'Hexagone* is used to distinguish continental France from its overseas *départements* and territories.[1] This geometrical description of things attempts to avoid the fuzziness of the simple word *France* but lacks its plenitude. The inhabitants of this puzzling land cannot agree upon a definition, for there is not one but several Frances.[2] What indeed have the rain-washed plains of Picardy in common with the luminous, fragrant, scrub-covered hills and gullies of Provence, or the snowcapped Alps with the Atlantic dunes?

A Crossroads

Geographers from earliest times have been fascinated by the situation of France. Lying as it does between two seas, no part of the country is

1. The inhabitants of territories such as Réunion or New Caledonia refer to France proper as the *Métropole*, or mother country, a reminder of the nation's imperial past; Corsicans speak of the *continent* and, sometimes with a touch of irony, of the *continentaux*, the Continentals.

2. Fernand Braudel, *L'identité de la France*, vol. 1, *Espace et histoire* (Paris: Arthaud, 1986), 27–31.

FIG. 2. L'Hexagone

more than 250 miles from the coast. It forms a natural bridge between the north and south of Europe and lies at the western extreme of the vast Eurasian continent. Moreover, invaders and merchants were quick to grasp the economic advantages of this crossroads between the Mediterranean Sea and the Atlantic Ocean, which is also a point of convergence for traffic from the east.

The earliest traces of human occupation of the land date back to the Lower Paleolithic (about 380,000 B.C.) and can be seen in Terra Amata near Nice. Skeletons of Cro-Magnon humans (35,000 B.C.), Homo sapiens who were hunters and fishers, were discovered by railroad workers in the Dordogne region in 1868. The famous cave paintings of Lascaux (15,000 B.C.), also in the southwest, are further reminders of France's earliest inhabitants. During the Neolithic period (5000 B.C.) invaders from the eastern Mediterranean made their home in the south of France, while others, from the region of the Danube, settled in the east. By 3000 B.C. mysterious megaliths and dolmens were being raised in Brittany—long before Stonehenge. Further invasions from central Europe took place in 2000 B.C. Meanwhile, the Greeks and Phoenicians, great consumers of tin from the British Isles, opened up trade routes to transport the ore from the port of Boulogne to Marseille with horses, a journey that took thirty days. Between the seventh and fifth centuries B.C., a horde of Celtic tribes, who spoke a variety of dialects of a common language, arrived from the east. One branch of these Celts came to be known as the Gauls. The French consider the Gauls their direct ancestors, though it was from Frankish warriors who crossed the Rhine in the fifth century B.C. that the country takes its name (France: land of the Franks).

In the best-selling comic strip "Astérix," the Gauls are portrayed as boisterous, undaunted beer drinkers who love a fight and good food (wine, first brought by the Greeks to Marseille, was not to become popular until after the Roman conquest).[3] In reality, they were an ingenious and industrious people who invented soap and were skilled wheelwrights and barrel makers. After the conquest of Gaul by the Romans, the latter relied on the Gauls not only for food supplies—wheat, flour, cattle—but also for pottery and jewelry.

The frontiers of the Gallic confederation and Roman Gaul encompassed a far greater entity than the present-day hexagon. The Roman

FIG. 3. Astérix. (Copyright © Les Editions Albert René.)

3. It has been said that it was the convivial wine that opened the road to the conquest of France by the Roman legions (Braudel, *L'identité de la France*).

Empire extended across what is now Holland, Belgium, and Switzerland and reached beyond the Rhine to the banks of the Elbe and the Danube. In A.D. 843 when Charlemagne's son, Louis the Pious, gathered 120 experts in Verdun to divide up his vast empire between his three sons, Francia Occidentalis fell to Charles the Bald. The kingdom of France

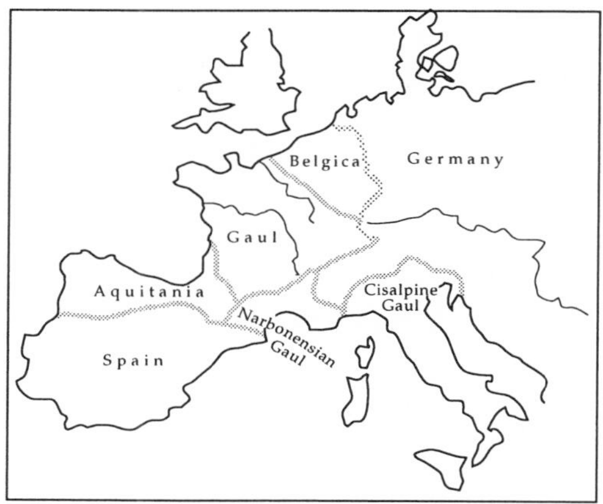

Roman Gaul circa 60 B.C.

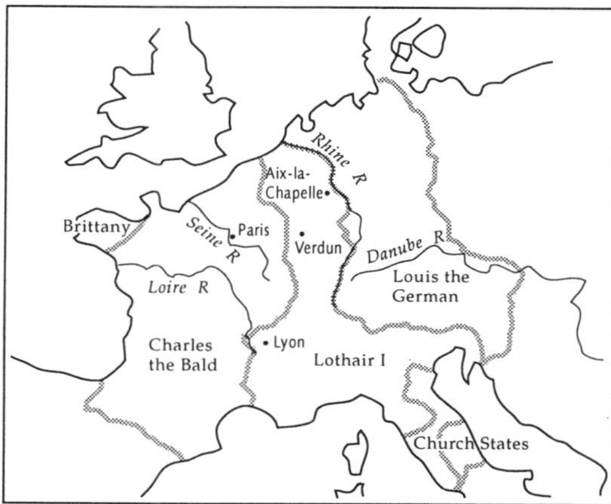

Division of Carolingian Empire by Treaty of Verdun, A.D. 843

FIG. 4. Caesar's view of Gaul (58–51 B.C.) and the division of Charlemagne's empire (A.D. 843).

that eventually issued from this territorial division (Nice and Savoy did not become French until 1860) corresponded more or less to the contours of the present hexagon, with its natural boundaries of the Mediterranean and the Atlantic, the English Channel, the Alps in the southeast, and the formidable barrier of the Pyrenees in the south.

France continued to attract merchants from the north, south, and east. Later on, in the twelfth century, the great fairs in Champagne, which lasted as long as seven weeks at a time, were genuine centers of international trade, where spices and silk from the Orient, Italian fabrics, English wool, Dutch linen, and furs from the Baltic were traded. Protectionism, so frequently an economic and cultural feature of the country since the seventeenth century, contradicts France's long tradition as a commercial crossroads.

The Hexagon in Figures

The hexagon today covers an area of 211,208 square miles, making France the second largest country in Europe after Russia. The largest distance across, both from the north coast to the Pyrenees and from Brittany in the west to Alsace in the east, is 625 miles (1,000 km), and France claims the highest peak in Europe west of the Caucasus mountains: Mont Blanc, in the Alps bordering Switzerland and Italy, reaches 15,771 feet.

The physical configuration of the hexagon has changed little over the past million years or so. Remnants of ancient mountain ranges dating from the Paleozoic era, more than 300 million years ago, are found in the hills of Brittany in the west of the country and in the Ardennes to the east, where no peak exceeds 225 feet. The wooded Vosges and the central plateau or Massif Central, which tends to be higher, belong to the same period. These old land areas became partially and intermittently submerged in the Mesozoic era 190 million years ago and furnished the raw materials for the Alps in the southeast and the Pyrenees in the south. These ranges, like the Jura and Corsican ranges, emerged during the Tertiary period, which lasted 65 million years. Then, 1 million years ago, nature put the finishing touches to the land. The return of a warmer climate after the major glaciations and the ensuing thaws carved out the rivers, lakes, valleys, inlets, estuaries, lagoons, and other natural beauties that attract sixty million tourists to France every year.

Of France's four major rivers, three flow west. The Loire, which is the longest at 634 miles, and the Garonne pour into the Atlantic Ocean; the Seine flows into the English Channel; only the Rhône, which flows out of Lake Geneva, goes south to the Mediterranean.

The country has the densest network of navigable waterways in Europe after Russia, concentrated in the north and east. The Canal du Midi links the Atlantic to the Mediterranean. Unfortunately, these rivers and canals are underexploited because they lack sufficient interconnections. Although there is a plan to connect the Rhine to the Rhône—a mere 150-mile gap in existing waterways separates the North Sea from the Mediterranean—water transport of merchandise, while nonpolluting and economical, accounted for only 7.3 percent of total freight transportation in 1989.

A Farming Paradise

Lying between the 42d and 51st parallels—Paris is at roughly the same latitude as Winnipeg, Canada, and Bordeaux as Minneapolis—France is blessed with a temperate climate. Indeed, however much the French grumble about changeable metereological conditions, which are the rule rather than the exception, the country knows none of the climatic extremes to be found in the United States.

The southeastern Mediterranean area, known as the Midi, and the southwest enjoy a subtropical climate, with average July temperatures of 74.5 degrees in the Midi. The coldest nonmountainous region is the extreme east, with average January temperatures as low as 32 to 28 degrees. Even within these zones altitude, latitude, orientation, and exposure can create microclimatic pockets.

The winds that blow in from the Atlantic, mild in winter, cool in summer, counter those from the interior of the continent. Winters can be harsh, but, generally, below-freezing temperatures are of short duration—less than a fortnight in most areas. The Mediterranean region and the southwest rarely get snow or frost. North of the Massif Central there are alternating spells of wet or dry cold in winter, humid or dry heat in summer. It rains most on the Atlantic seaboard: Brest, with an average rainfall of forty-five inches, gets more than twice as much rain as Marseille (twenty-one inches). The former has two hundred rainy days per year, the latter only seventy-six.

The variety of weather conditions together with the diversity of soil found in France make the country something of a farmer's paradise, where crops as diverse as citrus fruits, corn, beet, vines, and artichokes thrive in an area four-fifths the size of Texas. The four major river basins form rich alluvial plains where the greater part of French agriculture is concentrated. The bassin Parisien and the bassin d'Aquitaine in the southwest are particularly important. Of course there are poor lands, but 60 percent of French land is used for agriculture. France accounts for almost one-quarter of total EC (European Community) farm production. While this may be something of a liability in a Europe dogged with food surpluses, it makes it easy to understand why the country enticed invaders and immigrants from the earliest times.

Natural Resources

Apart from farmland and forests—woods cover more than a quarter of the total area—France has few natural resources. French coal, found chiefly in the north and east (Lorraine), has not been competitive in the industry for a long time, and the closing of the last mine in the north in late 1990 left only seven coal mines, employing a total of twenty-two thousand miners, still open. There are small oil fields in the southwest and to the east of the Bassin Parisien, but production is not significant. The natural gas pumped in the southwest (Lacq) meets less than one-quarter of domestic needs.

Bauxite, so-called because it was discovered near the picturesque Provençal village of Les Baux, permitted French engineers to play a role in the development of aluminum. (Pechiney, which has long been associated with the production of aluminum, became world packaging giant in 1989 with the buyout of American National Can Company that was to lead to an insider trading scandal.) Other minerals such as tin, lead, and zinc are found in small quantities in Brittany and the Massif Central.

The Lorraine region, which had iron ore in abundance (though of poor quality), was badly hit by the economic crisis of the 1970s that devastated the steel industry. Production dropped by 22 percent between 1970 and 1987. The north and northeast of France, together with Saint-Etienne in the center, which had been the flagships of the French mining and steel industry for over one hundred and fifty years, have suffered cruelly in the last two decades. The 1990 unemployment rate in the Nord Pas-de-Calais region was 13.1 percent.

One natural resource not lacking in France is water. The French were European pioneers in developing hydroelectric power. Firms such as

Merlin Gerin in the Alpine city of Grenoble, which was the cradle of the industry, export their know-how and equipment all over the world. Nevertheless, it is clear that France cannot rely on its limited natural resources to survive in the competitive business world of the 1990s. Even agriculture, one of its prime natural advantages, can no longer muster the strength. In the modern world it is brain power, skilled labor, innovation, and research that largely determine the capacity of a country to maintain and develop the quality of life of its citizens.[4] The challenges facing France on the eve of the twenty-first century will only be met if the jocular energy-saving slogan of the 1970s holds true: "We have no oil, but we've got ideas."

Defending the Environment

> A new nature will spring from our hands.
>
> —Georges Buffon (1707-88)

The great French monarch Philippe Auguste (1165-1223), who published regulations designed to protect the forests from overexploitation, and the unhappy King Charles, the Beloved, may have been the first environmental regulators in France. In 1415 Charles promulgated a law designed to prevent the pollution of the Seine. Today, the secretary of state for the environment has a whole arsenal of legislation to protect the air and water and control the disposal of waste. Until recently citizens did not feel overconcerned about ecological questions, which they consider it is the duty of the state to handle. By and large, it has not done a bad job, even if France has never been a paragon of environmental protection, on which it spends only 0.06 percent of the national budget.

Overall the situation is probably better than in most other European countries. Compared to the United States, France is not a throwaway society, and per capita consumption of energy and water is relatively moderate. French beaches tend to be less polluted than elsewhere, and forests have so far been spared large-scale devastation by acid rains. The country is well equipped for the disposal of toxic waste, and while pesticides and fertilizers are widely used in farming, consumption per acre corresponds roughly to the European average. The quality of drink-

4. Denise Pumain, Thérèse Saint-Julien, and Robert Ferras, *France-Europe du sud: Géographie universelle*, ed. Roget Brunet (Paris: Hachette/Reclus, 1990).

ing water as well as that of rivers and lakes also compares favorably to that in other countries in western Europe. Nature has endowed France with plenty of space, and the population density is comfortable. According to the latest report of the secretary of state for the environment, the country has a wonderful variety of landscape and a rich wildlife. In Europe only Russia has a greater diversity of mammals. Plant life too is abundant. The country boasts 40 percent of the various kinds of vegetation in the European Community, and there are as many species of flora in the Mediterranean region alone as in all Great Britain.[5]

Yet there is little cause for self-congratulation. The list of afflictions is long: barely tolerable noise levels in many places because of increasing air, rail, and road traffic, automobile pollution (the number of motor vehicles alone has increased 29 percent in the past ten years) owing, in part, to the reticence of consumers to use unleaded gas and catalytic converters; insufficient prevention of forest fires (nearly 400,000 hectares have gone up in smoke in the last decade), sewage pollution (two-thirds of the French live in homes that are not connected to a waste treatment plant); the destruction of sites of natural beauty because of the anarchic development of tourism; the increasing number of industrial pig farms that are a major cause of water pollution; the high-tension electric cables that disfigure the landscape; the railway lines for the high-speed train that cut through farmland and vineyards; the highways that eat up the land at the rate of ten hectares per kilometer of asphalt and threaten wildlife; the marinas and ports that destroy the ecological balance of coastal areas; the twenty-five thousand illegal trash heaps that dot the countryside; not to mention the looming problem of the disposal of nuclear waste for a country that has the highest density of nuclear energy installations in the world.

It is only of late that the public at large has become aware of environmental issues. The bearded, long-haired ecological pioneers of the 1970s that fought a losing battle against nuclear energy were not taken very seriously in a country where city dwellers who had fled the rudimentary comfort of rural France in the 1950s and 1960s were discovering the commodity of electric central heating. The squabbling among the ecology movements did not help either. However, the global awareness that followed the Chernobyl disaster has shaken somewhat the blind faith of the public in the atomic god. The comical reaction of the French

5. *Etat de l'environnement 1989* (Paris: Ministère de l'Environnement, 1989).

authorities, denying that France had been contaminated and proclaiming the safety of French power stations and military installations, did not convince anybody. A series of flaws in nuclear reactors, including Superphénix, the fast-breeder prototype, have since shown that the technology is not as infallible as the engineers pretend. Yet, the consensus that permits France to produce three-quarters of the electricity it consumes with nuclear power still appears to be very strong.

Population

The French take pride in their Gallic ancestry; the national emblem is the cockerel (in Latin: *gallus*), which came to be associated (at first derisively!) with the Gauls.[6] Yet, in spite of the efforts of the nationalistic extreme right-wing party today to "keep France French," it would be hard to find a homogeneous French population. No single race but between thirty and forty different ethnic groups—Ligurians, Iberians, Greeks, Teutons, and Romans, to mention but a few—have a valid claim to being the ancestors of the French. Even today one-third of the population has a first, second, or third generation foreign grandparent. France has always been a multiethnic, if not a multicultural, society, and as Pierre Miquel has pointed out it "was a melting pot long before the United States."[7]

The hexagon has a population of 56,556,000, including 4.4 million immigrants.[8] Up to the end of the seventeenth century France was the most thickly populated country in Europe and its monarch the wealthiest, thanks to the many taxes he exacted from his numerous subjects. In a rural society before the age of mechanization, a large work force was all-important. The big rural population constituted another of the advantages of the country. In the latter part of the nineteenth century, population growth stagnated, and only the massive arrival of immigrants prevented demographic decline. The percentage of the population of

6. Colette Beaune, "Les deux chants du coq gaulois," *L'Histoire*, January 1987, 112–14.

7. Pierre Miquel, *Vive la France* (Paris: Librairie Seguier, 1987), 19.

8. Population figures are those supplied by the 1990 census, undertaken by the Institut national de la statistique et des études économiques (INSEE). See "Recensement de la population de 1990," *INSEE Première*, no. 81, June 1990. The census is taken at irregular intervals in France. The previous one took place in 1982.

immigrant stock in France is the highest in the world after the United States and Canada. Yet, the Germans, the Italians, and the British outnumber the French nowadays.

In the aftermath of World War II France had 1.7 percent of total world population. Yet, in spite of the postwar baby boom, this figure has dropped to 1 percent in the 1990s owing to the higher birth rate in the Third World. It is estimated that thirty years from now the French will represent only 0.7 percent of world population, and there will be a lack of young blood essential for the economic vitality of the country. From this long-term viewpoint present immigration policy and latent racial prejudice could adversely affect France's ability to meet the challenges of the next millennium.

Average population density is 102 inhabitants per square kilometer, that is, 269 per square mile. The most thickly populated areas are the Parisian region of Ile-de-France, with 887 inhabitants per square kilometer—almost nine times the national average—followed by the Nord-Pas-de-Calais region (319). The *département* of Lozère has the lowest density, with 25 inhabitants per square kilometer, roughly the same as the United States overall. However, density in France is lower than the European average (163 inhabitants per square kilometer) and far below that of countries such as Germany, Great Britain, and Holland. Many Europeans perceive France, with its thinly populated rural and mountain areas, as a haven of peace off the urban, industrial track that runs from Glasgow to Turin.

2

Town and Country

Paris is the largest urban center in France, with a population of slightly over nine million, followed by Lyon, Marseille, Lille, and Bordeaux, in that order. Though Lyon and Marseille are the only two cities besides Paris to reach the million mark, this basically rural society has undergone profound changes since the 1960s. At the end of World War II, 36 percent of the working population still worked on farms; today, less than 7 percent is engaged in agriculture. In the period 1945 to 1973, the so-called *trente glorieuses* (thirty glorious years) of French industrial expansion, there was a massive move from the country to the cities and larger towns. Now 77.2 percent of the population lives in an urban center, officially defined as a town of more than 2,000 inhabitants. One-third of the population lives in city suburbs. Towns of fewer than 10,000 inhabitants have shown a very high growth rate over the past fifteen years. The 1990 census figures show that the population of cities of more than 200,000 inhabitants, which had slowed down in the 1970s, is growing again and that these towns "appear to be the powerhouses of urban growth."[1]

Housing and Housing Policy

In a predominantly rural society—nearly half the population lived on the land in 1914—housing and sanitary conditions generally left a lot to be desired. The rent freeze decreed by the government during World War I was designed to prevent unscrupulous landlords from exploiting the families of soldiers away fighting at the front. In the difficult economic situation that followed World War II a new law was voted that severely limited rent increases. (This law still prevails for a dwindling number of lucky tenants.) As a result landlords were unwilling to renovate their

1. Pierre-Alain Andiras and Jean-Paul Faur, "La population des régions," *INSEE Première*, no. 111, 1990.

tenements or invest in new property. In 1950 only sixty dwellings per one thousand persons were being built. In this still largely rural country one-third of the homes had no running water and one-quarter no indoor toilet. Telephones were a luxury.

To house the millions of people who were leaving the farms after World War II to take up jobs in the cities, as well as the immigrants attracted by the industrial boom, and to offset the effects of the 1948 rent law, the state was forced to invest heavily in social housing projects. Giant schemes were implemented quickly, but, unfortunately, French urban planners in postwar France had only retained the ideas of functionalism and zoning advocated by Le Corbusier (1887–1965), forgetting the novel use of space that inspired much of the great theorist's architecture.[2] The resulting standardized, dismal apartment blocks, which have become the *cités dortoirs* (bedroom communities) of the larger towns, are inhabited by manual and office workers, immigrant families, and the jobless. Nevertheless, in the 1960s people appreciated the relative comfort of these buildings, which had hot and cold water, bathrooms, and central heating.[3] The popular songwriter and singer Renaud wrote a satire on life inside a *habitation à loyer modéré* (HLM, rent-controlled dwelling), and the grim blocks of the 1960s are a familiar if not picturesque feature of French towns. France is not all châteaux and *jardins à la française!*

Between 1984 and 1988 private housing projects increased by 68 percent, while social housing start-ups decreased by 32 percent, but HLMs still house thirteen million people in France, that is, almost a quarter of the population, and they are still being built by some thousand nonprofit

---

2. "What was constructed was done so not only with cynicism, but also with foolishness, in a sort of stupid obedience to the ultra-rationalistic discourse on the housing machine professed by Le Corbusier, which was accepted by all, including those who were supposed to be in charge of housing the poorest." Roland Castro, "Banlieues, vers une nouvelle culture," in Verdié, *L'état de la France et de ses habitants* (Paris: Editions la Découverte, 1987), 23.

3. "The move from the slums to comfort took place amid general consensus. What is absolutely astonishing is that these places had to be occupied, that segregation had to creep in before people realized the intolerableness of the situation, namely, that this was not a city, even a poor one, but a simple storage area where people were stowed in hygiene and comfort but in which not the slightest quality associated with the city existed: privacy, strata, the opportunity to stroll about, quaintness, complexity" (Castro, *Banlieues*, 23).

High and Low Tech

It is possible that the opinions some Americans used to have about sanitary and hygenic conditions in France were propagated in the postwar period by tourists from the United States who, dreading "the Paris tummy," had a phobia about drinking water from the faucet.* Fortunately, these prejudices have largely disappeared, and the United States is nowadays a major importer of mineral waters, such as Perrier and Evian, from France.

Nevertheless, many visitors from the United States and northern Europe are surprised by public sanitary facilities. Even if the old *vespasiennes* in some cities are giving way to *Sanisettes,*† state of the art self-flushing, coin-operated toilets with background music, the *wc à la turque*—basically a square basin at ground level with a hole in the middle over which you crouch—that upset some foreigners but that the French consider more hygenic than ordinary sit-down toilets, have not disappeared. They can even be found in campus dorms—a proof that France is not all high tech. Yet, according to that excellent connoisseur of Paris, Alain Schifres, there are only two of the old *pissotières,* chanted by Henry Miller among others, left in the capital, and they have become objects of veneration for Japanese and American tourists.‡ Another reminder of tradition is the sharp-eyed *dame-pipi,* the terror of visitors with no small change, who is still around, though probably not for long. Yet another service occupation that has been sacrificed to the god of modernization!

*René Girard, "La différence franco-américaine," in *Demain la France* (Paris: L'Expansion, 1986), 225–32.

†In July 1992, the first *Sanisette* was inaugurated in front of Macy's in Manhattan, was filmed for television, and made the headlines of the *Washington Post* supplement.

‡Alain Schifrés, *Les Parisiens* (Paris: JC Lattès, 1990), 381. The humorist devotes a whole chapter of his best-selling book to the *wc à la turque* of the Parisian *bistrot,* complete with a sketch and instructions for use for the uninitiated. This is typical Gallic humor.

agencies with the cooperation of the state and local authorities. Financed by long-term treasury loans, they are designed to provide housing for low-income groups. As an official declared in 1989 at the HLM congress: "We were created so that there would be less inequalities in housing and so that quality housing would not be reserved for a minority."[4] Large-scale renovation involving insulation, decoration, and even landscaping is in progress to change the grim appearance of the

4. Josée Doyère,"Le Président de la République assistera à la clôture du congrès HLM," *Le Monde,* 29 April 1989.

existing HLMs. One million units are to be refurbished in the early 1990s.

Some attempts were made to break the uniformity of these *grands ensembles* and to make socializing easier, for example, the Villeneuve experiment in Grenoble,[5] but for a number of reasons, basically cultural, they have been a failure. The French home is still a (fortified) castle, and it must not be forgotten that for a population of fifty-six million France has thirty million pets, a sizable number of these being watchdogs!

If 70 percent of low-budget housing constructed in the sixties consisted of rentals, one out of three housing projects financed by HLM agencies now helps people to become the owners of the apartment they occupy. The French in this respect are more like the Americans than they care to think. They have a strong historical attachment to the notion of private property, and this, together with their peasant roots, makes a house and garden the dream of the majority of people; 55 percent of the French dwell in private houses, 45 percent in apartment blocks. Privately owned dwellings comprise 56 percent of all residences. More French than American families are homeowners. A record number of families in France (10 percent) also own a seasonal or holiday home. Descendants of peasants that most of the French are, they continue to "appropriate the territorial basis of their liberty" by becoming homeowners.[6]

Any understanding of the French value system is impossible if one forgets peasant roots: "The expression *être au loyer,* literally, 'to be on the rent,' which used to be applied to sharecroppers, is nowadays used for people who have not yet undertaken to build a home; *patronne, être patronne chez soi,* 'mistress,' 'to be mistress of the home' means something more than being the owner of property: it is to rule over your domain and to have the assurance that nobody can drive you out." The homes workers have built, writes Anne Gotman, gives them a status in society. It is the equivalent of land for the generation of their parents.[7]

In 1986 the right-of-center party that won the elections the same year decided to phase out the rent controls that had existed for forty years,

---

5. See Jacques Joly and Jean-François Parent, *Paysage et politique de la ville* (Grenoble: Presses Universitaires de Grenoble, 1988).

6. Michel Winock, "Liberté, égalité, propriété." *L'Histoire,* January 1987, 96–105.

7. Anne Gotman, *Héritier* (Paris: Presses Universitaires de France, 1988), 14–15.

and because of the abusive practices of landlords or, more often, the institutional investors who hold much of the property, prices in the larger cities skyrocketed. In Paris, where 76 percent of the population rents a home, prices rose by 7.4 percent in 1989. That was double the inflation rate. The average Parisian has to spend one-third of earnings on lodging. This helps explain much of the social unrest and the sporadic strikes by low-paid civil servants, office staff, and workers unable to afford housing in the capital. Employees earning small salaries have had to move out of the city. They spend more and more time commuting and are losing that "quality of life" the French are so attached to. However, it should be added that rents in some provincial cities may be half those in Paris.

When the Socialist government returned to power in 1988, it refused to reintroduce a rent freeze, but landlords may no longer raise rents indiscriminately. One of the basic conditions is that increases are only possible for new leases—but one Parisian in five relocates every year! Property prices in Paris are soaring too. In the Golden Triangle around the Champs Elysées one building was recently sold to an insurance group for Fr 200,000 per square meter![8] Average apartment prices have doubled in five years. In 1990, it was well nigh impossible to buy anything anywhere in Paris for less than Fr 10,000 per square meter. In the chic, residential areas like the sixteenth arrondissement (one of the city's twenty wards), where in the late 1980s the Japanese were buying a lot of property, average prices are two to three times higher. Housing is one of the major issues in France today, and land is so expensive in the Parisian area that the HLM agencies can no longer compete with private real estate agents ready to pay huge sums they can recoup in the form of high rents.

Exurbia

Some quarters in the cities and the immediate suburbs have, of course, luxurious condominiums for the affluent, but in the late 1960s ecological issues came to the forefront, and a certain disenchantment with urban life set in. The middle classes and workers who could afford it started to move outside the cities to buy or build a home in the surrounding villages. With land becoming increasingly expensive, people had to move farther and farther out of town, so that urban sprawl soon enveloped formerly rural communities. There has been some friction between the

8. One square meter is equal to 10.8 square feet.

newcomers and the villagers in places, largely due to the increased taxation necessary to provide schooling and other facilities for these neorurals, who also often got involved in local politics. In spite of this, and however much one may regret the disappearance of the old village fêtes, this movement has brought new life and new blood to villages that were becoming deserted. Beautiful stone farmhouses and other abandoned dwellings the early exurbanites shrewdly bought up have thus been preserved from decay.

"For the first time in over a century the population of rural France," says Annie Moulin, "has grown faster than in the urban communities."[9] In fact if the greater rural area, which includes towns of fewer than ten thousand inhabitants and their outskirts, is considered, the population of the French countryside—twenty-five million—is roughly the same as at the end of the eighteenth century. But in 1982 only 23 percent of rural inhabitants were farmers, and it is the neorurals who run the show. These have changed somewhat from those who fled to the countryside in the sixties. Dissatisfied with the existing economic setup and the consumer society, the former hoped to rediscover the age-old rural values of solidarity and mutual assistance. Not so today. The neorural families of the eighties and nineties have migrated for very personal reasons and tend to have a highly individualistic behavior. What they seek is a home of their own, a nonsalaried job, independence. Although this implies, in many cases, the development of an underground economy where moonlighting and tax dodging are common, the arrival of these young, well-educated immigrants could help revive the stricken rural economies if the mistrustful natives and the dynamic newcomers could cooperate in local development, as they sometimes do.[10] They might do well to take inspiration from the dynamism of the inner-city immigrant population, which seems to enjoy a genuine community life for the benefit of all concerned. (Alain Tarrius has shown the rich network of economic relationships and solidarity that exists between Maghrebian people living in Marseille and the surrounding region.)[11]

---

9. Annie Moulin, *Les paysans dans la société française* (Paris: Editions du Seuil, 1988), 241.

10. Joseph Catanzano, "Retour vers l'arrière pays" in *Cahiers de l'Economie Méridionale,* vol. 9 (Montpellier: University of Montpellier, 1987).

11. Alain Tarrius, "L'entrée dans la ville: Migrations et recomposition des tissus urbains à Tunis et à Marseille," *Revue Européenne des Migrations Internationales* 3, nos. 1, 2 (1987): 131–48.

Peasants, Ruralists, and City People

> The village feasts have become a commercial operation designed to attract a large audience from outside the local community. The attractions are more often than not standardized, pale copies of city feasts and of TV variety shows. The Saturday night dance has become a monstrous event everywhere. Majorettes in shakos and miniskirts, or traditional music groups, parade without much conviction in front of passive spectators. Some touristic villages call in professional organizers to contrive a *fête* "in the old fashion." Farmers will sometimes give a demonstration of farm work "of yesteryear," i.e., before the period of mechanization, with all the incongruities this implies. With a few awkward gestures they represent symbolically a whole way of life that their parents abandoned without regret in the fifties. They play the *paysans* just like the city dwellers expect to be shown. (Annie Moulin, *Les Paysans dans la société française* [Paris: Seuil, 1988], 243–44. Copyright © Editions du Seuil, 1988.

Although the oil crisis in the 1970s, with the increased costs of fuel for heating and gas for commuting, momentarily stalled this return to nature, there has been no significant movement back to the cities in recent years. In 1987, for the first time in its history, Paris lost part of its working population to the upstart French economic sun belt.

La Maison

One interesting difference from the United States is that in France new housing developments do not spring out of nowhere. They tend to develop only where facilities—a school, shops, medical care, utilities, and public transportation—exist. They are not built from scratch.

Another difference is the layout and style of the houses. As in most places in Europe wooden structures are rare, except for occasional chalets in mountain areas. Air conditioning is practically unknown and generally unnecessary. The French will usually build a house designed to last several generations. The typical structure is built of concrete and cement blocks (or bricks in some areas). Nowadays buildings are extremely well insulated, since tax breaks are granted for energy-saving construction. The AFME (Agence française pour la maîtrise de l'énergie) has done a remarkable job in encouraging people to reduce their consumption of energy. The wisdom of this policy was fully appreciated when the Persian Gulf crisis broke out in 1990.

Most houses in a development will have a personal style, though *villages pavillonaires* of identical semidetached dwellings are becoming more common. The building permit, delivered by the mayor, will require the homeowner to respect local or regional stylistic norms, usually discernible in the slant of the roof, the type of covering, or decorative elements (e.g., the *gênoise* or frieze of overlapping, curved tiles so typical of Provence). A quarter to half an acre of land will surround the house. Each plot is individually partitioned off. A high, evergreen hedgerow will generally separate next-door neighbors,[12] and there will inevitably be a vegetable garden. Living space in French homes tends to be somewhat cramped. The national average in 1990 was eighty-seven square meters (less than one thousand square feet), but, of course, the size of homes does vary enormously from the tiny studio apartment to the spacious private dwelling.

Home Financing

Building costs obviously vary a great deal from one region to another, but the average new apartment, outside the Ile de France can cost between seven thousand and twelve thousand francs per square meter of floor space. In 1989 in the Riviera towns of Grasse, Cannes, and Antibes the average price was between twenty thousand and forty thousand francs per square meter for a new apartment.[13] People will go to great sacrifices to build a home, particularly the lower income groups, who will sometimes spend a quarter or even a third of their annual earnings on mortgage payments. However, it is just about as expensive to rent as to purchase, and state aid for individual purchasers is the same as that offered to builders of social housing. This aid, which was partly designed to help the building industry and costs taxpayers between Fr 100 and 120 billion annually, helps citizens who otherwise could never have afforded a new home to buy or lease a house or apartment by offering them credit options, tax breaks, and interest bonuses. The system was

12. Henry Miller said the French build walls around their conversation as around their gardens. Is their legendary love of privacy changing? A surprising 56 percent declared in a survey in late 1990 that they perceived their home primarily as a place to exercise hospitality. Only 31 percent saw it as a comfy nest designed to protect their privacy. CSA/La Vie Poll, "Les Français et leur nid," *La Vie*, 8 November 1990, 63.

13. Michel Vives, "La fièvre de l'immobilier," *Le Monde*, 16 May 1990.

set up with the best intentions in the world, but because it encourages the purchase of new property, it has led to a paradoxical situation: home buyers are increasingly younger—between 1981 and 1984, 69 percent were under forty years old—and poorer (one out of two had a monthly income of less than three times the minimum wage). The state, in France, thus helps the poorest citizens to buy the most expensive housing, while in the United States the vast majority of first-time homeowners purchase a secondhand home.[14] A commission was set up in late 1988 to study a reform of the system, the ministry for housing being anxious to prevent the family and social hardships that present home-financing policy has brought about for many people unable to pay their mortgages.

Although France needs to build 350,000 new houses annually if it is to avoid a long-term housing shortage, ministerial preferences go to rehabilitating dilapidated suburbs and inner cities. Construction companies will be expected to devote at least 50 percent of their activity to this task in the coming years.

Cities

Milan Kundera, in his novel *The Unbearable Lightness of Being,* compares European and American architecture, suggesting that whereas in Europe beauty is in the mind of the architect before he creates his work, the American urban landscape "is beautiful almost by mistake."[15] Whether one agrees with this or not, it is a fact that urban development in France has rarely occurred by chance. From the Gothic cathedrals to Versailles and from the Paris of Haussmann (who redesigned the city in the nineteenth century) to Sarcelles,[16] it has always followed ideological principles of one kind or another: religious, monarchical, political, social. As Jean-Robert Pitte has pointed out, the city, in France, is rarely utilitarian: "The recipe of Manhattan combines the lack of space, modern building techniques, and a pinch of American vainglory; that of Sarcelles the urgent need to house the new Parisians of the early sixties and the

14. Josée Doyère, "L'Etat et les paradoxes de l'aide au logement," *Le Monde,* 9 September 1988.

15. Milan Kundera, *The Unbearable Lightness of Being,* trans. Michael Henry Heim (London: Faber and Faber, 1985), 101.

16. This working-class agglomeration of apartment blocks in the Paris region has become the symbol of what was worst in the architecture of the 1960s.

conviction that an ideal environment was being built for them in which people would learn to live in greater harmony."[17] Of course this ideal is utopian because it goes against the grain of the individualistic French character. In any case, as many of the jobs were located at a distance from the dormitory cities, their occupants were submitted to the grind of *métro, boulot, dodo* (subway, job, sleep) and had little time left for socializing.

There is no real equivalent in France of the American downtown, no strict separation between the business and residential districts of cities. Upper-middle-class apartments will be found over or next door to stores and offices in the town center. Downtown where property taxes, paradoxically, can be much lower than in some working-class suburbs. The poorer quarters are mostly inhabited by the elderly, the unemployed, and low-income families.

France, thanks to its unique housing policy, has been largely shielded from the inner-city problems that England and America have to cope with. Nevertheless, there are an estimated ten thousand homeless persons in or around Paris, and eighty thousand people, including whole families, are still housed in tawdry *hôtels meublés* (furnished apartments).[18] Outbreaks of suburban violence, which are becoming more frequent, suggest that France is paying today for its hasty construction program in the 1960s, which displaced the lower class and created suburban "ghettos."[19]

ZUP

The ZUP (zones d'urbanisation prioritaires) that were built to offset the housing shortage and to cope with the massive migration from the land are now almost deserted by the French lower, middle, and even working classes. They have become the lot of the poor, largely immigrant, population that has been forced to quit the renovated old quarters of the cities because of spreading gentrification and soaring rents. Out in their grey concrete wasteland, surrounded by beet fields, far from the con-

---

17. Jean-Robert Pitte, "Pour comprendre le paysage," *L'Histoire*, January 1987, 82–83.

18. Bernard Veillet-Lavalle, "Voyage au bout des garnis parisiens," *L'Evènement du Jeudi*, 21–27 September 1989, 48.

19. The definition of a ghetto in France is not quite the same as the U.S. or British definition. See chap. 12.

sumer palaces and glitz of the city, the jobless, poorly educated youth—the *zonards*—with no money and no future express their frustration in violence and delinquency. The window smashing and pillaging by uncontrolled teenagers from the ZUP during the student demonstrations in Paris in fall 1990 showed the French that segregation could exist in a country with a strong social awareness, and that even the laudable renovation of the HLMs, the new sports facilities, and social-assistance programs in the dismal bedroom communities are unable to prevent it. In an attempt to defuse the potential time bomb the ZUP conditions represent, the government voted an "anti-ghetto" law in late 1990 and set up a ministry of the city to tackle what is one of the most serious challenges to French social policy. Sixteen top priority districts nationwide have been earmarked for specific action, and a general mobilization of state and local authorities, HLM representatives, social workers, chambers of commerce, and local politicians has been decreed for four hundred of the most difficult urban districts. There is no alternative to this painstaking task, and during the parliamentary debate on urban policy in December 1990 the prime minister lashed out at the reticences of "this dear old country, always enthusiastic about solidarity as long as it is the others who make the first move."[20] However, in March 1991 a majority of deputies, not all of them Socialists, voted a law that stipulates that the wealthier municipalities will have to pay a special tax to finance the development of the poorer urban *communes* in the name of national solidarity.

If much attention has been focused on the trouble spots, it should not be forgotten that many of the *banlieues* (suburbs) in France, including some in the Parisian region, are agreeable spots to live in, and that their inhabitants enjoy an environment and quality of life that many city dwellers envy.

20. Jean-Louis Saux, "M. Rocard veut passer à 'l'ère industrielle' pour rénover les grands ensembles urbains," *Le Monde*, 20 December 1990.

3

Communications and Telecommunications

While the majority of French roads tend to be narrow by American standards, it should be remembered that France has the densest network in the world, and the general quality of the surface is outstandingly high, even on minor roads. However, until recent years France lagged behind countries such as Germany and Italy in the number of expressways that were being built. Thirty years ago there were only twenty miles of *autoroutes* in the west. In all fairness, it should be pointed out that transportation systems are more costly to develop in France than in either of the two neighboring countries because of France's size. In fact Italy and Great Britain together would fit neatly into the hexagon. Only very large countries, such as the United States or Canada, need to invest so much in road construction and maintenance. There used to be only a few roads linking east and west, and they were notoriously inadequate for the density of the traffic. In 1982 *l'autoroute* Bordeaux-Narbonne was finally completed, providing a fast link between the Atlantic and the Mediterranean coasts. With its 4,500 miles of expressways, France now has a more extensive network than Italy and should soon better Germany. An ambitious ten-year program involving the construction of an extra 1,690 miles of *autoroutes* was approved in 1988. By the year 2003 France will have more than 7,500 miles of major highways.

The aim of this plan is to put France squarely in the middle of a modern European road network between Italy, Spain, and Portugal in the south—a total market of 150 million consumers—and the countries of northern Europe. At present, traffic from Scandinavia, Holland, and Belgium tends to head south down through Germany and the Swiss Alpine tunnels, avoiding France. Eurotunnel (the Chunnel) and the addition of a complex system of interconnections between French expressways should allow the country to more fully play its role as a hub in the Europe of the 1990s.

The intensity of the squabbling over the towns to be served by the new roads gives an idea of the importance of communications for the future economic development of the different parts of the country: no expressways, no business! The scheduled links with the west of France are a vital element in this scheme, as all the European regions are vying with each other to attract foreign businesses and investment in preparation for the Europe without borders of the 1990s. Being a latecomer, France was able to benefit from the experience of other countries. The French *autoroutes* are not only beautifully landscaped but have attractive rest areas. However, there is some concern about the hazards to the environment of developing the road network on such a grand scale. Tolls can be relatively expensive (as much as 50 centimes per kilometer), as is gas, which costs between Fr 5.50 and 6 per liter in 1992 because of heavy taxation.

Transit Services

Transport has always been considered a public service in France, and while the taxpayer may grumble about the cost and deficits, there is no denying the quality of the service at affordable prices for all. Anyone who has ever used the New York subway will appreciate the general cleanliness and punctuality of the Paris, Marseille, Lille, and Lyon subways. Public transit in any sizable city is extensive and efficient, although the services may be crowded at peak time.

A good example of the value the French put on efficient public transportation is the *carte orange*, introduced in 1975, which allows Parisian commuters an unlimited number of trips on any Métro, bus, train, or Réseau Express Régional (RER) line. The RER is the fast intercity link in the Parisian area. In late 1990, the Ile de France region decided to make the system available to the more than half a million people who live in all the départements of the region, whether they use it for short distances (Fr 180 per month) or travel from one end of the region to the other (Fr 501). The *carte orange* is jointly financed by employers, who contribute one-third of the cost of the system, passengers, who contribute another third, and the region, which makes up the difference. It is expected that the new scheme will entitle ninety-five thousand employees who formerly were excluded from the system to obtain a partial refund (the legal minimum is 50 percent) of the price of purchase of the card from their employer. Weekly or monthly cards are available. The authorities are seriously considering making car parks in the vicinity of public transportation facilities available to cardholders so as to discourage them from taking their autos into the capital. The *carte orange* may even be extended to other large urban areas elsewhere in France.

In the larger towns special lanes are reserved for buses, and they have priority over cars when edging out of stops. Most of the bigger cities, but also medium-sized towns, have set up pedestrian precincts in the shopping districts. However, all these measures and the nightmare of parking have not shaken the French driver's stubborn conviction that the automobile is the most efficient means of transport. Carpooling being extremely rare, traffic can sometimes be chaotic. In the provinces only 15 percent of the population uses public transit, though the Paris figure is higher: 30 percent. In towns with a population of under thirty thousand the cost of the automobile to the community budget in terms of roads, maintenance, and machinery is 40 percent more than public transit, and in an attempt to promote public transportation some cities are supplying twentieth-century technology to nineteenth-century modes of transport. Lyon, for example, has just refurbished a cable railway dating from 1878.

A Streetcar Named TAG

Lille, Toulouse, Strasbourg, and Bordeaux have opted for a lightweight fully automatic subway called the VAL (*véhicule automatique léger*). Streetcars have reappeared in Nantes and Grenoble, and Saint-Etienne has extended its tramway system. The streamlined Grenoble TAG (Transports de l'agglomération grenobloise), inaugurated in 1987, with its special easy-access coaches for the handicapped, is attracting the attention of other European cities. Paris has adopted the system, built by Alsthom, for a link between Bobigny and Saint Denis. The TAG travels at an average speed of twelve miles per hour. This is slower than a subway (fifteen miles per hour) but faster than a bus. Equipped with antivibratory elastic wheels and powered by electricity, the new tram is comfortable, silent, and nonpolluting.

Le Car

Probably only the Americans have a greater passion for the automobile than the French. There is a car in practically every home, and almost 50 percent are two-car families. With over 494 vehicles per thousand people in 1989, there are obviously fewer autos in France than in the

Mass Transit versus the Automobile

The French goal of developing the highway network in the forthcoming years is somewhat ironic at a time when so much effort is going into promoting mass transit, but at least the problem is discussed. At the congress of the International Public Transport Union in Budapest in June 1989, the secretary general, Monsieur Pierre Laconte, declared that with the rise of individualism in the industrialized countries and the increasing use of autos the world's cities are suffocating and our forests dying. He went on to say:

> One person transported by bus requires one hundred times fewer square meters than the same person behind the wheel of his car. And the faster cars go, the more space they need. The indiscriminate use of autos is modeling our cities on the American system, a type of human settlement that was unknown before, sprawling across the land, with no community life, no heart; in other words, the contrary of a city. It is no life living in a town like Los Angeles, 150 kilometers long by 150 kilometers wide, because the highways have twelve lanes!

Commenting in *Le Monde,* Alain Faujas said that the American example was precisely the worst to follow:

> In fact the United States is among the countries that subsidizes public transport most (in 1982, 63 percent of the running costs came out of public funding), but it is also the one that makes the least use of it because it has overprivileged the private vehicle by not taxing gasoline and car sales enough. The scattered townships that result from this policy are an impediment to the development of mass transit because an RER network has no raison d'être amid the homes scattered in the green of New York state. (*Le Monde,* 20 June 1989)

The development of the nonpolluting TGV, of tramways, of automatic subways, and the overall quality of mass transit in France may be a lesson for other countries, if the French take a firmer stance on the spread of highways that the ecologists warn against. The new awareness of environmental issues may show that French technology and transport policy is indeed exemplary.

United States (759), but this is a higher figure than in Italy, Great Britain, or Japan. The country has a sad record of auto accidents, and nearly four hundred thousand people have been slain on French highways in the past thirty years. Nineteen ninety-one was considered a "good" year, with "only" 9,617 people killed and 205,968 injured—the lowest figure in thirty years! In 1990, more than ten thousand people were slain. There are twice as many traffic casualties in France as in England, and com-

FIG. 5. Road safety bill amended. First driver: The députés have watered down the bill! Second driver: Let's celebrate! (*Le Monde,* Copyright © Pancho 1989.)

paratively speaking, the United States has fewer road deaths for a greater number of miles driven.[1]

The main causes of road accidents, according to government officials, are drunken driving, which is responsible for fifteen deaths per day, and excessive speed—less than half the drivers respect speed limits. It is estimated that 3 percent of drivers on the road at any one time have a percentage of alcohol in the blood over the legal level of 0.5 gram per liter of pure spirits. At night 12 percent of drivers are over the legal level, and almost one in three between 1 A.M. and 3 A.M.[2] The car is the third greatest killer after cardiovascular disease and cancer. Seat belts are mandatory, and stiff fines have been introduced for traffic offenders, but nothing seems to reduce the depressing number of accidents. Probably speed limits are too high—eighty miles per hour on expressways, sixty-five miles per hour on two-way main roads, and, since December 1990, thirty miles per hour in towns. But the speed and response of engines is a major sales argument, and no government has dared oppose the powerful automobile lobby. In 1989 Parliament watered down a tough road-offence bill it was presented with. Neverthe-

1. Alain Faujas, "Un livre blanc pour une conduite automobile apaisée," *Le Monde,* 26 April 1989.

2. Ch. de Ch. "L'alcool au volant est réprimé plus sévèrement," *Le Monde,* 24 April 1992.

less, French carmakers agreed, in late 1988, to refrain from plugging speed in future commercials. A report published in 1989 declared that one in six drivers exceeded the speed limit on freeways, one in three on bypasses, more than one in two on main roads, and practically two in three on minor roads. The commission underlined the increasing gravity of traffic accidents and denounced this "intolerable modern barbarity." It pleaded for a European decision to reduce the power of cars rolling off the assembly lines and demanded the setting up of a special traffic police in France.[3]

Another cause of accidents mentioned in the report is the inadequate road network for modern traffic conditions, such as dangerous intersections and the beautiful plane trees that make the shady charm of French roads in summer but which were planted, in another age, too close to the verges. There are twenty-eight times fewer accidents on highways with one-way traffic than on two-way roads. The normal driving age is eighteen but, in an effort to teach young people caution, they may now drive at sixteen if accompanied by an adult driver.

Eurotunnel

A new alpine road tunnel, Le Tunnel de Frejus, linking France to Italy was inaugurated in 1980, but by far the most ambitious project so far is the Channel tunnel or Chunnel—*Eurotunnel* to the French—linking Calais in France with Folkestone in England. Work on the thirty-one mile underwater link at an initial cost of Fr 50 billion (£4.8 billion) got under way in 1987 and is to be operational by late 1994. Capital is provided by a joint Franco-British private corporation that obtained institutional financing and sold shares to the public in both countries at a unit cost of Fr 35.

The Chunnel, comprised of three separate tunnels, is bored out of the waterproof chalk at a depth of 130 feet below the seabed. Each of the outer tunnels is designed for one-way traffic in each direction. The center tunnel is for security and servicing. Vehicles will have drive-on access to the high-speed train shuttle from the French expressway network, and passengers will remain in their cars during the twenty-eight minute channel crossing. There will be vehicle and passenger shuttles

3. Alain Faujas, "De nouvelles mesures sont proposées pour réduire l'hécatombe routière," *Le Monde*, 3–4 September 1989.

Hullo Trouble!

Hey, kids! Hittin' the road today? You're damn well right. That's the real McCoy: Grab a bite to eat, knock back a glass, a stirrup glass—hey, pass the *Beaujolais!*—before chasin' all those bastards, they're gonna pay for it, just watch me, dawdlin' in the left lane. Hey, get the hell out of my way, you bugger! Yeah, that's the real McCoy, the real kicks, the feelin' that you're the lord and master of your little marvel, your darling, RENAULT 5, souped up Gordini style—submissive, fine-tuned, powerful. Jeez, what pickup! Lettin' yourself go on the freedom trail. Free, sure, free at last to kill scot-free. Go to it, boys, don't give a damn about the others. In France, that's a hell of a privilege. (Claude Sarraute, *Le Monde,* 13 May 1989. Copyright © The New York Times Syndication Sales Corporation. Claude Sarraute writes a racy, hard-hitting, daily column in *Le Monde.* The title of this excerpt comes from a popular slogan used to fight drunken driving: *Un verre ça va; deux verres: bonjour les dégâts!* which can be loosely translated: "A single, ok; a double: Hullo trouble!")

for tourists and separate trains to carry freight and trucks. It is estimated that thirty million passengers and fifteen million tons of freight will be transported in 1994, when the Chunnel is due to be inaugurated, and traffic is expected to increase annually thereafter. There are plans to extend Chunnel services to Amsterdam and Brussels.

In spite of the financial difficulties of Eurotunnel—shares have been wildly fluctuating and the cost had climbed to an estimated Fr 81 billion by mid-1992—progress by the British and French tunnelers is going ahead according to schedule. As of December 1990, with the completion of the fifty-kilometer service tunnel, it is theoretically possible to walk from France to England!

Railroads

The picture of a familiar, red diesel-powered *Micheline* chugging across a narrow bridge astride a lovely valley, featured in tourist posters a few years ago, is hardly representative of French railways today. While the train and the beautiful landscape can still be seen, France now has one of the most modern and efficient railway systems in the world as well as the fastest train—the bullet-shaped, high-speed TGV (*train à grande vitesse*) that zips along at 190 miles per hour. The TGV is the end product of a massive modernization program undertaken after World War II.

The war had left the railroad company in a sorry state, with 80 percent of its locomotives and coaches destroyed. Today one-third of the lines are electric, and these lines carry more than 75 percent of the traffic. Electrification of the system was possible thanks to the cheap energy furnished by the French nuclear power program. Electrically powered trains are economical because of their higher efficiency and are nonpolluting as well. The national railway company, or SNCF (Société nationale des chemins de fer), transports more than 2.5 million passengers daily—more than half of these in the Parisian area—and a half million tons of freight. In 1989, 800 million passengers were transported. Travelers appreciate the punctuality and comfort of French trains.

An Atlantic TGV line, to run from Paris to Hendaye on the southwestern border with Spain, already reaches Tours. A northern line linking Paris with the Chunnel and England is to be operational as of 1993, as will the Paris-Brussels-Amsterdam-Cologne-London tie-up with a train scheduled to speed along at up to 200 miles per hour. In all, the network already has seven hundred miles of rail. Indeed high-speed trains seem to be the answer to Europe's transportation needs. There is an ambitious European project to build ten thousand miles of lines for this rapid, nonpolluting, and economical means of transport by the year 2025. In December 1990, the EC Commission gave the go-ahead to a project that involves the construction of fifty-six hundred miles of high speed rail for trains traveling at 150 miles per hour to 190 miles per hour by 2015. In addition, ten thousand miles of existing lines will be upgraded to accommodate express trains (125 miles per hour).[4] In May 1992, a general agreement on the project to link the future French Eastern TGV with the German high-speed ICE (Intercity Express) network was signed between France and Germany. This will cut travel time between Paris and the major German cities drastically.

London will only be three hours from Paris by train when the Chunnel is completed. Thus, a Londoner will be able to hop on a train at 7 A.M. and be on the ski slopes in the heart of the Alps by early afternoon. Should the British invest in a high-speed link between Folkestone and London, the trip will be even quicker.

France is already working on third-generation high-speed trains. The Atlantic TGV broke the world speed record on 5 December 1989,

---

4. "La Commission de Bruxelles propose de construire 9000 kilomètres de lignes à grande vitesse," *Le Monde*, 7 December 1990.

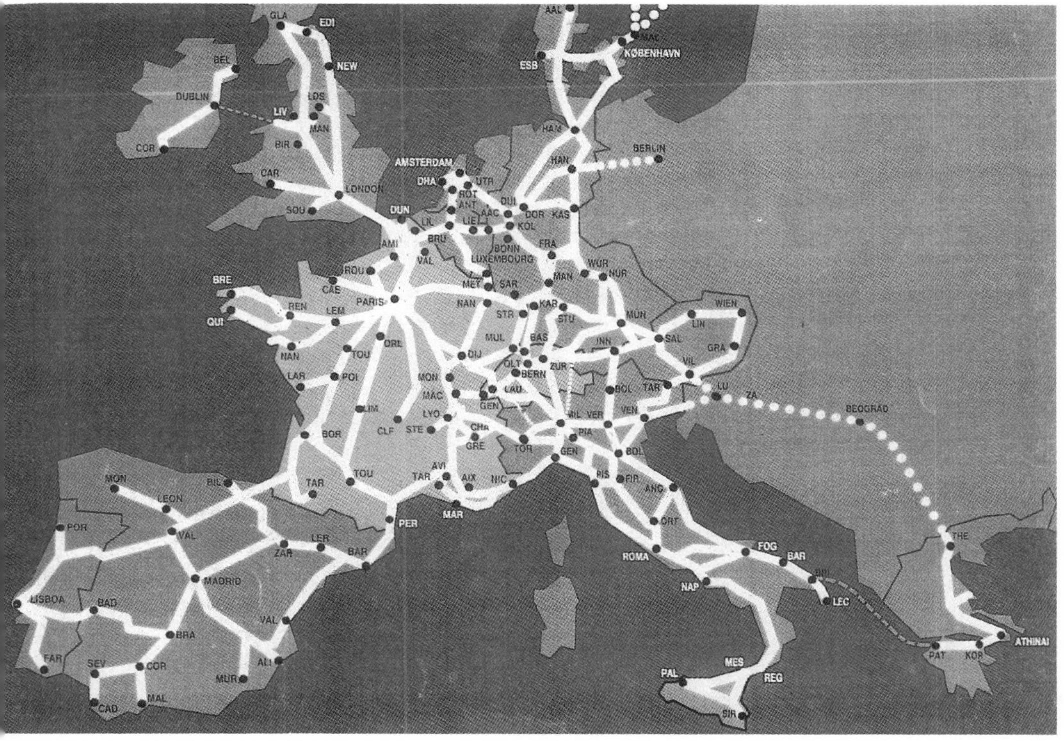

FIG. 6. High-speed European Rail Network of the Future. (Copyright © SNCF.)

reaching a top speed of 513.3 kilometers per hour (320 miles per hour). Its European rival, the German ICE, has a maximum speed of 407 kilometers per hour. The two main problems to be solved concern pressurization of passenger cars and the development of a standard electric current in Europe, where four different intensities of electricity are at present used. The French-British corporation GEC-Alshtom has already sold its technology to Britain, Spain, Belgium, and South Korea. In May 1991, the state of Texas opted for the TGV, dubbed the "Train of Great Velocity," that will link Dallas to Houston in ninety minutes at a speed of 200 miles per hour, if funds can be found for the project. GEC-Alsthom is negotiating with several other countries, including Taiwan, Canada, and Australia.

Some unexpected consequences of the TGV are worth mentioning.

One is that property prices have soared in some towns because of the business it generates, but it may also hurt the status of other towns or regions. The Paris-Lyon TGV has in no way prevented migration from the Morvan region. Another development, according to an SNCF survey, is that the high-speed train has actually increased centralization. "Turbo-executives" in Lyons, for example, increasingly hop on the train for meetings in Paris. Before the high-speed line was opened, the journey took nearly four hours; now it takes only two. Moreover, executives increasingly use the TGV as an annex of their office and can make phone calls during the trip.[5] The French have become more mobile than is generally believed, but one of the reasons for the popularity of the TGV is that it allows professionals in the provinces to spend the day in Paris and be back home for family dinner in the evening.

Air Transport

"Low traffic, high fares, prerogatives" was how the French business journal *L'Expansion* described European airways in September 1988.[6] With a potential population larger than that of the United States, the national airlines of the twelve European countries manage to carry less than one-fifth the total number of passengers transported by American companies. High fares offset low productivity but discourage would-be travelers. Nine out of ten French people have never taken a plane!

Until early 1990 there were three main airline companies in France: UTA, a long-haul carrier that was assigned all western Africa destinations in 1963; Air Inter, which was confined to domestic flights; and Air France, the national airline, set up in 1933. As France moved toward the 1993 single-market deadline, it hardly looked likely that three companies could survive in a deregulated Europe. Thus, when Air France acquired a controlling share of UTA in January 1990 and increased its holding in Air Inter, the news came as a welcome suprise. The national company became the seventh largest airline in the world in number of passengers transported per kilometer flown (47.5 billion annually) and the second largest in Europe after British Airways. However the European Community has taken steps to ensure that the national airline cannot mo-

5. SNCF:TGV Sud Est, Service des études, de la recherche et de la technologie. See B.C.,"Une génération de turbo cadres," *Le Monde*, 27 January 1988.

6. Airy Routier, "Air France, UTA, Air Inter, faut-il faire l'union?" *L'Expansion*, 9–22 September 1988, 115.

nopolize traffic in France, and the company is committed to opening up certain routes to competitors from abroad.

With the acquisition in 1992 of 37.5 percent of the capital of Belgian Sabena airlines, Air France has now the critical size necessary to compete in a deregulated Europe, but this will involve changing a number of bad habits. Repeated strikes reveal a serious management problem; productivity is low and the company has a record number of ground staff and on-board personnel—the service is indeed unbeatable! The *corporatisme* of French airline personnel and the lack of entrepreneurship of successive government-appointed directors of Air France are major obstacles to reform.[7] An example of this corporatism came in November 1990, when the company announced measures for restructuring the network and employees went on strike, protesting the shutdown of unprofitable international links with provincial cities, such as Nice, and the transfer of some personnel from Air Inter to Air France.

Despite the reluctance of the Socialist government to allow a nationalized company to raise capital from private investors—in fact, 30 percent private capital is authorized—Air France will inevitably look to private capital to insure its future development. Alain Faujas believes that the arrival of "normal" shareholders would be "a breath of fresh air" for the national airline and would lead to tighter control

> because the company is managed by a technostructure, where civil aviation administrators, trade unionists, pilots, and pure products of the seraglio hold sway. In this closed environment—now that they no longer fear competition on the home front and are protected from without by the government—they are in danger of losing touch with world airline realities and of believing that deregulation is a thing of the past. The eyes and the voices of private capital would be a precious antidote to these corporatist temptations.[8]

Paris has the second largest airport system in Europe after London,

---

7. *Corporatisme* refers to the clannish attitude of professional groups who exercise a monopoly in their profession and cling fiercely to their prerogatives, just like the corporations (trade guilds) of the ancien régime that were officially abolished on 4 August 1789. See the section "Fortress France" in chap. 17.

8. Alain Faujas, "Le rachat d'UTA intervient dans un contexte de déréglementation mondiale," *Le Monde*, 20 January 1990.

and the French are stepping up investment to be able to handle fifty million passengers as of 1993. A new extension is to be built as well as a TGV station so that passengers will be able to hop off the plane and onto the high-speed railway network.

Sea Transport

Despite its privileged geographical position "between two seas," and though almost 40 percent of French trade (in monetary terms) is carried out by sea, France is not a major maritime power. Its merchant fleet of 215 carriers ranked only twenty-third worldwide in 1989, that is, just after the Bermudas.[9]

In the 1960s and early 1970s great hopes were held out for the six principal French seaports, which account for 90 percent of the traffic: Marseille, Le Havre, Rouen, Dunkerque, Nantes-Saint-Nazaire, and Bordeaux. Major modernization programs were undertaken to increase their capacity. Because oil was the major energy source at that time, the ports were redesigned and extended to reduce the costs of handling it. French shipbuilding was the most technologically advanced in the world, and the French fleet had four of the world's largest tankers, with a capacity of 500,000 metric tons each. The oil crisis dashed these hopes, so that "years of technological innovation and massive investment were frozen."[10] Painful restructuring has taken place, and promising initiatives are being taken in other directions to offset the decline of the major French ports.

In 1974 the luxurious liner *France,* no longer profitable, was sold, putting an end to the era of floating hotels. Although many shipyards were closed during what was to be the bleakest period for French shipbuilding, Les Chantiers de l'Atlantique, in Saint Nazaire, and Les Chantiers du Havre, both remarkable for technological innovation, remain competitive in a market dominated by the Japanese. High-tech sailing ships such as the *Lafayette,* with its five masts and 250 square meters of sail, or the *Club Med 1,* the largest cruising ship with sails in the world (120 meters long by 20 wide), are opening up new opportunities for French shipbuilding.

In the short term, the opening of the Chunnel in 1993 is likely to

9. *La France en chiffres,* special number of *Science et Vie Economie,* 1991–92, 117.

10. Miquel, *Vive la France,* 379.

Marine High Tech

If French shipbuilding has suffered badly in the past fifteen years, France comes second only to the United States in the development of high-tech equipment for exploring the seabed. Comex, an industrial deep-water diving company, has almost 50 percent of the world market in this area. It has built the first autonomous, unoccupied submarine capable of exploring the seabed at depth of six thousand meters. Another firm, Intersub, located in Marseilles, has practically a monopoly on the inspection of off-shore platforms in the North Sea. IFREMER (Institut français de recherches sur l'exploitation de la mer) has built a manned bathyscaphe designed to reach a depth of six thousand meters, and Smal Industries has developed a two-seater submarine. The SMAL, which can safely take its passengers to a depth of fifty meters, can be used for leisure or the surveillance of underwater installations.

Another interesting piece of high-tech gear designed in France is the little ultrasonic transmitter produced by Comex-Pro that enables solitary transatlantic skippers to get back on their ship if they fall overboard. The device, no bigger than a cigarette pack, is triggered by water pressure. The sound waves are picked up by a receiver in the cockpit of the ship that then activates the automatic pilot and the tiller halting the boat. At the same time a relay ejects a self-inflating dinghy with a lifeline over the stern. All the skipper has to do is to climb onto the dinghy and pull back to the ship with the aid of the lifeline.

affect the cross-channel ferry link with Britain, which has been one of the mainstays of French passenger traffic. Eurotunnel expects to grab 70 percent of the traffic, but ferry companies believe *they* can hold on to 70 percent.[11]

The construction jobs created by the Chunnel have been a help to a stricken region, and property investment is pouring in. Housing and land is far less expensive than in affluent Kent on the other side of the channel, and when the Chunnel is completed, British employees who will have settled in France are expected to commute daily!

Telecommunications

Twenty years ago France's telephone system was so antiquated that it had become something of an international joke, and the tribulations of Fernand Raynaud, the popular music hall artist, trying in vain to get

11. Laurent Zecchini, "La bataille de la Manche a commencé," *Le Monde*, 24 September 1991.

through to "22 à Asnières" were barely exaggerated. In 1970 France had fewer telephone lines than did Greece! The changes that have taken place are impressive. In 1968 only 15.2 percent of homes had a telephone. Today the figure is 98 percent. With fifty main lines per one hundred inhabitants, France is among the best-equipped countries in the world and is pioneering a telecommunications revolution: *Télématique, Minitel,* and *cartes à puce* or "smart" cards have become household words. Nothing better illustrates the modernization of France than the truly spectacular developments that took place in telecommunications in the 1980s.

Although France ranks only eleventh worldwide for the density of its telephone network, it has one of the most sophisticated systems in the world. It has built a digital network that can carry voice, data, and audiovisual messages. In 1990 it became the first country in Europe to make an integrated services digital network (ISDN) available nationwide. This dial-up service, called *Numéris,* can transmit data files anywhere in France at fifty times the speed of ordinary modems. Unlike the telephone, distance is not taken into account in the billing, which makes this service very attractive to corporations. While cable television is not as developed in France as in other countries, Montpellier is the first city in the world to have optical fiber cables installed to carry phone services and TV programs through the entire city. The equipment manufacturer, Alcatel, which merged with ITT in 1986, holds 15 percent of the world market and 30 percent of the European market for switching equipment.

Smart Cards

It is difficult to find a coin-operated public telephone in urban France. France Télécom has installed vandal-proof card telephones nationwide. Smart cards, invented by the creative Roland Moreno, are credit-size plastic cards embedded with microcomputer chips. Phone users purchase 50-unit or 120-unit *télécartes* at a local post office, tobacconist, or railway station, then use them in the card telephones, each of which has a special smart-card reader.

Telematics and Minitel

Télématique is the French word coined to describe the combination of *télécommunications* and information technology, or *informatique.* It refers to the technology of transmitting data over telephone lines.

Minitels are lunchbox-sized, video-text terminals used widely in French homes and offices. Every month ninety thousand new Minitels are added to the five million already installed, and it is expected that by the mid-1990s one out of two telephone subscribers will have one. Whereas attempts to use video-text in other countries have met at best with a lukewarm reaction, the French operation has been a tremendous success thanks to the shrewd marketing strategy of the P&T (poste et télécommunications): in 1982, Minitels, which have a unit cost of $200, were provided free of charge to one million telephone subscribers in lieu of the cumbersome, printed telephone directories, the idea being to save forty thousand tons of paper annually (printed directories are to be phased out). Thus phone users had free directory assistance on twenty-five million numbers at their fingertips. The *annuaire electronique* was born! The electronic directory service encouraged many to try the Minitel, and before long they began to browse through the ancillary services that are not free: armchair shopping, weather reports, train and airline schedules, reservations; data bases that allow you to calculate insurance or the cost of highway toll from one city to another; educational services, entertainment, cooking recipes, and the scandalous flirt and blind-date services that contributed in no small way to the success of the operation in the early days. In 1990 Minitel connection time totalled over one hundred million hours. In 1991, more than fourteen thousand services were available that cover a whole range of subjects from the indispensable to the futile.

The charges vary according to the number dialed and the prices applicable for the service provided. When you use the Minitel, you have to pay France Télécom the price of your phone call to the service you wish to connect to and the cost of consulting the data bank, which is left to the discretion of the service. For Télétel 3 (*kiosque*) and a few other services, charges are based on connection time and appear on the subscriber's phone bill. France Télécom will return a percentage to the agent running the service. There is a basic connection fee of twelve centimes and charges range from thirty-six centimes to Fr 2.19. Early users were sometimes astonished by their phone bill, particularly if their kids were connecting to the numerous games available! Now they have grown wiser and more experienced. On average, Minitels are used 1.5 hours per month.

France Télécom has produced several new versions of the Minitel, from the improved basic model, the M2, which can be rented for less than Fr 20 per month, to the sophisticated laptop M5 that costs Fr 230

Some Minitel Services

Dialing Code	
11	Toll free for callers. The electronic directory generated 600 million calls in 1989. It is the most important data base in the world.
36-13 (Télétel 1)	This offers professional business services. A password is necessary.
36-14 (Télétel 2)	Professional services but also useful services for the general public: armchair shopping, transport, banking, and so on. One in five Minitel users subscribes to a banking service. 36-14 offers nearly five thousand services.
36-15 (Télétel 3)	Commonly called *kiosque*. Some of the most popular services in the early days were the *messageries* or message centers (particularly the notorious *messageries roses*, which put callers in touch with an anonymous correspondent for an "intimate" dialogue via Minitel). Games and information services were also very popular, but now connection to the *messageries* has dropped to fewer than three million hours per month as people become more aware of the practical rather than the entertainment value of Minitel.
36-18	Minitel to Minitel link designed for the deaf.
36-05	Toll free. The supplier of the service bears all costs.

to rent. Of the present five million Minitels distributed, about one million were rented in 1990. The basic M1 model is still available free of charge. Revenues already balance spending, and France Télécom's policy is to invest further for the sake of diversification.

At present, Minitel users can rent a smart-card reader to make stock and bank transactions or travel arrangements, but there are plans to equip future Minitels with a built-in card reader. It is hard to know if France's success with video-text is exportable. Great hopes were held out in the beginning, but there are many obstacles, including the absence of a European standard. Yet some countries are moving toward multistandard terminals, and the French Télétel is now interconnected with the Italian Videotel. Crossborder connection time amounted to 140,000 hours in 1990. Interestingly, the Italians, like the French in the early days, seem for the moment to be essentially attracted by the "fun" services.

Minitel pilot programs are already under way in Spain, Ireland, and Portugal. Sales efforts have been launched in several countries. The hopes placed in French-speaking Canada were dashed when the Canadians chose the Alex terminal, based on a U.S. standard launched by Bell-Canada. The American market is potentially enormous, but a wide variety of services already exist there for personal computer access. However, a Minitel network on French lines—Videotel—has been set up in Houston and another in Omaha in collaboration with the American company, U.S. West. France Télécom has also set up a software subsidiary in the United States called Infonet Minitel Services.

A New France

The past thirty years have seen profound shifts in French society, which is becoming more open, less "self-centered," and, perhaps, for the foreigner less "typical." Rural France is changing, apartment blocks are more common than chateaux, expressways crisscross the land; Eurotunnel, the TGV, the digital telephone network, and the Minitel are symbols of these changes. One may ask if the country buffeted by influences from the four corners of the globe is losing its soul in the process of modernization, as Lothar Baier has suggested,[12] or if France is simply rediscovering its ancient function as a crossroads after three hundred years of practically uninterrupted protectionism.

---

12. Lothar Baier, *Firma Frankreich* (Berlin: Verlag Klaus Wagenbach, 1988), trans. Jean-Luc Tiesset, *L'entreprise France* (Paris: Carlmann-Lévy, 1989).

PART 2

La Vie, L'Amour, La Mort

Plus je fais l'amour, plus j'ai envie de faire la révolution; plus je fais la révolution, plus j'ai envie de faire l'amour.

—Graffito at the Sorbonne, Paris 1968

[The more I make love, the more I want to make revolution; the more I make revolution, the more I want to make love.]

4

The Sexual Revolution

John Naisbitt in his book *Megatrends* points out that whereas the shift from an agricultural society to an industrial society in America took one hundred years, "the restructuring from an industrial to an information society took only two decades."[1] Nowhere else, except perhaps Japan, has the pace of change in the last fifty years been faster than in France. The country has practically leapfrogged from a centuries-old rural civilization into a postindustrial society.

Les trentes glorieuses, the "thirty glorious years" (1945–75) of French economic expansion, were brief in comparison with the industrial maturation of England and America. The French barely had had time to adjust to a postwar manufacturing boom when they had to readjust to the oil crisis bust before being hurled into the dizzy world of high tech. The pace of change has wrought havoc in every sphere of life. As Emmanuel Todd says, "Between 1974 and 1988 the slowdown in economic growth concealed the speed of social change. . . . Recent changes in the socioprofessional structure, in the level of education, in family, religious, and political behavior are such that it is legitimate to speak of a revolution in [French] society."[2]

The turmoil has not yet abated, and the major transformations taking place in life-styles and values can help explain the social tensions and contradictions of a society that has lost its traditional bearings. The life of the French from cradle to grave has been affected by these changes, one of the most notable of which is the so-called sexual revolution.

Claude Chabrol's 1988 film, *Une Affaire de Femme,* starring Isabelle Huppert in the role of Marie-Louise Giraud, a laundry woman who was executed in 1943 for practicing illegal abortion, is a reminder of the revolution in moral values that has taken place in France. Not only was

1. Naisbitt, *Megatrends,* 18.

2. Emmanuel Todd, "Une révolution toute neuve," *L'Expansion,* 21 October–3 November 1988, 104.

abortion legalized in 1975 for pregnancies of up to ten weeks, but since 1982 all the costs involved in the operation have been fully refunded under the public health system. Fewer than thirty years ago militants of the Family Planning Movement had to smuggle diaphragms into France. Today, both diaphragms and oral contraceptives are refunded by social security, and public television—admittedly in response to the scare of AIDS—is even promoting the use of condoms.

The sexual revolution came late to France. Whereas women in the United States won the right to vote in 1920, French women had to wait until 1944. Little progress was made in other areas until the 1960s. In an effort to stem the wave of illegal abortions, the first birth control center was set up in France in 1956—forty years after the United States—but the sale of contraceptives was forbidden until 1967!

The liberalization of contraception and abortion were the great victories of the women's lib movement in France, which opened a breach in a society where family ethics had scarcely changed since the nineteenth century. World War I had taken a tremendous toll on the population, and the 1920 law banning advertising for contraceptives had its logic. Though human losses in World War II were less drastic, the pro-Hitler Vichy government of Marshall Pétain (whose motto was "Work, Family, and Fatherland") did not condone "moral laxity."

Abortion

The current debate on abortion in the United States has had very little echo in France, where it was legalized in 1975. There has been reluctance by some physicians to carry out the operation and protest by minority groups who, in 1990, attempted to prove that the law violated human rights. The Council of State judged otherwise. In fact, in spite of a negligible number of agitators who have been trying to imitate pro-life groups in the United States, legalized abortion has never seriously been called in question, and the number of operations has been declining regularly since 1984. There were fears that the RU-486 drug developed by Professor Etienne Beaulieu—exaggeratedly dubbed "the day after pill"—and commercialized by the pharmaceutical group Roussel-UCLAF might make home abortions so easy that it would be used as a contraceptive. Pro-life groups, particularly in the United States, were so vocal that after an initial launching of the product it was hastily withdrawn from the market by the producers, who feared a boycott of their other products. This did not prevent Beaulieu from being awarded the coveted U.S. Lasker Prize for achievement in medical research. It was the minister of health who finally ordered the corporation to distribute the drug again, but very strict legal measures have been taken to insure against abuse and to prevent accidents. As she must for surgical abortions, the woman wishing to abort must undergo the standard interview and confirm her intention. The pill can only be taken in the presence of a doctor who has prescribed it in an authorized abortion clinic, and the woman must even sign a document declaring that she is taking the drug voluntarily and has been informed of its medical properties. It is not possible, therefore, to buy the pill over the counter.

With easy access to contraception and abortion, together with the spread of AIDS that is discouraging sexual promiscuity, one might ask if the family planning centers have any role to play nowadays. The pioneer center in Grenoble, where pregnant women from all over France sought aid in the 1960s and 1970s, still exists and continues—illegally—to help distraught Frenchwomen to obtain an abortion in England. Why? Simply because French law authorizes the operation only for fetuses of up to ten weeks. In Britain the limit for foreigners is twenty-four weeks. Does the fact that the authorities turn a blind eye to this practice indicate the high degree of tolerance of the French for personal choice in this matter, or does it show a lack of political courage, a fear to stir up trouble and reopen the wounds of the past?

The Battle of the Sexes

> It looks like we are aware of their superiority and that we want to prevent them from taking advantage of it.
>
> —Jean le Rond d'Alembert (1717–83)

Before the 1960s French women had very few formal rights. The Napoleonic Code of 1803 gave absolute power to the husband, who could demand divorce if his wife committed adultery, whereas the man could merely be subjected to a fine—and then only if the adulterous act took place in the home! This restriction was finally abolished in the late nineteenth century. Other laws were introduced that increased the rights of married women, but they had to wait until 1965 to be allowed to work or open a bank account without the consent of their husband! In 1970 "parental authority" (*autorité parentale*) over the children replaced

Much publicity has followed each time a woman has been able to break into a male stronghold such as the Paris *bourse* (stock exchange), where entrance was forbidden to them until 1968, and the first woman to be admitted to Ecole polytechnique in 1972 was hailed in the media. Yet, today, the prestigious school has only thirty female graduates from among the three hundred students who attend annually.

Today 44 percent of the working population are women. Yet many professions are virtually closed to women. Only one Air France pilot is a woman, and there is only one female préfet. In public and private corporations, in public administration as well as in worker unions, few women occupy key executive positions. Politics is the most misogynist of all: only three ministers in the twenty-nine member Balladur cabinet are women and there are only thirty-seven women in the 577-member National Assembly; 3 percent of senators are women. There are only five women among the 264 chief executives of the top twenty French corporations—four work in public relations and one in a legal department. 45 percent of working females are confined to 20 professions among the 455 that figure in the INSEE classification. Many are to be found in clerical and low-paid jobs and, even when they are executives, tend to perform a limited number of functions such as commercial or administrative ones in a limited variety of firms such as pharmaceutical, cosmetic, and publishing companies. On average, they earn 31 percent less than males, although the gap narrows to about 15 percent higher up the hierarchy.* Women have been worse hit by unemployment than men, and a larger number of them hold down precarious or part-time jobs, even though they are better educated in general.

There is no denying that barely disguised discrimination still exists in many professional fields, but things are slowly changing, and some professions such as elementary and secondary school teaching (relatively poorly paid, it is true) have a majority of women. Other jobs such as social workers and nursery school teachers have hardly any men, while more than 50 percent of liberal professionals are females. In fact the spouses of the latter, who are dependent on their wives, are seeking a new legal status! Educated women in particular are beginning to challenge their male counterparts, especially in private business, where one out of five corporations with more than ten employees is now controlled by a woman. Perhaps the most significant change is that female executives are no longer the objects of condescension, bemusement, or gratuitous aggressivity and are forcing recognition of their competence and pragmatism in a tough male environment where they cannot afford to make a faux pas. They have acquired a new self-assurance and authority and no longer need to hide their femininity and charm to command respect: "Nowadays they no longer want to sacrifice this essential part of their nature. From this point of view they are undergoing a major change

**Le Monde*, 14 February 1990.

because the successful woman is no longer the 'male-woman.'" Modern women "have acquired an extra dimension that leaves men somewhat at a disadvantage," writes Ségolène Royal. They manage to combine "a career, motherhood, and *vie affective* [emotional life]".† It might be hasty to conclude that the avant-garde woman is representative of the vast numbers of women in low-paid jobs who are not always so respected, but it would be hard to deny that some women are asserting a new feminine awareness and independence. A survey taken in 1987 showed that if a majority of women reject the erotic image French advertising tries obsessively to project, they have no complex about flaunting their femininity.‡

†Ségolène Royal, "Elles ne récriminent plus, elles assument," *Le Monde*, 9 March 1990.
‡IPSOS–*Le Monde* poll, 3–19 March 1987.

the term "paternal authority" (*pouvoir paternel*) in civil law. Full legal parity within marriage was finally achieved in 1985 with the publication of the Badinter law, which put an end to the last vestige of male domination, whereby only the husband was entitled to administer the property the spouses owned conjointly. In fact this law only made official what had become the new pattern of relationships within the family.

In the 1970s and 1980s, with a calm determination and self-confidence, French women chipped away at the prerogatives of a male society in the home, education, athletics, and the workplace and shook the conviction men had of their own superiority. Today, the sharing of household chores may not be perfect; discrimination in jobs and salaries has not disappeared in spite of legislation; sexual harassment by employers, rape, and marital abuse may still often go unpunished; but, by and large, the status of women in contemporary France has moved over the past twenty-five years from one of subjection to equality, or rather to recognition of a fundamental right to liberty of choice in matters such as procreation, career, and family life. As one of the few female Socialist deputies, Ségolène Royal, who was to become minister of the environment in the Bérégovoy cabinet in 1992, pointed out in a remarkable analysis in *Le Monde* for Woman's Day 1990, this has been the major transformation in womanhood: "If equality has not yet been achieved, female values are no longer ashamed to assert themselves. The desire for children has replaced abortion and the ethic of free choice has supplanted obsessive egalitarianism."[3]

3. Ségolène Royal, "Elles ne récriminent plus, elles assument," *Le Monde*, 9 March 1990.

It is in the name of free choice that contraception, abortion, and in vitro fertilization are not only available to French women but paid for under the social welfare system; that single mothers enjoy the same benefits as married mothers; that four months paid maternity leave is available for each birth; that publicly financed day-care facilities, though still insufficient in number,[4] as well as nursery schools allow working mothers to continue working; that leave of absence from work to look after a sick child is available to either parent; that raising children is considered a worthy occupation in itself; that a wife—or husband—who has worked on a permanent basis prior to becoming a parent is entitled to a regular income, albeit small, if she decides to give up her job to bring up her kids; that divorce by mutual consent and dual management of the children's well-being by divorced couples have been made possible no matter which partner has custody; and that discrimination in education or jobs is illegal.

The range of legislation guaranteeing sexual equality that has been passed in less than a quarter of a century has completely altered the status of women. It is in family matters and in relations with their male partners that they have been able to assert themselves most, although not always without suffering emotionally—as well as economically when they belong to low-income categories—after a divorce or separation.

Men have changed too and no longer feel obliged to hide feminine feelings such as tenderness, which has become a new expression of virility. The attentive husband and the "new fathers" of the TV commercials who bathe and change the children exist in a service society where intelligence and imagination have replaced physical superiority and lead to a new relationship between male and female, between father and children. But the battle of the sexes is not over in a society that has a long tradition of investigation in affairs of the heart, from the troubadour poets of the Middle Ages to Marguerite Duras. It is practically a specialty of French literature and movies.

4. The problem of day care is a serious one for many mothers, as was shown in the television program "Mediations" (TF1, 26 September 1989). Fifty-six percent of the 770,000 children under three cannot be placed in official *crèches* (kindergartens), and some 200,000 babies are confined to "unofficial" nannies. In a society that prides itself on egalitarianism, only a minority of mothers, more often than not the better-off, can actually get their children into state and municipally financed day-care centers owing to the shortage of places. This may also explain why so many women can work only part-time.

In France the struggle for sexual equality never exhibited the contempt for males that was sometimes present in feminist movements in other countries. As Evelyne Sullerot says: "In France there has never been between men and women that wall of mistrust, indeed hate, that is to be found in Anglo-Saxon countries, particularly the United States. Men and women in France have always tried to charm and seduce one another, have always loved to talk together, to eat together, to play all the variations of joys and pains together even during the years of feminist struggle."[5] However, Sullerot, who was the founder of the French Family Planning Movement, is so alarmed by recent legal developments that have tipped the scales in favor of women, and by the ferocity of disputes between men and women over child custody after separation or a divorce, that she has taken up the defense of husbands and fathers in her latest book, *Quels pères, quels fils?*[6]

Birth control, medically assisted procreation, and the new economic independence of women have given them the upper hand in the last resort and largely deprived men of initiative in these matters. In three out of four cases it is the wife who asks for divorce, and in 85 percent of the cases it is she who gets custody of the children. The male partner in a couple is no longer indispensable. As another sociologist puts it: "The father is the fuse. When there's a short circuit in the couple, he blows."[7]

As for women, their principal complaint is the unpreparedness of men to accept the new role they expect them to play. It is not so much the sharing of chores that is at issue, although women continue to bear the brunt of household work and child rearing. According to INSEE figures,

---

5. Evelyne Sullerot, *Quels pères? Quels fils?* (Paris: Fayard, 1992), 252.
6. See Sullerot, *Quels pères? Quels fils?* 114–15.

Paternity henceforth depends entirely on the mother, on her desire and on her relationship with the father. . . . Henceforth the woman is the decider. . . . [T]he man is the instrument she uses to become a mother. . . . After the birth of the child, the paternal role depends less on the father-child relationship than on the quality of the mother-father relationship. The couple has precedence over paternal consanguinity. If the mother no longer wants to live with her husband or male friend, the father will rarely be able to continue living with his child. If she does not care for him as a father, she can deprive him completely of relations with his son. . . . To enjoy the full status of a father today, it is henceforth necessary to please the mother before, during, and after.

7. Marie Chaudey, "Papa, comment tu as changé," *La Vie*, 30 March 1989, 57.

mothers devote six times more time to their children today than fathers. Indeed, husbands today only contribute six minutes more per day than their own fathers did to domestic tasks! Modern appliances have relieved women of much of the drudgery of housekeeping. Their main complaint is the males' refusal to recognize woman's several abilities, her triple role of mother, professional, and wife, which she often deems essential for her personal development. According to Ségolène Royal, if a man becomes a hindrance to the realization of her other two goals, the "superwoman" of today prefers to forego his services

> because nowadays woman too longs for the repose of the warrior, coming home to a joyful, gentle, tender, and courteous man (the eternal male?). She does not demand anything else from him. Neither domestic chores nor a fabulous social status, nor a breath-catching chic [*un look d'enfer*]. Only the loving presence of a distinguished guest. If not, solitude is better. But man has not understood. He still needs a dependent relationship to have a feeling of being "useful," by imposing upon himself obligations that woman no longer expects from him.[8]

This public plea for a quality love relationship is very much in the mood of the 1990s, but it is also very French. It would be difficult to imagine a female member of parliament in any other country writing with such intensity, in what is considered an intellectual newspaper, about affairs of the heart.

Sexual Mores in France Today

France has had no Masters and Johnson, and until recently there was very little reliable data on the sexual behavior of the French, as Professor Claude Got, a well-known advocate of sexual education in the schools, lamented in 1989, when he criticized the health authorities' bungling anti-AIDS advertising campaign promoting the use of condoms: "Lacking knowledge and serious thought [on the subject] we steer a course midway between religious, moralistic terrorism and the silly promotion of a gram of rubber by advertisers who have become our guides in matters of sexual education."[9]

---

8. Ségolène Royal, *Le Monde*, 9 March 1990.

9. Claude Got, "Nullité d'une politique," *Le Monde*, 1 November 1989. In a similar vein, Professor Got declared in a recent TV program that the minister

It was precisely this lack of reliable information necessary for a coherent policy in the battle against AIDS that prompted what was to be the most important study ever made on the sexual behavior of the French. The survey, launched by the ANRS (Agence nationale de recherche sur le sida) was carried out under the control of the INSERM (Institut national de la santé et de la recherche médicale). The sexual behavior of a large cross section of the population was analyzed following detailed telephone interviews with each of the twenty thousand persons who agreed to participate. All necessary precautions were taken to ensure that the collected data was as trustworthy as possible.[10]

In general, the findings—except for the influence of AIDS on the sexual behavior of the subjects, which the researchers were particularly interested in—confirmed the major trends that had been noted in a lesser study conducted by Dr. Pierre Simon twenty years previously: women on the average have sexual intercourse for the first time at seventeen

---

of education's decision to install vending machines for condoms in the lycées cannot be a substitute for proper sexual education. "La marche du siècle," Antenne 2, 3 March 1993.

10. Obviously the findings of a survey of this nature are based on the statements of the respondents. Two pilot studies carried out in 1990 indicated that the rate of acceptance of the questionnaire was identical for face-to-face interviews and telephone interviews that guaranteed anonymity. (As soon as the respondent answered "male" or "female" to the first question, his or her name and address were automatically erased by the computer. All the questions required a simple yes or no answer, or numbers, so that none of the responses could be understood by another person who might be present in the room.) The sample population of 20,055 persons age eighteen to sixty-five who had been residents of France for at least three years was chosen randomly from the France Télécom directory. (Only 20 percent of all the people contacted refused to take part in the survey.)

The study, which was carried out between September 1991 and February 1992, mustered twenty-three researchers (epidemiologists, demographers, and sociologists) from the major French research organizations and universities, and 110 interviewers. The first results of the inquiry were made public on 29 June 1992. There was a very high rate of response to the questions, even the most intimate ones, and a remarkable coherence in the responses for any given individual—it is difficult to lie for forty minutes! Variations from one interviewer to another were minimal, as were those between the results of the two polling institutes that participated in the survey. Despite all these precautions it is possible that there is a gap between the results of the study and the actual sexual behavior of the respondents, but the researchers feel that it cannot be a very large one. See Marie-Ange Adler, "Comment on fait l'amour en France," *L'Evènement du Jeudi*, 25 June–1 July 1992, and "Sujets à risques," *Le Monde*, 30 June 1992.

years of age and men at eighteen. The total number of sexual partners men tend to have as of twenty-five years of age does not seem to have changed very much: between twelve and fourteen on average; for women the figure is two to five, although women admit to having more sexual relationships than previously.

Information on younger teenagers (thirteen to eighteen years of age) can only be gleaned from studies that use sample populations that are very limited in number. One such survey for *L'Evènement du Jeudi* and *Sciences et Vie Junior* carried out in May 1992 showed that less than a third of the subjects interviewed had already had sexual intercourse. Fear of parental reprobation did not seem to be a very important factor for those who had not yet taken the plunge. Thirty years after the sexual revolution the behavior and attitudes of boys and girls—the rules of the mating game—do not seem to be very different from those of previous generations.[11] Love is one of the main values of young people according to all the surveys—but that is hardly a major discovery!

Attitudes and Values

Many of the taboos in sexual matters—taboos inherited from a conservative Catholic tradition and relayed strangely enough by the Communist Left, whose conception of family ethics was just as strict—have disappeared in modern France. Decision sharing has become the rule for the couple, and parents are less authoritarian and less inhibited with their children. There is general acceptance of people's right to live their sexuality as they think best—at least as far as heterosexual relationships are concerned. The French today are comfortable with displays of affection by couples in public, and no eyebrows are raised when women appear topless on beaches or tiny tots play in the nude at crowded seaside resorts. The obsessive use of sex in commercials that feminists elsewhere might find offensive to women does not seem to trouble anybody in France.

French people today put a high premium on sexual liberty, and in-

11. In the 1991 *Le Monde*-SCP Communication survey among teenagers in lycée, "love" ranked third in importance after "studies" and "friendship." "Money" trailed a long way behind. Monique Perrot-Lanaud, "Sexe, amour et lycéens," *Le Monde de l'Education*, May 1992, 34–49. See also Andrée Mazzolini, "Nous la génération Sida," *L'Evènement du Jeudi*, 25 June–1 July 1992, 76–78.

dividuals do not accept that parents, church authorities, politicians, or moralists dictate their behavior in these matters, as minister of the interior Charles Pasqua learned to his cost in 1988 when he tried to ban a number of pornographic magazines from newsstands, among them the respectable homosexual publication *Gai Pied.* The moralistic Pasqua became the laughingstock of the country. Even practicing Catholics pay no attention to the pronouncements of Rome on sexual morality, and the untimely remarks of the French bishops on the government's AIDS prevention campaign promoting the use of condoms received scathing criticism. Public tolerance in this area is very high in France, and the private lives of public figures give rise to no scandals, as they do in some countries.[12] Where else in the world could a reputed collector of pornographic literature have become a minister of education?

The French are very attached to the notion of civil liberty, and the law neither forbids nor condones any form of sexual behavior between consenting adults. This public tolerance—one of the many colorful terms for a brothel in French is *maison de tolérance*—which foreigners from more puritanical societies in search of adventure have often taken for permissiveness, always stopped on the threshold of the home, and it used not to be uncommon for a wife to cover up for an unfaithful husband

---

12. Questioned by the Anglo-American press in Paris in March 1989, on the "Tower affair," Michel Rocard, the French premier, visibly irritated, declared:

> One must never have touched a marijuana cigarette, even at the age of seventeen in high school; there's always an ex-student who is nasty and will tell tales. One must be of monastic fidelity toward one's wife. . . . We [the politicians] shall all keep on the straight and narrow when the level of hypocrisy declines, that is, when people will ask politicians to have the normal accepted behavior of the standard mores of the society in which they live—that includes those vaunted in television productions. ("M. Rocard, 'au train où l'on va' il n'y aura plus de ministres possibles," *Le Monde*, 6 March 1989)

Ironically, Rocard was to create quite a stir when he publicly announced his divorce from his wife in 1991, setting a precedent in French political life and breaking the self-imposed discretion of the press concerning the private life of politicians. The former premier's proclaimed concern for frankness, *le parler vrai*, possibly motivated this announcement, which was generally analyzed by pundits as an attempt by Rocard to ingratiate himself with public opinion for electoral purposes. In any case, reaction to the declaration was not so much approval or disapproval of the couple's divorce—after all, one in three French marriages ends in rupture—as bewilderment at the unprecedented announcement of the former prime minister.

to preserve the integrity of the *foyer.* Even today many foreign visitors, disconcerted by openness in sexual matters in France, would be wise not to make any hasty generalizations about the moral standards of the French.

Homosexuality: A Taboo Subject?

Open-mindedness toward sexual matters, especially in rural France and the smaller towns, is largely limited to heterosexual relationships. Although television has made a few laudable efforts to deal with the subject of homosexuality, there is little information on gay men and women in any of the recent books on French society, or even in the press in general, proving that it is still somewhat taboo in a sociopolitical environment that places such emphasis on the family.

In 1981, homosexuality became an election issue when ten thousand homosexual sympathizers demonstrated in Paris against discriminatory legislation. As a result, a law introduced by the Vichy government in 1942, which made homosexuality a crime, was abrogated and sexual majority for homosexuals was put on par with that of heterosexuals (fifteen years of age). Further, the mention that civil servants should be "of good morality" was struck from the statutes of public administration. Likewise in the new housing bill, the loi Quilliot (1982), the standard phrase referring to residence "en bon père de famille" (as an upstanding father) was removed. Police surveillance of homosexuals was also officially abolished in an administrative memorandum of the Ministry of the Interior in 1981, although the mysterious murder in 1988 of a gay activist and clergyman, Reverend Joseph Doucé, who was under police supervision at the time of the crime, raised some doubts about this.[13]

Despite these reforms, the tolerance of homosexual life-styles has its limits. For example, in 1992 one Socialist representative proposed to allow unmarried couples (homosexual or heterosexual) living together to contract a civil union in lieu of a marriage contract. Such a bill would give the same legal status and advantages in terms of taxation, inheritance, social security, and so forth to gay couples as to married couples. (For example, if a civil union were authorized, upon the decease of one member of a gay couple, the other could not be evicted from the couple's

13. Dominique le Guilledoux, "L'affaire Doucé et les renseignements généraux," *Le Monde,* 6 November 1990.

home by a landlord or relatives of the deceased.) The proposal met with considerable opposition. According to *L'Evènement de Jeudi,* the bill is unlikely to see the day: "In these times of panicky ethics, at ten months from the [legislative] elections, a representative who is a future candidate cannot afford to risk approving a law that officializes 'pansy marriages.' If the bishops have denounced a 'new attack on marriage,' a lot of other people have only retained this aspect of the bill."[14]

Public recognition of gays' rights has not notably altered attitudes toward homosexuality. Paris of course has a gay radio, Fréquence Gaie, and magazines such as *Gai Pied* can be found at newsstands everywhere. All the big towns have gay bars, restaurants, and night spots frequented mostly by males in search of adventure (lesbians tend to have more stable relationships). However, if it is relatively easy for artists to flaunt their homosexuality, it is a lot harder for manual workers to do so. Job discrimination, although illegal, definitely still exists; it would be risky for a schoolteacher, for example, to admit he or she was gay.[15]

It is difficult to find reliable statistics on the number of homosexuals. A survey carried out in 1985 by Dr. David Elia for IRMA (International Review of Medicine for Adolescents) revealed that 22 percent of young people between the ages of thirteen and twenty-two believe they are homosexual, a figure far higher than the roughly 10 percent in the adult population.[16] The ANRS survey on the sexual behavior of the French showed that homosexuals today are even more reluctant than in the 1970s to admit their homosexuality and that this reluctance probably gives an erroneous idea of their real number in the sample population. In 1992, only 4.1 percent of men (compared to 5 percent in 1970) and 2.6 percent of women among the more than twenty thousand persons interviewed admitted to being homosexuals—except for Paris and its surroundings, where the figures were double those in other places.

In May 1991, following a debate in the senate in the framework of the reform of the penal code, a majority of senators voted for what amounted to reintroducing the Vichy law abrogated in 1982, that is, homosexual relations with a minor (someone under eighteen years of

---

14. C. Salès, "L'union civile, un faux mariage pour de vrais droits," *L'Evènement du Jeudi,* 23 May–3 June 1992, 53.

15. Gérard Bach-Ignasse, "Vivre Homo," in Potel, *L'état de la France,* 53–54.

16. Anne Rousseau, "Le silence des homos," *Le Monde de l'Education,* May 1992, 39.

age—not fifteen as for heterosexuals) would be a crime punishable by two years of prison and a fine of Fr 200,000. Whatever the virtues of the legislation designed to protect young people from abuse by adults, the debate revealed the persistence of an ambivalent and somewhat disparaging attitude toward homosexuals. One senator remarked that opposition to the legislation "defied the common sense of the rural population. We do not want to introduce any form of discrimination. Homosexuality is not a crime, but it is something we do not want to see spreading around the country. Some people want to give us a guilt complex about this business. They are saying it is a horrible Vichy bill. . . . As for the silence of the penal code on this question during the Revolution, let's not forget that the code was drawn up by Cambacérès, whose nickname was Tante ["queen"] Hurlurette."[17]

In general, however, there seems to be greater understanding today for homosexual life-styles. The number of people (36 percent) who consider homosexuality as an acceptable expression of sexuality has increased since the 1970s (24 percent in 1973).[18] Nonetheless, though homosexual organizations have been in the forefront of the battle against AIDS, the gay community may become suspect again as the number of victims of the disease increases. The controversial decision taken in 1992 to ban traffic at night in the Bois de Boulogne in Paris, which a former minister of health, Michèle Barzach, described as "AIDS boulevard" on account of the number of transvestites who ply their trade there, may be an indication of decreasing tolerance for what are considered deviant forms of sexual behavior.

Violence and Pornography

The sexual revolution has been accompanied by an explosion of pornography. One of the main concerns today is that television and the Minitel have put an end to the distinction between public liberties and private liberty, and there is increasing concern about the evil effects on children at a time when latchkey kids are left to confront on their own television violence and soft porn.

The French magazine *Le Point* descibed a typical week's television

17. Gilles Paris, "La majorité sénatoriale rétablit le délit d'atteinte homosexuelle sur un mineur," *Le Monde*, 24 May 1991.

18. Gérard Mermet, *Francoscopie 1989* (Paris: Larousse, 1988), 50.

menu in October 1988. Selected viewers counted no less than 670 murders, 15 rapes (including sodomy and child rape), 848 fistfights, 419 shoot-outs or bombings, 14 kidnappings, 11 holdups, 8 suicides, 32 hostage threats, 27 scenes of torture, 18 drug cases, 13 stranglings, 11 war scenes, 11 striptease acts, and 20 torrid love scenes—though it was not the week of the monthly hard porn film on Canal Plus, the pay channel! Many of these programs are imported from the United States, and it is sad that the stereotype many less-educated French people should have of American culture comes from "Dallas," "Dynasty," and other such serials, which are merely "entertainment." It is also true that many French productions, while being less commercially successful, are not much better. A *Reader's Digest* poll in February 1990 showed that the French found the increasing number of commercials on TV more "hateful" than all the violence. 37 percent objected to the former and 35 percent to the latter. Only 6 percent objected to sex. The novelist Michel Tournier has declared that "a revolver is more obscene than a penis."[19]

The older generation is particularly upset by what they see on billboards, in movie theaters, and on television, but they do not dare to protest for fear of appearing old hat, or worse, of being lumped together with the extreme Right and its campaign to limit the liberty of expression so precious to the French.

The state plays a very ambiguous role. Thus while some films in movie theaters are banned to children under thirteen and others to those under eighteen, adult movies have been shown at prime time on television, and previews of films forbidden for children will be shown in movie theaters before a Walt Disney movie or at prime time on TV!

Le Minitel Rose

An astonishing book published in 1988 went as far as to accuse the state of connivance with porn barons. The author, Denis Perier, claims that the Minitel network was deliberately set up without any parliamentary control and a virtual monopoly organized by the state with certain press groups to exploit the *messagerie* services. After delivering Minitels free to French homes, the state-owned France Télécom claims it is a "neutral carrier"—"like a highway," in the words of its director—and cannot be

19. See Robert Solé, "La France sans carré blanc," *Le Monde*, 25 October 1988.

held responsible for the messages sometimes transmitted by prostitutes, pedophilites, and sadomasochists over the interactive network. The annual turnover of the *messageries roses* is an estimated Fr 1.5 billion shared by some thirty large groups and France Télécom.[20] Perier speaks of an abuse of power, or worse, "the moral decadence of the state." He claims that the Minitel was going to be nearly as big a commercial fiasco as the Concorde and that it was essentially the *messageries roses,* not the "electronic directory," that helped the successful launching of the operation. The conclusion of the book throws some light on the paradoxical conception the French have of the role of the state in matters of morality:

> Let's go deeper into this: is it the role of the state to contribute to an operation likely to be used as a support for illicit or amoral activities? In other words, does the state have a conscience? No! declare many citizens. To avoid interfering with personal liberty it should not intervene in ethical questions; it must remain neutral. This amounts to the denial of the very principle of a frontier between good and evil to guarantee against abuse by a public authority, in which case the administration can no longer be considered as acting solely in the common good. The state is no longer perceived as the incarnation of the community of citizens but rather more like some cold monster that it is better to shun.
>
> Finally, the most worrisome aspect of this case of the *messageries roses* is the moral decadence of the state and of the top administration that it cruelly highlights.[21]

Elsewhere, this well-documented book would have had the effect of a bombshell. Not so in France, where people seem blasé about scandals related to sexual questions, which they consider a private matter.

In 1992 the government slapped a 50 percent tax on telematic services with "a pornographic slant," and defenders of the *minitel rose,* including artists and intellectuals, signed public petitions in defense of the services. The minister of the budget, Michel Charasse, was accused of hypocrit-

20. Denis Perier Daville, "Le minitel rose et ses dangers," *Le Monde,* 5 December 1991.

21. Denis Perier, *Le dossier noir du minitel rose* (Paris: Albin Michel, 1988), 216.

ically arrogating the powers of censorship by deciding which services were pornographic and taxing them to fill the state's coffers, whereas it would be sufficient to apply existing legislation on prostitution and corruption of minors. Moreover, it was pointed out that the latest Minitel models have a special access code that could be used to prevent children from connecting to the porn services. The problem is that these more sophisticated models are not supplied free. In any case, according to a Louis Harris poll, the French are massively against banning the *messageries roses*. Only 2 percent of the respondents rate it as the first target for a ban, far behind violence in cartoons (46 percent) and advertisements for corridas, cigarettes, and so on, and even behind erotic films on television that everyone can watch.[22]

Paradoxically, in 1990, many French TV viewers were disturbed by a serious documentary entitled *L'amour en France*, which aimed to describe the sexual behavior of the French from the attitudes of tiny tots in nursery school to various types of adult relationships. In fact the main objection was that some viewers felt the youths interviewed had been manipulated by the film director and psychiatrist who produced the series. This was unfortunate, as Daniel Karlin's documentary raised important issues ranging from sexual education in schools, to teenage sex and the sexual lonesomeness of many people in France. (Does this explain the success of the *Minitel rose*?) The subject may have been too taboo for many viewers, although more than a third of them actually followed the series.

The French, like most people in the world, are rightly preoccupied about how children are treated but very often will refuse to see the beam in their eye. Unlike the United States little publicity is given to cases of perversion (child abuse, incest, rape) in the media. It is only recently that a hotline for victims of child abuse, Allo enfance maltraitée, was set up in Paris. Three to four hundred calls per twenty-four hours are recorded by the center. There were 100,000 calls in 1990 and double that number in 1991. While all these cries of distress may not be of equal gravity, the figure is still astonishing; sexual abuse beatings and incest—very often linked to overdrinking—are the main complaints. The fact that very often it is a third party such as a relative or a neighbor who reports the ill-treatment and furnishes his or her name shows a shift in

22. See Michel Colonna d'Istria, "Le minitel entre morale et taxation," *Le Monde*, 28 November 1991.

French attitudes to privacy in family matters and to denouncement, something French culture in the name of personal liberty is very loath to accept even for a good cause.

A similar trend is noticeable for rape and incest. Witnesses and victims are less reluctant than before to denounce their attackers to the police, who are more likely than before to enforce legislation. (Charges for rape increased by 143 percent between 1980 and 1990.) The subject of sexual harassment—in particular, the infamous *droit de cuissage,*[23] which is nothing more than the abuse of authority by male employers or superiors in order to seduce female employees—has given rise to new labor legislation and has been written into the revised penal code as well. Legislators have tried to make a law in keeping with French culture that will not be used by supporters of puritanical principles to denounce a man who tries to win the favors of a woman but that will prevent superiors from abusing their authority. These new trends show how much mentalities have changed since the beginning of the sexual revolution in France.

There are signs that Love with a capital L, said to have been dethroned by sex in the promiscuous 1970s and 1980s (in fact far less promiscuous than the media pretended), is once again the central preoccupation of the French. *L'Evènement du Jeudi* devoted a cover story to the subject in March 1990.[24] Tempting as it is to compare this to the moral revolution in the United States during the 1980s, the two trends have little in common for the simple reason that there is no equivalent of the Moral Majority in this secular society. It is in the name not of prudery but rather of a qualitative love relationship that the values of tenderness and fidelity seem to rate higher than sex today.

---

23. The legendary feudal right of an overlord to spend his vassal's wedding night with the bride.

24. Sylvie Blanc, "Ils sont heureux, ils s'aiment," *L'Evènement du Jeudi,* 8–14 March 1990, 54–65.

5

Demographics

> The room where the mother is to bring forth should be perfectly clean when her time comes; it shall be well aired. . . . The best way to do this is to light a blazing fire in the hearth. This will provide a strong current of air and help burn up the miasma.

La Vie

This 1914 Health Authority memorandum was still relevant in the 1950s in many parts of France, where 39 percent of births continued to take place in the home.[1] For a society in which one-quarter of the population was still engaged in agriculture, having a baby in the maternity hospital meant a month's absence from the farm. Thirty years later the rural population has shrunk, and less than 0.5 percent of babies are born at home. With an infant mortality rate of 7.2 per thousand births France does better than the United States (9.1 per thousand).

This change in the rate of home births is indicative of the many changes that have taken place in France since the immediate postwar period. Nevertheless, some writers say that hospital births have not necessarily made things easier for the majority of French mothers, who still bravely continue to give birth without the assistance of painkillers (in spite of the increasing number of episiotomies). Is this due to the callousness of male obstetricians, as has been suggested,[2] or has it something to do with the persistence of a rural mentality that sees childbirth as a natural process not to be interfered with?[3]

While the birthrate in France has dropped from the 1960s peak of 2.9 children per mother to 1.8 today, among the twelve EC countries

1. The memorandum is quoted by Bernard Lalanne, "Que reste-t-il de tout cela?" in *Demain la France* (Paris: L'Expansion, 1986).

2. Marie-José Jaubert, *Les bâteleurs de mal joli* (Paris: Balland, 1979).

3. Laurence Wylie, *Village in the Vaucluse* (Cambridge: Harvard University Press, 1958), 38.

only Ireland has a higher figure. Nevertheless, this rate is not sufficient to offset a rapidly aging population, which would require 2.1 births per mother to support them. An increase is unlikely to occur in spite of incentives, such as family allowances, to encourage couples to have more children. Marriage is on the wane, and married women are postponing their first child for as long as five or six years. Among married couples, DINKS (Double Income No Kids) and OINKS (One Income No Kids) are on the increase. Working women, abortion, and contraception are here to stay. However, it would be wrong to put all the blame for the decline in the birthrate on changing social standards. In fact, the one out of four children born out of wedlock today helps to maintain the number of births at its present level!

Marriage

Sociologists fiercely debate the causes of the demise of the traditional French family. Was it the 1968 student riots that shattered parental authority all over France? Was it the feminist movement? Urbanization? The automobile? The economic independence of women? Or pervasive materialism? Whatever the reason or reasons, the turning point for demographers came in 1972, when the birth and marriage rates toppled and divorce skyrocketed. While the average number of family members living under the same roof grew smaller, the number of people living alone increased. At nearly the same time there was a spectacular increase in unwed couples and single-parent families, leading to what have been described as "high-speed families of variable configuration."[4]

The venerable institution that has been the backbone of French society since the Middle Ages has taken a serious battering. In 1987 only 266,000 marriages took place in France, a drop of more than 30 percent since the early 1970s. In the years leading up to 1987 demographers expressed little hope for the future of marriage, and some made doomsday calculations, predicting that if the annual number of marriages celebrated in France followed the trend of the previous fifteen years, wedding bells would soon fall silent. In less than three decades, the tooting cavalcade of cars bedecked with white and pink carnations would no longer turn heads, offering a fleeting glimpse of marital bliss on a sunny Saturday afternoon in June. Yet the number of marriages in 1987 was a faint sign

4. Gérard Moatti, "La famille minimale," in *Demain la France*, 349–61.

Boy Meets Girl

Some recent studies illustrate interesting changes in dating patterns. In the seventy years between 1914 and 1984, with growing urbanization and the development of public dances, the most notable change was the decline in matches between neighbors. By the 1960s, however, public dances were losing ground as a trysting place. While these dances can still occasionally be found in working-class and rural areas, they are no longer the main place where couples meet. Family gatherings and the workplace have also declined as meeting spots. College, vacations, and clubs—while continuing to provide a place for couples to meet—are in fact losing their appeal. A sign of the times is that acquaintanceships made at private parties, in discos, and in public places are increasingly leading to marriage. People in the upper social classes tend to meet their future spouse in reserved social settings, whereas working-class couples tend to form in public arenas.*

Yet, it would be hasty to conclude that material considerations have little to do with marriage. People still overwhelmingly continue to marry within the social group within which they were raised. Only the nature of the possessions each partner tends to contribute has changed. As often as not a woman's "dowry" today consists of cultural and academic qualifications, while her future husband's salary scale, in place of the land and rents of the past, is also determined to a large extent by the degrees he holds.† Of course, the better educated tend to be wealthier as well.

Another trend is that couples tend to marry three years later than in the 1970s. For a first marriage nowadays the average age for the bride is 25.5 years, for the groom 27.5. More than 15 percent of couples have had children before getting married.

*Michel Bozon and François Héran, "La découverte du conjoint," *Population* vol. 6 (1987) and vol. 1 (1988).

†François de Singly, "Théorie critique de la homogamie," *Année Sociologique* 37 (1987): 181–205.

of hope for the nostalgic, because for the first time in fifteen years the figure showed a slight increase. (This increase was further confirmed in 1989 when 280,000 marriages were celebrated.) Had the wave of permissiveness in France subsided? Had the harsh winds of the recession driven the adventurers of 1968 back to the safety of the family haven? Had the spectre of AIDS chilled the hearts of the pleasure seekers? Or had a new understanding between men and women of the first generation of coeds reconciled individual aspirations with the demands of an institution that had ceased to be an absolute monarchy and received a new legal appearance? The questions are vain because a growing percentage of total couples is living out of wedlock. As Kriss Graffiti and Chantal Pelletier put it in their lusty *Et l'amour dans tout ça,* marriage is not coming back, "It's only going away slower, that's all."[5]

In a 1986 survey of French Catholics 87 percent of the couples interviewed declared they had had a church wedding after the mandatory civil ceremony at the town hall.[6] This is one of the paradoxes of a predominantly Catholic country where regular church attendance is negligible. It shows the strong influence of tradition even in a society in which the institution of marriage has lost some of its appeal to young people. The civil ceremony, presided over by the mayor in his tricolored sash, apparently lacks the solemnity that couples feel the commitment requires.

Divorce

In France one out of three marriages ends in divorce, although the rate is lower for some social categories such as farmers, shopkeepers, and manual workers, as well as in rural areas. This is one of the lowest divorce rates in Europe.

Originally a victory of the French Revolution, divorce was later outlawed under clerical pressure before its restoration in 1884. Divided on whether to consider marriage an indissoluble bond according to the teachings of the Catholic church or as a simple legal contract, French legislators have vacillated between conservative and liberal attitudes. The latter triumphed in 1976 when divorce by mutual consent was legalized—as it had been just after the revolution. Many saw a sharp increase in the divorce rate as a result of this liberal policy. However, the figures had begun to climb earlier. Moreover, about half the couples that divorce today still resort to the notion of matrimonial offence to justify their claim. In part, this is because it sometimes allows practical details such as joint property rights to be settled faster.

Until recently an odd legal disposition in France made it more rewarding for a couple with two children to be divorced than married, as

5. Kriss Graffiti and Chantal Pelletier, *Et l'amour dans tout ça?* (Paris: Balland, 1989), 25.

6. SOFRES–*Le Monde* survey, 8–13 September 1986. *Le Monde,* 1 October 1986.

New Patterns in Divorce

One of the important changes that has taken place in France in the past twenty years has been attitudes toward separation and divorce. Three new tendencies are worth mentioning: first, it is increasingly the wife who asks for divorce, which may show that French women feel freer, more independent, and more capable of managing on their own. This is probably not the only explanation. If the woman increasingly takes the initiative, it seems she is the one who is more involved in the marriage in the first instance and is therefore more exacting when marital conditions are not fulfilled. Moreover, she is almost certain to be awarded custody of the children.

Second, couples are divorcing sooner, at the average of four or five years after marriage compared to seven or eight years formerly. The children of divorce thus tend to be younger and the grandparents have to be called in to lend a hand with rearing the kids. "It is as if they are getting their own back for having had no say in the marriage decision," says Robert Solé.*

Children are no more an obstacle to divorce than they are a sufficient reason for getting married. In fact divorce seems to be more frequent for couples who have children before marriage or in families where there is not an adequate time lapse between the births of successive children. Indeed, "the decision to break up seems increasingly to spring from selfish considerations on the part of the couple."†

Once bitten twice shy. The third trend is that divorced individuals no longer tend to remarry. In the past, French people used to divorce after a disappointing marriage so as to make "a new start" with another partner. Twenty years ago twice more divorced couples remarried than today. In 1987 the figure was 16.6 percent, and in one out of two cases the new partner was unmarried.

**Le Monde*, 11 July 1985.

†Patrick Festy and Marie-France Valetas, "Le divorce et après," *Population et Société* 215 (INED, July 1987).

ex-husband and wife could each claim a separate tax break per child, whereas a married couple was only entitled to a deduction after the second child. This law was altered in 1986, and while the new legislation does not penalize divorced couples, it has put low-income married couples on a better footing by entitling them to an allowance for both children.

In the majority of cases, child custody is given to the ex-wife, partly because it is considered shameful for a woman not to demand it (tradition in this respect is still strong in spite of feminism), partly because judges tend to have a preference for mothers or, possibly, because of "sexist antifather prejudice." As they are generally not in favor of the idea of "Ping Pong children," they will most often refuse joint custody. However, the 1987 law that allows divorced couples to have an equal say in all major decisions concerning each child's welfare, no matter who has custody, should theoretically make it easier for fathers to play their role after a divorce.[7] If the children are mature enough, the judge is required to grant them a hearing before deciding on custody.

While divorce figures are alarmingly high (one out of two marriages in Paris breaks up), there have also been recent signs of a slowdown. Are people rediscovering the value of conjugal fidelity, as some commentators feel?

Unwed Couples

One of the most striking demographic shifts in France in the last decade has been the sharp increase in the number of couples living out of wedlock. The number doubled between 1976 and 1986 to reach more than one million in the 1990s. (Nobody knows the real number. Some demographers feel that this figure is underestimated.) While this is lower than in some Scandinavian countries, it is proportionally higher than in the United States (2.2 million couples in 1986) and is a record for a Mediterranean country with a strong family tradition. Fifty-seven percent of the couples that got married between 1980 and 1985 had lived together beforehand—75 percent in Paris.[8] In 1989, 23 percent of young adults in the twenty to twenty-four-year age group who were living together were unwed.[9]

The decrease in the number of divorced couples who remarry offers a partial explanation. Nonetheless, in one-third of the unwed couples today the male partner is under twenty-five years of age. While essentially an urban phenomenon that developed among the more educated classes, it has spread to rural areas and to other social groups as the

---

7. In her latest book (in which she defends fatherhood) the sociologist Evelyne Sullerot has demonstrated that divorced and, especially, unwed fathers who have separated have little or no chance in practice of exercising this right if the mother refuses to cooperate. Sullerot, *Quels pères, quels fils?*

8. Henri Leridon and Catherine Villeneuve-Gokalp, "Les nouveaux couples: Nombre, caractéristiques et attitudes," *Population* 2 (1988): 331–74.

9. Guy Desplanques and Michel de Saboulin, "Les familles ajourd'hui," in *Données Sociales 1990* (Paris: INSEE, 1990), 276–84.

stigma of living out of wedlock has vanished. In a poll taken in 1986 only 7 percent of those interviewed condemned it outright.[10] In another survey 69 percent of young people between the ages of thirteen and nineteen did not think it was necessary for a man and a woman living together to be married.[11] Parents have largely accepted this to preserve their relationship with their children, and it is not uncommon for them to help the young unmarried couple financially either by paying their rent or offering them room and board. An expression has even been coined to describe these young dependent couples: *les bébés couples* (the baby couples).

Sociologists point out that many unwed couples today have simply postponed marriage for practical reasons, or feel that it is necessary to cohabit before making this commitment so as to reduce the margin of error in their choice of a lifetime companion.[12] Others, they say, feel that such a long-term commitment is beyond them; the baby boomers have come of age in a society where instant gratification has replaced lifelong dedication. Yet others have become disillusioned with the capacity of political, social, and religious institutions to respond to the aspirations of the individual. Authenticity is the name of the game for these lovers; being true to oneself and to others is one of the major values among young people in contemporary France.[13] It is felt that the formal obligations of a marriage contract are an obstacle to an authentic relationship between two people, who do not need a legal document to love each other. The sexual liberation of young people, the economic independence of young women, and the removal of legal barriers and social taboos have done the rest. (Significantly, as Louis Roussel points out, derogatory terms such as *fille-mère, bâtard,* and *concubin* are no longer widely used.)[14]

Yet, just when unwed couples have become socially acceptable demog-

---

10. *Figaro Magazine*–SOFRES, June 1986, quoted by Mermet in *Francoscopie 1989*, 107.

11. *Le Parisien*–CSA, March 1987. See Mermet, *Francoscopie 1989*, 107.

12. The 1990 INED report shows that this is something of an illusion: 15.6 percent of the couples who live together before getting married are divorced ten years later, compared to 12.3 percent of those who did not cohabit before the wedding.

13. See Daniel Linnart and Anna Malan, *Fin de siècle, début de vie* (Paris: Syros, 1990).

14. Louis Roussel, *La famille incertaine* (Paris: Editions Odile Jacob, 1989).

raphers wonder if a turning point has not been reached. The authors of a study published in 1988 suggest that this might be due to the high level of unemployment among the young. The latter are tending to leave home later, and having no financial security, they are loath to strike up an unmarried relationship. The same report shows that these relationships are de facto marriages. As proof of this the authors point out that the number of children born out of wedlock multiplied by 2.5 between 1975 and 1985. Indeed, in spite of the development of contraception and abortion the number of children born out of wedlock in France today has shattered wartime records. One in three children is born to unmarried parents. The phenomenon is not confined to urban areas nor to any single social class, which shows the widespread acceptance it enjoys. (It was not always so. In the early 1950s what used to be called illegitimate births accounted for 7 percent of the birthrate. These mostly occurred in the working classes, and fingers were pointed at the "culprits.")

In the 1988 study 28 percent of the couples already had a child, 38 percent wished to have one, and only 10 percent did not want to have children. For 33 percent the principal complaint against marriage was that it makes separation more complicated. Nevertheless, 42 percent declared they were willing to marry. The authors of the report concluded that "living out of wedlock was not synonymous with free love." People, they said, just want to keep their options open.[15]

Singles

In any society in which the majority of people are married, singles are often regarded with suspicion or mockery. A French tradition once required women who were still single on their twenty-fifth birthday to don a carnival hat on Saint Catherine's Day.[16] While the custom is disappearing, public dances called *le bal des Catherinettes* still takes place in some rural areas on 25 November. Were all the *Catherinettes* in contemporary France to attend there would not be enough hats to go round—and if all the single men attended there might be more wedding bells!

Singles today—divorcés and divorcées, confirmed bachelors, jilted lovers, and single parents—are no longer regarded with suspicion (except

15. See Leridon and Villeneuve-Gokalp, "Les nouveaux couples," 367.

16. Saint Catherine, the patron saint of milliners, is portrayed wearing a bonnet in popular iconography.

perhaps homosexuals). They are so numerous that they have become marketing targets in everything from condominiums to frozen foods and dating services. Demographers worry about the long-term effects on the birthrate and sociologists about the pattern of social relations.

Single Mothers

The term *single mother* includes women whom statisticians consider as a single group for their convenience. The widow may have little in common with the unhappy teenager who is pregnant or with the independent woman who has chosen to lead her own life. As Robert Solé says,

> What has the Maghrebian woman who has found herself alone from one day to the next with five children in common with Brigitte T., an attorney who has practically kicked out her husband? The latter has moved to the end of the block to take up abode in a studio apartment. Why not divorce? They do not see the necessity for the time being. Extremely concerned about the welfare of their children, they have found a modus vivendi. The father babysits twice a week and two weekends every month. So, he comes home and the mother contrives to sleep somewhere else those nights. However, in practice, it is she who has the burden of the children.[17]

In any case the fact remains that, according to the latest figures available (1982), more than 600,000 French mothers were rearing their children on their own. While the number of widows had decreased since the 1975 census, there was a 40 percent increase in the number of divorcées and a 50 percent increase in other single mothers. All the pointers indicate that the phenomenon is even more widespread today, since the number of children born out of wedlock doubled between 1982 and 1986, according to INED (Institut national d'études démographiques).

The vast majority of single mothers endure material hardship. They account for two times more of the work force than married women. The majority have low-paid, unskilled jobs. Frequently they have no car and have difficulty in reconciling work and child care. Alimony, when they are entitled to it, is often small and was often unpaid until a 1987 law authorizing garnishment of pay by the Children's Allowances Offices.

17. Robert Solé, "La nébuleuse monoparentale," *Le Monde*, 29 April 1986.

She Had a Baby on Her Own

It was in those crazy years
When pops were no longer pop'lar
She had a baby on her own.
She picked the dad scientifically
For his genes and zodiacal sign
She had a baby on her own.

She hurries from December to summer
From nanny to baby-sitter
From Pamper packs to 4 o'clock bottle
And she smokes, smokes, smokes—even at breakfast.

She undoes her huge bed on her own.
She undoes her huge bed on her own.
She lives just like in those magazines
Where men and cash come easy.
She undoes her huge bed on her own.

And she hurries all day:
Garage, gym, the blues alone
And her pals who weep for hours on the phone
She assumes, 'sumes, 'sumes her new femininity.

—Jean-Jacques Goldman, 1987. Copyright © JRG Editions musicales

As in the United States, there are more and more women living below the poverty level.

Some experts have tried to make a distinction between wanted and unwanted pregnancies among single women, but, as one sociologist remarked, new stereotypes have developed. When a single woman belongs to the middle classes, pregnancy is necessarily desired: "With the availability of contraception and abortion one can no longer afford to say that having a baby was not deliberate." On the other hand, in the poorer classes, it is harder to admit that a child born out of wedlock was desired, as the unwed mother will have to solicit financial aid and allowances.[18] Whatever the reason, the price of their courageous decision is costly for single women in material and emotional terms.

18. Marie-Claude Betbeder, "Les mères volontaires," *Le Monde Dossiers et Documents*, March 1987.

Single Fathers

The French film *Trois Hommes et un Couffin,* which later inspired the American version *Three Men and a Baby,* was a box-office hit in France. This lighthearted view of the plight of three bachelors saddled with a baby girl depicted a situation that is not uncommon. About seventy-five thousand Frenchmen bring up their children on their own, and only a minority of these are widowers. However unprepared single dads may be (or pretend to be) for child care, paradoxically, things appear to be easier for them than for single mothers. They tend to lean more on their relatives—one out of five lives with his parents compared to one out of fifteen unmarried mothers. They are seen as more creditworthy by landlords and bankers and are likely to enjoy greater esteem. People are more ready to pity or admire them for having the courage to bring up their children.[19] The bungling dads of *Trois Hommes et un Couffin* were national heroes!

La Famille

In spite of the myth of "gay Paris" cherished by foreigners since strait-laced Victorian times, France as a whole never was—and probably is not today—as promiscuous as visitors would like to think and as the French themselves often pretend.[20] Contraception, abortion, divorce, and unwed couples have not destroyed the family but rather introduced new models that coexist with the units institutionalized by civil or religious matrimony. As sociologist Agnès Pitrou says, "The capacity for resistance of family ties that in the past twenty years have absorbed the shock of teenage pregnancies, cohabitation, trial marriages, single-parent families, separation, test-tube babies, and adoption obliges one to take into account the apparently 'essential' nature of these ties, even at a time when relationships based on free choice rather than constraints are being advocated."[21]

---

19. Robert Solé, "Familles sans père," *Le Monde,* 29 April 1986.

20. Guy Nevers, *Les Français vu par les Français* (Paris: Barrault, 1985), 38.

21. Agnès Pitrou, "Dépérissement des solidarités familiales?" *Année Sociologique* 37 (1987): 210. According to Emmanuel Todd these ties have been traditionally more close-knit in the south of France than in the north, where the nuclear family encouraged early emancipation of the children. In contemporary society the "extended family" tradition of the Midi, with its greater solicitude

Historically, the family has played a very important role in French society. Under the absolute monarchy it mirrored the organization of the state—the pater familias ruled over the members of his household just as the king ruled over his subjects. The Napoleonic Code consecrated fatherhood—the famous *puissance paternelle*, tempered by the revolutionary idea of equity husbands were supposed to be endowed with. Yet the shock waves of the past thirty years that have destroyed the traditional family have not altered the particular status of the family in the French value system:

> In France the family occupies a specific place in the hierarchy of national values . . . If all the countries in Europe have taken measures in favor of families (housing and children's allowances, aids for the elderly), none of them openly claims, as France does, a family policy. Since the Liberation, this is a stake in the game for all the political parties. And in no other democratic country does one find a High Council for Family Affairs and Population under the auspices of the president of the Republic, a sort of moral guardian of the existence of the family.[22]

The child is still central to the French couple's vision of life, as has been the case since the nineteenth century. The observation of an interviewee in the 1951 Columbia University study of the French family would appear to be valid today: "A Frenchman does not live in the moment. For a Frenchman life is more profound and ample [*plus large*]. He has a view of life *totale et en profondeur*—a more global attitude toward life [than the American]. One doesn't think of one's own life, but of that of one's children, first and foremost."[23] While accomplishment for the majority of French women was linked solely with family life until the 1970s and 1980s, it would be hasty to conclude from the number of women in the work force that children are no longer the driving force for the French couple. While the rise in individualism in France over the past two decades has affected all the traditional institutions—church,

---

for children, may explain the higher level of education and the new dynamism of the south. Todd, "Une révolution toute neuve."

22. Martine Segalen, "Les métamorphoses de la famille," *L'Histoire*, December 1991, 47.

23. Mead and Metraux, *Themes in French Culture*, 6.

political parties, marriage—children, though fewer in number, would still appear to be essential to the French idea of happiness. What else explains that the birthrate continues to be one of the highest in Europe, even though comparable financial rewards for childbirth exist elsewhere, and countries with such a strong family tradition as Italy or Spain are having fewer children? What else explains the high percentage of children born out of wedlock in spite of the availability of contraception and abortion? What else explains that unmarried couples tend to behave more and more like those who are married? Commenting on a 1975 INED survey in which two-thirds of the respondents declared that for two persons to marry without the intention of having children was not a real marriage,[24] Louis Roussel wrote in 1989, "No real marriage without the intention of having children, no real family without children. More recent studies seem to indicate that, in France, at least, a majority of people still subscribe to this opinion."[25] In a survey taken in 1987, 93.6 percent of girls and 88.2 percent of young men aged sixteen to twenty-four declared they expected to have children one day.[26] DINKS and OINKS are likely to remain a minority.

Nevertheless, it may well be that the reign of the child as central to the modern couple's vision of happiness is coming to an end. According to Louis Roussel: "He [the child] is a member of the family grouping in his own right but is no longer sovereign. He possesses rights corresponding to his age. However, he has ceased to be the one that conditions all the decisions that are taken." In spite of the obvious love of parents for their offspring, says Roussel,

> the majority of our contemporaries no longer believe that the happiness of their children suffices to make them happy. They are always ready to make "sacrifices" for them, but if the child becomes an obstacle to their own happiness, they take it badly. They continue sometimes to claim that the child is a privileged partner, but more often than not they organize their life according to other priorities.[27]

---

24. Louis Roussel et al., "Le divorce et les Français, (2) L'expérience des divorcés," *Cahiers de l'INED,* no. 72 (Paris: Presses Universitaires de France, 1975).

25. Roussel, *La famille incertaine,* 156.

26. BVA-*Le Monde* 1987, "Jeunes, oui au mariage," *Le Monde Dossiers et Documents,* December 1987.

27. Roussel, *La famille incertaine,* 185.

Although profound changes have taken place in the French family structure in the past thirty years, *la famille* continues to rank very high in the value system of young people, who seem more loath than ever to leave their *foyer.* Three-quarters of unmarried young people aged eighteen to twenty-five live with their parents, and half of the same age group refuses to leave home even when they have a job. When the young adults actually quit their parent's nest and become independent through marriage or a stable sexual relationship, they tend overwhelmingly to maintain close links with their family—a phenomenon more pronounced in France than in most industrialized countries. In fact, this is one of the great obstacles to the geographical mobility that corporations and the administration for thirty years have been encouraging without much success.[28] French attitudes to family legacies, the importance they attach to family furniture that is passed on from one generation to the next, the home that is built to last for several generations, are other indicators of the importance of continuity embodied in the French vision of life that the Columbia University study underlined.

The Older Generation

For demographers one of the most worrisome phenomena in contemporary France is the rapidly aging population. While not a recent development—the trend began in the second part of the nineteenth century with the declining birthrate and was only momentarily stalled by the post–World War II baby boom—France ranks seventh in the world among the countries having the greatest number of old people, and in three decades will have a far older population than the United States. 18.7 percent of the inhabitants are already over sixty years of age—14.2 percent over sixty-five—and even if the present birthrate of 1.80 is maintained, it is projected that by the year 2020, the oversixties will account for one-quarter of the population. The number of people under twenty years of age has dropped from 34.2 percent in 1900 to 27.4 percent today, while 58.4 percent of the inhabitants are in the twenty to sixty-four age group. Thus, although the population of France is increasing

28. While the French become more mobile, they also seem to become more gregarious. On average, people tend to live less than seven miles from their nearest relative nowadays. Hervé le Bras, "Une société à deux vitesses . . . de migration," *Le Monde,* 6–7 January 1991.

and should continue to do so until the year 2020, when it is expected to reach sixty million inhabitants, this increase is entirely due to the longer life expectancy—80.9 years for women (almost a world record) and 72.7 years for men.

Economic and Social Consequences

The economic and social consequences of this demographic shift are already making themselves felt. Retirement payments and health care for the aged are becoming an increasing financial burden for the social security system. The hospital structure is often inadequate to care for the very old—there are not sufficient beds and few suitable wards for terminally ill patients. Gerontological research is underdeveloped. There are not enough homes for the elderly, and they are expensive, so that a number of old people are confined to mental hospitals for no other reason than because these establishments have vacancies and entitle patients to 100 percent social security coverage! Less dramatically, consumer habits are changing, and it is forecast that by the year 2005 medical expenses will eat up the largest portion of household budgets.

Purchasing patterns also change with age, the older generation preferring to shop in small stores rather than in supermarkets. The elderly have become the targets of tour operators and the media, and they are great consumers of audiovisual equipment.

For economists, the long-term consequences of the aging working population are worrying. In less than five years one out of two jobs will be held by a person over forty years of age. In a rapidly changing world where flexibility, innovation, training, and geographical and professional mobility are the keys to survival, an older active population is a serious handicap for France. At the same time, the well-intentioned lowering of the retirement age in 1981, to sixty—or 37.5 years of work—has created a new category of senior citizens ill prepared psychologically for a sedentary life. Contributing to this was the economic crisis of the 1970s and early 1980s, when many workers in their fifties were laid off, partly to make room for the young jobless, which put an extra charge on the social security system. While many of the elderly are poor, overall senior citizens have never had it so good financially, and their situation is enviable compared to that of the numerous young people who start off in life on the dole lines.

Solitude

One of the most devastating social effects of old age in contemporary France is loneliness, which is something of a taboo subject in an era of mass communication. (Gérard Mermet, author of *Francoscopie*, has dubbed modern French society "the excommunication society".)[29] The age-old solidarity between generations is disappearing, and many older people experience deep solitude, which may explain, in part, the number of domestic animals in France. More seriously, the over-fifty-fives commit almost half the total number of suicides recorded each year. The majority of these suicides are committed by males living in rural areas, and frequently occur after the death of a spouse. France's suicide rate for the elderly is two to three times higher than in neighboring countries. Josiane Andrian, a researcher at the CNRS, asks if this means that French society is incapable of looking after its weakest members.[30] It is true that there has been a spectacular development of *clubs de troisième âge* (senior citizens' clubs) that help to offset the isolation of the elderly. The very success of these associations over the past decade, even in rural areas, shows the revolution that has taken place among the older generation, as French society had never been very club oriented.

The New Grandparents

The new nuclear family tends to have closer links with the extended family—parents and grandparents in particular—than postwar developments would lead one to expect. Indeed, thanks to longer life expectancy, 75 percent of French families today have three generations, and half the twenty-year-old age group has two living grandparents. *Grandmère* and *grandpère* are discovering a new role, important if more discrete. They tend to act as "shock absorbers" and life savers when troubles arise for the couple or when bearings are lost. Although the authoritarian relationship of the past has disappeared, *grandpère* is often the only figure of authority for the younger children in a society where parents have become increasingly tolerant, and *grandmère* is always around to lend a helping

29. Gérard Mermet, *Francoscopie*, 167.

30. Josiane Andrian, "Un suicide rarement évoqué: Celui de la personne âgée," in *Vieillir Ensemble* (Paris: Hôpital Paul Brousse, 1989).

hand with the housework and children in times of stress or distress.[31] Parents have had to adjust to the value system of their adult children. But the extent to which they are willing to make concessions for deviations from their own moral standards to preserve their privileged relationship with their own children points more to the strength of family ties in contemporary France than to a change in values on their part.[32]

La Mort

Life expectancy varies from one socioprofessional category to another, with teachers holding the record of 78.2 years for males. At the other end of the scale, unskilled laborers average nine fewer years owing to work accidents, working and living conditions, and health habits (55 percent of heavy drinkers and smokers are manual workers).

The principal causes of mortality in France are cardiovascular disease and cancer, followed by automobile accidents and respiratory disorders. Although 36 percent of deaths are caused by cardiovascular disease, this figure is lower than in Britain, Germany, Canada, or the United States, where the disease causes twice as many deaths. Is this due to the more balanced diet of the French? While the abuse of alcohol and tobacco still cause numerous deaths, the French are smoking and drinking less than before, and a fitness movement is leading to a new awareness of the importance of health and body care.

Less than 10 percent of all deaths are of a violent nature (accident, suicide, or murder), but they account for 70 percent of deaths for the

---

31. See Ségolène Royal, *Le printemps des grands-parents* (Paris: Presses Pocket, 1989).

32. Louis Roussel points out that touchy subjects are carefully avoided in regular family meals between parents and their married children: "The disagreements between generations, which are nowadays latent, would have led to open conflict and even rupture at the beginning of the century. Today they are concealed by harmless remarks about sports topics, movies, fashion, and the weather. It is possible to argue safely about these subjects and to try to prove one's point without threatening the unity of the family." The only source of friction that sometimes does arise concerns the upbringing of grandchildren, but if the older generation dares broach this question, they are quickly put in their place: "A passing disagreement between two generations, some will say. Who cannot perceive that this point is central and sums up, in a way, two different cultural worlds." Roussel, *La famille incertaine*, 181.

fifteen to twenty-four age group—a 15 percent increase since 1960. The number of suicides tripled for this age group between 1960 and 1985, and the official figures (nine hundred per year) probably underestimate the real number. Suicide is the second cause of death for young people after traffic accidents. The High Council for Family Affairs and Population (Haut conseil de la famille et de la population) stresses the vulnerability of "young people who have moved, who are school dropouts, who are from a poor sociocultural background, when their families are upset by the illness of one of the parents, when they are hospitalized or when the parents have separated."[33]

Every year thirty-six hundred young people in the fifteen to twenty-four age group are slain and 31,800 injured on French roads. Mopeds are the dream of fourteen-year-olds and a common birthday gift. High-powered motorbikes are involved in many accidents. The High Council for Family Affairs considers the speed of vehicles as the main cause of traffic accidents and criticizes the tendency of the French "to close their eyes on the deep reasons that have made French roads so unsafe and that are 'objectively' so well tolerated by the population and institutions as a whole." The report published in October 1988 goes on to say that road accidents, like suicide, drugs, and unemployment, reveal "the inability of our society to open the doors of adult life to its youth."[34] The tolerance of the French toward dangerous driving is matched only by that of Americans toward the sale of firearms.

Funeral Rites

Although 75 percent of the French say they would like to die at home, 80 percent die in hospitals or homes for the elderly. Cremation is not very widespread—6.37 percent of all funeral ceremonies in 1990.[35] The French have a stronger attachment to funeral rites than they do to baptismal and nuptial rites. Although they may never have gone to church, the majority of the deceased will receive a religious burial. Yet another contradiction of this supposedly rationalist nation is that tradition re-

33. Robert Solé, "Jeunes Français en danger de mort violent," *Le Monde,* 22 October 1988.

34. Solé, "Jeunes Français."

35. Between 1989 and 1990 the number of cremations increased by 18.5 percent. "Crémation: les chiffres de 1990," *Funéraire Magazine,* May 1991, 28–29.

mains strong even when religious rites are devoid of any real significance for a secular society. In France, chrysanthemums are associated with death, and on 1 November, All Saints' Day—a national holiday—the vast majority of the French will commemorate their dead relatives and pay a visit to the cemetery, laden with pots of chrysanthemums. The day is often a pretext for families to gather over a good meal. There is something vaguely primitive and pagan in these commemoration rites celebrated on the day before the Catholic All Souls' Day.

This overview of demographic trends suggests that the changes that have taken place in France in the space of three decades have outwardly transformed the life of the French people from the cradle to the grave. However, the hopes and aspirations of individuals do not seem to have been changed. Fascinated by progress and not wanting to be left out of the transformations taking place in the world around them, the French seem incapable of turning their backs completely on the past. One is reminded of Paul Valéry's remark from the 1930s about the difficulty we moderns face in adjusting to cultural upheavals: "we walk backwards into the future."[36]

36. This was one of the recurrent themes in the essays of the prolific poet and philosopher, Paul Valéry (1871–1945), who urged the young people of France to exercise their intelligence, as athletes exercise their muscles, so as to be able to apprehend cultural change. The quotation is from *Discours de l'histoire prononcée à la distribution solennelle des prix au Lycée Janson de Sailly, Oeuvres,* vol. 1, *Essais quasi politiques* (Paris: Librairie Gallimard, 1957), 1135.

PART 3

The Sweat Shop

Only those who wish to fool the people wish to keep them ignorant.
—Napoleon

6

From Early Education to Collège

France is an indivisible, secular, democratic, and social Republic. It guarantees, before the law, the equality of all its citizens without distinction of origin, race, or religion. It respects all creeds.

—Article 2 of the constitution of 4 October, 1958

The French prize education more than anything else except perhaps politics—and sometimes it is hard to draw the line between the two. Few subjects are likely to stir up more controversy, as politicians have often learned to their cost. In the last twenty years all the major political upheavals in France were sparked by educational issues.

The School War

It is impossible to understand the philosophy and values of French education or the violent outbursts that mark discussion in contemporary France without some knowledge of its troubled history. Before the French Revolution the parochial schools had a monopoly on education, and the Jesuits jealously guarded their prerogatives not only vis-à-vis the schoolmasters but also in dealing with men like Jean Baptiste de la Salle and his disciples, who purposed to teach catechism to the children of the poor and—worse—in French rather than in Latin. Nonetheless, under the ancien régime there was general consensus about the purpose of education—that it was to form upstanding Christian citizens.

The revolutionaries saw a different value to instruction. They realized that the success of their enterprise depended on educating the whole population, and they actually enacted a short-lived law instituting compulsory schooling. They even toyed with an ambitious project of special spartan institutions where children would learn "republican virtues." The agitation of the times prevented the revolutionary school from making much headway in practice, but the experience persuaded people that education could do more than simply transmit knowledge: education had the power to change society. Henceforth schooling would be at the center of political debate in France, and the so-called school war between the advocates of secular and parochial education is still alive two hundred years later.

The Republican School

Napoleon, who saw the threat the school war could be for the authority of the state, tried to gain control of the educational system at the start of the nineteenth century but was unable to break the influence of the clergy because of a shortage of secular schoolteachers. Thus private institutions—mostly Catholic—continued to exist alongside the state schools. Throughout the nineteenth century the political struggle between the partisans of the Republic and those who favored a royalist restoration supported by the Catholic hierarchy brought the school war to a head. The latter half of the century saw the victory of the anticlerical republicans (1879), who, like the revolutionaries before them, perceived education as a means to impose the secular value system they deemed essential for their political survival. Those diehard republicans, known as *les Opportunistes* (1879–99), set up schools from which not only the clergy but also God was banished: "They were convinced that Catholic schools were 'mental incubators' designed to breed antirepublican and antimodernist ideas."[1] Those were the heydays of secular schooling, and the schoolmasters whom the poet Charles Péguy hailed as "the black hussars of the Republic" were the highly esteemed, albeit poorly paid, mentors of universal values. Catholics continued to demand the liberty to educate on Christian principles; even today, the expression *école libre* designates a private school.

Theoretically, the separation of church and state in 1905 should have put an end to the school war, but in 1959 the strong Catholic lobby managed to get state funding for private schools as a reward for service to the community. This seemed to indicate that a dual system was henceforth unnecesssary—at least from a financial point of view. However, when the Socialists proposed to merge the public and private educational systems in 1984, a million defenders of private schooling

---

1. Gordon Wright, *France in Modern Times*, 4th ed. (New York: W. W. Norton, 1987), 236.

Private Education in France

13.4 percent of elementary schoolchildren and 20 percent of high school (lycée) pupils attend private schools. At least one in three French students over eighteen has had some of his schooling in a private establishment. They follow the same curricula as their counterparts in the public schools apart from religious instruction, which in itself is not always mandatory. The majority of the private institutions have a contract with the state and get state funding. According to the type of contract the latter will not only pay the salaries and social security costs of accredited teachers but also subsidize busing and scholarships for the needy pupils. This is the case for most of the Catholic schools.

Teachers in private schools under contract, appointed by the school with the agreement of the rector of the *académie* (school district), who represents the state, do not have tenure like their colleagues in public schools. They are often less qualified too. Private education in France, therefore, is not necessarily synonymous with high-quality education, although some schools have stiff screening procedures and expel students who are doing poorly. Still a pupil who is required to repeat a year in a public school will often bypass that by registering in a private school, particularly when repeating a year for the second time!

Although the majority of the private institutions are Catholic schools, they will accept children from nonpracticing families. Except in the northwest (Brittany) and the east (Alsace), where there is a long tradition of Catholic schooling, parents usually choose a private school for practical reasons such as stricter discipline and tighter control of pupils during recreation. In addition, working couples unable to help their kids with their homework appreciate the after-school organized study periods and the fact that their children are in safekeeping until a parent can get home from work.

Postsecondary Private Schools

A number of postsecondary institutions designed to provide professional or technical training are privately run, including all the business schools under the aegis of local chambers of commerce in the major cities, the so-called *écoles supérieures de commerce*, and a few highly prestigious grandes écoles.

In general they are a mixed bag and have sprung up to cover areas of study neglected by the universities in the past. Unfortunately, publically funded universities do not have the extensive alumni and professional networks or the comfortable financing available to private schools.

---

marched through Versailles, forcing the government to withdraw the proposed bill.

In 1992, the Socialist Jack Lang, shortly after becoming the fifth minister of education in ten years, decided to bury the hatchet of war by agreeing to pay Fr 1.8 billion in arrears due by the government to private schools under contract. He also made a number of concessions concerning salaries, state funding of social security, and retirement payments for private-school teachers. Above all, he officially recognized "the contribution of private schooling to national education," thereby shattering one of the founding myths of the French Left.

It is too soon to tell if the school war is definitely over, but it is true that in recent years it is pragmatic not ideological reasons that have determined parents' choice of schools, whether public or private, for their children. What counts is the establishment's rating in terms of the outlets it offers to students. The 1984 demonstrations were clearly a refusal by people to allow their liberty of choice to be restricted by the rigidities of l'Education nationale.

In a country where the number of churchgoers represents a minority, the Catholic hierarchy still wields considerable power in the area of education. For example, the church has torpedoed the projects of successive governments to alter the weekly school schedule. As a result of a concession wrenched from the republicans, a law promulgated in 1882 stipulated that one day per week other than Sunday should be set aside for religious instruction. In 1972 Wednesday was designated as the free day, with additional classes Saturday morning to make up the difference. Since then there has been increasing tendency to move the Saturday morning classes to Wednesday. In June 1990, the bishops demanded that a half day be set aside for religious instruction if the government authorizes the shift of Saturday classes to Wednesday.

The Muslim Veil

While secular education in France evolved largely as an anticlerical reaction in the nineteenth century, some groups today interpret the separation of church and state as excluding not only religious instruction, but the expression of personal religious faith by individual students. As the so-called incident of the Muslim veil illustrates, this position may compromise the ideal of tolerance the state schools are meant to promote and which are clearly expressed in article 2 of the constitution.

In 1989 three Muslim girls were expelled from a public school when they refused to remove their veils in class. They were accused of provocation and proselytism. The incident sparked a violent public debate involving politicians, cabinet ministers, educators, and intellectuals.

The minister of education prudently referred the matter to the Council of State, and the latter even more prudently ruled that the veil should be banned only if its use tended to provoke or proselytize, leaving the ministry and school officials to decide case by case. Incongruously, Socialists and Communists, who defended the expulsions as necessary to secular education, found themselves in the company of the racist extreme Right; meanwhile the pro-Left immigrant association *SOS-Racisme* condemned the intolerance of the public school; feminists declared the veil was the symbol of male domination of Arab women; and the Catholic hierarchy used the opportunity to point out the inadequacies of an educational system that fails to include a religious dimension.[2]

The narrow definition of secular schooling that surfaced in this quarrel was not that of the founder of secular schooling, Jules Ferry, who in 1881 declared—he was referring, of course, to Christianity, not Islamism—"Yes, we favored the anticlerical battle, but the antireligious battle . . . never!" Indeed, extreme reaction and racist overtones to justify or invalidate the expulsion decision stirred up antagonisms that observers of the French scene were beginning to think had disappeared from a society that seemed tired of conflict.

The historian Mona Ozouf explains the school war as the inability of the French to come to terms with conflict. On account of its troubled development, secular education has always been on the defensive, and any challenge to it is perceived as an attack on the republican form of government: "The intolerance of French society toward pluralism, the extraordinary attachment of the French to unity also comes from this [defensiveness]. Today, the consensus on the institutions and on the republican form of government is such that we need no longer fear for them."[3] Nevertheless, the incident of the Muslim veil shows just how fragile French society remains two hundred years after the Revolution.

2. The problem of religious culture is one of the key questions in the debate on schooling. According to a poll (SOFRES-*Le Monde,* 24–29 September 1988; see *Le Monde,* 5 October 1988) two out of three people favor teaching comparative religion in public schools. However, if church leaders would like to insist on the ethical dimension of such courses, supporters of a lay society feel that only the historical and cultural aspects should be taught. This issue is debated in other countries too, but the peculiar status of religion in France, the question of the place of catechism in school settings, and the troubled history of relations between church and state make it an explosive one.

3. Mona Ozouf, "Pourquoi l'école de Jules Ferry divise la France," *L'Histoire,* February 1990, 44–52.

It is sad that some of the most progressive opinion makers inadvertently joined forces with the racists when one of the major challenges facing France was to accept the expression of different cultures and opinions.

From Nursery School to Collège

Taylorism

The vast majority of French young people attend public elementary, secondary, and higher education institutions, where education from kindergarten through university is free, curricula are defined nationally by the Ministry of Education, all teachers are appointed by the ministry, and all degrees have the same value whatever institution delivered them.

French education is therefore highly centralized, a heritage from Napoleonic times, and has accumulated the advantages and drawbacks of centralized systems in general. In theory at least, global standards of excellence can be defined and tightly controlled; all pupils have the same possibilities for study; all enjoy the same professional opportunities. However, this top-down system is bureaucratic and cumbersome. A former minister once described l'Education nationale as one of the world's top employers along with General Motors and the Red Army. The organization is indeed Tayloristic.[4] It lacks flexibility, tries to put everyone in the same mold, becomes obsessed with numbers to the detriment of people, and fails, as will be seen, to provide the equality of treatment it so loftily proclaims as a priority.[5]

Mandatory Schooling

The right to education is a tenet of the French constitution, and school is compulsory up to the age of sixteen. Twenty years ago a little more than one-third of youth over sixteen continued school; today, more than two-thirds of seventeen-year-olds attend. Fifty-eight percent of an age

---

4. Jean-Louis Peaucelle, "Détayloriser l'Education Nationale," *Le Monde*, 16 June 1989.

5. Michel Crozier's analysis in *La société bloquée* (Paris: Editions du Seuil, 1970) is still one of the best. For example, "Nobody seems to be worried by the paradoxical coexistence of the most elitist system with the most egalitarian" (156).

group actually reaches the final year of high school, but the Socialist government's aim was to reach 80 percent by the end of the century. This objective will be difficult to achieve unless drastic reforms are undertaken to reduce the number of pupils eliminated by the present system. In addition, present spending on education, which amounts to 6.3 percent of the gross domestic product, will have to be increased considerably. According to one group of experts, if the goal of 80 percent is to be achieved, spending on education will amount to Fr 576 billion by the year 2005 instead of the Fr 398 billion spent today. This figure was considered so outrageous that the conclusions of the study group were not made public.

La Maternelle

In France, practically all three-year-olds go to day school, but only 35.8 percent of two-year-olds attend, since priority is given to the former when places are limited. Overall, 98 percent of children between three and five are in school in France, compared to 50 percent in the United States. The hours are similar to elementary school—8:30 A.M. to 11:30 A.M. and 1:30 P.M. to 4:30 P.M.—but canteens and cots for napping are generally provided. The architecture, the playgrounds, and the furniture are designed for children, and the highly trained schoolteacher is assisted by a helper. Nursery schools are never confined to church basements or to poorly qualified teachers. Preelementary schooling is one of the enviable aspects of the educational system. Few other countries in Europe, and that includes France's rich neighbor, Germany, offer such remarkable facilities free of charge to working mothers. This is one explanation for the greater number of women in the work force in France. It also explains why female absenteeism from work is not a serious problem. In 1990 a report distributed to members of the U.S. Congress by fourteen American child experts declared that French nursery schools were among the best in the world.[6] The focus is on socialization through play and manual activities designed to stimulate the intelligence of the pupils. It is regrettable that in elementary school the socialization process very soon becomes secondary to information overload.

6. Ch. de Ch., "Un rapport au congrès fait l'éloge des écoles maternelles françaises," *Le Monde*, 5 July 1990.

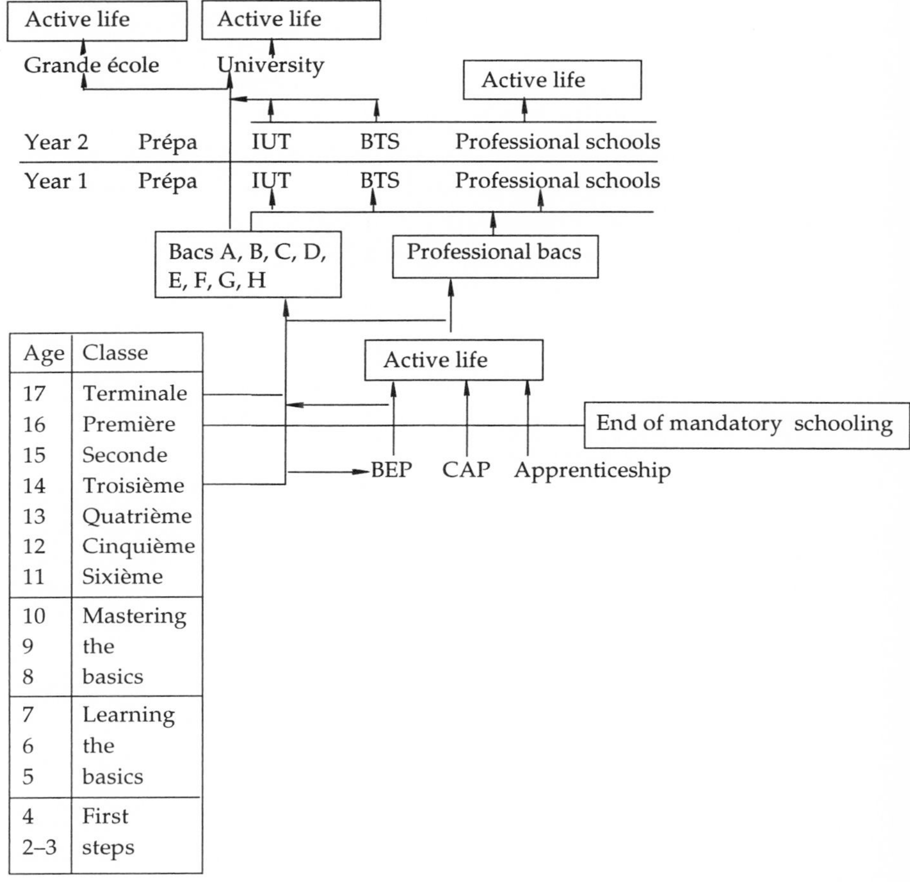

FIG. 7. The French educational system

Elementary School

Elementary school lasts five years, from age six through age ten, but many pupils are older than ten when they leave, as it is not uncommon for some to repeat a class. Such repetition can be fatal to the child's scholastic future. Of the 10 percent of pupils who repeat their first year of elementary school, during which they are expected to learn to read, only 5 percent graduate from high school. In fact, only two out of three schoolchildren actually make it to secondary school at the usual age of eleven, and of these, only one in five comes from a less-favored socio-cultural environment.

Thus the educational system, designed to be egalitarian, becomes elitist and socially discriminatory from the early years. In addition, there are important geographical variations in the rates of success or failure: almost one out of two students graduates from high school in the south, and only one out of three in the north.

The reasons for this waste of intellectual resources are many. The whole approach to education is, for better or worse, very different from the American approach, which the French, and indeed many Americans, criticize for the small amount of information taught.

Full Heads

John Dewey's statement that education is "a process of living and not a preparation for future living" could hardly be further from the present-day concept of education in France, which is based first on the acquisition of theoretical tools, and second on skills for adult use. It has not always been so. Rabelais preferred a "well-made head to a full head," and Célestin Freinet (1896–1966) emphasized the "how" rather than the "what" in teaching. Yet his method has enjoyed more success abroad than in France. In fact he was ousted from the public school, and l'Ecole Freinet was a private institution that became a model of pedagogical training for teachers from many countries. Threatened with closure in 1990 because of a shortage of cash, it was bailed out by the government, which decided to transform it into an experimental public school. Some findings of a University of Bristol comparative study of elementary schoolteachers in Great Britain and France, published in February 1992, showed that if 46 percent of British teachers saw their main task as developing pupils' intelligence, only 17.6 percent of the French teachers surveyed subscribed to this view. 56 percent of French teachers, compared to 14.7 percent of English, stressed the importance of academic knowledge. Moreover, 23.2 percent of French teachers were concerned about preparing pupils for adult life at this early age, compared to only 3.6 percent of British teachers.[7]

---

7. Patricia Broadfoot and Marilyn Osborn, *French Lessons: Comparative Perspectives on What It Means to Be a Teacher* (Oxford: Triangle Books, 1992).

Talking Heads

The results, of course, do not always correspond to the expectations of the curriculum. In the best of cases the system ultimately produces those brilliant French engineers and thinkers that the rest of the world admires, those highly educated statespeople, those cultivated men and women perfectly at ease with abstract concepts, capable of distancing themselves from the gritty contingencies of a problem and placing it in a theoretical framework to better analyze it. As Bertrand Girod de l'Ain, a specialist in education at the University of Paris, has pointed out, these are precisely the type of intellects our high-tech society needs in great numbers: "Today's world, science and corporations have become powerful consumers of abstract thinking, of intellects capable of analyzing increasingly complex situations. And this is something Europe knows how to do, and perhaps better than others, thanks to an elitist secondary school system aided by a teaching profession of incomparable intellectual quality."[8]

This intellectual procedure is fascinating to observe, even if the practical implications sometimes get lost en route. The painstaking, pragmatic British or American approach to problem solving is more laborious and less intellectually satisfying. Probably the most effective engineers or

---

See Linda Blackburn, "French Shrug Off Parents' Power," *Times Educational Supplement*, 28 February 1992, 5.

8. Bertrand Girod de l'Ain, "L'élitisme exacerbé," *Le Monde*, 30 June 1989. Yet according to Edgar Morin, French intellectual training, which teaches children from an early age to have "clear and distinct ideas" and separate the simple from the complex, that is, to "separate what is interconnected, to unify what is multiple, to eliminate whatever introduces disorder or contradictions in our understanding" might not be the most suitable today. The crucial problem of our time, he says, "is the necessity of a mode of thinking geared to facing the challenge of the complexity of reality, that is, capable of grasping the links, interactions, and mutual implications, the multidimensional phenomena, those realities which are at one and the same time connected and discordant." The sociologist criticizes all that has been undertaken in the name of rationality and that has led to "alienation from work, dormitory cities, subway-job-sleep, serialized leisure, industrial pollution, degradation of the biosphere, the omnipotence of nation-states possessing annihilating arms." Is that really rational? he asks: "Isn't it high time to reexamine a mode of reasoning which has nurtured in its bosom its worst enemy, which is rationalization." Edgar Morin, "La démocratie cognitive et la réforme de pensée," *Le Monde*, 23 September 1988.

executives today are precisely those nurtured in the elitist French system whose training is completed in the American corporate, scientific, or academic world, where they acquire the professionalism so absent from their education. They are certainly those who can command the highest salaries in Europe.

Elitism and Illiteracy

However, French intellectual training does not always have such happy effects, and for ordinary young people the modern world also requires more practical skills. The educational system, designed to produce an elite, has been slow to adapt to the democratization of schooling, to the hordes of boys and girls from a varied sociocultural background who attend today's school. Twelve percent of each age group quit school with no qualification whatsoever; this figure has not changed in the past ten years.

Alarmed at the rates of functional illiteracy (one out of five adults has trouble reading or writing with ease) and the number of children (an estimated 20 percent) who have not mastered the three Rs by the time they reach junior high (*collège*), the second Socialist minister of education during President Mitterrand's first term in office in the mideighties, promoted a laudable if misguided "back to basics" policy in elementary school in the name of updated Republicanism under the bizarre slogan of *élitisme républicain.* Jean-Pierre Chevènement declared: "The guiding principle of the Republic is not wealth, good fortune or heredity; rather it is based on equal opportunities for all and individual merit."

The basic inequalities the system engendered were thus underlined, but the solutions proposed were hardly appropriate. Chevènement recommended concentrating on the three Rs to the detriment of manual and artistic activities and, under parental pressure, encouraged home assignments that had been banned from elementary education for thirty years.

Neither he nor his Conservative successor, René Monory, who was to face the massive student demonstrations of 1986, made any attempt to tackle the problems of objectives and curriculum content, of teaching and study schedules that ignore basic psychological findings concerning child development. All these are highly explosive questions, concerning as they do parents and teachers, not to mention powerful economic influences, such as publishers of schoolbooks, and the directors of ski resorts who want their say in the organization of vacation periods. The hapless Alain Savary, Mitterrand's first education minister, was genuinely preoccupied by these issues but fell victim to the school war and the Versailles demonstrations in 1984 and had to be replaced. Chevènement, understandably, did not reopen the file on program content.

The main criticism aimed at curricula is that they are too exhaustive and far beyond the capabilities of the average student to digest. The result is that, in scientific courses, for instance, except for the very bright pupils, most are able to learn formulas by rote but cannot really apply them. In other words, they do not learn to think.[9] The programs are designed to select at a very early age the whiz kids who will follow a fast track to higher education. All attempts to lighten the work load to date have met with fierce opposition from teachers and, paradoxically, from parents, who fear their offspring will not be sufficiently prepared for the competitive job market. Indeed even pupils will ask teachers for more work, more home assignments, and assessments!

Scheduling

French elementary schoolchildren have the longest workweek in Europe: twenty-seven contact hours, that is, six hours per day from Monday through Saturday except for Wednesday, which is free, as well as is Saturday afternoon. Twenty-seven hours for six-year-olds! This is more than nineteen-year-old German high school students get. Add on to that homework, private piano or dance lessons, commuting time, and one can appreciate why school vacations in France tend to be longer than elsewhere. France has the shortest school year in Europe (175 days) to offset the stress of the crazy work schedule. Transforming the rhythm of schooling is one of the touchiest issues. The French have been talking about it since the nineteenth century! They have marched through the streets for far less. In fact they are more likely to protest if any steps are taken to solve this nagging problem. Where is their legendary Cartesianism?

Contrary to a widely held cliché, the French, though Mediterraneans, are not at all "laid-back." In France, parents and children live at a hectic pace. Maybe this explains why they are so impatient, why they drive so fast. Is this where they get their zest for life, why they put such a

9. See Sylvestre Huet and Jean-Paul Jouary, *Sciences: Les Français sont-ils nuls?* (Paris: Jonas, 1989).

Les Vacances

The importance the French attach to family vacations is a major obstacle to reorganizing the school year, and the tourist industry exerts considerable pressure on the Ministry of Education when the negotiations on holiday dates take place. Already the midterm February and Easter vacation dates are staggered to ensure a longer season for the ski resorts, which could not accommodate a holiday rush of all the French at the same time!

The right to vacations is not written into the constitution, but it is a privilege the French, with their more than five weeks of annual paid vacation, refuse to let anyone tamper with. Six out of ten people go away for a holiday at least once a year, shattering the myth of the stay-at-home French. A cultural explanation for the importance of holidays in the value system might lie in attitudes toward health care, where restorative vacations are deemed essential for "charging the batteries again." Of course it is a vicious circle. Frenzied spurts of activity require "time to decompress" as the popular saying goes, and then the lost time must be made up by investing even more in work which, in turn, requires a further break!

Whatever the reason, it is strange that a nation so deeply attached to the welfare of the family and children should impose upon its youth a workweek that many adults would find exhausting. French children today no longer work in coal mines or sweat shops as they did at the turn of the century, but the grueling school week takes a heavy psychological toll in terms of stress and exhaustion.

---

high price on leisure? Is this also why they are the greatest consumers of tranquilizers in the world?

Be this as it may, they find all sorts of pretexts for not altering the daily, weekly, and yearly school schedule, at tremendous social and psychological cost to French youth. The main argument is that it is impossible to lighten the curricula without producing a nation of *idiots,* as the French pride themselves on their intelligence and culture. All French children are expected to learn to read at the age of six so that they can get down to the serious business of studying. Yet, psychologists have pointed out that there are important variations in the age at which children learn to read. The child who has not mastered reading after the first year of elementary school will, therefore, have to repeat the year and is likely to lose his or her self-assurance. This also jeopardizes the child's scholastic future.

The fourth minister of education of the "Mitterrand decade," Lionel Jospin, anxious to neutralize the potential time bomb represented by increasing exasperation with the educational system, made prudent efforts at reform. One of his prime objectives was to give priority to the needs of pupils rather than those of the educational machine that has sacrificed generations of children. In this scheme, early education is divided into three cycles: a first cycle for children under five (*cycle des apprentissages premiers*); a second cycle for children between five and eight (*cycle des apprentissages fondamentaux*), during which pupils acquire basic skills like reading and writing without having to worry about repeating a year; and a third cycle for children aged eight to eleven (*cycles des approfondissements*). While parents, many of whom saw in this reform a chance for their children to learn to read from the age of five, were enthusiastic, some educational experts feared that by introducing reading too early the final year of *maternelle*, at present a time for socialization, would become a minielementary class. However, the main aim of the new system, which is likely to take years to be fully institutionalized, is to take into account the variable learning pace of pupils and put an end to the negative experience of repeating classes at an early age.

Throughout the educational system parents have little or no say in matters concerning curriculum content, and teachers, who have survived the elitist mill themselves, see no reason to reduce the work load. Later, in secondary school, many teachers—particularly those who teach subjects at the top of the hierarchical scale, such as math and physics—try to protect their own turf and will refuse to make concessions toward lightening the program. In 1990 the minister of education, true to his philosophy of curricula streamlining, and despite the protestation of teachers and school editors, declared that physics and chemistry would no longer be taught during the first two years of secondary education. Detractors suggested that the decision was dictated not by pedagogical motives but by the difficulty of recruiting teachers.

Updating the curriculum is another difficulty. Books are supplied on a loan basis to every single schoolchild up to the age of sixteen, so the major French publishers have a vested interest in education. The cost of changing manuals—largely developed with publishing interests in mind—can be exorbitant for schools, so program changes are very costly. This is another deterrent to reform.

Changing the daily school schedule would necessarily have repercussions on the daily life of parents as well as of children. Were schools open only in the mornings, as in Germany or in Italy, what would become of the children in the afternoon in a country where two out of three women in the twenty-five to fifty age group hold jobs? In Mediterranean fashion, children are emancipated much later than in Anglo-Saxon countries, and parents worry about latchkey kids. Extracurricular activities would increase the work load of teachers, who, even in the unlikely event that they accepted working more—or differently—would expect to be remunerated in consequence. As they are already poorly paid and increasingly difficult to recruit, little hope for reform lies in this direction in the immediate future. However, Minister Jospin, undaunted, circumvented the rigidities and corporatisms by incentives that were likely to appeal to the younger generation of teachers such as the special allowance for those willing to assist in organizations that run after-school activities: sports associations, computer and science clubs, holiday camps for young people, or the Scout movement.

Secondary Education

Secondary schooling lasts seven years, from age eleven to eighteen. It is divided into two cycles, each in a different establishment. The first four years are spent in collège (junior high) and the last three in lycée (high school). Classes are designated by ordinals that run from *6ème* (*sixième*), the first year of collège, to *1ère* (*première*), the second to last year of lycée, the final year being called *terminale*. The work load gets heavier—twenty-five to twenty-eight contact hours in collège and as many as thirty-five in lycée, plus from three to ten hours of home study depending on the class. The weeding-out process continues, and only 50 percent of an age group will obtain the coveted terminal examination called the *baccalauréat*, or *bac*, for short, which is required to register at university. This is four times more than in the 1960s but reveals the extent of the reforms that will be necessary to meet the proclaimed goal of 80 percent. Only one out of nine pupils takes the examination at the age of eighteen, which means that it is not infrequent for many to repeat a year or more.

Le Collège

Up to the late 1970s pupils were segregated early, and only a minority could make it to the lycée and go on to take the baccalauréat. In 1975, a well-intentioned reform designed to put all pupils from ages eleven through fifteen on an equal footing was introduced; the so-called *collège unique* (single-track collège) or CES (*collège d'enseignement secondaire*) was born. A decade and a half later the assessment of this generous project is disappointing. Only slightly over half of the pupils go on to lycée, and the chances of children from disadvantaged social backgrounds of reaching the *bac* are scarcely better than before the reform. According to one report, the CES "produces more social inequalities in two years than all the previous schooling."[10] The reasons range from the inability of teachers to deal with pupils of mixed ability to curriculum content maladapted to mass education, and biased, elitist orientation procedures. The introduction of "new mathematics" and linguistic concepts at an early age stresses abstract intelligence and symbolic language out of the reach of many children. The sad thing is that by setting its sights too high the reform gave an inferiority complex to many pupils. It jeopardized the development of technical vocations, when it did not completely discredit occupational courses that became the dumping ground for those not fit to pursue the lycée track. Segregation crept in by the back door, and informed parents knew that by having their children study German—reputedly difficult—as a second language, rather than Italian—reputedly easy—their child would be in a "good" CES or at least a "good" class.[11] When word got round of this and the "dunces" also wanted to learn German, the only solution left was to choose Latin as an elective subject to be with the cream! All attempts to reform the CES so far have failed because teaching continues to be curriculum centered rather than pupil centered, and nothing has prepared secondary teachers for the challenge of mass education.

Technical Education

Mandatory schooling finishes at sixteen years of age; the advanced pupils will go on to the ordinary lycée (*lycée d'enseignement général*) and the general baccalauréat or to the technical lycée (*lycée d'enseignement technique*) to study for one of the numerous professional baccalauréats, some

---

10. Marie Duru-Bellat and Alain Mingat, *Réduire les inégalités sociales et scolarisation*, Institut de recherches sur l'économie de l'éducation, Dijon. See Philippe Bernard, "Le collège unique n'existe pas," *Le Monde*, 17 March 1988.

11. In spite of restrictions it is much easier to attend a public school outside one's catchment area in France than in the United States.

of which are becoming increasingly valuable on the job market. One million pupils will have little choice but to go into apprenticeship and try to obtain a CAP (*certificat d'aptitude professionel*) or a BEP (*brevet d'études professionnelles*) at a *lycée d'enseignement professionel*, commonly known as the LEP. In fact many of them will not even finish the four years of collège, having attained the age limit before. In France less than one-third of all workers—31 percent—possess a basic professional diploma (CAP) compared to 67 percent in Germany.[12] Today 12 percent of young people quit school with no qualification whatsoever.

The BEP and CAP, though better than nothing, are not very useful, although attempts are being made to respond to local needs for skilled tradesmen. Germany has an excellent apprenticeship system with nearly two million pupils, the majority of whom obtain a technical diploma that is highly valued on the job market. In France, vocational training is scorned in an educational system that has been largely cut off from the economic environment and confuses professional success and personal development with the possibility of obtaining a white-collar job. At the same time no other country has invested so much in technical schooling. Elsewhere the bulk of training is carried out by industry, possibly with better results. It has never been a priority of French manufacturing, which rewards manual skills poorly. The result is that CAP and BEP pupils frequently learn a trade with outdated machinery, or worse, train for professions that they did not really choose in the first place and for which there is not a very high demand. Many of them are far from being skilled when they leave the LEP and join the ranks of unemployed youth that account for 25 percent of all the jobless in France. (The German figure is 8 percent for this age group.) One hundred thousand pupils quit vocational training annually with no recognized qualification whatsoever. The advantage of taking the BEP over the CAP is that it allows pupils to get back on the bac track, usually by means of the professional baccalauréat. BEP pupils refuse the negative orientation procedures and overwhemingly want to continue their studies if the latter are adapted to their capacities. Yet industry bosses warn that they will probably not be able to absorb the flow of *bachéliers* that the system is supposed to produce by the turn of the century. Only 29 percent of the

12. Jean-Jacques Salomon, "La capacité d'innovation," in *Entre l'état et le marché*, ed. Maurice Lévy-Leboyer and Jean Claude Casanova (Paris: Editions Gallimard, 1991), 15–58.

Worlds Apart

The divorce between the business world and the educational system

> dates back to the beginnings of free, mandatory, secular schooling, when the black hussars of the Republic set out to raise the educational level of the nation while at the same time attacking what they considered the destructive influence of the church and bourgeois capitalism. This education, which aimed to impart the social and ethical value system of the Republic, deliberately removed from economic life, never managed to adapt itself to the needs of those, workers or technicians, who were unable to pursue the classical path designed for the education of the elite.*

The industrial world resigned itself to this situation, which dispensed it from the obligation of financing the training of its employees. Moreover, Taylorism, which required minimal manpower for mass production, facilitated industrial expansion. So the only areas in which the business world really required the cooperation of the schools to teach skills were the building trade, restaurant services, hairdressing, and small traditional shopkeeping—the prestigious business school, HEC (Hautes études commerciales) used to be known as *l'école des épiciers* (the grocers' school). Even today industry trains only 10 percent of all the apprentices; the rest are trained in commerical services and the trades (*l'artisanat*).

Worker unions too have never been very keen to see corporations meddling in the education of young workers. They feel that the training may be too job-specific, more advantageous to the corporation than to the trainees. Yet, since the 1960s, industry has been sharing the cost of technical education.

Though the historical mistrust between employers, educational authorities, and the worker unions has not entirely disappeared, industrial restructuring, on the one hand, and the high unemployment rate among school leavers, on the other, seem to have convinced all concerned that it is time to get their act together. That is the real significance of the 1992 apprenticeship bill.

*Valérie Devillechabrolle, "Deux routes longtemps parallèles," *Le Monde*, 10 April 1991.

---

active population today actually possesses the baccalauréat diploma. How will the business world be able to cope with the arrival of an overeducated but ill-adapted 80 percent of an age group who will not be enticed by run-of-the-mill administrative positions or the skilled, indeed even unskilled, jobs that will continue to form the bulk of the needs of industry for some time?

Only 240,000 French youth are registered in practical training programs in industry. They attend apprenticeship centers (*Centres de formations d'apprentis*) controlled by l'Education nationale, where they receive a general education in French, math, administration, and labor legislation—a French speciality. They also get some courses in technology, but two-thirds of their practical training is given in the workplace under the supervision of a skilled worker (*maître d'apprentissage*). Most apprentices will take a CAP. One of the major goals of the short-lived Cresson government (May 1991–April 1992) was to double the number of apprentices by the year 2000. In June 1992, a bill on apprenticeship designed to confer the same educational value to practical training within the corporation as to that provided in the school system (CAP or professional baccalauréat), was approved by the national assembly. In the course of the debate, Martine Aubry, minister of Labor, employment, and professional training in the Bérégovoy cabinet, pointed out that one of the main goals of the bill was "to convince young people and their families to deliberately opt for professional training rather than having it imposed upon them following a setback [in the school system]."[13] Thus the Socialists seem to have discreetly shelved the overambitious idea they launched in the mid 1980s of bringing 80 percent of an age group to the baccalauréat.

Les Compagnons

Foreigners, aware of France's reputation for quality craftsmanship, are sometimes surprised to learn that technical training is in such a sorry plight. After all, did not French craftsmen lend a hand to rebuild Charleston after the devastation caused by Hurricane Hugo in the United States? The explanation is simple: these *maîtres artisans* perpetuate the tradition and skill of the *compagnons* who built the Gothic cathedrals. They are members of a hierarchical, somewhat secret society, with strict discipline and strange initiation rites, who are trained in a special boarding school in Paris and then spend one or several years touring France to learn their craft from older members who are the very best in their trade. To qualify for the title of *compagnon* the candidate has to produce a chef d'oeuvre of outstanding craft. Needless to say, they form a small professional elite.

---

13. Frédéric Bobin, "Mme. Aubry veut rendre l'apprentissage plus attractif," *Le Monde*, 19 June 1992.

7

From Lycée to Université

The lycée for pupils of sixteen to eighteen is the last lap of the hurdle race for the bac. The first year of lycée is called *seconde,* during which all the pupils take the same courses, mathematics, physics, biology, French, history, geography, physical education, and two foreign languages. At the end of *seconde* they have to choose in which area they want to specialize for the final two years of lycée. A letter of the alphabet corresponding to each major designates the type of baccalauréat the student will ultimately take: languages and literature (A), economics (B), mathematics and physics (C), biology (D), engineering (E), and the various technical bacs (F, G, and H). The amount of time devoted to the core courses formed by the subjects studied in *seconde,* plus philosophy, which is taken in the last year of lycée (France is the only country in the world to make philosophy mandatory for all pupils), will vary from one area of specialization to another, as will the total number of hours given to electives (not more than one or two). Some pupils will have as many as thirty-five hours per week in the classroom. The minimum is twenty-five from Monday through Saturday morning.

Scheduling is complicated, some lycées having as many as two thousand pupils, and it is not uncommon to have two-hour classes (the standard period is one hour). It is also not rare for a student to start at 8 A.M. and finish the school day at 6 P.M. with perhaps one or two free periods in the course of the day. If commuting is taken into account—school buses are available to all students—this can mean a workday of twelve hours!

Discipline is pretty relaxed outside of class. Smoking is now forbidden inside the buildings but tolerated in the playground. Lovebirds will be seen necking openly in the corridors. In the classroom, teachers can rely only on their personality and the work load to keep noses to the grind. The approach is directive, with a lot of chalk and talk because of the obsession with getting through the nationally defined yearly program.

The Baccalauréat

> Exams are the only opportunity mortals get to know a few things for a few days.
>
> —Paul Valéry

Though the bac, like the SAT in the United States, is required to register at university, the comparison stops there. There are few or no multiple-choice questions, and the candidate is expected to call all the knowledge ingested over the years in areas as diverse as philosophy, math, physics, biology, economics, history, geography, foreign languages, and literature. The written tests, as well as oral tests in some subjects, run for three weeks and are nationally organized. (Incidentally, most of the lycées will be closed for classes during this period, giving an extra three weeks vacation to pupils not taking the exam!) An examination board in each area, presided over by a university professor, awards or refuses the diploma on the basis of overall results. Anguished parents and candidates wait for hours in the street in front of the local lycée waiting for the results to be posted. There is great excitement, as well as tears and wringing of hands for those who have failed, when the list is finally posted. (Now the results are also available on Minitel.)

The examination involves many education officials and teachers throughout the year to prepare and administer it to some 600,000 candidates. More than two thousand questions have to be written in the various subject areas. Candidates have an assortment of twelve "official" foreign languages to choose from, together with thirty-nine optional languages. Teachers must be designated to prepare the questions in each of the twenty-five *académies* (local educational districts). Copies have to be corrected anonymously by teachers external to each lycée, and the latter have to move around from school to school to administer the oral tests—at great expense to the ministry (the total cost of running the examination is about Fr 180 million). Finally, the school year, already the shortest in Europe, loses three weeks while the exams are taking place. The system works like clockwork, but it is expensive and time-consuming. Yet there is tremendous pressure from parents and teachers to maintain the bac. More than one minister of education has suggested replacing the baccalauréat by some simpler arrangement, for example, by allowing students who satisfy requirements to obtain credit throughout their schooling. This, according to one ministry official, would "enable precise objectives to be evaluated as well as [allow us] to know what is being evaluated." Yet no minister has had the courage to take the drastic step of reforming the bac that has existed for so long. Not even enterprising Jack Lang, who exclaimed on French television (Antenne 2) on 15 June 1992, "Why abolish the bac, this two hundred year-old historical monument that many [countries] are envious of?"

It is hard for a foreigner to appreciate the symbolic significance possessing the baccalauréat has for the French. Worthless as the document is on the job market, the loss of prestige associated with not having one's bac, in the French value system, is catastrophic, and parents feel ashamed if their child fails. After all, those who pass have survived the obstacle race for twelve years; they are among the five out of ten pupils of their generation to be thus distinguished. While not necessarily forming part of the elite, since some bacs are more elitist than others, they have still got their options relatively open. Those who fail cannot register in any university, and their prospects are limited in a country where levels of remuneration are so closely linked to educational achievement. Moreover, the baccalauréat is frequently a minimum requirement for even clerical jobs and jobs in public administration that, though poorly paid, offer a guarantee of permanent employment. France has probably the best-educated civil servants in the world.

Results are getting better year by year thanks to nudges from the ministry and more leniency on the part of correctors. Yet, nearly 30 percent of pupils who actually sit for the exam still fail. A frequently heard complaint is the ignorance of today's youth, who seem to know so little compared to previous generations of French teenagers. However, a well-documented book published in 1989 entitled *Le niveau monte* (*Standards on the Rise*) tried to show that, in spite of all the moaning by their elders, today's kids in fact know more than children in the past. If it is true that most secondary school pupils today would be incapable of rattling off the list of départements or *sous-préfectures* that was among the requirements for the coveted *Certificat d'Etudes* formerly delivered at the end of elementary school, which has a special place in the heart of the older generation, the statistics tell a different story. At the end of the nineteenth century 60 percent of pupils quit school without any diploma. Today's figure is 20 percent, although standards have risen in the meantime. The level of math required in some baccalauréat sections today is equivalent to what used to be demanded of engineering graduates only a few years ago. The new history program takes on nothing less than "the construction of the contemporary world, the world today, and France since 1945" and covers international issues involving geo-strategy, communication, science, and religion among other things. Even some history teachers have argued that in spite of their excellent training they might not be up to teaching such a vast subject. In fact it is amazing that so many pupils actually manage to handle questions of the complexity of those given in the bac.

The real problem is the high demands made by the school on the average young person. All too often those who are judged unfit are steered into a blind alley. The authors of *Le niveau monte* plead for establishing a cultural minimum attainable by all rather than worrying about the standard of those who will make it anyway: "a minimum baggage that the worst school leaver from the worst collège [junior high] should possess." This implies nothing short of a cultural revolution after years of elitism.

Classes are generally very large, about thirty-five pupils. The unmotivated tend to suffer in silence.

All lycées have a lunch room, but recreation facilities or places for socializing, such as clubrooms, are absent or shabby. Libraries tend to be overcrowded, and during free periods pupils have nowhere to go. Thus cafés or game arcades in the vicinity of secondary schools have a captive clientele. The spartan material conditions of study prompted massive strikes and demonstrations in 1990.

As there are magnet collèges there are also magnet lycées, the reputation of which is founded on their location (is it mainly an upscale, working-class, or immigrant population?), oral tradition, the number of *agregés* (highly qualified teachers), or the establishment's ranking on the bac achievement scale published annually in the press. Informed parents, particularly schoolteachers, whose kids have better results overall than any other socioprofessional group, are familiar with all the subtleties of the system and the numerous ruses, such as the choice of electives, that can get their children into a prestigious lycée outside their catchment area.

Super Bac

The choice of baccalauréat, determined more by the pupil's performance at school at the age of sixteen than by his or her desires, was designed to develop the appropriate profile for the various specializations proposed by the institutions of higher education. Thus, those with a bac A could pursue studies in languages or literature and in many of the social sciences (politics, law, psychology, etc.). Bac B students could specialize in economics; bac C in science; bac D in medicine, pharmacy, and so on. In theory, the different baccalauréat majors are equal and automatically open the doors to higher education in the corresponding field of study; in practice some are more equal than others, and there is an undisguised hierarchy dominated by the "super bac," bac C (mathematics and physics), while the bac G (business administration), at the other end of the scale, is practically worthless. This means that to have the greatest possibility of continuing the university studies of one's choice, be it medicine, business, politics, or engineering, or to have the slightest chance of getting accepted into a preparatory class for the prestigious *grandes écoles*—the royal road—and even many two-year postsecondary professional courses, the bac C is practically a must.

The bac C was initially designed to encourage students to take up engineering and scientific studies. Indeed, in their two final years of lycée the pupils get up to sixteen contact hours per week in mathematics and physics plus as many hours of general subjects. However, with the bent for elitism in French education, the original purpose got lost in route, with the result that France is still short of scientists. In other words, many pupils who do not have an interest in pursuing a scientific career are taking the bac C (recently being challenged by the professional bac E for engineering) simply because it opens all doors, and they are grabbing places designed for students with other majors who cannot compete when places are limited.

Mathemania

Math has replaced Latin as the yardstick of excellence in France today, and, faced with a choice, even literary screening panels, all other things being equal, will choose a candidate with a bac C rather than one with a bac A because they know that the former has run the gauntlet and is likely to be a workaholic. Of course there are brilliant, well-rounded students among them—the best literary students as well as the best math students will follow this path—but many are mediocre mathematicians who owe their diploma to their score in the general subjects or to perseverance and private coaching. Others offset their lack of general culture by their skill in math and physics.

The first year of lycée, when pupils leave the relatively protected environment of a small CES, can be a pretty grueling experience. Their future is largely decided in the space of one short year at the critical stage of adolescent development. From the very start of *seconde*, which is supposed to be *indifferenciée* (i.e., there are no majors), math and physics teachers, bent on finishing their program and with their sights already set on choosing the elite who will be capable of majoring in these subjects the following year, have no time to bother with the laggards. They are soon left behind and thus condemned to choosing other majors on the hierarchical scale, which is itself founded on the math work load they offer. The pecking order is roughly bac C to bac D to bac B to bac A. The system favors the gifted or those mature enough to adapt to its constraints. As in collège choices that determine educational opportunities or career paths are largely negative. One wonders what affects this may have on personality. One thing is certain—young people generally do not have the self-assurance of American teenagers. Many develop a guilt complex about their scholastic aptitude that is hardly conducive to a "can-do" attitude and personal development.

While France definitely does not have the serious problem of declining educational standards frequently denounced in the United States, it would be rash to assume, as the French often do, that it has the best system in the world. Mathematical specialists are among the first to worry about the excessive role math plays in orientation. They are also concerned about the misconceptions pupils have about mathematics, which is not perceived as discovery learning but as a purely formal exercise that leaves little room for the experimentation and reflection a genuine scientific approach requires. Finally, the exaggerated status of math in the curricula has not encouraged teachers to question their methods. There is an almost total absence of thinking on pedagogy in this area, which demotivates even further students who have difficulty in assimilating the subject, while comforting the others in ready-made answers to problem solving. According to Marc Legrand, a professor at the University of Grenoble who has been one of the rare math teachers to question the existing pedagogy, pupils tend to perceive the exercises as some sort of a magical sleight of hand: "Fashioned by the school system, they have a tendency to believe that it is enough to pull a rabbit out of the hat to make things work." He goes on: "Scarcely 20 percent of the young people that graduate from the scientific grandes écoles or universities have acquired a genuine mathematical turn of mind. The others work like automats."[1]

In any case, high math input cannot be the only criterion of excellence, and probably the vast majority of professionals in the contemporary world need not be mathematical geniuses. The social consequences of this unhealthy hierarchy are far-reaching because young people are conditioned to choosing majors that they are not necessarily motivated by, and the gap between science and humanities is wider than ever. The trouble is not that France produces too many engineers and scientists but that the bac C has failed to encourage enough genuine scientific vocations while favoring the development in other spheres—medicine, business, economics, politics, the social sciences in general—of a narrow technical if not technocratic approach to issues that neglects the human factor. Sixty percent of holders of super bac take up nonscientific studies

---

1. Philippe Bernard, "Les mathématiques victimes de l'école," *Le Monde*, 17 December 1987.

afterwards. The prestigious commercial schools only recruit 13 percent of economics majors (bac B). Meanwhile, France's notorious labor relations are largely due to the neglect of human resources. Students with a literary background who might make excellent managers, international negotiators, or communication specialists are sacrificed at an early age to the god of mathematics and have little chance of competing for the best schools. As Frédéric Gaussen has pointed out, there is no counterweight in the humanities to the excessive technicity the country's most prestigious institutions of higher education encourage.[2]

Teachers and parents are so obsessed with the baccalauréat that it becomes hard for pupils to be indifferent. During the school year teenagers have little time for socializing if they want to fit in even a minimum of sports or hobbies. Yet, dropouts are rare. Home assignments take up a lot of time, and a large number of pupils—one out of two according to a survey taken in 1990—will pay for private coaching in one or more subjects.[3] This can only mean that there is something seriously wrong with the program or the teaching, if not both, because it shows that 50 percent of the learners at one time or another during their schooling feel stranded. It also shows the stress pupils are under to succeed.

For those that get the coveted bac, 71 percent of those enrolled in 1992, the choice is supposedly very wide, but, in actual fact, it turns out to be quite narrow except for the pick of the bunch. While the diploma is the sesame that opens the doors of postsecondary and university studies, it does not mean that pupils are free to choose their career path. In other words it is not sufficient to have majored in a given area to be able to continue in this field afterward. Even the technological institutes (*Instituts universitaires de technologie* or IUT), similar to the British polytechnics, designed to train industrial, scientific, and business technicians in two years, have strict entrance requirements, and one has a better chance of being accepted with one of the general bac majors (D, B, or C) than with a professional baccalauréat. It is obvious that French universities have their fast track too, but as long as the economy was booming and the numbers of pupils reaching higher education was

---

2. Frédéric Gaussen, "Renouveau des humanités," *Le Monde*, 22 April 1989.

3. Dominique Glasman, *Les cours particuliers: première phase d'une recherche dans la région Rhône-Alpes*, Université de Saint-Etienne. See Christine Garin, "Le virus du cours particulier," *Le Monde de l'Education*, September 1990, 50–51.

limited, screening by certain institutions was not an issue. Most graduates, even if they had not been able to pursue the studies of their choice, had little difficulty in finding a job. This is no longer the case today. High unemployment, the growth in the number of pupils earning a baccalauréat, the limited resources of the universities, and indeed the increasing professionalization of academic courses that demand high intellectual input have left by the wayside those who did not or could not choose the right track in lycée, the vast hordes of pupils herded into baccalauréat sections that offer little prospects for the pursuit of university studies. The university is supposedly open to all, but on account of limited facilities and staffing there is a disguised screening in many faculties, while others become the dumping ground for all those that have nowhere else to go. How many students who want to study business or science end up by registering in psychology or sociology? The result: a huge undergraduate failure and dropout rate, particularly among first-year students.

After much hesitation, Lionel Jospin decided in 1991 to launch a timid reform of education in the the lycées. It is being phased in by the new right-wing minister and should offer a broader choice of electives for the baccalauréat by 1995. The goal is to lighten somewhat the weekly work load and introduce greater flexibility than the present bac straitjacket permits by offering the students a wider range of subjects—majors and minors—to choose from within a given field of study: scientific studies, social and economic studies, technological studies, literary studies. It is hoped that this will put an end to the hierarchy the present system has engendered. Another innovation is the introduction of mandatory modules for small groups of students, that is, tutorials where they will learn how to learn. Welcome as it is, this reform is unlikely to change things very much, as it makes no attempt to address the highly explosive issues of course content and the baccalauréat—the major obstacle to genuine reform, but politically taboo.

The Fast Track: Les Grandes Ecoles

In France, contrary to the situation in other countries, the prestigious institutions of higher education have developed outside if not in opposition to the university. The famous Collège de France that still exists today was founded in 1530 to teach Greek, Hebrew, Latin, and mathematics. The erudites were paid directly by the Crown so that they could be entirely

Age		School	Class
		Grande école	
22		Third year	
21		Second year	
20		First year	
		Classes préparatoires (prépa)	
19		Second year	
18		First year	
		Lycée	
17		Seventh year: baccalauréat C	Terminale
16		Sixth year: première S	Première
15		Fifth year	Seconde
		Collège	
14		Fourth year	Troisième
13		Third year (choice of electives to be in a "good" class: German or Latin)	Quatrième
12		Second year	Cinquième
11		First year	Sixième

FIG. 8. The fast track

independent from the clique of theologians that ran the Sorbonne. The first grandes écoles—Polytechnique and l'Ecole normale supérieure—were set up in 1794 with the avowed aim of responding to a need the university was incapable of fulfilling. One of the most prestigious business schools in France today, HEC (Hautes études commerciales), founded in 1881, long a lackluster institution for *fils à papa,* was reorganized in the 1960s on the American model and created a dynamism that the stuffy French academic world was incapable of generating. The ENA (Ecole nationale d'administration) also developed outside the university. Most of the grandes écoles are not under the control of the Ministry of Education but of other ministries such as Industry and Commerce, Agriculture, or Telecommunications.

Les Prépas

One cannot go directly from lycée to grande école, the one exception being Sciences-Po, the private Parisian Institute of Political Science, which is, moreover, the only establishment that enables pupils who are not math wizards to envisage a career in management and is a useful steppingstone for ENA as well. The normal fast track is the baccalauréat (preferably bac C) and two years of grueling preparation in the *classes préparatoires aux grandes écoles,* where candidates are prepared for the competitive schools. There are scientific, business, and literary classes or *prépas.* The latter aim for l'Ecole normale supérieure, at which so many famous French intellectuals were trained—although now the school turns out mostly *agrégés* who will help perpetuate elitism when they go into teaching later. To be selected for these cram classes that exist only in the "best" lycées, candidates must have perfomed above average in the baccalauréat. Unwilling or unable to bear the self-discipline required by a forty-hour schedule plus the twenty to thirty hours of weekly home study necessary to having any chance of getting into the more prestigious schools, many will drop out of *prépa* and be content with lesser ambitions. Only about one in ten candidates will get into Ecole normale, while only about one-third of scientific pupils will be accepted by a grande école, and half of those who do manage to make it will have repeated a year of *prépa.* Business schools offer slightly more openings. The famous Parisian lycées, Montaigne, Henri IV, and Saint Louis bag the best places. The not-so-smart—if they can get transfer credit—will end up as university seniors glad to have avoided the bane of the overcrowded, mixed-ability, first- and second-year classes that are the lot of the majority of lycée pupils who continue their studies.

The best prépa students, destined to form the future elite, get a good grounding in the liberal arts and can expound on any topic at the drop of a hat, leaving foreign observers dumbfounded by their erudition and skill in rhetoric. They acquire a capacity for seizing rapidly a situation, for synthesizing it—the famous exposé in three parts with three subsections in each part!—and proposing a solution in record time.

The Making of the Elite

The French meritocracy is educated essentially in a handful of grandes écoles situated in or around Paris, which provide the administrative, political, and industrial leaders of the nation, that is, the members of the so-called *grands corps,* which some thirty envied graduates join each year. They are akin to the top civil servants of the ancien régime and ensure the continuity of the state as ministers come and go. They themselves tend increasingly to move back and forth between the public and private sector. The two main schools are Polytechnique, founded by Napoleon to train engineers, and the ENA, which was set up in 1945.

Les Polytechniciens

The graduates of Polytechnique, a sort of military academy for the whiz kids, are known as "Xs" from the emblem of two crossed canons they wear on their parade uniform. After two years of high-level education in scientific and general subjects at the school in Palaiseau in the suburbs of Paris, the majority will specialize in engineering at the Ecole des mines or l'Ecole des ponts et chaussées and later go on to hold key administrative or industrial positions. Half of all industry bosses in the seventy top French corporations have come from the *grands corps,* and the CEO of eight of the nine top enterprises is an "X." The major state-controlled companies are administered, for better or worse, by *polytechniciens.* They are the men behind the TGV, the Minitel, and Superphénix, the fast-breeder nuclear reactor.

Les Enarques

ENA graduates, known as *énarques,* monopolize the highest administrative functions, and many have become ministers, indeed prime ministers, like Jacques Chirac and Michel Rocard in the eighties, or even president of the Republic, like former President Valéry Giscard d'Estaing in the 1970s. This is not surprising, since they are the backbone of the ministerial cabinets and rule over the Inspection des finances; the Cour des comptes, the auditing body that supervises state spending; the Conseil d'état, which handles disputes between the state and citizens—it is about as close as you can get to the seat of power—and the diplomatic corps. The Commissaires de la République will also be *énarques.*

The ENA was set up in 1945 to train top civil servants with management rather than technical skills. They dispute power with the polytechniciens, who sometimes have the same hunting ground, particularly in private corporations. All the members of the *grands corps* have extensive networks that they can rely on for personal and professional maneuvering.

Of course, only a tiny minority of Polytechnique and ENA graduates, la crème de la crème, manage to become *corpsards.* Their ranking in the exit exam determines their future position in the administrative hierarchy, and the rigidity of the system allows little opportunity for climbing the rungs of the ladder afterwards. At worst, the less brilliant will enjoy a comfortable sinecure for the rest of their lives.

On account of the shortage of engineers and top managers in France today—largely due to the low ouput of the elitist educational system—headhunters dispute the graduates of other grandes écoles, who can command fabulous starting salaries in spite of their lack of experience. All told the network produces about fifteen thousand engineers and twelve thousand managers annually, when the country needs about twice that number.[4] It is little wonder that ambitious young people should set their sights at an early age on the fast stream. It is an open race, but naturally some sociocultural environments are more favorable than others to nurturing the future elite, and children of working-class parents have a very slight chance of reaching the top. Self-made men like Jacques Delors, president of the European Commission, or Premier Pierre Bérégovoy, who started in life with a CAP in fitting and machining, are the exceptions that confirm the rule.

The exit examination at the ENA consists of solving in six hours a complex administrative problem with the aid of a dossier. The assumption for the future énarque is that given a good report, prepared by his subordinates, he can treat any problem no matter how difficult in six hours! This is perhaps the main grief with the French elite, who are first and foremost *hommes de dossier,* that is, dossier men. They have a

4. Grande école students (engineering and business) account for only 7 to 8 percent of the total number of students registered in higher education. *La France en chiffres,* 18.

developed sense of organization, they are able to delegate responsibility, they know how to command, and they are mobile and adaptable, but their training "underestimates systematically the value of experience, of technique, of analytical rigor, of attention to detail and exhaustiveness."[5] It neglects the value of discussion, something practically unknown in French education. It only accepts one mode of reasoning—intuition is suspect—and does not encourage decision sharing that is often time consuming. *L'efficacité avant toute chose* (effectiveness above all else) is a common expression that shows a French obsession with productivity that is largely of the intellectual kind. The elite tend to ignore human factors, real-life situations, and are not very good listeners. The grande école system explains both the brilliant technical achievements in telecommunications, aerospace, railways, and the enormous commercial fiascos of French industry such as Concorde, cable TV, and Superphénix.[6] Things are slowly beginning to change with the increasing internationalization of science and business and the development of foreign alliances. This cross-fertilization of the elite (Airbus Industries is a good example) should give the French the professionalism that has so far been lacking in their training.

Indeed, there is increasing criticism of the dilettantism of the elite and of the quality of the education they are receiving. A survey taken in January 1990 showed that one out of two students skips courses and less than one out of five believes that school is giving them a sound technical training.[7] Yet they have unlimited confidence in their operational capacity in spite of their lack of experience! The majority of business school alumni are attracted by finance and management consulting. They want nothing to do with selling, while the future engineers show little enthusiasm for careers in production and want positions in management and consultancy. Quality of life has become the new value of the pampered elite. For the moment they can dictate their conditions to employers. For how long? Much will depend on the capacity of the university to produce top-quality graduates in sufficent quantity to regulate demand.

---

5. Laurent Cohen-Tanugi, "Les règles du poulailler," *Le Monde*, 10 May 1990.

6. See François de Closets, *Tant et plus* (Paris: Grasset-Seuil, 1992).

7. Anne Fohr, "Portraits de jeunes gens pressés," *Le Nouvel Observateur*, 26 April–2 May 1990, 39.

Degrees and Salaries

Salary scales in business and industry are more closely linked in France than elsewhere to the number of years of postsecondary education. Thus bac+2 (i.e., two years of higher education) is worth less than bac+3, in turn less than bac+4 and bac+5 on the job market. Professional training neither brings the same status nor the same rewards as theoretical studies. As economist Jean-Jacques Salomon says: "The disdain for technical jobs that pervades our educational system, even the best schools, has led to 'devaluation' of professional training." There is an imbalance between technical education and general education. Yet, "this imbalance precisely goes against the hierarchy of functions upon which the successful performance of industrial corporations depends to a large degree."[8]

Generally speaking, no level of professional experience or technical competence can offset the money value of the diploma one possesses. This not only hampers career prospects for those with a shorter education but is often a source of professional demotivation and embitterment. For instance, a supervisor with ten or fifteen years of experience may earn less than the graduate fresh from university whom he or she is expected to train! The economist Philippe d'Iribarne has shown how the relationship between degrees and salaries is conditioned by the French "honor code" that has given rise to an extremely subtle hierarchy, as portrayed in the INSEE's inventory of professions: "Just try to explain to a Dutchman the difference between a cadre and a non-cadre!"[9]

Another consequence of this hierarchy is that everybody naturally wants to accumulate as many marketable diplomas as possible. As a result postsecondary courses have a glut of candidates that they are unable to absorb. This is true not only of engineering and medical schools but also of shorter two- or three-year training courses for health, business, and other service technicians. The BTS (*brevet de technicien supérieur*) classes open to postbaccalauréat students in some lycées or the highly successful university institutes of technology cannot cope with the demand. Originally designed to train technicians in two years, they have been caught up in the race for higher qualification. As they only

8. "La capacité d'innovation," 36–37.

9. Philippe d'Iribarne, *Le chômage paradoxal* (Paris: Presses Universitaires de France, 1990), 91.

pick the best students and as the ambition of the latter is to continue their studies, these institutions no longer fulfill their primary role. Students who do not meet the stringent entrance requirements based on their bac results and lycée records have little choice but to join the ranks of the hundreds of thousands of French university students, who have only the choice between the "open" literary, psychology, sociology, and economic departments that will weed out those that do not have the profile to continue studying in these areas. In the Rhône-Alpes region, for example, 40 percent of undergraduates are eliminated after two years. This is a huge waste of the intellectual resources of the nation.

Coca-Cola Universities

If the grandes écoles have spacious buildings and a campus life on the American model with their initiation rites of doubtful taste (*le bizutage*), galas, and clubs, French universities in general tend to be shabby, overcrowded, and dismal. There is no graduation ceremony and students may have to wait as long as a year after graduating to receive their diplomas due to bureaucratic delays. They have no personal tutors, as in Britain, and teachers tend to be aloof and indifferent. First-year students are largely left to their own devices to glean information on schedules, course content, and lecture rooms. Assessment is often byzantine, or at least the criteria are not always clear. Poorly stocked libraries are open for a limited number of hours during the day and closed during vacations. Dormitories have only minimal comfort, no individual telephones, and limited supplies of hot water for showering. There are long queues in the campus restaurants, and napkins are rarely supplied. Social life is gloomy. The list of grievances is long after twenty years of neglect of French universities financed almost entirely by public funds. In 1988 France only devoted 6.28 percent of its GDP to education in general and less than 0.5 percent to higher education, compared to 1.5 percent in the United States.[10]

Yet, if all the seventy-seven universities have been notoriously short

10. Gross domestic product (GDP) refers to the total value of products and services produced in France, including that of foreign companies established in France. Gross national product (GNP) refers to the total value of products and services produced by French corporations, whether they are situated in France or abroad.

Age		Years of Study	"Cycle"
		University	
25		Eighth year: bac + 8	doctorate, equivalent Ph.D., Doctor of Medicine (8 years min.)
24		Seventh year: bac + 7	doctorate (7 years min.)
23		Sixth year: bac + 6	Pharmacy
22		Fifth year: bac + 5	Magistère, DESS, DEA , dentistry (five year min.) engineering degrees—*3ème cycle*
21		Fourth year: bac + 4	Maîtrise—*2ème cycle*
20		Third year: bac + 3	Licence—*2ème cycle*
19		Second year: bac + 2	DEUG-DUT —*1er cycle*
18		First year: bac + 1	DEUG-DUT—*1er cycle*
		Lycée	
17		Seventh year: baccalauréat A, B, C, D, E, F, G, H or professional bac	Terminale

DEA: Diplôme d'études approfondies (roughly equivalent to a Masters degree). Necessary to undertake doctoral studies

DESS: Diplôme d'études supérieures specialiséés (also roughly equivalent to a Masters degree in a variety of specialized fields such as law, economics, business)

DUT: Diplôme universitaire de technologie. A two-year degree conferred by an IUT

FIG. 9. The organization of higher education

of cash and if the working and living conditions of students have deteriorated with the development of mass education, the "productivity" of the system has offset to some extent the material shortcomings. When one considers that many French universities have a budget ten to twenty times smaller than American institutions of comparable size, it has to be admitted that they manage remarkably well despite their handicaps. Three-quarters of the students actually get a degree, even if they do not always take the shortest route, and those who fail still find a job more easily than pupils who have only the baccalauréat.

French academia has no Harvard or Cambridge. There is no Ivy League—all universities being supposedly equivalent in an educational system that prides itself on egalitarianism. This means that a doctorate from the Sorbonne, for example, is theoretically of no more value than a doctorate delivered by any provincial university, all degrees bearing the national stamp. In 1986, the Ministry's proposal to have national degrees bear the name of the university by which they are conferred, the so-called Devaquet reform, was one of the major causes of student protest that almost toppled the government. Of course there is a hierarchy among the universities and faculties, but it is hypocritically denied because it goes against the proclaimed egalitarianism.

The myth of equality of opportunity has been confused with the privilege for all of continuing their studies as long as possible because of the close link between remuneration and the accumulation of degrees. As a result each of the seventy-seven universities has been expected to train both top-level professional and researchers as well as students with lesser career goals. The notion of uniformity has prevented the setting up of a diversified university system on the American model catering to the needs of a public with varied capacities and ambitions. In 1986 students marched through the streets in defense of equality of opportunity with banners that said "This is not America" and "We don't want Coca-Cola universities," blind to the fact that, on the one hand, it is harder to enter higher education in France—the bac is the sine qua non—than in the United States and, on the other hand, that the dumping grounds many university departments constitute have nothing to envy in the performance of the worst colleges in the United States. According to a report by the National Committee for the Evaluation of the University published in 1990, many students take three, four, and even five years to get their DEUG (*diplôme d'études universitaires générales*), which should normally be obtained after two years. On average, students presently take more than three years to get this diploma.

A New Chance for the Universities

The Devaquet reform and the massive 1986 student demonstrations that forced the government to shelve the draft bill had the merit of forcing all the players (politicians, academics, and students) to recognize the perversion of a system that, under cover of equality of opportunity, is discriminatory and inefficient. The controversy also made it clear that "the quality generation" of the late 1980s and early 1990s expected a lot from the university. Students who had toiled for their baccalauréat would no longer be content with the overcrowded amphitheaters and the inadequate facilities or accept being parked in departments that offer few career opportunities.

Contrary to a widely held cliché, the quality of university graduates in many sectors is on a par with and often superior to that of the grandes écoles prodigies. Major corporations are turning more and more to the universities to find skilled technicians as well as the talent they need for research and development. The latter are seizing the chance to respond to a demand that the prestigious schools are incapable of satisfying on account of their limited supply, not to mention the exorbitant wage demands of their alumni—from Fr 150,000 to 200,000 per year for a twenty-three year-old with no experience!

Of late, the university has been catching up and has created its own "schools" that coexist with the more traditional faculties. Many of the engineering schools are excellent. The University of Dauphine in Paris with its six thousand students has become a reputed European business school. Many of the universities nowadays have business programs on a par with, if not better than, those offered by the network of commercial schools (*écoles supérieures de commerce et d'administration des entreprises,* or ESCAE) run by the chambers of commerce, which, incidentally, play a far more important economic role in France than their counterparts in the United States.

At the same time scientific and business programs are getting increasing aid from the private sector in the form of cash and equipment. IBM, Digital Equipment Corporation, Hewlett-Packard, Rank Xerox, and Bull have united their efforts to set up high-level research and development programs in four Parisian universities. The executives of these and other companies are bringing their professional know-how and commercial expertise to students across the country. The mutual distrust between the academics and the industrial/business world is disappearing. Researchers no longer lock themselves up in their ivory towers, and in the midst of the overall impoverishment of the university system, some French institutions have nothing to envy foreign counterparts in terms of equipment and training. The grandes écoles cannot always stand the

The Devaquet Reform

During the brief spell of conservative government (1986–88) René Monory, minister of education, proposed a reform of higher education drawn up by then Secretary of State for Universities Alain Devaquet. The three points in the Devaquet reform that particularly angered students were: (1) possession of the baccalauréat would no longer automatically allow them to register at university (2) degrees, while continuing to bear a national seal of approval, would also indicate the name of the university that conferred them (thus making official the disguised hierarchy among institutions of higher education—there would be "good" and "bad" universites) (3) tuition fees that cost about Fr 500 per year at that time could be increased to as much as three times that amount.

Another provision of the reform implied increased power for the conservative professors at the top of the academic hierarchy, whose prerogatives had been confiscated by Monory's Socialist predecessor.

The reform was clearly an attack by the political "liberal" Right on the egalitarian principles defended by the Left, just as the 1984 attempt by the Socialists to merge the public and private school systems was an attack on the *école libre* defended by the Right. Massive student demonstrations broke out all over France, and the Chirac cabinet withdrew the reform bill when a student was beaten to death by riot police.

---

comparison where research is concerned—many of the business schools do no research at all and their graduates have to go to university to pursue postgraduate studies. This has not been the least contradiction of French education: the prestigious schools have had limited research and the universities limited prestige!

Still, the task facing the government is gigantic. French higher education today is at a turning point after two decades of pinching and scraping and a huge waste of limited resources because of the unpreparedness of freshmen in many study areas who are the victims of the skewed orientation at lycée. Mr. Mitterrand made education the top priority of his second mandate, and the educational budget is now even bigger than that of national defense. A complete overhaul of the system is under way, and there seems to be general consensus on the role of postsecondary institutions in modern French society. Improved career orientation, quality training at all levels, and a network of specialized institutions catering to the diverse professional and academic goals of students are the central pieces of the reform. Mr. Mitterrand himself has lashed out at the "private hunting grounds" of the grandes écoles, and *prépa* classes are being urged to open wide their doors. New university institutes of technology are being built, and new teacher-training centers, designed to give all teachers from kindergarten to university a basic training in pedagogy have been set up.

Universities are being given increasing autonomy in the framework of the new five-year development plans that have replaced the annual state funding. Regional groupings of institutions designed to form quality hubs in a European context—The Universities 2,000 project—are being set up, and the bulk of research spending is no longer confined to the Parisian centers. The regions are being invited to contribute to the development of higher education, which means greater decentralization and integration with the local economy, even if it is too soon to expect the ministry to abandon central control. Among students there is even a new awareness that quality education is expensive and a willingness to pay more for it, even if this involves borrowing money. This is an entirely new attitude in France.

Minister Jospin even had a project to reduce the undergraduate failure and dropout rate by replacing the fixed menu at present available to freshmen by an à la carte system that would allow greater flexibility in the choice of credits. Student organizations were opposed to this plan, which they claimed would actually restrict their choice of subjects. After the 1993 legislative elections this controversial project was shelved by the new Right-wing minister, François Bayrou.

The single market and the numerous European programs such as ERASMUS (European Action Scheme for the Mobility of University Students), COMETT (Community in Education and Training for Technology), and LINGUA (designed to encourage the teaching and learning of at least two EC languages throughout the Community) are powerful incentives for change, as students become familiar with other educational systems. The politicians at last seem to have measured the importance of education for the future of France. However, a sustained budgetary effort will be necessary over many years to make up for the long recession in state investment, and new sources of financing such as local government funding will have to be found if 80 percent of an age group are to pursue their studies after the baccalauréat. New buildings totaling one and a half million square meters need to be constructed by the year 2000, and 500,000 square meters of derelict buildings have to be renovated. Dormitory accommodation for thirty thousand students will have to be provided by 1995. Overall spending on education has increased sharply—Fr 247.8 billion in 1991, that is, nearly 20 percent of the national budget and 6.7 percent of gross domestic product. In 1991 every person in France contributed an average of roughly eight thousand francs to the educational system. Higher education received 14 percent of funds. Yet, despite increased spending since 1989 higher education still represents only 0.4 percent of GDP, a ridiculously small figure compared to the United States, Britain, or Japan.

The urgency of reform and the new realism of students seem to have pushed the ideological battles that have been one of the salient characteristics of French universities into the background. Yet, education remains a potentially explosive issue, and the government is treading warily the thin line between screening and orientation as well as between decentralization and state control, which are related to the sacred egalitarian principles. The ability to reconcile the theory and practice of equality of educational opportunity with the new economic circumstances of the 1990s that require an increasing number of qualified professionals is one of the major challenges facing France today.

PART 4

The Wheel of Fortune

Money doesn't make the person who hasn't got any happy.

—Boris Vian

8

Wealth and Equality

France went right from a taboo about money to the cult of it.
—Alain Minc

The French have always had a rather ambivalent attitude toward wealth, and this would-be egalitarian society has never been able to get rid of the fundamental suspicion about money that medieval preachers instilled. Molière's miser, Harpagon, sacrificed reputation, virtue, and honor to it, while the poet and critic Nicolas Boileau (1636–1711) declared that it turned a gentleman into a scoundrel. Montesquieu, the great eighteenth-century philosopher and political theorist (whose portrait adorns the 200-franc bank note!), observed that "money is only estimable when it is scorned."

French capitalism is probably the most uncompromising in the world. The Revolution was fought to put an end to the privileges the wealthy enjoyed, and for two hundred years money—if you were among the lucky few to have any—was something to be tucked away in the legendary woolen socks of French peasants but certainly not something to brag about. Not that money was despised. Only superior minds wealthy in the bargain, like Montesquieu, could afford to do that. But the subject was taboo, personal.

Laundering

Paradoxically, it was the Socialist government that came to power in 1981 that broke down the self-imposed discretion of the French in money matters. Following its disastrous handling of the economy on generous if misguided egalitarian principles during its first two years in office, it made an abrupt about-face in 1983. In haste to prove they could govern as well as the right-of-center parties that had run the country for forty years, the Socialists carried out a major laundering operation on what the Left had always considered as "filthy lucre." With the help of appealing commercials the Socialists urged the middle classes to join the genteel world of high finance for the common good, by investing their extra money in newly nationalized enterprises instead of vulgarly hoarding it. Stories of money-makers filled the pages of news magazines, and Bernard Tapie, a brash corporate raider, ran his own TV show vaunting the new business mentality.[1] Almost overnight several million ordinary people who had never possessed stock in their lives invested their savings on the Bourse and glued their eyes to the CAC index. Newsstands offered an array of financial magazines and fledgling investors exchanged tips. Casinos were refurbished. One-armed bandits were authorized for the first time in France in 1988 under the brief spell of Right-wing government, and new money-making games were launched on a national scale, turning the country into a sort of vast Monte Carlo with the benediction of the Socialists. TV games like "Wheel of Fortune," which offset their lowbrow content by offering fabulous prizes, shadowed the stuffy word quizzes that had so long been the fare of TV viewers and enjoyed enormous popularity with a nation supposed to be finicky about easy money. Never before in the history of France had the "Western influence" been so powerful. The Americanization of France in the 1960s had not affected the overall value system; the French had subscribed to American management methods, listened to American music, consumed Coca-Cola but had remained conservative in money matters. Henceforth they would be income conscious.

Though perhaps ironical, it was logical that the Socialists should have initiated this financial revolution. Only they were in a position to absolve the French from the sins of capitalism. With the return of the right-of-center party to power in 1986 money making became increasingly acceptable, and the Left (which had sold its soul) was no longer in a position to rebuke—supposing it still wanted to. The Socialists' rehabilitation of money in the value system of the French was to have far-reaching social, economic, and political consequences. The Left, in the long run, was to lose more than it gained from its well-intentioned efforts to persuade its supporters to finance economic recovery. During the student uprising in 1990 the rallying cry of the supposedly idealistic youth was: *"Du pognon!"* (Bucks!) showing how deep the transformation of mentalities had been in the previous decade. The pragmatism of the young people today

1. Bernard Tapie was to become the controversial minister of city affairs in the Bérégovoy cabinet.

contrasts with the idealism of their "ancestors" in 1968, suggesting that "the Golden Age was the age when there was no gold."

But have the French no qualms about this glorification of money? A certain number of indicators suggest that the transformation of mentalities has been far more superficial than the pollsters suggested and that the flamboyant 1980s are giving way to questioning in the 1990s.

The first alert came with the minicrash that hit stock markets worldwide in 1987 and sent some of the newly converted *capitalistes* scuttling for cover when they suddenly experienced the risk of investments. While there was a reassuring absence of panic among the majority of inexperienced investors, it did tamper their enthusiasm. As Bruno Frappat wrote:

> Culturally, in the broad sense of the term, the stock exchange crisis may tone down, for the time being, the glorification of money that has been chanted for a few years. Far from living according to the old Christian idea that money is dirty and all wealth illegitimate (or at least to be hidden), French society had discovered—under the Left!—the virtue of getting rich, the nobility of financial pursuits, and of the adventures of cash flow. Money-making held its head high. A situation that America had been familiar with for decades was finally tolerated here. . . . But deep down, especially among the "small fry" who had been pompously requested to join the financial family and who are being begged today to accept ruin with good grace, there is a feeling that there's something rotten in the kingdom of money. . . . Perhaps a new distribution of values, in every sense of the term, will arise from all this chaos. This financial unrest may provide the opportunity for cultural reassessment. It would be the only positive effect of this disaster.[2]

But if some of the French were hurt in their pockets, others were hurt in their souls by the new value system. In 1989, an insider trading scandal involving personalities close to the president, who has professed a scorn for money all his life, rocked the Socialists' reputation for integrity, and Mitterrand, criticizing the pervasive materialistic standards of conduct, lashed out at "money vultures," "easy money," and "gangsterism of the strongest," using a terminology that the new, pragmatic Left—la gauche

2. Bruno Frappat, "Le chaos et le bémol," *Le Monde,* 1–2 November 1987.

champagne—had wiped out of its vocabulary and that only he with all his presidential authority could still venture to use.[3]

If money is a taboo subject, it is because wealth is more likely to stir up resentment than admiration in a society obsessed with the idea of equality. Indignant employees at the state-run TV network went on strike in 1989 when they heard that a star anchorwoman, Christine Ockrent, had been hired for the sum of Fr 100,000 per month. Shortly after, in the heat of a strike at the Peugeot plant, information leaked out about the salary of the CEO, Jacques Calvet, actually a modest one by European or American standards for someone in his position—Fr 185,000 per month—causing an uproar in the media. Yet, things may be changing. In 1990 when Antoine Riboud, CEO of BSN, the big French food conglomerate, committed the indelicacy of making public on TV (*L'heure de Vérité*) his annual earnings of Fr 5.5 million, there were no protests, only amazement. Is this a sign that people are finally ready to accept that professional competence should be rewarded? This event was singular enough to make the headlines in a country where the earnings of top executives are a tightly kept secret.

Formerly the "worth" of a person had nothing to do with his paycheck, and a poorly paid tax official could talk man to man with a wealthy *rentier.* The status conferred by being a member of the civil service and working for the common good offset the difference in income. In the new value system status has become synonymous with income, so people are no longer ashamed to talk about their salary. If their remuneration is high, it shows just how good they are at their job; if it is low, it shows that they are underpaid for the work they do. Many people are no longer ashamed to show their paycheck. At the end of 1990 *L'Evenèment du Jeudi* presented a cover story on "How much your neighbor earns." The reporters questioned people directly about their earnings—an unheard of indelicacy in France—and very few refused to answer.

Haves and Have Nots

By promoting a value system based on money, the Socialists have destroyed a form of cultural identification, a brand image, that had been

3. In fact, the president's warning went unheeded. Following this, a long series of financial scandals were to ruin the Socialists' reputation for integrity and contribute to their crushing defeat in the 1993 legislative election.

theirs for more than one hundred years. With the Communist party having lost all credibility in France today, there is no longer anyone to plead the cause of the poor—a situation the extreme Right has been quick to exploit politically. In a society where money is becoming the supreme goal, the underprivileged feel frustrated by the ostentation of the well-off at a time when the former are urged to be more productive and competitive:

> The decline of Marxism, the economic crisis, the gradual glorification of the market, the social advantages of profit making have relentlessly legitimized wealth and its symbols and discredited poverty, synonymous with failure and uselessness. The winners, the conquerors, have become the models to be imitated, the supporters of overall prosperity; champions on top of that, symbols of luck and success; while the outcasts, the misfits, the poor, have put on the downcast expression of losers, of those who have nothing to lose and who can do nothing about it. And the Socialists themselves, discovering the charm of the capitalistic system and striving to manage it intelligently, have not avoided the tendency to wrap wealth in the cloak of virtue and beauty.[4]

The republican ethic of liberty, equality, and fraternity that graces the frontons of town halls all over France is losing its lustre. What liberty does a social outcast enjoy? asks lawyer and writer, Jean-Denis Bredin.

"Liberty, Inequality, Fraternity"

This was the surprising title of a report in France's leading business magazine, *L'Expansion,* in March 1990, while *L'Evènement du Jeudi* ran a cover story on spreading inequality in the "disastrous 1980s." The event that sparked these alarming articles was the updated edition of the INSEE's *Données sociales* and the publication of the latest report on the eighties by the CERC (Centre d'étude sur les revenus et les coûts). All the indicators show that after a decade of Socialist leadership the rich are getting richer and the poor poorer. For the well-off the high interest rates of the 1980s meant high dividends, while the increase in value of real estate meant higher rents and more profit. As former prime minister Michel Rocard was forced to admit: "Money begets money." Between 1980 and

4. Jean-Denis Bredin, "Les champs ouverts au socialisme . . . ," *Le Monde,* 22 March 1990.

1990 the value of real estate was multipled by 3.5; that of securities and bonds by 5; and, although the number of middle-class people who own stock has almost doubled since the early 1980s, the bulk of investments is still in the hands of the traditionally more privileged classes (industrialists, businessmen, senior executives). Meanwhile a low inflation rate and high interest charges penalize home buyers with a limited income and saddle them with debts, while reducing the availability of affordable rentals. High unemployment and a taxation system that favors those with most property also contribute to inequalities that the government has tried to attenuate with the "tax on large fortunes" (*impôt sur les grandes fortunes*) and social cushioning for the needy, but the gap between rich and poor continues to grow wider.

In his book, *L'argent fou* (*Crazy Money*) Alain Minc, businessman and self-appointed guru on social issues, who can hardly be suspected of socialist leanings, declared, "We are witnessing the end of the great egalitarian movement that emerged after the war from which the huge middle class sprung." In fact, Minc is worried that the reign of "king money" may sound the death knell of capitalism in France. The only answer to its reign is: "virtue, more virtue, always virtue."[5] He is shocked by the cynicism and corruption of the business world, tax dodging, kickbacks, illegal political handouts, insider trading, at a time when the gap between rich and poor is growing wider. Minc is not convinced of the virtues of trickle-down theory: "The rich are getting richer, the not so rich are consuming; as for the poor . . . they are hidden from view, sunk in a distant, invisible counter-society."[6]

Salaries and Income

The average net monthly wage in 1990 after the social security contributions due by all employees had been deducted was slightly over Fr 9,000. Women average 30 percent less than men, partly because they work less overtime and occupy positions in traditionally low-paid sectors of the economy, partly because of sexual discrimination in spite of equal pay legislation. Salary scales are increasingly linked to levels of education: for each additional year of study there is a corresponding increase in pay, and the higher educational qualifications a person possesses, the less chance he or she has of being jobless. However, as the INSEE points out, there has been a steady decline in the market value of university

5. Alain Minc, *L'argent fou* (Paris: Grasset, 1990), 16, 8.
6. Minc, *L'argent fou*, 83.

1. Private Corporations	
Managers (*cadres*)*, senior professionals	Fr 19,394
Technicians, supervisors	Fr 10,450
Clerical staff and shop employees (*employés*)*	Fr 6,925
Skilled workers	Fr 7,250
Unskilled workers	Fr 6,190
2. Civil Servants	
Senior managers (*cadres*)	Fr 14,740
University professors, researchers	Fr 13,970
Elementary teachers, collège teachers	Fr 9,110
Police officers, prison wardens	Fr 9,500
Clerical staff (*employés*)	Fr 7,090
Blue-collar workers (*ouvriers*)*	Fr 6,910

* A *cadre* is defined as a person in a position of management or control; an *employé* is a person who works in an office or a store as opposed to an *ouvrier* who works in a factory or on a working site. However, it is extremely difficult to understand the hierarchy of professions (a municipal street sweeper is not an *ouvrier* but an *employé*), and the subtle differences in status which are reflected in salary scales and pensions. (See chap. 20).

FIG. 10. Average monthly salaries in 1990. The tables show net salaries, that is, after deduction of social security contributions and retirement payments. Gross before tax earnings will be 17 to 22 percent more. (*Sources:* CERC and *INSEE Première* 156, 1991.)

degrees over the past fifteen years compared to the diplomas awarded by the grandes écoles.[7] On the other hand, a lot of college graduates, especially in public administration, who occupy positions that do not require very high educational qualifications are badly paid. The gross minimum wage or SMIC was Fr 5,760 per month (Fr 34 per hour) on 1 July 1992.[8] This means a take-home pay of roughly Fr 5,000 when the worker has paid his share of social security charges.[9]

7. Christian Baudelot and Michel Claude, "Les diplômes paient-ils de moins en moins?" in *Données Sociales 1990,* 103–8.

8. SMIC (*salaire minimum interprofessionel de croissance*). The minimum wage for 169 hours of work per month is fixed annually in July by the government in terms of the increased purchasing power of the average hourly wage earned by workers. When prices rise by 2 percent, it is automatically increased. In July 1991, 8.6 percent of all wage earners were being paid the minimum wage.

9. In July 1990, on average 7.8 percent of workers in industry, and 14.4 percent in the services were being paid the minimum wage. In some industries (textiles, clothing) the proportion was 26.2 percent, and reached 28 percent for employees in hotels, bars, and restaurants. In businesses employing less than ten workers 12.2 percent of men, and 25.5 percent of women were earning the minimum wage. *Tableaux de l'économie française* 1991–92. (Paris: INSEE, 1991), 84. The statistics are based on data available on 31 May 1991.

Food	
Milk (liter)	Fr 5.60
Eggs (doz.)	Fr 13.60
Bread (baguette)	Fr 3.50
Steak (kilo)	Fr 92.60
Services	
Movie ticket	Fr 38.00
Medical visit (generalist)	Fr 90.00
Local 'phone call	Fr 0.73
Miscellaneous	
Gasoline (liter)	Fr 5.80
Newspaper	Fr 6.00
Gauloises bleues (packet)	Fr 5.50

FIG. 11. Prices of some commodities and services in 1991. Spending on the home, inclusive of rent or mortgages, utilities, and local taxes accounted for 29 percent of family budgets in 1989, an increase of 22.4 percent per person in ten years, reaching Fr 1,850 on average per person per month. This is a lot more than the French spend on food (20.5 percent), transportation (14.5 percent), and clothing (8.3 percent), for which expenditure was respectively 25.4 percent, 14.3 percent, and 10.3 percent ten years ago. The minimum wage in 1991 was Fr 32.66 per hour. (See Mireille Moutardier, "Le budget habitation," *INSEE Première* 164, 1991.)

Disposable Income

When considering salary scales in France, it is important to bear in mind the distinction between basic wages and disposable income. Because of the peculiarities of French taxation and the extensive redistribution of funds in the form of social security benefits—allowances of various kinds, unemployment payments, health care, and pensions—someone earning a lower salary may have a disposable income proportionally higher than a person with a better remuneration. For instance, the allowances and tax breaks given to an average working-class family with four children increase ordinary family earnings by two-thirds. Broadly speaking, these transfer payments account for almost one-third of total revenue. They have increased by 5 percent in less than ten years and have in no small way contributed to the higher standing of living retired people now enjoy. Still, according to INSEE, large families, in spite of these transfer payments, continue to have the lowest standard of living. One in six

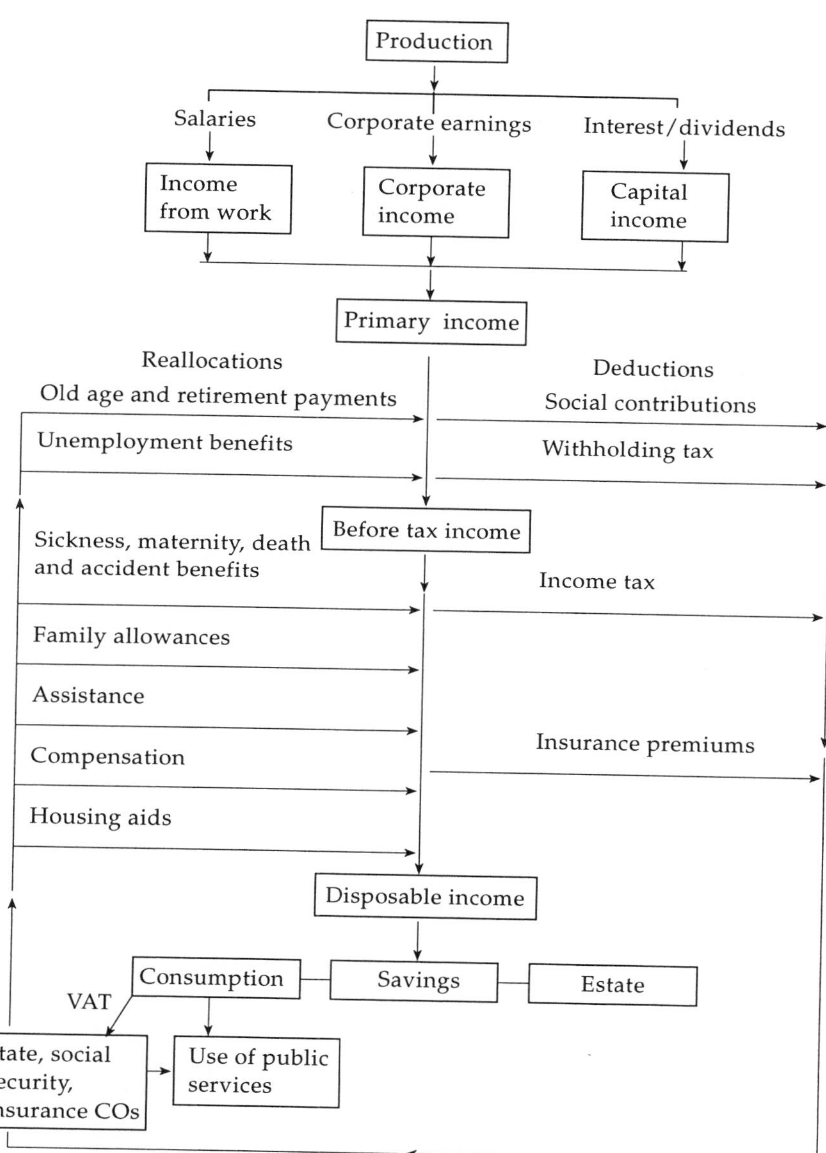

FIG. 12. Disposable income

French families is classified as a low-income household (defined as earnings totaling a mere 50 to 60 percent of the median income), one of the main causes of poverty being unemployment. Immigrants and older people living in rural areas are also likely to be poorer. In developed countries it is usually the older generation or large or single-parent families that are worst hit by poverty. France stands out as an exception to the rule insofar as the older generation (over 65s) are more sheltered than elsewhere thanks to the *minimum vieillesse* available to the elderly.[10]

The Socialists did nothing to narrow the gap between high and low salaries. Even the right-of-center governments that ran the country before the eighties had an incomes policy that tended to reduce the salary range. In the 1980s the gap widened as private enterprises encountered enormous difficulty attracting the talented executives and technicians they needed to cope with a buoyant economy. At the other end of the scale there was no dearth of unskilled workers, and demand for them declined. In 1991, the top 10 percent of male wage earners received an annual net salary of Fr 217,300 while the lowest earning 10 percent received a mere Fr 67,000 per year.[11]

Industrial workers in France are among the most poorly paid in Europe, and the government keeps a tight check on salaries generally, particularly on those of state employees.[12] Thus, there is intense dissatisfaction among wage earners, who feel that they are paying for the inherent weaknesses of the French economy. Due to the lack of a com-

---

10. Jean-Robert Suesser, "Pauvres en France et ailleurs," in *Données Sociales 1990*, 150–55.

11. INSEE. See *Le Monde Dossiers et Documents-Bilan Economique et Social 1992*. The statistics are based on data available in 1991.

12. Wages tend to be low because of the high social security charges employers have to pay. Among the twelve European Community countries only Spain, Greece, and Portugal pay lower wages, and, in terms of purchasing power the median hourly wage procures only Greek and Portugese industrial workers do worse than the French. (EUROSTAT, *Populations et Conditions Sociales* 8 [Luxembourg: L'office des statistiques de la communauté européenne, 1990]). One ECU (european currency unit) is equal to seven francs. The median hourly wage in France is 6.2 ECUs. However, international comparisons are delicate. French workers pay little or no income tax compared to those in Denmark, for example, where wages are high (11.1 ECUs per hour) and taxes too. French trade unions always complain about how poorly paid workers are, forgetting the low rates of income tax and the extensive social protection they enjoy. On the other hand, employers complain about the high social security charges they are required to pay, forgetting the low salaries.

petitive manufacturing industry, an inefficient educational system, and a cumbersome bureaucracy, keeping the French franc strong boils down to wage restrictions. Of course the minimum wage is there to ensure that workers are not exploited, but there are numerous ways of getting round it—trainee workers (jobless youth and laid-off employees who have no other solution) and part-time workers unable to find a permanent job earn less than the SMIC, which imposes an hourly rate of payment and not a monthly wage.

After the Socialists' conversion to economic realism the necessity of an incomes policy was struck off the agenda. Their technique was rather social cushioning for the needy such as the provision of housing for the destitute (*loi Besson*) and the RMI (*revenu minimum d'insertion*, minimum integration income), financed by the solidarity tax on large fortunes—more than Fr 4.3 billion—payable by a mere 0.6 percent of taxpayers. These policies had mixed results.

A Minimum Income for All

In December 1988, to alleviate the hardship of the jobless who had exhausted their possibility of obtaining an extension of their unemployment benefits, as well as to help the very poor, a RMI of Fr 2,000 for a single person was made available to all the population over twenty-five years of age—or those under 25 with children—whose total revenues did not exceed that sum. (The larger the family the higher the rate, but income from other sources, e.g. family allowances and, partly, housing allowances, are taken into account in computing the rate.) The system was designed as a safety net for those that slip through the mesh of social security aids. No resident of France (including foreigners who have resided in the country for three years) should henceforth—on paper at least—be completely destitute. By July 1989, 268,000 were receiving the RMI. To the surprise of the specialists three-quarters of the beneficiaries were persons living alone, and about half of them were under thirty-five years of age, showing the toll unemployment was taking on young people. Seventy-seven percent of the beneficiaries were jobless receiving no unemployment benefits.[13] By 1992 more than a million people had benefited from the system.

13. Vincent Poubelle, "Les bénéficiaires du revenu minimum d'insertion," in *Données Sociales 1990*, 425–27.

The minimum integration income is designed essentially to tide people over until they find a job or some suitable remunerated occupation, such as working for a non-profit-making association, doing community work, or retraining. Thus far "integration" has been the weak link in the system. Much seems to depend on the creativity and dynamism of the local authorities, who are commited to coming up with suitable occupations for the beneficiaries. (In 1991 the state had to step in to make up for their lack of imagination.) In spite of the deficiencies of the system,[14] one shudders to think what would have been the plight of the beneficiaries of the RMI if all the political parties had not for once forgotten their ideological differences and taken concrete action to alleviate the human suffering brought about by extreme poverty.[15]

Taxation

> In the reign of Louis XV, Madame Du Deffand declared, "They tax everything except the air we breathe"—a situation that was to come about under the Revolution when they put a tax on doors and windows.
>
> —Jacques Bainville

France has one of the most bizarre tax systems in Europe. Not the least oddity is the option available to all taxpayers to pay their income tax, if they so wish, in three annual installments—in February, May, and October—rather than having it automatically deducted from their monthly paycheck. The lamentations of the French on those fateful dates are probably louder than elsewhere in the world when the time comes to cough up for the public good. The image of the tax collector in the collective consciousness is associated with the hated tax farmers of the

---

14. Chantal Euzeby, *Le revenu minimum garanti* (Paris: Editions la Découverte, 1991).

15. Poverty is increasing throughout the EC. If the EC definition of the poverty level (i.e., earnings totaling a mere 50 percent of the median income per household) is retained, then there are forty-four million people living below the poverty line in the EC. Studies have shown that the situation would be worse were it not for the numerous "safety nets" set up in the member states. Yet, before the RMI was introduced in France, four hundred thousand people were not receiving any social welfare, almost one million jobless were not receiving any unemployment benefits, and between two hundred thousand and four hundred thousand people were homeless (Euzeby, *Le revenu minimum garanti,* 72).

ancien régime that bled the citizens in the king's name. Yet, income tax in France accounts for barely 20 percent of total tax revenues. It is insignificant compared to the sums deducted from paychecks in the form of social security contributions and represents less than one-half of the amount they pay in the form of TVA (*taxe à valeur ajoutée*, a value added tax, basically a uniform nationwide sales tax) and is even lower than the taxes levied by local authorities, the so-called *quatre vieilles* (the four old ones) introduced two hundred years ago: residential tax (payable by houseowners and tenants alike); property tax; land tax; and the professional tax—formerly known as *la patente*—payable by all those who run a business of any size or kind. All told, the burden of taxation in France—44 percent of GDP—is heavier than the European average (40 percent) and much more so than in the United States or Japan.

French Taxation and the EC

One of the prime objectives of the EC Single Act (1985–86) was to set up a single domestic market by abolishing crossborder obstacles to the free movement of goods between the EC countries. These obstacles were differing national TVA rates and excise taxes. With the single market there would be no exportations as such between the member countries. TVA on goods would be paid at the rate of the country they were purchased in. France, which had very high rates ranging from a basic rate of 5 percent to 33 percent, was particularly worried by this proposal, as customers were likely to shop elsewhere.

Following intense lobbying by France and other countries, the Brussels commission decided instead to first harmonize European taxation. The various national TVA rates would be gradually narrowed down to two rates by 1993: a reduced rate of 5 percent and an ordinary rate of 15 percent. In addition the notion of exportation between EC countries and payment of TVA at the national rate would be maintained until 1997.

To the surprise of all, by mid-1992, France had achieved the EC objectives concerning TVA, and its industry is now in a more competitive position. However, as TVA accounts for 45 percent of budget receipts the country ran up an official deficit of Fr 131.7 billion in 1991. In addition, France was forced to make painful adjustments in other areas such as the capital gains tax. As of 1990 capital is free to move wherever it wants within the EC, and there is no reason a French citizen should

TVA and Other Taxes
Some TVA Rates (1993)

Ordinary rate: 18.6 percent (manufactured goods and most services). Accounts for about 80 percent of all TVA collected
Lower rate: 5.5 percent (food, books, theater tickets)
Upper rate: 22 percent (autos, furs, jewelery, porn films, lottery tickets)

Other Taxes

gasoline: 75.94 percent	auto insurance: 35 percent
tobacco: 75.03 percent	fire insurance: 30 percent

not purchase insurance in Britain or buy stock in Germany, Spain, or Luxembourg, where interest is tax free. To prevent a drain of capital, tax rates on fixed interest securities such as bonds and treasury bills has already been lowered from 27 percent and 34 percent to 17 percent, and the withholding tax on retained earnings from 47 percent to 34 percent. The paradox is that these measures were taken by a Socialist government that would have never dared make such concessions to capitalism had it not been for the constraints of the single market. (This accounts for the tensions within the party between pro and anti-Europeans.)

With the drop in TVA and other taxes sacrificed to European integration, the dilemma for the government is to find other sources of tax revenue. But where?

An Unfair System

According to the liberal experts who met in Paris in October 1989 to debate this subject, the "egalitarian philosophy of taxation" is a distortion of one of the principles of the Declaration on the Rights of Man, which specifies an equitable sharing of the tax burden among all the citizens.[16] In twentieth-century France, this has been taken to mean that the minority should pay for the majority. Thus French taxation is not only odd; it is also unfair. The tax burden is far from being equally shared. Practically half the population pays no income tax whatsoever, and 1

16. See Paul Fabra, "Justice fiscale et lutte contre les inégalités," *Le Monde*, 10 October 1989.

percent pays a quarter of the total; 10 percent of taxpayers pay two-thirds of all income tax collected in France. It has been suggested that some income groups, at present exonerated, should be asked to contribute something, even if it were a symbolic sum, for the sake of fairness. But this would be a highly unpopular political decision. If so many less well-off people receive exemptions, it is largely to offset some of the concessions made to the better-off.

There are other discrepancies in French taxation. Ten percent of French households pay more than half the total property tax. Fifty-eight percent pay less than one-tenth. One in five home owners pays no property tax whatsoever. Local taxes vary enormously from one part of France to another, and these are higher in the Paris suburbs than in the city. The inhabitants of Montpellier and Toulouse pay stiffer local taxes than residents in Paris or Lyons. Professional tax rates are higher in the underindustrialized Languedoc-Roussillon region than in the wealthy Ile-de-France, and 0.7 percent of all corporations pay 64 percent of the total sum collected.[17] According to *Le nouvel observateur,* if the total amount of taxes in one form or another (social security contributions, local taxes, excise taxes, and TVA) as well as consumption patterns are taken into account, the disparity in the treatment of the French citizen is even greater than it appears at first sight. Some professional categories are, in the words of the reporters, "clobbered" (engineers, industrialists, middle executives, and technicians), while others get off light (farmers, sole tradesmen, shopkeepers). Although members of the liberal professions pay relatively high taxes, they too can more easily cover up earnings than salaried personnel. Surprisingly, these professionals rank second for income but only sixth for taxation. These disparities can be explained in part by the different professional health plans. Nonsalaried people pay lower social security contributions than salaried employees—33 percent on average for a member of the liberal professions and 50 percent for the latter, employer's contributions included—even if they do sacrifice some social benefits. Progressive income tax rates offer another explanation. Although the top rate has been lowered from 65 percent to 56.8 percent, good salaries are heavily taxed and one does not need to earn a lot to find oneself in the 45 percent bracket.[18]

---

17. François Grosrichard, "Taxe professionnelle, l'Arlésienne de la péréquation," *Le Monde,* 3–4 March 1991.

18. *Le Nouvel Observateur,* 2–8 February 1989. The following are some examples of taxation for salaried people: For an annual net income of Fr 120,000

While savings are equitably taxed, it is true that low-income groups do not pay any taxes on their meager savings thanks to the Blue Savings Book (*le livret bleu*) delivered by the caisse d'épargne and La Poste with its exoneration limit of Fr 100,000 for a single person.[19] Family members can have one book each, but naturally this is an option of which the better off can take advantage.

The French taxation system is particularly unfair not only because of the unequal distribution of the tax burden but also because the bulk of tax levies proper—45 percent—comes from TVA, which is the same for rich and poor alike. In order to offset the drop in TVA income inevitable with the advent of the single market, the obvious solution would be to increase taxation on the wealthy, to extend the present wealth tax to include works of art as well as corporate assets such as plants, land, and machinery; and to raise capital gains tax and property taxes, as well as death duties, from which 88 percent of the French are presently exempted. Not only would these measures be unpopular, they would also be counterproductive, since the economic machine needs the investment of the wealthy to function.

Moreover, things are not so simple as they seem. Death tax in France, for example, is higher than in most industrial countries in terms of percentage of GDP: 0.34 percent compared to 0.26 percent in Britain and 0.24 percent in the U.S.A. Wealth tax and death tax

in 1988 a married couple with no children paid 21.1 percent of their gross annual income in social security contributions and income tax combined. If their net income was Fr 240,000 they paid 25.5 percent of gross income and if it was Fr 480,000 they paid 30.9 percent. See *Bilan Economique et Social 1990,* 184.

19. The caisse nationale d'épargne (national savings bank) network that offers fixed tax-free interest—4.5 percent in 1992—on savings up to one hundred thousand francs per person deposited in a *livret bleu* account has traditionally been the major collector of funds in France—funds that are administered by the Caisse nationale des dépôts and that are used for financing social housing programs. In recent years with the development of investment funds that offer higher tax-free interest people have turned away from the *livret*—77 percent of families today possess one compared to 82 percent in 1986. This trend, if it continues, could have dramatic consequences for the financing of the HLM building programs. While the French tend to save less than the Japanese or the Germans, the savings rate of families in France—12.4 percent—is far higher than that of American households (4.2 percent)—see *INSEE Première,* no. 184, 10 March 1992.

combined, France has the heaviest taxation: the equivalent of 0.44 percent of GDP more than the amount levied in most industrialized countries.[20]

The newly introduced wealth tax designed to finance the RMI for the destitute also goes against the tendency in other European countries to reduce this type of levy. Finally, the four local taxes in France bring in more than income tax, which is quite unique in Europe, where the former are based almost exclusively on income and corporate profits.

The problem of taxation accounts for much of the unrest in French society today. While corporations are proclaimed the powerhouses of economic recovery and prosperity, they feel hampered by an anachronistic tax system that penalizes their development and competitiveness. Individuals also feel frustrated on account of the inequity of the system. Fiscal policy encourages demagogical behavior on the part of politicians and helps explain the antagonisms and latent tensions among social groups: the cynicism, the petty jealousies of daily life, the mistrust, the self-righteousness so often dressed up as concern for the underdog to cover self-interest. Taxation, because it is the one instrument that can insure a more equitable distribution of national wealth without necessarily jeopardizing the economy, as can be seen from the example of countries like Norway and Sweden, is at the core of the debate on equality.

The Socialist government made prudent efforts to reform. A more equitable though controversial plan to establish local residential tax rates on incomes rather than on an estimation of the rental value of property was in the pipeline, and the CSG (*contribution sociale généralisée*), voted after a tough battle with the parliamentary opposition in late 1990, is a first step toward a more equitable sharing of social security contributions. The CSG is, in fact, a disguised tax designed to consolidate the financial basis of the welfare program.[21] The Socialists also toyed with the idea of making it mandatory for income tax to be deducted directly from salary, putting an end to the option of paying in three annual installments so as to speed up collection. More surprising—and

20. Alain Vernholes, "Les effets ambigus de la fiscalité," *Bilan Economique et Social 1990,* 183–84.

21. Jean-Michel Normand, "La contribution sociale généralisée," *Le Monde,* 13 November 1990.

more questionable—was the Socialists' sale of assets belonging to state-owned enterprises to finance the budget deficit.[22]

Patrimony

The wealth of the French includes their salaried or nonsalaried revenues, social security benefits, and their possessions generally referred to as *patrimoine* (patrimony)—a hoary term that designates a family trust handed down from one generation to the next.

Under the old monarchical regime there were various traditions of heredity. In the southwest of France the firstborn male inherited everything, in Alsace it was the youngest son, in Brittany and the north the legacy was divided equally among all sons.[23] The revolutionaries advocated splitting up the estate equally so as to prevent the accumulation of wealth by the nobles that the old system permitted. Mirabeau declared: "There are no more firstborn, no more privileged persons in the great national family, neither should there be any in the little families that form part of it." Robespierre said it would put an end to a form of paternal authoritarianism that France had inherited from the Romans.[24]

The Napoleonic Civil Code of 1804, in a spirit of equality, guaranteed the same rights of inheritance to all the offspring, leaving only a tiny part of the estate to the discretion of the testator. This did not happen overnight. Many resisted the new system, and even today some remnants of the older tradition still persist in rural France. However, in the vast majority of cases the rule of equality prevails. The legal situation—but not necessarily the usual practice—is very different in the United States and England, as the testator is completely free to decide whom to will property to. Children can be disinherited, and contrary to France, where taxation favors the transmission of one's estate to one's direct descendants, no distinction is made between direct and indirect heirs in calculating the amount of death tax due. In France, it is impossible to disinherit one's children, but, of course, there is no obligation to bequeath anything to anybody. This means that once a bequest is made (or if no

22. The deficit of the national budget is quite small in fact—2.6 percent of GDP in December 1992—compared with countries such as Great Britain, Germany, or the United States (4.7 percent in fall 1991).

23. Denis Kessler and André Masson, "Le patrimoine des Français," in *Données Sociales 1990,* 156–66.

24. See Gotman, *Héritier.*

will is made—only 20 percent of the French make one), the children all have an equal claim to their share. The testator may only dispose freely of one-third of his estate if he has two children and one-quarter if he has three, for example.

Of course, like many of the egalitarian principles the French cling to this does not always make their system more equitable. For instance, a son who has married a wealthy woman or who has earned high academic qualifications is entitled to the same amount as a brother or sister who has not had the same opportunities. Neither has the system put an end to family feuds, particularly where large fortunes are involved. The battle among the Rémy-Martin heirs (the makers of the famous champagne and cognac) has been going on for over a quarter of a century, and there have been thirty-two law cases between them so far. The affair has been dubbed "Dallas in Charente." The famous Petrossian caviar inheritors are also involved in a major lawsuit. But even when the inheritance is of no great value, there are occasional family feuds over who gets the antique wardrobe or the automobile.[25]

More worrisome in France is the tendency of corporation bosses with a major holding in the enterprise they have founded to put one of their children at the head of the business before retiring, even if the latter is totally incompetent. A number of French firms have run on the rocks as a result of this practice, though dynasties such as Michelin are evidence that the practice can work. Some recent examples of corporations that have been entrusted from father to son are Bouygues (construction engineering), Lagardère (Matra-Hachette: hightech and publishing); and Trigano (Club Méditerranée).

Sixty percent of the French will receive at least one legacy in their lifetime, even if it be a negligible one, and most remain very attached to the principle, although they do tend to feel more than a little guilty about it. After all, it boils down to an arbitrary distribution of wealth that contradicts the notion embodied in the constitution that all are born equal. Inheritance continues to be a very taboo subject in modern French society, and the division of an estate among the heirs obeys certain rules. The living have a deep respect for the home, objects, or money they inherit, which are not disposed of or used in haste nor in an indiscriminate way that would be an offense to the memory of the deceased. If the windfall is large enough, preference will go to refurbishing or buying

25. Gotman, *Héritier*, 148.

a home, sometimes a holiday home, or putting the money in a savings bank. It will not be gambled on the stock exchange, and, contrary to practice in the United States, inherited money will rarely have to be used to finance the schooling of one's children.

It has been suggested that inheritance relieves pressure on the social security system by offering a safety net to many who would not otherwise have a roof over their heads. Yet, patrimony is one of the principle causes of inequalities in French society today. Ten percent of the wealthiest families in France possess 54 percent of gross assets. This is a far greater discrepancy than that which exists between salaries, where 10 percent of the top wage-earners account for only 28 percent of total income.[26] Yet, there is much less public tolerance for inequalities in salary than for those due to inherited wealth. There is no death tax on bequests to direct descendants that total less than Fr 275,000, and above that sum there are various tax breaks available. The maximum rate is 40 percent (compared to 90 percent in the United States and Britain). It is not possible in France to delay payment of death tax by leaving money to a trust. There have been various timid attempts at reform, but the subject is politically explosive, on account of the popular acceptance inheritance enjoys, so that no government has dared take the drastic measures necessary to reduce the inequalities the system generates in French society.

Alain Minc points out that attitudes to patrimony in France reveal more about the profound nature of French society than "the thousand and one national traits" designed to pinpoint the difference between "an egalitarian, petit bourgeois France and a liberal, aristocratic England." Contrary to the prevailing view among people from all sides of the political spectrum in France, Minc believes that wealth earned is legitimate and inherited wealth illegitimate because it breaks the rules of the liberal game based on personal merit, that is, on one's contribution to society. There is no merit involved in inheritance, which is revered by the French whereas wealth earned is suspect. (Is this because *patrimoine* is perceived as old, unostentatious wealth in a value system inherited from a peasant society unlike the money of the *nouveaux riches*?) Thus while the country may pay lip service to free-market principles and maintain an unhealthy admiration for money-makers, French society, according to Minc, has not changed fundamentally. Whether one sub-

26. Stefan Lollivier and Daniel Verger, "Le patrimoine aujourd'hui," in *Données Sociales 1990,* 167–70.

scribes or not to his ideas on economic liberalism, it is hard to disagree with him on this point:

> Without any doubt this is the only area where French attitudes have not changed for one century and where, moreover, no public debate has been demanded. Nothing will change in this matter for decades: as soon as the question of *patrimoine* arises, the progress accomplished by society has little influence. Without any doubt this amounts to a virtual intellectual regression; the very same people, liberal and open-minded about everyday events, become, suddenly, brutally conservative in the presence of the traumatizing association of money and death.[27]

27. Minc, *L'argent fou,* 100.

9

The Price of Health

We consume, they prescribe, it pays.

—Béatrice Majnoni d'Intignano

Sécurité sociale in France, familiarly known as *Sécu,* should not be confused with Social Security in the United States, founded in 1935. Although the French themselves tend to identify it essentially with health care, family allowances, and retirement benefits, it is in fact a blanket term covering all types of social funding, including state aid for the unemployed and the needy. All inhabitants of France obtain, in one way or another, these financial benefits even though they may also have some form of private insurance.

Compared to other industrialized countries, particularly Britain and Germany, social insurance in France got off to a late start. Social security as it exists today came into being only in 1946, three years after the Beveridge report led to the setting up of the welfare state in Britain.

Peculiarities of French Social Security

The French system, like the Dutch, is exceptional in Europe, insofar as it is financed almost entirely by employers and the working population and not by general taxation as in other countries, where public funding tends to be higher.[1] (In France, a levy on employers and employees is pooled and paid out to claimants.) Another distinctive feature is its extraordinary complexity. On account of the troubled history of social insurance in France, opposed for different reasons by partisans of a liberal economy and worker unions alike, it was not possible in 1946 to set up a uniform system. Thus it was only progressively that the entire pop-

1. A major difference from the Dutch system is that in France the bulk of contributions are paid by the employers, whereas in Holland employees and employers contribute about the same amount.

ulation came to be covered. Even today, within the general social security system there are a myriad of special plans (*régimes*) catering to the various socioprofessional categories who wanted to preserve privileges they had obtained prior to the 1946 reform. Not all pay the same subscription rates nor receive the same benefits. Thus an office employee, for example, will not be entitled to the same advantages if he or she works for the national railway company (SNCF), the Banque de France, or a large store. Nevertheless, seven out of ten people are covered by the basic system known at the *régime général*, designed for salaried employees working in private corporations.

In theory, everyone in France nowadays is covered by social security, yet some sixty thousand people for one reason or another, principally the difficulty of decoding the system and handling the paperwork, are left out. Tragic as this is, it is a far cry from the thirty-seven million Americans who have no health insurance.

Social Security and Equality

The dream of the founders of social security in postwar France was to set up a uniform system, so that there would be social equality among French citizens. Yet while this scheme, combined with taxation, does help to regulate the economy by aiding the jobless and by narrowing the gap in disposable income between those in low-paid jobs and those earning larger salaries, the program breeds inequalities. Although higher income groups contribute more, they also tend to consume more expensive health care; and the better paid people are, the more sick leave they seem to take. Some workers receive higher medical reimbursements than others thanks to their professional *régime*. Financial rewards for bringing up children (family allowances) vary with the number of offspring, and families with three or more, as well as single-parent families, do better than others. Perhaps the greatest inequalities are linked to the pension plan, since contributions, benefits, and even retirement age—sixty for some, fifty for others, and even forty for dancers at the Paris Opera!—differ widely from one profession to another. There are no less than 120 special plans, and many of those who obtain the highest benefits not only enjoy the longest retirement but contribute over the shortest period. At the other end of the scale some pensioners who have no supplementary retirement plan receive as little as Fr 2,500 per month.

		Fr per Month
Minimum income for elderly	Individual	2,763
	Couple	4,958
Sickness benefits	Minimum	1,161
	Maximum	5,055
Work accident benefits		
First 28 days: 50 percent of salary	Maximum	18,198
After 29th. day: 2/3 of salary	Maximum	24,264
Allowance for disabled adults		2,763
	Third party allowance	1,845 to 3,691
Family allowances (couples with children)	Two children	566
	Per extra child	726
Infant allowance		
From fourth month of pregnancy to third month after birth		813
From fourth month after birth to three years (means test)		813
Single parent allowance, three years maximum	One child	3,450
	Per extra child	885
Parental allowance for bringing up three or more children. Maximum duration: three years per child (Available to couples)	Full rate, i.e., if one parent stops work completely for the entire period.	2,524
Unemployment insurance		
Basic allowance if conditions are fulfilled	Minimum	3,456
Allowance for those who no longer fulfill conditions (valid one year)	Ordinary rate	2,150
Unemployment assistance		
Allowance for job seekers (valid 6 months)	Youth aged 16-25	1,245
	Single mothers	2,622
	Others	1,311
RMI (Minimum integration income)	Single person	2,000
	Couple with child or single parent	3,000
	Per extra child	600

FIG. 13. Some social security benefits. (Adapted from *Données sociales*, INSEE 1990.)

Health Care: How the System Works

Social security is not state run. It is managed by a joint committee of elected members of worker organizations and employers who negotiate agreements between representatives of the medical profession and the various *régimes.* Practically all French physicians have an agreement with the social security organization that defines basic fees for health care at all levels. (The state keeps a close eye on costs so as to keep a rein on inflation and guarantee the availability of medical treatment for all.)

Doctors, whether generalists or specialists, have a choice between two sorts of agreement. They can choose either to apply the social security tariffs strictly or to charge higher fees. Whatever price patients pay, they are always reimbursed at the predetermined rate. Health care is not entirely free and, except in the case of the needy, has to be paid for on the spot, as do prescription drugs. The patient then sends the bill to the local social security branch office to obtain a refund. This involves much paperwork and bureaucracy.

Regular medical care is reimbursed 75 percent, major surgery 100 percent, and medicine 70 percent (40 percent for drugs prescribed for treatment of lighter ailments). A consultation with a generalist applying the basic rate in 1992 cost Fr 100; a specialist was allowed to charge Fr 140. These rather low fees tend to encourage physicians to multiply the number of consultations needlessly.

In addition to paying for social security the majority of people contribute to a mutual insurance organization for their profession called a *mutuelle,* which will "top up" the sum to be refunded by the medical insurance organization, so that in many cases total reimbursements will amount to approximately 80 percent of the cost of treatment. People too poor to pay the difference receive state aid. Seventy-two percent of additional health coverage is provided by the *mutuelles.* On account of their policy of mutual assistance these cannot list preferential tariffs for specific risks like the private insurance companies, whose clients tend to be younger. They thus frequently have the charge of the older, high-risk population that consumes much health care.[2]

Unlike the British system, where patients have little choice concerning doctors and hospitals, the French social security leaves people free to

2. Jean-Luc Volatier, *Les modes de protection sociale* (Paris: Centre de recherche, d'étude et de documentation en économie de la société), 1990.

FIG. 14. Although it's not quite reasonable from an economic point of view, we'll keep you a bit longer. (*Le Monde,* Copyright © Pessin 1990.)

choose their physician, who is not a civil servant but a member of a liberal profession. They also have a choice between private and public hospitals and are entitled to the same reimbursements for each, although, of course, a stay in a private hospital may be more costly overall. The French prize the personal relationship with a physician and freedom of choice, which is becoming even rarer in America for corporate employees with the development of health maintenance organizations (HMOs) and preferred provider organizations (PPOs). Likewise, the waiting lists and long lines for medical care so common in Britain are unknown in France, which has a dense regional network of private and public hospitals, many with state-of-the-art medical equipment. In fact, the system suffers from overcapacity, and to offset soaring costs—empty beds cost money—patients, particularly older people and children, are sometimes hospitalized without real medical necessity. In spite of the student quotas in medical schools, there are also too many physicians—twenty thousand in 1989 according to one professional organization.[3] Another problem is the high concentration of physicians in some parts of the country

3. Guy Herzlich, "Le CSMF juge nécessaire de reconvertir 2000 médecins," *Le Monde,* 12–13 February 1989.

while other areas have very few. One solution for the glut of doctors (the national average is one per four hundred inhabitants) might be to develop preventive health care on the lines of the HMOs in the United States. Many younger doctors are having to struggle to make a living. A survey published in the professional review *Le Généraliste* in December 1990 revealed that three thousand doctors earn less than the SMIC.

A series of strikes by hospital interns in 1989–90 marked the negotiations between the social security organization and the medical profession. With all the belt-tightening, the interns no longer want to make a career in the public hospitals. They were protesting a government decision that would limit the number of doctors allowed to charge the higher rates since, in some parts of France, it is increasingly difficult to find a physician who accepts the basic tariff. The growing number of doctors—sometimes without any particular qualification—and, particularly, of specialists opting to apply the higher rates is worrisome and could jeopardize the financial stability of the health care system. The dilemma for the government is how to reconcile free medical treatment for all with an income in keeping with the qualifications of physicians.

Still, if some doctors, especially interns, are badly paid, the majority are not. The average purchasing power of practitioners increased by 13 percent between 1980 and 1990, and it remains one of the most lucrative liberal professions—Fr 24,000 net per month for a generalist; Fr 37,000 for a specialist.[4]

The French today enjoy an enviable level of health care—doctors will make home calls even for minor illness—and have a very strong attachment to their *Sécu*, which they believe is the best in the world. It covers the cost of everything from transportation by ambulance to splints, from in vitro fertilization (fifteen thousand births since the first test-tube baby was born in France ten years ago) to AIDS, and patients are spared the financial worry of major operations. Yet, while France ranks third in the world for health expenditure, Fr 573.4 billion, 8.9 percent of GDP, it is only fifteenth among the developed countries for reimbursement of medical treatment In 1991, the Sécurité sociale only refunded 73.6 percent of health care spending by the French, whereas in 1980 the figure was 76.5 percent.[5]

4. Jean-Michel Normand, "Le pouvoir d'achat des practiciens libéraux a progressé de plus de 13% entre 1980 et 1990," *Le Monde*, 29 October 1991.

5. Jean-Michel Normand, "La Sécurité Sociale rembourse de moins en moins les frais de santé," *Le Monde*, 19 May 1992.

Health care	Family	Old age	Unemployment
State subsidies 1 percent	State subsidies 9 percent	State subsidies 5.5 percent	State subsidies 45 percent
Employee contributions 27.7 percent	Employee contributions 7.3 percent	Employee contributions 39.7 percent	Total employee and employer contributions 55 percent
Employer contributions 66.2 percent	Employer contributions 80.8 percent	Employer contributions 52.4 percent	

FIG. 15. How social security is financed. Miscellaneous financial sources (taxes, interest, etc.) make up the difference in each category. In all, employers contribute between 42 and 52 percent of social security charges and employees between 17 and 21.9 percent. (Adapted from *Le Monde Dossiers et Documents*, February 1988. Copyright © The New York Times Syndication Sales Corporation.)

The Funding of Social Security

Both employers and employees contribute to the financing of the four major welfare programs: health, old age, unemployment, and the family. Of course the system is based on a great illusion, because it is ultimately wage earners who pay for everything. Instead of paying higher salaries corporations pay a large share of the welfare program for their employees. Social security amounts to one-third of the French employers' wage bill. (Economists speak of a "deferred salary.") This explains the low rate of income tax in France and the proportionally high rate of social security contributions.

High labor costs have often been put forward as one of the major causes of the lack of competitiveness of French industry, yet, all told, the combined cost of salaries and welfare contributions make average labor costs in France comparable to those in many of the major industrialized countries. However, it does act as a deterrent to employment. To remedy this situation the Rocard government decided in 1988 to reduce and even abolish for two years under certain conditions the contributions due by smaller businesses and tradespeople (*artisans*) who take the commitment of hiring a first worker. The state assumes these costs instead.

An assessment undertaken by the Ministry for Labor in 1990 showed that thirty thousand new jobs had been created under this plan during the previous year. This would seem to confirm that high social security costs do discourage employment.

Because they pay less in direct taxes, the French feel they are getting a better deal, and, while bitterly opposed to tax increases, they more readily swallow social security hikes—and there have been several since 1980. It is significant that the Rocard government called the new tax introduced in 1990 *contribution sociale généralisée.*[6] When a reluctant child does not want to swallow a pill, the best thing is to serve it with a spoonful of jam! However, people are beginning to wonder if the redistribution of income by means of transfer payments is as real and as equitable as they have been led to believe.

Funding is the main problem of social security. Medical costs have skyrocketed with the modernization of the hospital network, high-tech expensive medicine, the greater availability of physicians, and the excessive consumption of health care and drugs, for which the French hold a world record. In 1987 the minister of health, Philippe Séguin, put it bluntly to his fellow citizens: "If the French prefer to eat drugs rather than beef I don't see why I should try to stop them. All I ask them is to take responsibility for their choice." In 1990 medical expenditure amounted to Fr 9,537 for every man, woman, and child in France.

Sooner or later the French will have to come to terms with the spiraling costs and define limits. (Should vaccination for venereal disease be free? Should in vitro fertilization be so generously refunded? Will the system be able to withstand the explosion of AIDS?) Yet, there was protest when one minister of health deemed it necessary to limit the use of the very expensive Eprex drug for the treatment of kidney ailments. Administering the drug to all patients would have cost one billion francs. As Professor Béatrice Majnoni d'Intignano says, arguing for tighter control of medical expenditure, it is high time to question the overcon-

6. The CSG, voted by Parliament in late 1990, may be considered a first step toward public financing of social security. The euphemism "generalized social contribution" is designed to hide the fact that this is actually a new tax payable by all and not just by the working population. (Capital gains and pensions are subject to the new levy.) A standard rate of 2.4 percent is now applied to all gross earnings. The Right, who opposed this levy introduced by the Socialists, doubled it after the 1993 elections thus increasing the tax burden of the French by 50 billion francs.

sumption of medical treatment the profession is encouraging: "Why are there so many cesarean sections and appendicitis operations in France?" she asks. "Why are pregnancy ultrasounds increasing by 15 to 20 percent per year for a number of childbirths that remains stable? Medical techniques are becoming money-makers: electrocardiograms, gastrointestinal endoscopies. Tariffs are slow to catch up with productivity gains, and those who prescribe them perform them; they can thus multiply them ad infinitum."[7]

Several measures have been taken in recent years to reduce spiraling costs, and the government is trying to develop a new awareness among providers and consumers of health care. One innovation has been to include the figure corresponding to the employer's contributions in the gross salary printed on the employee's paycheck, so that the latter can measure how much social security is really costing in terms of salary. Following tough negotiations with representatives of the medical profession, a bill designed to curb spending by demanding a new cost awareness from the 108,000 liberal practitioners in France was presented to the national assembly in June 1992. The bill proposed introducing annual negotiations between the medical profession and the social security organization so as to put a ceiling on expenditure for the following year. This would require nothing short of a mental revolution that liberal practitioners and their patients did not seem to be ready for. Fearing a motion of censure by the assembly, the government finally withdrew the bill, jeopardizing any chances of curbing the spiraling cost of health insurance that was thirty billion francs in the red by mid-1992.

Not that health care is devouring the major part of social security spending. The main cost—44 percent of total expenditure—is pensions, the amount of which it is not possible to reduce, although reform is necessary in this area too.[8] As Prime Minister Michel Rocard said in 1990: "In twenty years the system will blow up and there will be enough

7. Béatrice Magnoni d'Intignano, "Médecine libérale: le débat confisqué," *Le Monde*, 24 February 1990.

8. The French pension plan is based exclusively on the principle of redistribution and solidarity between generations, that is, the working population finances the pensions of the retired. (Their contributions are not put by for their own retirement, as in a system based on capitalization.) Obviously, in times of high unemployment and of an ever-growing number of retired persons (chap. 5), the active (working) population is being bled to support the inactive. In 1990 INSEE forecasts showed that pension contributions, which now total 16.3 percent

to blow up the five or six governments who are going to have to deal with it."[9] It is also difficult to skimp on unemployment benefits—7 percent of total expenditure—of which many jobless are already deprived. Reforming the children's allowances by introducing a means test, though unpopular, might save some money, but it is obvious that the necessary curbing of medical expenses that account for 33 percent of social security spending is the safest option for the politicians.

The deficit of the social security program—FR 15.7 billion for 1992—is worrisome. However, the shortfall is not a real deficit but a fictional one, because before the end of the fiscal year precautionary measures, such as an increase in contributions or savings on services, are taken to ensure that the books balance. In comparison, the deficit of the state budget—a real one!—was Fr 226.4 billion in 1992.

The necessary reform of social security is a politically explosive issue because of the symbolic significance of the program for the population. Few of the French would be willing to accept another system, as all the surveys show. The worker unions who control it oppose reform, and the medical profession in the area of health care is corporatist. This will

---

of earnings, would increase to 40 percent by 2040 if nothing was done to remedy the situation.

In 1993 the new Balladur cabinet, with the support of a comfortable parliamentary majority in the postelectoral "grace period" overhauled the system. The annual amount of a person's pension is henceforth determined by computing the average of the retired worker's top earnings over a period of twenty-five years instead of ten as previously computed. Moreover, while the new measures to not affect people's sacrosance right to retire at sixty, in order to be entitled to the full social security pension they will have to pay into the system for 40 years instead of 37.5 before. If these conditions are fulfilled social security will provide 50 percent of the total and a mandatory supplementary pension plan provides another 25 percent. The retired person will thus receive 75 percent of his or her best salary average. In fact even under the more generous system prevailing in 1988 only three-quarters of male and one-third of female pensioners had accomplished a career entitling them to a full pension. Their average retirement benefits amounted to Fr 6,500 per month. This would seem to indicate that under the more stringent conditions of the new social security plan even fewer workers will obtain a full pension. Future generations of retirees are likely to be less affluent than those of today. INSEE, Denis Kessler, "L'avenir des retraites," *Economie et Statistique* 233, June 1990. See also Jean-Michel Normand, "La fausse querelle des retraites," *Le Monde*, 5 February 1990.

9. Jean-Michel Normand, "La bombe à retardement des retraites," *Le Monde*, 13 February 1990.

undoubtedly be one of the major debates in the 1990s in France, if some government—Left or Right—has the courage to tackle the problem.

Nowhere are the contradictions of French society more apparent than in their attitudes to money, inheritance, taxation, and social security, and nowhere is the gap between rhetoric and action more flagrant. This nation of individualists, fiercely attached to private property and selfishly guarding personal privilege, has, at the same time, a strong sense of solidarity, as their generous support of *Sécu* shows. The French are too lucid about their individualism, their *péché mignon* (peccadillo), and have too much respect for the dignity of other individuals not to be genuinely concerned about the poor, the handicapped, the elderly, and the unemployed. They are aware that there is no knowing to what extremes their self-interest may take them and seem secretly glad that they can unburden themselves of the task of helping their fellow humans by confining their expression of solidarity to social security or the state, with which they entertain an ambiguous relationship. Deep down they know that a regulator is necessary. Indeed they expect the state to set the example, to propose an ideal to them, but at the same time they want to cling to their privileges and refuse the state the means (taxation) to ensure the *solidarité* (fraternity) necessary for national cohesion.[10] On account of these contradictions there is little likelihood that either American-style liberalism or a Swedish type of socialism will ever see the day in France, which will continue to live with its contradictions.

10. The word *solidarité* (community of interests) that became the buzzword of the Socialists in the 1980s has replaced the revolutionary *fraternité* but lacks its emotional appeal—an indication of the conversion of the idealistic French Left to political realism?

10

Health and Body

Pleasure has its soldiers: many of them remain on the battlefield.
—Abbé de Condillac (1715–80)

AIDS

Among the industrialized countries France ranks second after the United States in the overall number of AIDS cases, the Parisian and Riviera areas having the highest concentration. In September 1988 there were 4,900 AIDS patients in France. The minister of health issued a graphic warning to the population by declaring that within three years more people would die of AIDS than from traffic accidents. His warning was lost on the wind. In 1993 there were more than 24,000 cases and an estimated 300,000 carriers of the disease.[1]

AIDS, which at first affected primarily marginal groups such as drug users and homosexuals, is now affecting heterosexuals and every social class. Indeed, in France as elsewhere, homosexuals were the first to take precautionary measures, and the unrestricted sale of syringes in pharmacies—which had been forbidden in an effort to stop drug abuse—is helping reduce the number of victims among drug addicts, who now tend overwhelmingly to purchase their own needles.

France has been in the forefront of state-funded AIDS research from the very beginning. In 1983 the virus called LAV, which was thought to cause the disease, was identified by Professor Luc Montagnier at the Institut Pasteur in Paris. Yet, in spite of this head start in research, it took the government five years to work out a coherent prevention policy. The dilemma was that there was only limited scientific data available at that time on the sexual behavior of the French.[2] After timid attempts to

1. Gérard Badou, "Sida le pire est devant nous," *L'Express*, 25 February–3 March 1993, 49.

2. The only available information before the vast 1992 report on the sexual behavior of the French was the Dr. Pierre Simon study (1972). Ironically, the United States, the country of the landmark Kinsey reports (1948 and 1953), is

promote the use of condoms for sexual intercourse, the minister of health discovered in 1987 that a number of the brands sold on the French market were of inferior quality and unreliable! There is no French manufacturer, the sheath not being a popular contraceptive device in France in spite of the British slang term, "French letter," for it.[3] The negative reaction of the Catholic hierarchy to a discreet advertising spot on public television promoting safe sex showed how difficult it was for the government to inform teenagers about the potential dangers of sexual promiscuity.[4] If the

---

no longer in a position to launch large-scale studies of sexual behavior. Two recent projects have been shelved under pressure of the Moral Majority. In 1989, a survey by University of Chicago researchers was torpedoed by Senators Jesse Helms and William Dannemeyer, who claimed it would increase the acceptability of sex outside marriage and "legitimize homosexual behavior." In 1991, another large-scale survey on teenagers, commissioned by the National Health Institute in an attempt to work out a coherent policy for teenage pregnancies and AIDS prevention, was abandoned. *L'Evènement du Jeudi* remarked: "Today, the American government has pulled off the feat of launching an AIDS prevention campaign in which the words *sex* and *condom* never appear in posters and television spots." See Pierre Cayrol, "Etats-Unis: le sexe interdit," *L'Evènement du Jeudi*, 25 June–1 July 1992, 61.

3. Familiarly called *capote anglaise* in French! Condoms are frequently associated with lechery and particularly repulsive to the younger generation. As a young man declared "A condom, it's like taking a shower with a raincoat, it stops everything" (Catherine Erhel, "La peur du Sida ne passe pas par les adolescents," *Libération*, 8 November 1988, 33). Still, the ANRS survey already quoted showed that about half the young people in the eighteen-to-nineteen-year-old age group with a single sexual partner were using condoms in 1992, while they are less frequently used by the older age groups. Heterosexuals with more than one sexual partner seem to be less conscientious in this respect: 39 percent of males and 58 percent of females declared they never had intercourse during which a condom was used. This would seem to indicate that the impact of the AIDS prevention campaigns, which got off to a late start in France, has been greatest among the younger generation despite their repugnancy for this type of protection. An INSERM survey in the Parisian region among teenagers (average age seventeen) showed that only 23 percent considered the use of condoms incompatible with love but nearly half of the sample population found it embarrassing to buy them in a supermarket or pharmacy. Fifty-nine percent of the respondents said that while they thought the initiative of using a condom should be taken by males, it was not easy for them to suggest this to their female partner. The INSERM survey was carried out by France Lert and Brenda Spencer. See "Les adolescents et le préservatif," *Le Monde de l'Education*, May 1992, 48.

4. The slogan of the campaign was "Le Sida ne passera pas par moi" (I won't let AIDS get through). In this first campaign condoms were mentioned but never shown.

bishops' criticism was understandable, the circumspection of the health authorities was surprising in a supposedly secular society where it is almost impossible to sell anything without an appeal to the libido and where the *messageries roses* of the Minitel are so popular. In all likelihood this prudence was prompted not by prudery but by the embarrassment of promoting a means of protection often associated with birth control in a country that has a strong probirth policy. In this respect, the preoccupations of the secular state meet those of the Catholic hierarchy. In fact, in 1992, the launching of an advertising campaign promoting contraception for young people was postponed by Prime Minister Bérégovoy, who criticized the campaign slogan: "La contraception pour ne penser qu'à l'amour" (Contraception to be free to concentrate on love). Yet, shortly after, the minister of education and culture announced that vending machines for condoms would be installed in lycées across the country with the prior agreement of parents and teachers.

While all cases of AIDS contamination in France have to be notified to public health authorities, the declaration is anonymous. In late 1988 the National Commission on Data Collection and Liberty authorized the setting up of a data bank on the disease, but information could only be recorded with the written consent of informants. Diagnostic tests are carried out in public health facilities and, on a voluntary basis, in special testing centers that guarantee anonymity. Costs of tests are fully refunded by social security. Some people, including doctors, have been advocating mandatory premarital and prebirth testing, but this is opposed on the grounds that it would be in vain, as AIDS cannot presently be cured. Further, this might lead to discrimination for jobs, for example.

In January 1988, the government finally got round to setting up a National Fight-AIDS Agency (Agence nationale pour la lutte contre le Sida) to study the financial, social, and medical consequences of the disease and make proposals. In a country that prides itself on personal liberty people are very concerned about the question of AIDS victims' rights on account of the taboos surrounding this illness, so a reputed anthropologist, Madame Françoise Héritier-Augé, was appointed to head the national AIDS council.

The typical French low-key approach to crisis situations may explain the lack of instances of emotional public reaction to AIDS that have occurred in the United States, in spite of the extreme Right's call for isolating victims from the rest of the population in special *Sidatoriums.* When a former minister of education attempted to prevent an elementary-schoolteacher who had AIDS from obtaining tenure on the grounds that he was physically unfit, parents made no protest when he was later reinstated by his successor, who feared the measure would be seen as discriminatory, although it was prompted by purely financial considerations on the part of the ministry. The results of a survey published in *La Recherche* (July–August 1990) indicate a high degree of public tolerance toward persons with AIDS. 87.2 percent of the respondents declared that someone with AIDS arouses in them feelings of "compassion and solidarity," and 93.5 percent think that persons with AIDS deserve the best treatment available under the social security system. In February 1993 the minister of health Bernard Kouchner announced that all those infected with the HIV virus would henceforth be entitled to 100 percent social security cover for treatment.

Scandal

The lack of a coherent prevention program in France may be partly to blame for the spread of AIDS, but this administrative blundering is nothing compared to the scandal of the contamination of nearly 50 percent of French hemophiliacs and of several thousand transfused persons in the early 1980s. The matter would only be sad were it not that contaminated blood was *knowingly* used for transfusions between 1983 and 1985. The scandal, which erupted in 1991 and led to a sensational court case in summer 1992, revealed a series of medical, scientific, administrative, and political blunders committed in the name of financial considerations and misplaced chauvinism. According to the medical correspondents for *Le Monde*, Jean-Yves Nau and Franck Nouchi, this huge scandal "in which blood, death and money are amalgamated, is very French, since the state—in its role of trustee and monopolist—is in part directly responsible."[5]

To understand the issue it is necessary to know that the CNTS (Centre

5. The medical supplement of *Le Monde* dated 6 November 1991 contained a number of articles on the scandal that the author has used, particularly those by Jean-Yves Nau and Franck Nouchi, the newspaper's medical correspondents. An article by Professor Claude Got, "Tirer les leçons d'un scandale," was also helpful as was Jérôme Strazzula's "Les enseignements du sang contaminé," in Cordellier, *L'état de la France 1992* (Paris: Editions la Découverte, 1992), 77–78. For detailed information see A. M. Casteret, *L'affaire de sang* (Paris: Editions la Découverte, 1992).

national de la transfusion sanguine) that has the monopoly of the collection of blood in France is one of those myriad non-profit-making associations allowed by a law dating from 1901. This type of association, which enjoys considerable autonomy, is often the only means of getting anything done in a country where state-run services are sometimes inefficient. The paradox is that the state itself, when it wants to escape the prying of public accountants, will contrive to set up *une association 1901* just like a group of *boulistes* or fishermen. The CNTS is such an association, to which the state has entrusted the collection of blood in France. The idea was to set up a monopoly that would guarantee national independence in this area. The French blood transfusion program, based on the gratuitous donation of blood with a guarantee of anonymity (as is the case for the donation of all body parts), is exceptional and has enjoyed a reputation for altruism and generosity since the setting up of the CNTS in 1975.

If the CNTS authorities could be excused for distributing contaminated blood before 1983, when little was known about the virus, why did it do so between 1983 and 1985, when specialists were already aware of the dangers of contamination? And why did it continue collecting blood from the high-risk population? (Quite a lot of the blood is collected in prisons.) The answer is edifying: the testing of donors was delayed for economic and protectionist motives, that is, to spare social security money and to give l'Institut Pasteur time to develop a French test, although an American one was already available.[6] Another rather astonishing point is that the screening of donors would be going against the altruistic ethic of the blood transfusion centers. The decisions that were taken at various levels showed misjudgment and incompetence. According to a report by a senatorial commission of inquiry, "industrial logic

6. The controversy between l'Institut Pasteur and Professor Gallo of the U.S. National Cancer Institute, who claims to have discovered the AIDS virus first, has given rise to a complex transatlantic dispute that has not yet been settled. See John Crewdson, "The Great Aids Quest," *Chicago Tribune*, 19 November 1989. In these circumstances, it is perhaps understandable that the French government did not want to see the American corporation, Abbot, which had developed a test in the meantime, cashing in on the fruits of the Pasteur Institute's discovery while Diagnostics Pasteur was trying to develop its own test. The government of the time was clearly responsible for retarding approval of the Abbot test for blood donors.

led to neglect of certain deontological rules," that is, rules of moral obligations.[7]

In 1992, Bernard Kouchner, minister of health in the Bérégovoy cabinet, publically asked pardon for the errors that had been committed. Decisions have been taken to reform the blood transfusion organization, and in a break with French medical tradition the rights to compensation of all who were contaminated, which will cost taxpayers billions of francs, were finally recognized in 1992. Will this open the door to a rash of malpractice suits, which are practically unknown in France? Another consequence may be that the somewhat idealistic, benevolent French approach to the donation of blood and body parts, based on a state monopoly guaranteeing national independence and solidarity, has seen the day. Private foreign interests are watching developments keenly with an eye to the huge potential market for plasma and body organs in France.

Les Paradis Artificiels

According to a report published in 1990 by the Institut des hautes études de la sécurité intérieure, drugs, together with AIDS and terrorism, figure among the main anxieties of the French, although in reality they represent a very low risk for individuals in general. On the contrary, people are only slightly frightened by the prospects of daily dangers, such as traffic accidents. In other words, phenomena that make the headlines are not nearly as serious as people's avowed fears may lead one to believe. This is particularly true of drugs.[8]

There are an estimated 150,000 drug addicts in France, but a four-year study undertaken for INSERM on consumption by teenagers showed that although one in eleven young people is addicted, the number has stopped rising. The survey revealed that 2.7 percent of first-year junior high school (collège) pupils and 19 percent of final-year lycée students had tried drugs at least once.[9] If children from disrupted households

7. Jean-Yves Nau and Franck Nouchi, "Le rapport de la commission d'enquête senatoriale sur la transfusion," *Le Monde*, 19 June 1992. See also Franck Nouchi, "Des documents confirment que l'autorisation d'un test de dépistage du sida avait été retardé pour des raisons protectionnistes," *Le Monde*, 2 April 1993.

8. Eric Inciyan, "Une radioscopie des peurs des Français," *Le Monde*, 4 July 1990.

9. Jean-Michel Costes, "La toxicomanie: Un difficile passage à l'âge adulte," in *Données Sociales 1990*, 258–61.

FIG. 16. By the way, how are you doing at school? (*Le Monde*, Copyright © Plantu 1989.)

tend to be more vulnerable than the population at large, a previous INSERM report showed that nearly half of the victims of drug abuse live with their families.

Consumption patterns tend to vary with age, the undertwenties preferring to sniff glues and solvents or smoke joints in their late teens; heroin tends to be more widespread in the twenty-to-thirty-year-old age group; while many older adults in France are addicted, without always being fully aware of it, to tranquilizers and pep pills. France has the highest consumption in the world of benzodiazepines (tranquilizers). Fifteen percent of medical prescriptions order them for use, often in association with other hypnotic drugs. It is estimated that 33 percent of the population consumes such pills more or less regularly.

French legislation makes no distinction between hard and soft drugs, and the former (heroin, cocaine, LSD) are not widely used. Less than 2 percent of schoolchildren have tried them. While the overall consumption of cocaine is increasing in France, it has not reached the alarming proportions it has in the United States with its six million drug addicts, and the country has so far been spared from the ravages of crack. However, in the annual report of the Centre Marmottan in Paris for 1991, Professor Claude Olievenstein, who has run this free-drug treatment center for twenty years, declared that it had been a catastrophic year: "there is far more heroin in 1991 than in 1990 and 1989. There is a dual development of drug abuse and social dropouts in the large city suburbs. . . . Heroin is everywhere. But there is an increasing number of addicts among the underclass and the ethnic minorities."[10]

In France it is illegal to be in possession of, consume, or deal in drugs. Dealers may incur a prison sentence of up to twenty years. Users, if convicted, undergo mandatory medical treatment that may replace imprisonment, although, in fact, this concession is not always used because of reluctance of doctors and psychiatrists to take charge of the culprits. Frequently too there is no real medical follow-up. Yet the French approach to the problem of drug abuse, which strives to steer "a middle course between law and order, public health and the respect of individual liberty," is not the worst.[11] Rehabilitation and treatment are considered more important than punishment for people suffering from social maladaptation, while the use of exceptional measures likely to represent a danger for democracy are avoided.

There have been some new approaches to the treatment of addicts such as controlled distribution of the substitute narcotic methadone. In an attempt to halt the spread of AIDS among drug users there is unrestricted sale of syringes in pharmacies, and there are an increasing number of centers where addicts may exchange used needles for new ones. There has also been some debate about legalizing the use and sale of drugs to break the power of the dealers. It has even been suggested that the state should set up a monopoly of the drug trade and fix prices in much the same way as it does with the tobacco monopoly it runs. Adversaries fight this project on legal, psychological, and economic grounds. But the ultraconservativism of French drug policy compared to Holland's or Spain's came under fire in 1993 when former minister of health, Bernard Kouchner, criticized the "arrogance" of the political Establishment and the "complacency" of medical officials.

Alcohol

France holds the world record for per capita consumption of alcohol, even if this rate is decreasing. In 1985 French adults over twenty years of age

10. "Le rapport annuel du Centre Marmottan," *Le Monde*, 11 March 1992.

11. Catherine Troutman, president of the Antidrug Movement. See Béatrice Batman, "La mission de lutte contre la toxicomanie met l'accent sur la prévention," *Le Monde*, 28 October 1989.

consumed on average the equivalent of 19.6 liters (5 U.S. gallons) of pure alcohol per person annually. This was 6.5 liters (1.5 gallons) less than in 1970.[12] Though people are drinking more beer now, wine continues to be the main alcoholic drink, and increasingly good wines are replacing the table wines of the past. Health authorities have long worried about the excessive consumption of alcohol, which is directly responsible for 13,600 deaths a year—to which should be added 14,000 alcohol-related cancer deaths and numerous work and traffic accidents. It is estimated that drivers with an alcohol level of more than 0.8 grams are involved in two out of five road deaths.

Regular drinkers, that is, those who drink between one and four glasses of an alcoholic drink per day, are most often male farmers, foremen, and *cadres* ([lower] executives), while overdrinkers (more than five glasses per day) are most frequently to be found among farmers, tradesmen, shopkeepers and small business proprietors, and skilled and unskilled workers.[13] Twice as many men as women consume alcohol regularly, which helps to explain the eight-year gap in life expectancy of men and women in France.

Consumption patterns are changing too: today only 18.5 percent of French people declare they drink wine daily with their meals, compared to nearly 33 percent ten years ago. Moreover, 50 percent of the French state that they never drink wine.[14] Meanwhile, social drinking is increasing as well as the consumption of beer and spirits.

While wines, even fine wines, are relatively inexpensive, nonalcoholic beverages tend to be costly, and there is a dearth of water fountains so that people are often tempted in this way to drop into the "café," where not only coffee and refreshments but also alcohol is for sale. The legal drinking age is eighteen, but this is not always enforced. A person of any age can go into a supermarket and purchase liquor. Cafés and *bistros* are open from six or seven in the morning until late at night, but there is

---

12. Nicole Guignon, "Alcool et tabac," in *Données Sociales 1990,* 254–57.

13. Within some of the socioprofessional categories, the percentage who consume at least one glass per day are foremen 58.3 percent; farmers 54.9 percent; *cadres* ([lower] managers, supervisors, technicians), 53.6 percent. Those who consume more than five glasses are among farmers 25.9 percent; tradesmen, shopkeepers, and small business proprietors 25.5 percent; skilled workers 24.3 percent. INSEE-SESI survey, *Etude des conditions de vie,* 1986–87. See Guignon, "Alcool et tabac," 256.

14. "Alors que la production augmente les Français boivent moins de vin," *Le Monde,* 12 July 1990.

hardly a direct link between the high consumption levels for alcoholic drinks and the opening hours of these establishments. A sign of changing social behavior is the disappearance of many bistros, cafés, and brasseries—some five thousand per year—that have been forsaken for fast-food places and *croissanteries* or affected by new consumption patterns. The aperitif that used to be drunk in bars is now more likely to be consumed at home, and people buy their beer in supermarkets rather than at the local. When they do go out to drink, it is now less frequently wine or aperitifs that they take and more often beer, coffee, fruit juices, and mineral water. These account for 60 to 80 percent of the turnover for beverages in some bars.[15]

In France, as in many Mediterranean countries, there is no "pressure" on clients to consume. People may spend a lot of time in a café without drinking that much. Teenagers, for example, mostly hang round bars to sip coffee, meet friends, and play pinball or *babyfoot*. This is probably due in part to the long school day and the absence of suitable conditions and facilities for socializing in the school setting. (It also allows them to loosen the grip of their family.)

Tough new antitobacco and antidrink legislation that puts strict limits on advertising for cigarettes and alcohol has been voted by the National Assembly. As of 1993 all advertising for cigarettes is banned on billboards, on television, and in the movies. However, as a concession to the vine growers lobby, alcohol may be advertised on delivery vans, and on billboards in vine-growing regions, in brochures sponsoring cultural events, and in newspapers and magazines for adults. Though wine sales continue to increase because of exports abroad, producers fear that the new law will affect their lucrative business. Hubert Bouteiller, who heads the very important Bordeaux wine professional group the Conseil interprofessionnel du vin de Bordeaux, declared in a press conference in January 1991:

> We are entering a phase that can be qualified as a moralizing one, according to a logic imported from the United States. The authoritarian ban on advertising for tobacco and alcohol is, in fact, nothing but one of the skillfully presented forms of standardized behavior that will affect other aspects of our private and social life in the future.[16]

15. Annick Cojean, "La déprime des zincs," *Le Monde*, 30 June 1992.

16. Jean-Yves Nau, "Les professionnels du vin de Bordeaux réaffirment leur opposition à la loi Evin contre l'alcoolisme," *Le Monde*, 18 January 1991.

Despite this appeal to the United States as a negative example of moralistic intrusion into free choice, the Socialist government's stance on alcohol as a risk to health remained firm to the end.

Tobacco: A State Monopoly

An estimated sixty thousand premature deaths in France every year are caused by the abuse of tobacco, the consumption of which is increasing, largely because of a lack of a clear governmental policy in the matter. The country is one of the smallest tobacco producers in the world, and production, which was traditionally concentrated in small family farms in the southwest, in Alsace, and in the Rhône Valley, began to attract larger farming units in the 1970s. Tobacco is a high added-value product, and growers, though numbering just fifteen thousand in all, represent a powerful prosmoke lobby. Moreover, it is hard to expect stringent antismoking measures, since SEITA (Service d'exploitation industrielle des tabacs et allumettes) is a state-controlled tobacco company that enjoys a manufacturing monopoly with a turnover of Fr 10.3 billion. It employs sixty-two hundred people and runs six tobacco factories as well as three match plants. The famous Gauloises are among the world's five or six top-selling brands, and the gentian blue pack of the Gitanes with the gypsy woman is well known to smokers everywhere. However, if many a visitor's first impression of France used to be the clinging odor of dark tobacco in the airport lounge, six out of ten smokers nowadays smoke Virginian cigarettes. *Les blondes* are ousting *les brunes.*

SEITA is the heir to the royal monopoly set up by the statesman and financier Jean-Baptiste Colbert in the seventeenth century to ensure the state got its due from tobacco consumption. In the late nineteenth century the manufacture and wholesale distribution of matches was added. Following French membership in the EC the company maintained its monopoly on manufacturing but had to give up its role as an intermediary for the retail distribution of tobacco products from other EC countries. In 1970 it lost its prerogative as exclusive buyer of raw tobacco from the growers, but it still maintains close relations with them. Previously SEITA workers were state employed, but nowadays they have a special status. The enterprise enjoys financial autonomy within the limits of state control. The latter appoints the CEO and board of directors as well as a comptroller.

In every country tobacco is a major source of tax revenue for the state. If cigarettes are less taxed in France than in most countries, it is basically because the government has a vested interest in tobacco consumption and does not want to kill the goose with the golden egg. SEITA contributes 2.4 percent of total tax revenue. However, under the twin pressure of EC health concerns and an extraordinarily powerful anti-smoking lobby, things are beginning to change. Moreover, SEITA is diversifying into agrofoods, textiles, and smart cards such as *télécartes* and parking cards. Soon 30 percent of turnover is expected to come from activities other than tobacco production.

For a number of years TV, radio, and billboard tobacco ads have been banned, and in movie theater commercials pictures of cigarette packs or of actors smoking are forbidden. Advertisers have also been limited in the amount of space they can buy in printed publications. Of course, there being no limit to the ingeniousness of admen, ways were found to work round these rules: Philip Morris offered discounts to movie-goers, the Marlboro cowboy was there but with no cigarette; Peter Stuyvessant and Gauloises advertised exotic travel. In 1991 the government decided, albeit reluctantly, to go a step further. A sharp price increase was put on cigarettes, and as of 1993 all advertising for tobacco, including sponsorship of sporting events by cigarette manufacturers, is forbidden. In December 1992, a decree designed to protect nonsmokers was published. Smoking is henceforth severely restricted in corporations, schools, transportation, and public places such as restaurants or bars. This was a big step to take in a country where 40 percent of adults smoke.

According to Minister of Health Claude Evin, who introduced the new anti-smoking legislation (*loi Evin*), tobacco consumption has not globally increased in France in spite of intense advertising but neither has it decreased. The minister's aim was to protect the younger population. While adult males are smoking less, there is a tendency for females to smoke more, and the number of young smokers is rising. 90 percent of these start smoking in their teens; 60 percent at the age of thirteen.

Never was the ambiguity of the French approach to tobacco consumption more apparent than in early 1991, when SEITA, in an attempt to take market share away from its foreign competitors—the state no longer permits the company to run up a deficit—tried to launch a new cigarette aimed at young smokers under the label of Chevignon, a manufacturer of modish teenager leather jackets and accessories. A state-controlled enterprise had thus decided to encourage young people to smoke in defiance of the recently voted laws of the same state! The minister of health publically denounced the company, but the cigar-smoking minister of the budget, Michel Charasse, defended SEITA's marketing strategy! However this incident, which has led to a judicial inquiry, should not hide the courage of a government, less hypocritical than the authorities in some countries where stronger antismoke lobbies exist, that has taken the commitment to ban all advertizing for tobacco in the interest of public health. Would such a ban be possible if the tobacco industry instead of being a state monopoly had been in the hands of greedy private corporations?[17]

17. There seems to be little likelihood for the moment of tough EC legislation on the lines of the loi Evin because European advertising and manufacturing lobbies oppose it. While the EC Parliament—which has little effective power—has voted a ban on all advertising for tobacco products, the Brussels Commission has balked at implementing this legislation. Moreover, it should not be forgotten that the EC gives considerable subsidies to tobacco-growers—1.3 billion ECUs (Fr 9.1 billion) in 1991.

PART 5

Social Relations

I prefer to look after myself rather than others, in case they say: why is he interfering?

—Jules Renard (1864–1910)

11

Community

If family and relatives are among the stongest links between individuals in France, nearly one out of two French people belongs to an association of one kind or another: sports and cultural clubs, self-help groups, organizations devoted to a cause (churches, political parties, worker unions), or defense groups (for consumers, immigrants, the environment). While associations that provide for leisure activities, particularly sport clubs, grew considerably in the 1980s, militant organizations stagnated or declined. Trade unionism is at a low ebb: only 10 percent of the working population is a member of a union. Consumer associations have few members, and only one in ten French adults belongs to a parent-teacher association.[1] Barely 3 percent of French adults are members of an environmental defense group, and while it is sometimes possible to muster large numbers of protesters for a specific cause such as the rejection of a highway project in the name of environmental protection or the defense of the immigrant population, there is little enduring support for the majority of associations of this type. After an initial show of indignation and *solidarité* people return to their individual occupations. This is sometimes seen as a rejection of traditional structures and institutions in favor of a more pragmatic and less ideologically inspired activism on the British or American model. The *restaus* (restaurants) *du coeur,* the student and worker *coordinations,* illustrate this new approach to issues, *solidarité* without militantism, a way of being involved without being co-opted.

Religion

> France, what have you done with your baptism?
>
> —Pope Jean Paul II

1. See Laurence Haeusler, "Le Monde associatif de 1978 à 1986," in *Données Sociales 1990,* 369–70; and Jean-Luc Volatier, "Associations: Loisirs en hausse, militantisme en baisse," in Cordellier, L'état de la France *1992,* 111–12.

When Pope Jean Paul II uttered these words at Le Bourget during his first visit to France in 1980 before a crowd of some 500,000 faithful, he was referring to the long tradition of Catholicism in France, the founding act of which was the baptism of Clovis in A.D. 496.[2] France was known for centuries as *fille aînée de l'église,* that is, elder daughter of the church, not because it was the first country to embrace Christianity but because for thirteen hundred years (until 1790) Catholicism was "the religion of the nation and an essential element in its identity."[3] But France was to be an independent if not rebellious daughter from an early age. If that peculiar brand of French Catholicism called Gallicanism was the expression of the refusal of monarchs to allow Rome to meddle in the affairs of the country by appointing prelates, religion helped consolidate French centralization from the fifth century, when the shrewd Frankish king, Clovis, perceived the temporal benefits that could be drawn from Christianity, which was already firmly anchored in Gaul and had offered many martyrs to the faith. However, during the Revolution the church played the losing card, and Catholicism was to lose its status as the official religion of the state in 1830. Yet, in spite of the anticlericalism of the nineteenth century, the churches continued to receive state funding under the terms of the Concordat (1801), inspired by Napoleon, until the separation of church and state in 1905. (Due to an accident of history, a trace of the old order still persists in Alsace and Lorraine, where priests, as well as pastors and rabbis, are officially appointed and remunerated by the minister of the interior in his capacity as *ministre des cultes,* or administrator of church affairs.) Until recently the tolerance of other religions, more often than not seen as a threat to the integrity of the nation, was limited, as persecuted Huguenots, Calvinists, and Jews learned to their cost. Today the secular dogma of the Republic (liberty, equality, fraternity), which paradoxically owes so much to Christian principles—does this explain in part why it was readily assimilated?—is no less binding than Catholicism. Yet, reticence or hostility toward Islam, the second religion of France with three million followers, by a lay society that proclaims tolerance as a virtue and the emergence of the traditionalist movement, *le mouvement intégriste,* founded by Monseigneur Lefebvre, the dissident Roman Catholic bishop, show just how unsure the French are of their identity and values.[4]

2. He repeated this idea in 1986 in Annecy: "Christians of France, what have you done with your baptism?"

3. René Rémond, "La fille aînée de l'église," *L'Histoire,* January 1987, 118–22.

4. The *mouvement intégriste* founded by Monseigneur Lefebvre started as a reaction to the liturgical reforms introduced by the Vatican council. The 1968

Catholicism is no longer the religion of the nation nor an essential element of the national identity. The Roman Catholic church is one of the institutions that has suffered most from declining participation. Religious practice has reached an all-time low. The French are Catholic more by tradition than by conviction. Thus if between 70 percent and 80 percent of the population says it is Catholic, one in four of these so-called Catholics is not convinced of the existence of God! Forty-two percent never pray and 90 percent never read the Bible. Although the figures for church marriages (70.4 percent) and baptisms (67 percent) have been relatively steady since the 1970s, the number of regular churchgoers has declined sharply.[5] Half of French Catholics set their foot in a church only on the "big occasions," that is, for births, marriages, and funerals; 13 percent attend service once a week, compared with 49 percent in the United States according to a Gallup poll;[6] and 19 percent attend "from time to time." French Catholics probably pay the least attention of all to the pronouncements of Rome in matters related to what

---

turmoil in France convinced the bishop of the need to return to tradition. He was against the "new cathecism," mass in French rather than in Latin ("Let me celebrate the religion of my forefathers"), priests wearing suits instead of soutanes, and "the general dissolution of morals" that he saw as an outcome of the teachings of the council. In 1969, in defiance of the pope he opened a traditionalist seminary in Ecône, Switzerland. He was finally excommunicated by Pope Jean Paul II in 1988 after proceeding to consecrate four dissident bishops despite a papal injunction. Monseigneur Lefebvre died on 25 March 1992. The traditionalist movement, comprising some five hundred priests and seminarists, continues in spite of the schism. The church of Saint-Nicolas-du-Chardonnet in Paris, where masses are celebrated in Latin, keeps the traditionalist flame burning, but there are isolated followers of the movement among Catholics all over France. In some respects the *intégristes,* who are close to the extreme right-wing political movement of Jean-Marie Le Pen, perpetuate the violent counterrevolutionary tradition of French Catholicism that the prewar Action Française shamefully exploited. (It was an *intégriste* who bombed the movie theater where Martin Scorcese's film *The Last Temptation of Christ* was showing.) The traditionalists are an embarrassment to French bishops, who must tread warily whenever they make a public statement on moral issues to avoid being accused of pandering to the "moral minority."

5. The figures on religious practice are from the following surveys: SOFRES–*Le Monde–La Vie,* September 1986, *Le Monde,* 1 October 1986; IPSOS–*Le Monde*-RTL, September 1988, *Le Monde,* 5 October 1988; SOFRES–*Le Monde–La Vie*–France Inter, September 1990, *Le Figaro,* 28 November 1990. See also Zohor Djider and Maryse Marpsat, "La vie religieuse: chiffres et enquêtes," in *Données Sociales 1990,* 376–79.

6. Louis Harris, *Inside America* (New York: Vintage Books, 1987).

they consider personal and family ethics: contraception, abortion, premarital sex. This was confirmed by a SOFRES survey for the excellent television program "La Marche du Siècle" and published in *Le Figaro*. The findings suggested that the opinions of practicing Catholics in such matters as abortion and premarital sexual relations are increasingly similar to those of the rest of the population. (According to Cardinal Lustiger, archbishop of Paris, it is nevertheless necessary to stress another result of the survey, which showed that French people increasingly expect the church to "enlighten" them on matters of private morality without imposing "precise obligations.") But even in other questions, such as the celibacy of the clergy or the ordination of women, the French do not generally agree with the conservative attitude of the pope.

Catholic militantism, symbolized by l'Action Catholique, which contributed so much to reconcile secular society with the church, the spiritual with the material world, has declined, and no longer seems to be a priority today for the bishops essentially preoccupied by the necessity of a spiritual revival—this was the message of Pope Jean Paul II to the French—in a society that considers the church as a sort of sacramental self-service.

In 1992 a group of Catholics in Paris took the initiative of a television campaign to promote the celebration of Easter. It was the first time in France that TV spots were used to market religion. A lot of people questioned the wisdom of this innovation, which seemed to reduce religion to a product. Church authorities were careful to emphasize that it was a private initiative.

Even if the 140 ordinations that took place in France in 1989 showed an increase for the first time in fourteen years, the number of religious vocations is tiny nowadays in a country that used to train so many missionaries, and it is difficult for the elderly clergy to manage the work load. There are only 24,800 priests today—one per twenty-four hundred inhabitants compared to one per six hundred at the beginning of the century. Many churches that had to be locked during the week to prevent theft are no longer open even on Sundays, particularly in rural areas, and the aging priests are so few in number that many have become overworked itinerants in charge of more than a dozen scattered parishes where they say mass in turn to a handful of mostly elderly parishioners. In some larger départements, particularly in the Parisian region, there is sometimes only one priest for seven thousand inhabitants. It would be hard to deny the dedication of the poorly remunerated French clergy—

they earn between forty-five hundred and fifty-four hundred francs per month—whose only resource is their spiritual strength in a society of pervasive materialism and broken community life. Yet, in times of distress anyone, churchgoer or not, is sure to get a sympathetic hearing from the local *curé* (priest), who still plays a vital role as a spiritual guide, particularly in rural areas.

In the 1980s there was much talk of a spiritual revival, even if many of the signals were coming from outside the established religions[7] or from religions that had hitherto had only a limited number of converts, such as Buddhism. The generosity of young people moved by poverty in the Third World, as well as by the so-called new poor on their own doorstep; concern about racial discrimination; the growing membership of movements like the Boy Scouts that have been traditionally close to the church in France;[8] a revival of prayer; and charismatic groups seemed to be the signs of a return to a less materialistic if not more God-fearing society. After the massive demonstration in favor of the *école libre* in 1984, the Catholic hierarchy jumped into the breach left by the apparent collapse of the secular value system promoted by the Socialists, assuming, perhaps, that the hour had come to reinstill a sense of purpose into French society, and church leaders made a series of rash public pronouncements that were perceived as pandering to the moral minority, that is, the *intégristes*. There was violent public reaction to the condemnation of Martin Scorcese's movie *The Last Temptation of Christ* by the archbishop of Paris, a statement that many felt had comforted the traditionalists who burned down the theater in Paris where it was showing; and to the opposition of the Assembly of French Bishops to the abortion pill RU-486 and to the government's anti-AIDS campaign promoting the use of condoms. The statement by the bishop of Lyon on the Persian

7. This has been particularly true for French Protestantism. In 1987 the American evangelist, Billy Graham, rallied more than 100,000 people to the five prayer meetings he gave in Paris. Meanwhile Pentecostalists and Assembly of God congregations are spreading. This charismatic Protestantism is a break with institutional Protestantism in France, which has historically had a strong political involvement characterized by the values of liberty, tolerance, individualism, pluralism, and modernity. See Henri Tincq, "L'embellie protestante," *Le Monde,* 1 November 1991.

8. There are two scout movements in France, the very traditional *Scouts d'Europe,* in which the Catholic clergy is very active, and *Les Scouts de France,* which is a secular movement.

FIG. 17. Cartoon that appeared after a time bomb exploded in a Parisian movie theater during Martin Scorcese's *The Last Temptation of Christ.* The sinner: Of course I had to go and see the film to place the bomb. . . . (*Le Monde,* Copyright © Pancho 1988.)

Gulf crisis—"rather war than dishonor"—also created an uproar. The resulting misunderstanding showed the gap that still exists between the bishops and a population that has been shaped by a long history of anticlericalism. French Catholics accept readily enough the social mission of the church, its pronouncements on arms sales, racism, human rights, nuclear deterrence, and unemployment, but deny it any authority in cultural and private matters. Only one bishop, Monseigneur Jacques Gaillot, has courageously taken a stance on most of the moral issues and problems facing the church in contemporary society that is opposed (often diametrically) to official doctrine. Protestant leaders, though their following is small—there are only about 850,000 Protestants in the Lutheran, Reformist, and Evangelist churches combined—show themselves to be much more progressive and tolerant in these matters.

The sort of psychosis that takes hold of the intelligentsia and politicians in France where religion is concerned should not hide the overall indifference of the population. At worst the man in the street will have a mocking look when the *curé* is mentioned. The real dilemma for the clergy is how to assert their moral authority in a society that has lost its bearings and where religious heritage is often the subject of mockery or artistic expression of doubtful taste in advertising and movies: the inevitable gourmet monk that adorns camembert boxes or liqueur labels; the heroine of *Une Affaire de Femmes* reciting a version of the "Hail Mary" that is blasphemous for practicing Catholics. In fact, in October 1991 Monseigneur Joseph Duval, archbishop of Rouen and chairman of the Conference of French Bishops, at the plenary assembly in Lourdes criticized very strongly advertisers who have "laid their hands on pictures and the symbols of religion to use them in such a way that they are misrepresented and made to look ridiculous." He was referring to the controversial Benetton ad portraying a nun kissing a priest and the Manix slogan for condoms that used the biblical phrase "Love one another."

With the weakening of ideology, the rise of *intégrisme* (fundamentalism)—not only Muslim but Jewish and Catholic as well—and the complexity of ethical issues for which a lay society has no easy answers—surrogate motherhood, frozen embryos, euthanasia—there is a feeling that the spiritual dimension of humans cannot be ignored. This led to increasing cooperation between the Socialist government and church leaders—for example, the historic agreement on *l'école libre* signed by the minister of education and culture in 1992—even if the grass-roots militants did not always approve. Yet, it would be as hard to expect the Grand Orient of France, the powerful masonic lodge that has been in the forefront of all the recent battles in defense of lay society, to renounce its beliefs as it would be to expect the Catholic hierarchy to turn its back on Rome in order to appeal to the secular value system that has become an essential part of the identity of the French. France, which is never at a loss for paradox, is not only elder daughter of the church but also elder daughter of secularism.

Worker Unions

In 1990 Renault, the very symbol of all the nationalized industries in France, opened its doors to a private investor, Volvo, which henceforth controls 25 percent of its capital. At about the same time, the decision was made to close down the auto plant in Billancourt that had been "the social laboratory of France."[9] These two events mark the end of an epoch in the history of French industry and of a certain form of trade union action in which social protectionism did not exclude, indeed was

9. Daniel Labbé and Fréderic Périn, *Que reste-t-il de Billancourt?* (Paris: Editions Hachette, 1990), 7.

based on, tacit acceptance and defense of a production model (Taylorism) even after this model had manifestly become obsolete. The last stand of a handful of militant strikers in Billancourt in 1989, completely out of touch with the desires of the workers they proclaimed to defend, was a pathetic symbol of the misadventures of French worker organizations.

France has the lowest rate of trade union membership in Europe, 10 percent of the working population in 1989, according to a CREDOC survey.[10] Public companies and the civil service are the main strongholds of the five principal labor confederations. Fewer than 6 percent of the employees of private corporations hold union cards. Workers are entirely free to join or not, and membership can never be mandatory as it sometimes is in the United States. Globally membership has declined since the beginning of the 1980s. The massive layoffs in industry, the shift from a blue-collar to a white-collar society that has blurred the boundaries of social class, the glorification of the corporation, and the rise of individualism have been the main external factors. However, the stubborness of the militants, the disputes between the reformists and the radicals, and the lack of funds have also contributed to the waning influence of trade unions, which were forced to accept the relentless wage freeze imposed by the Socialists (whom they had helped bring to power) and were unable to limit the spread of forms of employment that offer few prospects. The cumbersome centralized organizations lost touch with the realities of the shop floor. Bent on preserving their turf, they refused in general to accept the new economic deal. The 1982 reform of labor legislation that permitted decentralized negotiation of salaries by corporate bosses meant that collective bargaining lost some of its purpose. Indeed the uncontrolled strikes of 1987 called into question the very legitimacy of the confederations, although it did not really threaten their existence.

Les Coordinations

From 1986 to 1988 a wave of wildcat strikes broke out in France, inspired perhaps by the successful organizational pattern of the student protest drive that forced the government to back down on its proposed educational reform bill in 1986. The lycée students had proved that a flexible,

---

10. *L'évolution du monde associatif de 1978 à 1986* (Paris: Centre de recherche pour l'étude et l'observation des conditions de vie, 1989).

bottom-up strategy was more efficient than a top-down, Parisian-based approach, and the hundreds of local free-discussion coordinations hooked up to each other by the interactive Minitel were the real powerhouses of the movement. These long, drawn out strikes by union and nonunion workers in transportation and in the postal services, social security employees, and nurses did not unduly strain the patience of the public, who showed a certain resignation if not sympathy with the strikes. Neither the government nor the labor unions, short-circuited by the spontaneous coordinations, seemed capable of responding to these local initiatives. Unfortunately, the exorbitant wage demands shadowed the more fundamental question posed by the absence of any scheme for the management of human resources in the public service. The "Rocard method" finally got the better of these conflicts, and the black sheep that were lured back to the fold of the official organizations in the final negotiation stage had to be satisfied with minimal concessions.[11] This thinly disguised defeat of the coordinations has not improved the image of the trade unions, which seemed more intent on preserving their monopoly than furthering the cause of the strikers. In 1992 the roadblocks set up by French truckers opposed to the new driving licence with deductible points for traffic offences, *le permis à points,* which paralyzed France for more than a week, was also a grass-roots reaction by "the highway serfs" (Mitterrand) that recalled the strategy of the coordinations. And again, the scarcely representative trucker unions signed a compromise with the transport authorities, to the bitter disappointment of the protesting truck drivers on the road blocks.

The highly conflictual nature of social relations in France today is due to the breakdown of the institutions—churches, political parties, worker unions—that have traditionally played the role of intermediaries. The coordinations are an attempt at direct democracy, at power to the people who are concerned by the decisions that are taken on high, but they are basically *corporatiste* because the *solidarité* expressed by the individuals in this new form of collective protest is limited to the group they are defending. (For example, the nurses' coordination refused to allow their claims to be examined with those of the medical helpers.)

11. The so-called Rocard method was an approach to industrial strife implemented by former premier Michel Rocard. It consisted in allowing isolated social conflicts to simmer and then when the danger of a general conflagration was imminent to grant selective minimal wage increases to those workers earning the lowest wages, thus purchasing industrial peace.

The approach and the methods (use of the media) of the coordinations is close to the American idea of lobbying, which has a derogatory connotation in France, where the idea of the common good, guaranteed by the state, is supposed to prevail over the private interests of pressure groups—and generally does. (The government stood firm on the new driving licence in the name of improved road safety.) This does not mean that there are no lobbies in France but that their methods, particularly those of the institutionalized lobbies, are less transparent, and the interests of the community at large are often sacrificed to the idea the top administration has of the common interest, which leaves little place for citizen action and participative democracy.[12] The French nuclear energy program, which has opposed a handful of ecologists to the powerful Atomic Energy Commission and the EDF (Electricité de France), is one among many examples of how decisions affecting the community are sometimes handled in France. It shows how an institutionalized lobby, in this case the engineers of the Corps des mines, can obtain "consensus by default."

---

12. See Jean-Dominique Giuliani, *Marchands d'influence: les lobbies en France* (Paris: Editions du Seuil, 1991).

12

The Right to Be Different

Nowhere is one *more* of a foreigner than in France. Nowhere is one *better* a foreigner than in France.

—Julia Kristeva

France has a long tradition of immigration (chap. 1), and racism is no new phenomenon. Immigrants in any country have rarely enjoyed the same status as the so-called natives, and neither U.S. nor French society seems to be the real melting pot that has often been proclaimed. The veneration enjoyed by celebrities from abroad—famous artists, musicians, writers, athletes, and researchers—should not hide the fact that many foreigners have always been held in suspicion by the average citizen. The medieval overlord confiscated their possessions when they died; in the fourteenth century Philippe le Bel deported the Jews to lay hands on their capital, and in the seventeenth century the power of the "Italian clan" at the court of France gave rise to bitter xenophobic feeling among the people. Nevertheless, under the ancien régime foreigners who were badly needed in the armies, in business, and in the arts were under royal protection and often enjoyed special privileges.

Until the second half of the nineteenth century the typical immigrant was a soldier or a member of the cosmopolitan intellectual or business elite, if not a political refugee. With the industrial revolution, engineers, mechanics, and skilled workers began to join the ranks of the bankers and merchants who had arrived in the previous period and had contributed to the development of industry. Then the inexorable demographic downturn that set in after 1850 completely changed the professional profile of the new arrivals. The immigrant worker burst on the scene. Between 1851 and 1876 the number of immigrants increased by 25 percent. All in all, the country showed a remarkable capacity for integrating the new work force, but whenever the labor market contracted, ingrained mistrust and hostility broke out, as in the 1920s. In spite of that, France had for a time the highest rate of immigration in the world. By 1931, immigrants accounted for 7 percent of the total population, a figure similar to today's, which should help to put the current debate on immigration in proper perspective.

Racism

The short supply of labor in France, the aging work force, and industry's largely unavowed aim of undermining the trade unions' demand for better pay and working conditions have always been the principal motives for employing immigrant workers. This, in turn, has led to a latent hostility to foreigners that manifests itself every time the natives feel menaced in their jobs, pay, or working conditions. Yves Lequin describes the brutal treatment of Italians and Belgians at the hands of French workers at the turn of the century. Ten immigrants were slain in a manhunt in the south of France in 1893. In the mining town of La Mure near Grenoble in 1901 the natives organized what they called "bear hunts," chasing immigrant workers from their homes, terrifying their families, and burning their belongings.[1] The 1930s were a particularly somber period, as the national and international crisis stirred up xenophobia that was to culminate in the shameful behavior of the Vichy government, which withdrew French citizenship from fifteen thousand naturalized immigrants and handed over sixty thousand to sixty-five thousand Jews to the Nazis, who sent them to the gas chambers.[2] When one is aware of this, it is easy to understand the gravity of Jean-Marie Le Pen's miserable pun in 1988 on the name of Michel Durafour, the Jewish minister of labor in the Rocard cabinet, or his remark that the Holocaust was nothing more than "a point of detail."[3]

1. Yves Lequin, "Métissages imprudents," in *La mosaïque France: Histoire des étrangers et de l'immigration en France*, ed. Yves Lequin (Paris: Larousse, 1988), 389–410.

2. Yves Lequin and Dominique Schnapper, "Les chemins de Vichy," in Lequin, *La mosaïque France*, 411–28.

3. The word *four* means "oven." Le Pen was referring cynically to the gas chambers. A professor at the University of Lyon, a member of the so-called revisionist school, has even written a thesis that attempts to prove the gas chambers did not exist!

Le Front National

Jean-Marie Le Pen's extreme-Right-wing National Front (FN) movement, which he founded in 1972, is a populist party that recruits many of its supporters in urban working-class districts with high unemployment, where tensions run high between the native French and their North African neighbors. This voluble, mudslinging politician exercises a certain magnetism over his supporters and is a master of proposing pat solutions to complex political and social problems. Some examples taken from his election canvassing propaganda in 1988:

Problem: France is [dixit Le Pen] swamped by immigrants.
Solution: Send them back to where they came from; make it more difficult to acquire French citizenship.
Problem: Security.
Solution: Reintroduce the death penalty; deport illegal immigrants and foreign delinquents.
Problem: Social security deficit.
Solution: Discriminatory treatment of foreigners.
Problem: Housing.
Solution: Give prority to French citizens over foreigners.
Problem: Unemployment.
Solution: Priority of French citizens for jobs.[4]

False Solutions

It is easy to refute these arguments but hard to convince people that they are false because logic has little to do with the spell cast by Le Pen. France needed the immigrants in the postwar period and like the rest of Europe dogged with a declining demography, still needs them today. The recent economic recovery has been accompanied all over Europe by an increase in the influx of illegal immigrants. The aging work force and the small desire of European youth to do the lowly,

4. These and other proposals in a similar vein were among the fifty measures designed "to contribute to the solution of the immigration problem" presented by Le Pen's lieutenant, Bruno Mégret, at the Front National symposium in Marseille on 16 November 1991. Many of them also figured in the FN's party platform for the 1993 legislative elections.

sometimes—though not always—badly paid tasks, explains why the job supply—the real, not the theoretical supply—is increasing all over Europe and why Europe, in extremely technical areas, relies largely on immigration.[5] Thus Le Pen's proposal of giving priority to French citizens for jobs is a false solution, like most of the others.

It is relatively easy to acquire French citizenship, and official policy in this respect is far more lenient than in Germany, for example. The *jus soli* of the ancien régime, which states that anybody born in France is automatically French unless he or she relinquishes citizenship, and the *jus sanguinis*, put forward by the revolutionaries, which stipulates that any child of at least one French parent is to be considered French, both play a role in the naturalization process. In addition, the foreigner who marries a French citizen can claim French citizenship if the couple has lived together as husband and wife for six months. This has led to a number of "marriages of convenience."

Not only the FN but also the conservative Right-wing parties in a vote-catching maneuver have campaigned for tighter measures, proposing, in particular, an oath of allegiance on the American model. Why, they say, should the majority of foreigners become French practically without realizing it? They point out that while the revolutionaries maintained the *jus soli*, the Napoleonic Code stated that the children of foreigners born in France were expected to make a formal claim before becoming French citizens. In 1889 this provision was abolished. The historian Pierre Chaunu has criticized the very idea of dual allegiance.[6] Indeed, many foreigners have dual citizenship, and young Algerians may choose to do their compulsory military service in Algeria or in France. The historian declared: "A fatherland is something you choose." However, opponents point out that such an oath, which would be mandatory at the age of sixteen, would be humiliating for children brought up and educated in France and would, in fact, be an obstacle to integration.

A relatively high percentage of immigrants is involved in delinquency and crime but only when compared to the crime rate of the total population of French citizens. If a parallel is drawn with the comparable

5. Alain Murcier, "L'Europe face aux immigrés," *L'Expansion*, 17 May 1990, 60–67.

6. Pierre Chaunu, "Une patrie, cela se choisit," *Les Cahiers de l'Express* 3, April 1990, 76.

Foreigners and Delinquency

Raw statistics about rates of delinquency in the foreign population have to be handled with care. For example, according to official figures, in 1990 one-third of the prisoners in French jails were foreigners, and between 1974 and 1990 their number tripled, while the number of imprisoned French multiplied by 1.4 over the same period. But this is a simplifying view of things. As a recent study* demonstrates, in order to have a true picture of the situation it is necessary to take into account the demographic structure of the foreign population behind bars, the types of crimes they are guilty of, and the attitudes of the police and judges who deal with these delinquents. The study by sociologists Pierre Tournier and Philippe Robert shows, first, that there are more males in the foreign population than among the French and that they are younger—two factors that increase the likelihood of imprisonment. Further, there are more manual workers and jobless in the foreign population†—just as among people incarcerated; second, many of the imprisoned foreigners are in jail simply because they are illegal immigrants (they represented 27.7 percent of all imprisoned foreigners in 1989); third, the chances of foreigners of being charged by the police and convicted by judges are greater than those of the native French because, on the one hand, during identity checks to hunt down illegal immigrants, the police will more easily uncover other crimes perpetrated by foreigners; on the other hand the types of crime committed by the foreigners (theft, assault) are easier to track down than fraud, tax-dodging, or traffic offences more commonly found among the native population. Finally, judges more easily resort to detention pending trial for foreigners than for the French. In 1986, 40.5 percent of detained foreigners were awaiting trial compared to 27.4 percent of the French behind bars. Philippe Bernard and Anne Chemin, commenting on this study in *Le Monde*, said that the statistical instruments at present used would need to be seriously overhauled in the light of these findings if we are to prevent "the misleading figures on foreign delinquency from fueling xenophobic polemic or embarrassed silence."‡

---

*Pierre Tournier and Philippe Robert, *Etrangers et délinquance: les chiffres du débat* (Paris: L'Hartmann, 1991).

†Two-thirds of immigrants are men. Fifty-five percent are under forty years of age. Fifty-six percent are workers (1991 figures). More than two-thirds have no diploma, or at most, an elementary school certificate. See Christian Monade, "La condition immigrée" in Cordellier, *L'état de la France* 1992, 139–44.

‡Philippe Bernard and Anne Chemin, "Les faux-semblants de la délinquance étrangère," *Le Monde*, 5 December 1991.

native French social group—poorly qualified, low-income males in the eighteen-to-thirty age group—the difference is not so obvious.[7]

Le Pen's proposal for solving the deficit of social security is amusing when one realizes that while immigrants pay the same contributions as the French they are not entitled to the same benefits. They are expected to contribute to the national pension plan, but if they return to their homeland they relinquish their rights. Having on average more children than the French, they get more funds in the form of family allowances, but if their families remain in their homeland as is often the case, the rate is established on the home country rate, which is systematically lower than the French rate. The same goes for health coverage for family members not residing in France. Social security saves a billion francs annually in this way!

The problem of housing in Paris and the major cities is distressing not only for immigrants but also for the poorer French citizens: the unemployed and low-income families. However, it is downright malevolence to suggest that foreigners get a better deal or that they prevent the French from gaining access to social housing. Illegal quotas for immigrant families are openly or surreptitiously introduced in many places, even in Communist-run municipalities, and in Paris, where 20 to 30 percent of the demand comes from immigrants, only 5 percent is met. INSEE statistics show that immigrants are seven times more likely than French to have temporary housing. They are six times more likely to be living in overcrowded apartments and twice more likely to dwell in homes lacking in comfort.[8] Fifteen percent of single immigrant workers are housed in the 660 "homes" (foyers) that offer only minimal amenities, not to mention the shanty towns populated by many of the *harkis*, the Algerian refugees—in fact, French citizens—who were rewarded thus for siding with the French during the Algerian war of independence.[9]

---

7. Evelyne Fallot, "La mauvaise réputation," *Les Cahiers de l'Express*, 3, April 1990, 26–28.

8. Claude Taffin, "Le logement des étrangers en France," INSEE, *Economie et Statistique* no. 242, 1991. See also Christian Monade, "La condition immigrée," in Cordellier, *L'état de la France* 1992.

9. Officially the *harkis* are "repatriated French Muslims." In the summer of 1991 violent demonstrations by the younger *harkis* in the south of France brought to the fore the plight of this community ignored, for different reasons, on both sides of the Mediterranean. While France has spent considerable sums in assistance programs—a necessary but hardly sufficient solution—a report commissioned by the prime minister in 1991 stressed that the *harkis* have accumulated

The leader of the FN is careful to point out that he is neither racist—he finds the term *imprécis*—nor anti-Semitic, but with his anti-immigrant diatribes, he has helped to exude these twin poisons in French society with such mastery that little heed is paid by people to the gangrene that is spreading across the country: academics who blandly refute the Holocaust, a flourishing business in reprints of Nazi publications, a certain complacency about thinly disguised racist opinions. In spring 1990, the desecration, by unidentified individuals, of the Jewish cemetery in the southern town of Carpentras—home of one of the oldest Jewish communities in France—where tombstones were smashed and the corpse of a recently deceased old man was dug up and impaled on a parasol stick, was only possible in a society where racism is taken for granted. The anti-immigrant rantings of the FN and the insidious allusions to Jews have contributed to develop a climate of mistrust and violence toward out-groups, who have become the victims of gratuitous assaults and insults to which public opinion has been slow to react.

Overreaction

The sort of paranoia about immigration promoted by Le Pen has little justification. Of course, France is the European country with the greatest number of immigrants, but after all they account for less than 7 percent of the total population—hardly a threat to the ethnic predominance of the French. It is true that an estimated thirty thousand illegal immigrants are arriving annually and that France will have to stem the tide sooner or later, but this is no reason to give up attempts to integrate the existing immigrant population, to avoid the development of urban ghettos, and to provide fairer opportunities for education.

It is true that the *official* jobless rate among this unskilled, largely uneducated population is higher than for the French, but since 1974 the

---

all the handicaps of those in dire difficulty: "pauperism, massive failure rate in schools, catastrophic unemployment, delinquency, as well as phenomena of racism and exclusion." *Les fils de harkis,* the sons and grandsons of those Algerians who sided with France during the Algerian war of independence, have fully accepted their parents' commitment to the French cause and are claiming the same respect, rights, and opportunities for *harkis* as for other French citizens. See Alain Rollat, "L'histoire refoulée des harkis," *Le Monde,* 7 August 1991; and Anne Tristan, "Les rêves déçus et la colère rentrée des harkis," *Le Monde Diplomatique* August 1992, 12–13.

proportion of foreigners in the working population has practically been unchanged—6.5 percent in 1990. The new immigrants are mostly women and children allowed to enter the country under the family reunification legislation. In the lean 1970s and early 1980s, an average 70,000 per year quit the country, many under golden handshake schemes set up by the government to encourage workers to return to their homeland. This figure had fallen to 33,000 by 1985 with the big shakeout in the auto industry, and in 1990, there were only 421 freely chosen, financially aided departures. More significant are the "disguised departures" of foreigners from the labor statistics through naturalization, or the retirement of the older unskilled generation, which has brought younger, better trained and educated foreigners on the job market. While many immigrants are still confined to assembly line and construction jobs, there has been a noticeable shift, and employment patterns are slowly conforming to those of the native French, that is, feminization and a growth in service jobs and self-employment.[10]

Second-generation immigrants—the so-called *beurs*—are beginning to enter traditionally closed professions such as teaching, the police, and public administration. Nonetheless there is a real difficulty for these children of Maghrebian parents, who are disadvantaged by the elitist educational system but probably no more so than the native French underclass.[11] The same could be said for housing, the other major problem of the poor, whether immigrant or French. It is hardly surprising that education and housing should be the major solutions proposed by pro-integration groups like France Plus whose leader, Arezki Dahmani, a professor at the University of Paris, is himself a *beur.*

The most pressing problem is to dedramatize issues that the FN has exaggerated, but this is difficult in the political context. While few of the French would subscribe to the more radical of the fifty measures proposed by Le Pen's party to solve the immigration problem, such as withdrawing citizenship from all the immigrants naturalized—some thirty thousand per year—since 1974, segregation in schools, or abolishing the *jus soli,* the danger is that these proposals will be discussed and because they are

10. Guy Herzlich, "Les sentiers de traverse de l'intégration," *Le Monde,* 21 February, 1989.

11. *Maghrebian* refers to the inhabitants of Maghreb (Al Marhrib al 'Aqsa), that is, Morocco in Arabic. Today the Maghreb powers include the northwest African countries of Morocco, Algeria, Tunisia, Libya, and Mauritania.

Les Beurs

Beur is a slang derivation of *arabe* and refers to the children of North African immigrants brought up in France. Not to be confused with the word *beurre* (butter)—pronounced in the same way—which is "a greasy oily food substance" as Begag and Chaouite ironically observe, pointing out that the word is frequently misspelt by French journalists. The term *beur* was coined by teenagers in the Parisian suburbs but perhaps has a deeper significance than people generally think. The second-generation immigrants do not feel entirely French but neither do they feel Arabic. "I am *beur* means I am neither here nor there. Unclassifiable. Have no desire to be [classified]." Beur has a charming feminine form, the diminutive *beurette.* See Azouz Begag and Abdellatif Chaouite, *Ecarts d'identité* (Paris: Editions du Seuil, 1990), 9–10, 83.

discussed become acceptable. Politicians from Left and Right, even those who hold or have held the highest offices and can hardly be suspected of racism, such as Edith Cresson, Jacques Chirac, and Giscard d'Estaing, have all proved that they are not indifferent to the sensitivity of public opinion to Le Pen's arguments. Their "slips of the tongue" seem to legitimate measures that would otherwise be unmentionable.[12] Moreover, the FN, by pushing up the stakes—some of the fifty measures are completely unrealistic, such as giving a special label to products "produced in France by *French* workers"—may simply want to increase its chances of getting its main program accepted.

All in all, the French have made a laudable effort to integrate the 1.5

12. In summer 1991 former prime minister Jacques Chirac said he "understood" French people who had to put up with the "noise and stench" of their immigrant neighbors. Shortly after, Socialist premier Edith Cresson declared she saw no reason why illegal immigrants should not be packed back to their homeland "on chartered planes," thus approving a posteriori a much-criticized measure effectively taken by Right-wing minister of the interior, Charles Pasqua, in 1986. In fall 1991, former president of the Republic Valéry Giscard d'Estaing spoke of an "invasion" of immigrants and said it was time to abolish the *jus soli* so that French citizenship could only be acquired by *jus sanguinis,* that is, by having a French parent. This is one of Le Pen's prime goals. All of these slips, which were followed by rectifications in the press, were made in preelectoral periods. Nevertheless during the 1993 elections campaign the Right wingers made no secret of their intention to change the *code de la nationalité.* Pasqua was reappointed minister of the interior in the Balladur cabinet, destroying any illusions people might have to the contrary.

million Maghrebians who have arrived in less than half a century. As has been pointed out, "The 16 laws, 79 bills, 62 decrees and 220 instructions promulgated on this subject between 1981 and 1986 have enabled a lot to be accomplished."[13] However, in 1986, in the interval of right-wing government during President Mitterrand's first term in office, the repressive Pasqua law, designed to stop the flow of illegal immigrants, pushed the solution of social integration (housing, schooling) into the background. Upon the Left's return to power in 1988, their first step was to abrogate the Pascua law and vote a new, less repressive one, the loi Joxe. However, the legal and administrative measures that were taken in the interim to control the immigrant population created a climate of suspicion and clouded the other efforts made by the Socialists to work out a coherent approach to the problems posed by immigration. One of their more interesting initiatives was the High Council on Integration (le haut Conseil à l'intégration) set up by former premier Michel Rocard in 1989. The high council, with its nine members of differing political opinions, is a sort of think tank on integration. It would be a pity if the government elected in 1993 interfered with the necessary reflection on this complex process, because the main obstacle to integration in France is not political, social, or economic but cultural.

Integration

France has never been a multicultural society. Unlike the United States it assimilates individuals, not ethnic groups. In the words of former prime minister Michel Rocard, it cannot be "a juxtaposition of communities." It is a country that "stresses adherence to common values." As Robert Solé, explaining Rocard's position, remarked, French society "should not imitate Anglo-Saxon models that allow ethnic groups to barricade themselves in geographical and cultural ghettos leading to soft forms of apartheid."[14] In France the ghettos are not ethnic but social, that is, determined by the income level of the inhabitants (the existence of a minimum *integration* income shows that Maghrebians are not the only ones in need of integration in France) rather than by the color of their skin:

---

13. Guillaume Malaurie and Sylviane Stein, "Des papiers avant tout," *Les Cahiers de l'Express* 3, April 1990, 99.

14. Robert Solé, "Un modèle français d'intégration," *Le Monde*, 7 December 1989.

> A ghetto is a quarter defined by the national origin of its inhabitants. In France, the municipalites have always taken care to prevent quarters whose inhabitants belong to a single ethnic group from being established. There are quarters with a large number of immigrants, but people of different nationalities live there together, and there are always French people. There are no ghettos in the English or American sense. And it is in fact this absence of ghettos that allows children to mingle in schools.[15]

France looks with suspicion even on native minority cultures like those of the Basques, Bretons, or Corsicans.[16] Foreigners are expected to fit into the French mold, French thought processes, the French value system. In the French colonies of West Africa in the last century little black children recited by rote the opening lines of *Le Petit Lavisse:* "Long ago our country was called Gaul and its inhabitants were called Gauls. Our country has changed a great deal since then and we bear scarcely any resemblance to our forefathers the Gauls"! As was pointed out in an article in *Historia,* children of immigrant descent—one-third of the population in French elementary schools today—learn nothing about their ancestors. Even the most recent history textbooks begin with the ritual chapter on the Gauls.[17]

Previous tides of immigrants of European origin have gradually been assimilated in spite of initial hostility. Poles, Italians, Portuguese, and Spaniards are largely respected citizens today. Never until recent history has France had to face the arduous task of integrating a population whose language, religion, customs, and traditions are so foreign as those

---

15. "La France a mieux réussi que ses voisins." Dominique Schnapper, research director at L'Ecole des hautes études en sciences sociales, interviewed by Carole Barjon for *Le Nouvel Observateur,* 23–29 November 1989, 76–77.

16. During preliminary negotiation on the bill designed to grant increased autonomy to Corsica, the introduction of the term "the Corsican people" (*le peuple Corse*) into the bill's new statute proposal for the island created quite a stir. Favored by the Socialists, Communists, Corsican autonomists, and liberals, the expression was unacceptable to the conservatives. Approved by the National Assembly in 1990, the expression was declared unconstitutional in 1991 by the Constitutional Council, and the "Corsican people" disappeared from the new statutes for Corsica, baptized *collectivité territoriale* in 1992, that is, a territorial collectivity having a certain autonomy but forming an integral part of the French nation.

17. Suzanne Citron, "Nos ancêtres les Gaulois," *Historia* 2 (1989): 4–14.

The Immigrant Population

There have been three big waves of immigration in the twentieth century. The first occurred from 1921 to 1931, that is, just after World War I, in which 1.5 million Frenchmen lost their lives and another million were maimed for life. The principal national groups of this period were the Italians, followed by the Poles, the Spaniards, and the Belgians, who had already been predominant in the late nineteenth century. In 1946, after World War II, Spaniards, Italians, and Portuguese were the most numerous. In 1960–73, during the great French economic boom, there was massive immigration from North Africa.

In 1974 immigration was officially suspended, but some 100,000 foreigners a year continue to enter the country legally with a work permit through family reunification programs—37,000 in 1990—or as refugees. Nowadays, the Portugese are the largest single national group of immigrants, but the combined North African population (Algerians, Tunisians, Moroccans) represents more than 40 percent of the immigrant community.

of the Maghrebians. It was all very fine to live with "these people" in colonies dominated by the French. It is a different kettle of fish when your next door neighbor, a "guest worker," keeps you awake at night during Ramadan or insists that his daughters wear a veil to school, or demands permission to build a mosque on your doorstep. There are limits to exotism! After all, when in France do as the French do! Nothing in their education or upbringing has prepared the French public for this cultural shock. They have always believed that France was the center of the world. They feel threatened in their very essence and conjure up images of Islamic fanaticism and terrorism that they believed Charles Martel had eradicated for good more than a thousand years ago at the Battle of Poitiers!

However, this stereotype of the ethnocentric Frenchman, like all stereotypes, is unfair. Not only because many of the French, particularly young people, have foreign friends and respect their life-style; not only because the number of interracial marriages (8.7 percent)—a quarter of which involve Maghrebians—is higher than that in the United States (1 percent);[18]

18. Malaurie and Stein, "Des papiers avant tout," 101. See also André Lebon, *Immigration et présence étrangère en France 1990–1991: Les données, les faits* (Paris: La Documentation Française, 1992). According to this study more than twenty-six thousand interracial marriages were performed in 1989, that is, 9.3 percent of all marriages.

but because few nations, as Julia Kristeva has shown, take on so honestly the debate on racism.[19]

In many countries foreigners or out-groups are treated with cynicism, disdain, or indifference. As long as they do not upset the peace, as long as they stay in their ghettos, they can smoke, drug, and drink themselves to death. "I'd like to give Mr. President my honest regards for disregarding me," sings Tracy Chapman with her tear-wrenching voice. Never in France. The stranger is an object of curiosity, of hate or of love, never of indifference. By their very nature, the immigrants challenge the whole concept of the unity of the national culture that successive monarchs and the Republic have striven to preserve with the massive assent of the population. The long tradition of nationalism in France, according to Julia Kristeva, is very different from, say, the German Romantic concept based on the "cult of blood" and the cult of a "mystical language" that was to degenerate into Nazism. President Mitterrand sums it up nicely: "France is first and foremost a land, a history, a culture."[20] Race is not the distinctive feature of French patriotism.

Openness

The French preoccupation with the idea of nationhood corresponds to their obsessive questioning of their identity. In his scholarly *Nous et les autres*, Tzvetan Todorov traces the debate on the dual concept of ethnocentricity and universality from Pascal and Montaigne to Rousseau, Montesquieu, and Lévi-Strauss.[21] No nation has striven more to understand its uniqueness and thus to position itself in relation to other nations: Frenchness versus foreignness. This public debate explains the singular status of the foreigner in France: "in the presence of so much national and nationalistic candidness (*transparence*) the foreigner feels he is ignored, unrecognized, nonexistent: there is no room for him, he can only survive by relinquishing his identity, by becoming French," says Kristeva. "Yet," she goes on, "there is an advantage in this exclusion. In France,

19. Julia Kristeva, "Les deux défis de l'identité française," *Le Monde*, 21 February 1989.

20. André Fontaine, Jacques Amalric, Jean-Marie Colombani, "Un entretien avec M. François Mitterrand," *Le Monde*, 20 June 1990.

21. Tzvetan Todorov, *Nous et les autres* (Paris: Editions du Seuil, 1989).

the foreigner becomes less hypocritically and less shamefully than elsewhere a subject of debate. He is not invited to [French] homes and he has no legal status, but he exists because he preoccupies. Moralists, jurists, artists make a 'problem' of him."[22]

The debate on foreigners questions a person's capacity to mingle with others (rather than parking them in a ghetto). It is not only a political and legal question but a question of ethics as old as human existence: "From this point of view," writes Kristeva, "the debate on foreigners in France has the privilege of representing an advanced stage of civilization, which allows one to hope that the best possible solutions will be found to guarantee, not only social but also political and cultural liberties for foreigners."[23]

Hands off My Buddy

There has been a shift in the French approach to the question of how to deal with foreignness since the early 1980s, when, following the second oil crisis and soaring unemployment, the problem of immigration was brought into public focus by the FN. In the euphoric aftermath of Mitterrand's election and a Socialist National Assembly majority for the first time in the history of the Fifth Republic, reaction to Le Pen—he scored his first political success in the city hall elections in 1983—was healthy, exuberant, and generous. SOS-Racisme, a multiracial group that counted numerous celebrities among its members, epitomized this spirit with its famous badge, *Touche pas à mon pote* (Hands off my buddy). Harlem Desire, a philosophy graduate born to a French mother and an Antillean father, seemed predestined by his very name (authentic) to become the president of the association, founded by a group of "buddies" in 1984. The movement was to symbolize the new media-centered, good-humored approach to improving the image of minority groups. The writer-philosopher Bernard-Henri Lévy and the film star Valérie Kaprisky were among early supporters. Meanwhile, singers Jean-Jacques Goldman and Daniel Balavoine moved thousands of fans with their lyrics stressing the richness of ethnic diversity, while Renaud's mordant "Hexagone," which had been banned from the radio in the 1970s because it was considered unpatriotic, was on the lips of every teenager. Coluche, the popular

22. Kristeva, "Les deux défis."
23. Kristeva, "Les deux défis."

music hall artist, engaged in boisterous, disparaging criticism of the nationalistic mentality with coarse Gallic humor: "Why is the cock the emblem of the French?—Because it is the only animal that can crow with its feet stuck in dung." Coluche, who ran for the presidency in 1981 and campaigned on television with a feather adorning his behind—the cockerel!—was killed in a motorcycle accident in 1988 but continues from beyond the grave to represent for teenagers the joyous antidote to Le Pen.

In the early 1980s there was an openness, a joie de vivre, among the antiracist supporters that has since disappeared. The four and a half million French people who voted for Le Pen in 1988, Islamic fanaticism (terrorism, the Salman Rushdie death threat), and the Persian Gulf War have poisoned the debate. SOS-Racisme, which was able to muster three hundred thousand supporters to a rock concert with the group Téléphone in place de la Concorde in Paris in 1985 and grill *merguez* (spiced sausages popular in Algeria) in front of the uptight Maxim's restaurant, keeps a lower profile today. In spite of its ambiguous defense of the right of Muslim children to wear the veil in school, inspired by the tactical consideration that tolerance is the best means to combat Islamic fundamentalism ("Blue jeans will end up by ousting the *tchador* (veil)," declared Harlem Desire), the strategy of the movement has changed.[24] The exalted cry of "Multicultural youth are the France of tomorrow" has given way to "Integration works when you do something about it."[25] SOS-Racisme is now dealing with the more humble but no less effective task of building up a network in the urban trouble areas to facilitate the everyday task of integrating the immigrants into the French social fabric. The *maisons des potes* (buddy homes) offer a variety of services, ranging from helping children with their schoolwork to the sale of concert tickets. Meanwhile France Plus is patiently pursuing its strategy of gaining a hearing in local politics: "One *beur* elected is better than several antiracist demonstrations."[26] Five hundred second-generation immigrants were elected in the last local elections. The antiracist groups are no longer proclaiming the "right to be different." Even the right of foreigners

24. Philippe Bernard, "Le recentrage de SOS racisme," *Le Monde*, 2 July 1991.

25. Bertrand le Gendre, "A quoi sert SOS-racisme?" *Le Monde*, 9 January 1990.

26. Robert Solé, "Un entretien avec le président de France Plus," *Le Monde*, 7 April 1990.

to vote in local elections, long promised, but never accorded by the Socialists and a major source of politicking, is no longer considered a priority by those working in the field.[27] Slowly but surely the extraordinary national cohesion is exercising its power of attraction to the detriment of multiculturalism. This trend is in conformity with the long history of immigration in France. Of course there is resistance as the sporadic outbreaks of violence in the ZUP show and the anti-immigrant ticket of Le Pen is still likely to pay electoral dividends, as the results of the 1992 and 1993 elections have proved. But integration seems inevitable in the long run. The question is: at what price?[28]

Europe

Does this mean that the foreigners have been had, that the only way to have peace is to conform, that multiculturalism has no place? Probably. Yet, some people are beginning to question the viability of the French approach for the long run. Can a France called upon to relinquish its nationalism in a united Europe afford to turn a blind eye to the powerful east-west, north-south migratory movement? Can a rich, rapidly aging Europe, which according to United Nations projections will account in twenty years for only 4.7 percent of a world population that will have grown 39 percent, afford to ignore the message that illegal immigration is sending? The European democracies, says researcher Jacqueline Costa-Lacrou, should construct a Europe where crossborder mobility will not be limited to a privileged few, a Europe in which "cleavages between a

27. Many *beurs* deny these organizations, which receive governmental subsidies, the right to speak in the name of an extremely diverse population. The second-generation immigrants are far from forming a homogeneous group, and their self-designated representatives, sometimes referred to as the *beurgeois* (a pun on "bourgeois") by fellow *beurs*, have received no popular mandate. Thus, "Nobody can prove, for example, that the young girls of Maghrebian origin are for or against wearing the veil to school" (Azouz Begag and Abdellatif Chaouite, *Ecarts d'identité* [Paris: Editions du Seuil, 1990], 85). Likewise, it is difficult to know the real sentiment of the *beurs* concerning the right to vote in local elections. But this does not excuse the refusal of the French to envisage this reform. A golden opportunity to further integration was lost with the constitutional amendment necessary to permit the ratification of the Maastricht treaty, when even the right of other Europeans to vote in France was only reluctantly admitted!

28. Begag and Chaouite, *Ecarts d'identité*, 9.

cosmopolitan elite, a fourth world 'nailed to the ground,' and an illegal underclass will have to be avoided."[29] This implies a much broader vision than the present tracking down of illegal immigrants authorized in the Schengen agreements.[30] It also involves the question of improving relations with the national populations. What are the limits to multiculturalism? Does respect of ethnic difference mean that European countries should condone practices such as genital mutilation or polygamy?[31] A "clearly defined contract of citizenship based on the rights of Man" may offer a badly needed legal framework for multiracial Europe but will it end intolerance in an area where the respect of strangers, says Julia Kristeva, begins with the acceptance of our own strangeness?[32]

---

29. Jacqueline Costa-Lacrou, "Pour 'un nouveau contrat social' européen," *Les Cahiers de l'Express*, 3, April 1990, 105.

30. The agreements (1985 and 1991) first signed in Schengen (Luxembourg) between the Benelux countries, France, and Germany, later joined by Italy, Spain, and Portugal, are designed to harmonize legislation on immigration in the countries of the signatories. An immigrant entering any one of the countries will require a standardized visa valid for all. In addition, if he or she is declared a persona non grata in any state, that person will be banned from all the member states. There will be close cooperation between the signatories of the agreement, and an SIS (Schengen Information System) will be set up containing data on hundreds of thousands of people suspect to the authorities (people the police are looking for, undesirable individuals, or those who are to be under surveillance). There will be penalties for airline and maritime companies transporting travelers who do not have the required immigration documents. One of the main goals of the agreement is to define which country will grant political asylum, so that applicants will not be passed on from one country to another, but in fact this will probably limit their chances of obtaining satisfaction. The addendum to the 1985 convention was signed by France in July 1991. See Danièle Lochak, "La politique de l'immigration au risque des amalgames," in Cordellier, *L'état de la France 1992*, 560–65.

31. In matters of marriage and divorce foreigners residing in France are governed by the legislation of their home country. Muslim law (e.g., the right to repudiate one's wife, polygamy) and customary law (genital mutilation) are obviously in conflict with French legislation. Without actually recommending the British and American practice whereby foreigners are submitted to the same legislation as the citizens of the country of residence the High Council on Integration has urged tighter measures be taken by the application of existing laws on human rights, and law and order. Philippe Bernard, "Le Haut Conseil de l'intégration estime que les beurs devraient faire leur service militaire en France," *Le Monde*, 6 February 1992.

32. Julia Kristeva, *Etrangers à nous-mêmes* (Paris: Fayard, 1988), 269.

PART 6

Right, Left, and Center

In two centuries 1787 to 1987 the Americans have had only one constitution and twenty-six amendments. In France, over the same period, we have lived under three monarchies, two empires, five republics, without mentioning the "French State" of Vichy. We have used up thirteen written constitutions without counting the additional decrees and amendments.

—Robert Badinter, president of the Constitutional Council

13

The Fifth Republic

In recent history, no nation in the world has had such a varied political experience as France, and it is hardly surprising that the former Eastern bloc countries should be asking the French for advice on how to draw up their new constitutions. The French may not be able to tell the Hungarians and Romanians what to do, but at least they can show them what not to do!

It is significant that French has no specific term to translate the concept contained in the English word *policy*, which suggests a pragmatic course of action. *La Politique*, that is, politics with a capital *P*, is at the core of French thought processes, however much pundits may deplore the increasing apathy of the political scene today. Ideas and attitudes concerning the most innocent issues are still mentally cataloged "Right" or "Left" even if the differences between the parties representing these concepts are no longer clearcut and if the class war is considered a thing of the past.

In fact that is precisely what bothers the French, who are losing their traditional bearings and have so far found nothing to replace these ideological references. Moreover, they find nothing in the present-day political scene to quench their thirst for exaltation and polemic. There is no longer any *grand dessein*—no enemy on the doorstep to be attacked, no empire to be defended or dismantled, no reconstruction to be undertaken, no Gaullian ambition to admire or criticize—only the humdrum management of inflation and the growth rate.

Not that there is a dearth of issues: education, poverty, unemployment, the environment, unresolved ethical questions linked to medical progress (frozen embryos, surrogate motherhood, euthanasia), drugs, violence, immigration are all in need of attention. But these issues are considered more civic than political questions according to a new French view of things. It is politics with a small *p*. Some commentators, like Alain Duhamel, are delighted with this disarming of traditional politics, in which they see an opportunity for the development of greater participative democracy on the U.S. model, a new approach to issues in which ordinary citizens have a greater say in decisions that concern them directly. However, others like sociologist Alain Touraine, while welcoming the demise of party politics that subject the desires of the people to an ideology, warn against the dangers of the widening gap between politicians and society: "France has become Americanized and is drawing farther and farther away from the social democratic model, that is, the bond between the social players and the political agents. This Americanization has many advantages, but it bears negative effects that have marked American social and public life for a long time: violence, racism, the indifference of public opinion to political issues."[1]

Such indifference, which is indeed taken for granted by the average U.S. citizen, is a totally new phenomenon in France. This probably explains the alarming headlines and overreaction of political commentators. Yet, it might be hasty to predict the death of politics in a country nurtured on ideological divisions for two centuries. The old political cleavages have the habit of springing up when they are least expected, as Right- and Left-wing governments learned to their cost in the 1980s. Opinion polls regularly show that the French favor the development of a less conflictual society (*une société plus consensuelle*) on what they call "the Anglo-Saxon model." Yet, as one journalist points out, when the Right-Left border becomes blurred, when a Socialist prime minister strives to develop consensus, the response is "boredom, indifference, or resignation, indeed even sarcasm. Just as if the French who used to complain about the 'war of words' between political parties preferred it to the Anglo-Saxon model. Just as if the voters, deprived of their old bearings—or refusing to accept the new—were becoming skeptical and ill-humored."[2]

The present-day political division of France between Right and Left is not a recent phenomenon. Contrary to the United States, which is gun-shy of ideology but at home with a capitalistic value system, there has never been an ideological consensus on the type of society the French want, although nearly all political parties pay lip service at least to the Republican ideals of liberty, equality, and fraternity printed in large letters over the entrance to every one of the 36,394 town halls across the country.

---

1. Alain Touraine, "Aux portes de la violence," *Le Monde*, 7 May 1988.
2. Jean-Louis Andréani, "M. Rocard dans les turbulences," *Le Monde*, 6 December 1989.

The Revolution overthrew the monarchy, putting an end to a system of government founded on the privileges of the ruling classes (aristocracy and clergy), but consensus on Republican values can only be said to have been achieved in the late nineteenth century when the Catholics abandoned the royalist ultras to join (albeit reluctantly) the ranks of the Republicans.

While the possibility of a restoration of the monarchy today is very remote, at least two political parties in democratic France—the Communists and the extreme right-wing National Front—subscribe to ideologies that seem to imply authoritarian regimes. On the other hand, the constitution itself, fashioned by Charles de Gaulle for himself in 1958, gives greater powers to the executive than in most other Western democracies, and the president of the Republic, elected directly by the people, is said to be a "constitutional monarch." Nevertheless, the French seem to be at home with a constitution that has survived the troubled withdrawal from Algeria, the major political crisis of the 1968 student riots, the left-wing electoral victory of 1981, and the acid test of *cohabitation* from 1986 to 1988, which proved that power sharing between a right-wing prime minister and a left-wing president was possible.[3] Indeed it is ironic that the incumbent president, the Socialist François Mitterrand, who was bitterly opposed to the 1958 constitution because of the preponderance it gave to the head of state—it legitimized, he wrote, "a permanent coup d'etat"—should be one of its staunchest defenders today.[4] Whatever its drawbacks, it has to be admitted that the constitution accomplished what it set out to do. Only the Third Republic lasted as long as has the Fifth, and none has enjoyed greater institutional stability.

---

3. The crushing defeat of the Left in the 1993 legislative elections may put unprecedented pressure on the president. Only time will tell if Mitterrand's second cohabitation with a right-wing parliamentary majority will survive the inevitable tensions. Cohabitation between a Republican president and a Democratic Congress in the United States poses no such difficulty because, unlike France, the executive is not responsible before the House of Representatives and cannot be overthrown with a vote of no confidence. In addition, there are no highly structured political parties that impose a strict voting discipline on their members. (Many of the forty-three French deputies who dared defy their party's policy in the Persian Gulf crisis were treated as outcasts by their respective parties.) Finally, in the United States, "the search for a necessary compromise is considered the very essence of democracy, which is conceived only in terms of victory or defeat in France." Alfred Grosser, "L'héritage gaullien assumé," *Le Monde*, 4 September 1985.

4. François Mitterrand, *Le coup d'état permanent* (Paris: Plon, 1964).

Two Hundred and Forty-six Varieties of Cheese

The first French republic (1792) ended in the revolutionary bloodbath and fell into the hands of Napoleon Bonaparte (1799). A coup d'etat, by another Bonaparte, put an end to the short-lived Second Republic (1848–52). The third, which had 110 different governments in seventy years (1870 to 1940), was seized by Marshall Pétain in occupied France, while the fourth (1944–58), notorious for the instability of its successive ministries and incapable of solving the Algerian crisis, turned itself over to a retired general who made no secret of his intention to bridle Parliament and set up a strong executive branch. The history of the Republic in France seems to suggest that the French are incapable of reconciling democracy and efficiency. That is what de Gaulle set out to do, and that is what distinguishes him from his dictatorial predecessors. It was to be the aim of the constitution of the Fifth Republic, inspired by its first president, who felt it was necessary "for new democratic institutions to offset, in all independence, the consequences of our perpetual political agitation."[5]

De Gaulle had little faith in the capacity of his so-called Cartesian compatriots for self-government. "How can you govern a country with 246 different varieties of cheese?" was one of his more picturesque observations. Deep down the French themselves subscribe to this self-caricature, which flatters their individualism and may explain, in part, why four out of five voters ratified a constitution that is potentially dangerous. President Mitterrand himself has declared, "These institutions were dangerous before me; they will be after me."[6] But the personality of General de Gaulle—the hero of mythical dimensions of the French Resistance, the "savior" emerging like some twentieth century Joan of Arc from the history of the nation, whose integrity and unadulterated love of his country could not be questioned—and his pledge of allegiance to the Republic, were apparently a sufficient guarantee for the voters in 1958.

Three Palaces for the People

America has the White House and Capitol Hill. France is governed from three Parisian palaces.

---

5. Excerpt from de Gaulle's famous speech in Bayeux on 16 June 1946, in which he outlined his conception of the future constitution of France.

6. Quoted by Jean-Yves l'Homeau, "Une institution devenue mitterrandienne . . . ," *Le Monde*, 23 January 1988.

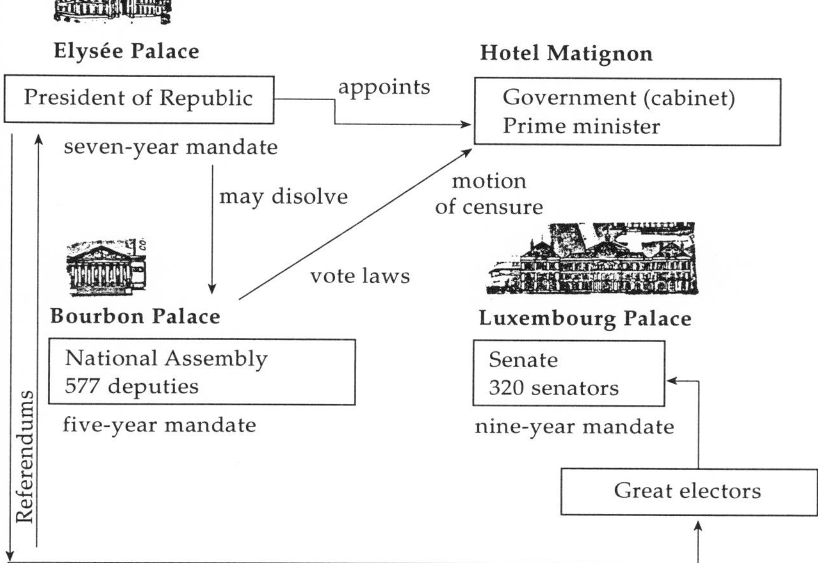

FIG. 18. Three palaces for the people

Executive Powers

The Elysée Palace: The President

> The president of the Republic can do everything; the president of the Republic does everything; the president of the Republic substitutes for the government, the government for the Parliament, therefore, the president of the Republic substitutes for the Parliament; the president of the Republic takes care of everything, even the parks on the banks of the Seine![7]

This was how then Socialist *député* (member of the National Assembly) François Mitterrand ironically described the presidency at the National Assembly in 1979, less than two years before he was to replace Valéry Giscard d'Estaing as fourth president of the Fifth Republic. The situation has not changed fundamentally since that date, and the man who

7. Jean-Yves L'Homeau, "Le gardien laisse sa marque," *Le Monde Dossiers et Documents: Bilan du Septennat*, 1988, 36–40.

fought the constitution for twenty-three years has not undertaken any major institutional reform. The regal trappings of the presidency have not disappeared, and Plantu, the genial cartoonist of *Le Monde*, has immortalized the double "reign" of Mitterrand the First and Mitterrand the Second.

The 1958 constitution and the amendment of 1962, which provides for the election of the president by universal suffrage, give a status to the presidency that no other European democracy confers. The president is over and above the political parties and is accountable only to the people. This one person represents the nation to the same degree as the 577 members of the National Assembly! The president cannot be impeached except for "high treason." Only the president is entitled to organize a national referendum on the draft of a bill—a referendum that can be taken as a plebiscite for the president in office.[8] Moreover, if the president feels that Parliament is encroaching on the powers of the executive, the issue can be referred to the Constitutional Council—originally conceived as "a canon aimed at Parliament"—of which the president designates three of the nine members including the head.[9]

He also appoints the nine members of the High Council of the Magistracy, which is a disciplinary body for court judges. In France, judges are appointed by the Garde des sceaux (high chancellor) who, as minister of justice, owes his own appointment to the president of the Republic. As history professor Alain Monchablon states, "Historically, in France, the magistracy has never played a major role in the defense of civil liberties." They have always been very close to the executive, and in 1941 only one magistrate refused to take the oath of allegiance to the Vichy regime. The others swore "fidelity to the person of the head of

8. According to the constitution, referendums should be held on the initiative of the Parliament or premier and *organized* by the president. In fact de Gaulle personally decided on each of the referendums that took place under his presidency.

9. The Gaullist constitution made a distinction between the *domain of law* (article 34), within which Parliament was free to legislate, and the *domain of regulation* (article 37), within which the executive could act through decree. Throughout the 1960s the main role of the council was to "police the frontier" between law and regulation. See John T. S. Keeler and Alec Stone, "Judicial-Political Confrontation in Mitterrand's France," in *The Mitterrand Experiment*, ed. George Ross, Stanley Hoffmann, and Sylvia Malzacher (Oxford: Polity Press, 1987), 161–81. The Constitutional Council today has a far less restricted role. (See the last section of this chapter.)

state."[10] Magistrates, appointed and not elected, are considered high-level civil servants. Politicians always fear that they may abuse their power and set up a "government of judges." The corollary of this is the thorny question of their independence.

The prime minister, designated by the president, and the *gouvernement*, that is, the cabinet or policy-making body consisting of senior ministers, share the executive powers with him but depend for their survival on the person in the Elysée Palace, who can change the government (cabinet) at any time, although, theoretically, it is the National Assembly that has the power to overthrow the premier. In practice, no premier has ever refused to comply with the presidential request to step down, although they may smart under the humiliation as both Michel Rocard and Edith Cresson did. In this respect, the British prime minister, who is only responsible to Parliament, enjoys far greater autonomy than the French one. Also, French prime ministers have usually had little say in the appointment of cabinet members. Even the right-wing prime minister Jacques Chirac had to seek presidential approval for some of his appointees in 1986. However, the Right made it quite clear before the second cohabitation period in 1993 that the President would have no say in cabinet appointments.

Contrary to the practice in other countries, the head of state—in whose absence no decision can be taken—presides over the weekly meeting of the Conseil de ministres, that is, the Council of Ministers. (While the term *ministre* is often translated in American English by "secretary of state"—e.g., ministre de la défense, secretary of state for defense—a *sécrétaire d'état* in France has a slightly lower status than a minister and does not attend the council unless invited.) The presidential signature is required for decrees drawn up by the Council of Ministers, even those concerning the appointment of top civil servants. This includes highly sensitive posts such as those occupied by the CEOs of nationalized industrial groups. On the other hand the president can refuse to sign the ordinances submitted by the government—as Mitterrand did for the privatization ordinances submitted by Chirac—and can order a law to be reexamined before promulgating it. The head of state can even dissolve the National Assembly and, in extreme circumstances, use the emergency powers conferred by the constitution to take any measures deemed

10. Alain Monchablon, *Le livre du citoyen* (Paris: Editions la Découverte, 1987), 155.

The Odd Couple

The position of premier in the Fifth Republic is a coveted one because it is the natural stepping stone to the presidency. (By the same token, the party leadership is important because it is a springboard for the position of premier.) This means that the prime minister is a potential rival of the president in office, and the more efficient or popular the former is, the more the latter fears a "stab in the back." Georges Pompidou set the example by announcing he would run for office before de Gaulle had declared the race had started.

Pierre Servent* analyzes three phases in the relationship between the odd couple that the president of the Fifth Republic and his prime minister represent. After the initial honeymoon, the relations turn sour, and the end result is divorce. The "unnatural" union between François Mitterrand and Michel Rocard confirmed this analysis. Their turbulent relations prior to 1988, when Rocard was tempted to run for the presidency, did not prevent a two-year honeymoon, as the popularity ratings of the couple indicated. However, a number of barely concealed criticisms of governmental policy by the head of state in 1990 showed the increasing tension between the premier and the president and divorce was inevitable. Had the wily Mitterrand made his enemy premier the better to crush him—the "kiss of death" technique† that he has so often used in his political career?

Mr. Rocard's successor, Madame Cresson, was to have the shortest honeymoon, although her relations with the president remained good to the end. Her dismissal after ten months illustrates another function of the prime minister, which is to serve as a shield, indeed a scapegoat, for the chief of state in times of difficulty. Madame Cresson's departure from Hotel Matignon after the disastrous performance of the Socialists in the regional and cantonal elections in March 1992 was thus necessary to mask the president's share of guilt in the downfall of the Socialists.

Of course, as the title of Pierre Servent's book—*Oedipus at Matignon*—indicates, the relationship between "the couple" is more like a father-son relationship in which the son tries to kill his father than a marriage contract in which each partner has the same rights and duties.

*Pierre Servent, *Oedipe à Matignon* (Paris: Editions Balland, 1989).

†Franz-Olivier Giesbert, *Le Président* (Paris: Editions du Seuil, 1990), 74.

necessary in the interest of the country. While these latter powers, which were used by de Gaulle to fight threatened subversion during the Algerian crisis, are temporary, they really authorize the use of dictatorial methods. Finally, the president is chief of the armed forces and alone can decide the use of the nuclear bomb. The preeminence of the presidential role was confirmed during the Persian Gulf War, when all the operational decisions were taken at the Elysée and the prime minister was reduced to supervising the nonmilitary aspects of the crisis.

The list of presidential prerogatives shows how successful the founder of the Fifth Republic was in his attempt to replace an omnipotent Parliament by an omnipotent president, a far cry from Clemenceau's cynical assessment of the role of the head of state: "There is only one organ as useless as the prostate; it is the president of the Republic."[11]

Introduced as a temporary expedient, the seven-year presidential mandate replaced the four-year term in 1873 and persists to this day in spite of the promises of all de Gaulle's successors to reduce it to five years. Public opinion would seem to favor a reduction. According to a 1984 poll 64 percent of those interviewed were in favor of a five-year mandate.

Hôtel Matignon: The Government

The presidential palace, the Palais de l'Elysée, has got what pundits frequently refer to as *l'annexe.* This is the city mansion, Hôtel Matignon, which is the headquarters of *le gouvernement* (the cabinet). The main aim of the 1958 constitution is to "allow the government to govern." Although the government emanates from the presidency, the constitution gives considerable powers to this part of the executive branch, especially where Parliament is concerned. As master of the parliamentary timetable the government engineers most legislation, since it decides when its bills should be discussed. In fact it is misleading, in the Fifth Republic, to use the term *executive* for the government, which not only executes laws but makes them.[12] There are only a small number of private members' bills: "More than nine out of ten laws are of governmental origin, and the legislative role is increasingly limited to exercising the right of amendment."[13]

If Parliament is uncooperative or stalls on issues, the government can even bypass parliamentary debate by issuing decrees. The thorny aspects of bills opposed by the National Assembly will frequently become law

---

11. Monchablon, *Le livre du citoyen,* 95.

12. Jean-Louis Quermonne and Dominique Chagnollaud, *Le gouvernement de la France sous la Vème République,* 4th ed. (Paris: Dalloz, 1991), 207.

13. Alain Duhamel, "La sclérose des institutions," *Le Monde,* 30 October 1989.

this way. Another procedure the executive can use for the sake of expediency is the vote of confidence on legislation it wishes to push through. This is the famous—or infamous—article 49.3 of the constitution, which has been likened to the serial number of a six-shooter. It is designed "to shoot down" the opposition. Highly controversial decisions are thus taken with little or no parliamentary control, because bills that are made an issue of confidence are considered adopted unless a motion of censure is put forward in twenty-four hours and adopted by an absolute majority. In this way, "a decision as essential as the setting up of the nuclear deterrent force" was adopted without any parliamentary vote![14] Of course, if the deputies refuse to approve the government, it can be overthrown. However, the presidential prerogative of dissolution of the National Assembly is a powerful incentive for recalcitrant members of the majority, their allies—or even the opposition—to toe the govenmental line. Another gambit that may be used for the sake of expediency is the take-it-or-leave-it *vote bloqué* (package vote), which allows the government to bypass article-by-article discussion of a bill.

For a foreign observer of French institutions the question that springs to mind is why de Gaulle bothered to set up two executive branches—the presidency and government—considering the omnipotence of the president of the Republic. Yet, article 20 of the constitution clearly states that "the government decides and implements national policy." Legend has it that when someone suggested amending the constitution to put an end to this ambiguity, de Gaulle tugged his suspenders and answered that it was necessary to preserve "all the elasticity" of the original text. As Jean-Marie Colombani has pointed out, that was what made cohabitation between a Socialist president and a right-wing government possible between 1986 and 1988.[15] This was also to be the case after the victory of the right wing in the legislative elections of 1993.

Legislative Powers

The Bourbon Palace: The National Assembly

The National Assembly has 577 members elected for five years by the people. The presidential prerogative of organizing a referendum and the

14. Monchablon, *Le livre du citoyen,* 113.

15. *Le Monde Dossiers et Documents: Les Trente Ans de la 5ème République,* September 1988, 1.

election of the president by the people mean that Parliament is no longer the sole representative of the nation. The nature of the French constitution and the electoral system favor bipolarization, the development of two major political blocs. On the one hand, the government needs the support of a strong majority, and, on the other hand, the opposition needs to be united to effectively counterbalance the preponderance of the executive. This tends to aggravate the cleavage between Right and Left. The smaller political parties are wooed by both, and they have little choice but to support one or the other. They thus become the arbiters between the extremes, and the whole art of government in France consists in treading the thin line between Left and Right, in other words, governing from left or right of center.

The father of the French constitution set out to bridle Parliament and succeeded admirably. The trouble is that issues that never make it to the National Assembly tend to explode in the streets. The unexpected outbreaks of social unrest, the massive demonstrations that from time to time threaten the government in power, the periodic strikes are signs of the exasperation of voters who are without a political hearing. Of the hundred or so laws passed each year, 90 percent are government initiated, although the number of private members' bills that never reach the floor of the National Assembly exceed in number the bills proposed by the government. If it is true that the Third and Fourth Republics mocked the voters with a parliamentary majority they had not even voted for as a result of party maneuvering, the National Assembly in the Fifth Republic has become merely an echo chamber for governmental policy. In these circumstances, it is hardly surprising that absenteeism is very high. Historian and politician Jean-Noel Jeanneney relates that one day an eminent industrialist who was a *deputé* created "quite a stir" when he arrived in the middle of a session and had to be accompanied to his seat, having no idea where it was![16] Officially a representative should be present in the assembly to vote but proxy voting is common practice.

The National Assembly is not entirely powerless and has, for example, the right to propose amnesty—a privilege it does not always use judiciously, as a recent example shows. (The amnesty granted in 1989 to politicians involved in illegal political fund-raising has poisoned public debate and discredited the assembly.) The National Assembly can also censure the government. To do so, at least 10 percent of the deputies

16. Jean-Noel Jeanneney, *L'argent caché* (Paris: Le Seuil, 1984), 54.

must lay down a motion of censure (article 49.2). If in the ensuing ballot a majority of the representatives vote in favor of the motion, the government has to resign. (Abstentions and absences are counted as positive votes for the government.) On account of the bipolar political setup, reflected in the composition of the assembly, this is difficult to pull off, and only one of the motions of censure voted over the past thirty-two years actually worked. This was in 1962, when the National Assembly refused to approve de Gaulle's referendum on the question of the election of the president by the people (formerly he was elected by an electoral college of ninety thousand leading citizens, of which a majority were mayors of smaller, politically conservative, rural municipalities). Undaunted by this defeat, de Gaulle promptly dissolved the assembly, and in the ensuing elections, an overwhelming Gaullist majority came to power and ratified the referendum, a triumph for the general! As political commentator André Laurens wrote, "the French [thus] approved twice the presidentialization of the regime."[17] In 1992, the newly appointed Bérégovoy cabinet was within three votes of being overthrown on a motion of censure laid down in reaction to "the government's brutal announcement of the reform of the [EC] common agricultural policy." This was the closest shave for any cabinet in thirty years.

Checks and Balances

The constitution of the Fifth Republic is a subtle and unique blend of authoritarianism and parliamentary democracy. Before granting full powers to General de Gaulle in 1958, the National Assembly of the time laid down a certain number of democratic principles that de Gaulle accepted (appointment by the president of the Republic, approval by the assembly). Whatever misgivings one may have about the functioning of the institutions, one has to admit that ultimately, as in any democracy, power is in the hands of the voters. The "elasticity" of the constitution permits a wider interpretation of the text than might appear at first sight. Thus, while the French president appears to have dictatorial powers since he can dissolve the National Assembly, things are not so simple in practice. For example, in 1986 when the right-wing coalition ousted the Socialists and their Communist allies in the legislative elections, François

17. André Laurens, "L'élection du Président au suffrage universel," *Le Monde*, 29–30 March 1981.

Mitterrand, the Socialist president elected in 1981, still had two years left in office. This was the first time in the twenty-three year history of the Fifth Republic that the National Assembly majority was of a different political cast from the president of the Republic, and François Mitterrand had four options: resign; dissolve the National Assembly and hold new elections with the thin hope of obtaining a left-wing majority; appoint a left-wing or middle-of-the-road prime minister; or appoint a right-wing prime minister.

Had the president adopted one of the first three solutions, he would have shown himself to be a "Socialist" and partisan president rather than the impartial *président de tous les français* that all his predecessors had always proclaimed themselves to be. Public opinion would never have tolerated this abuse of presidential prerogative. Consciously or unconsciously, the voters, by returning a right-wing majority, seemed to be seeking a new balance of power between the executive branch and the National Assembly, as all too often in the Fifth Republic the assembly had become simply an echo chamber for governmental/presidential policy.

Nevertheless, as subsequent events showed, the French did not seem to want to go back to the parliamentary instability of the Fourth Republic, when there were twenty-five different governments in the space of thirteen years. The sometimes clumsy attempts of the impulsive, right-wing prime minister appointed by Mitterrand, Jacques Chirac, to undermine presidential authority probably explain, in part, his defeat in the 1988 presidential election. In a memorable preelection debate on public television, Chirac, stung by his adversary's sarcasm, addressed the outgoing president as "Mister Mitterrand"—instead of *Monsieur le Président*—while the latter continued to counter with the respectful (and in this case, ironic) *Monsieur le Premier Ministre.* Apparently the French were shocked by this act of lèse-majesté on the part of Chirac, and the president was announced winner of this decisive debate.

In any case, Mitterrand was reelected, putting an end to cohabitation. Yet, when he dissolved the National Assembly to try to impose a left-wing majority, the voters did not give the Left the landslide victory it expected. The right-wing majority in opposition held 268 seats in the 577-member National Assembly and prevented the government from treating the assembly high-handedly. Informed public opinion thus counterbalances the risks of abuse inherent in the 1958 constitution.

The composition of the 1988 assembly showed the political maturity

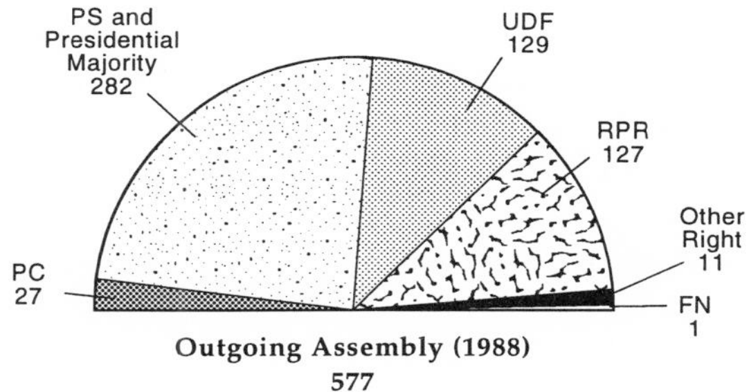

Outgoing assembly (1988)

PC; PS including Left-wing radicals and presidential majority; UDF; RPR; other Right (non-affiliated); FN.

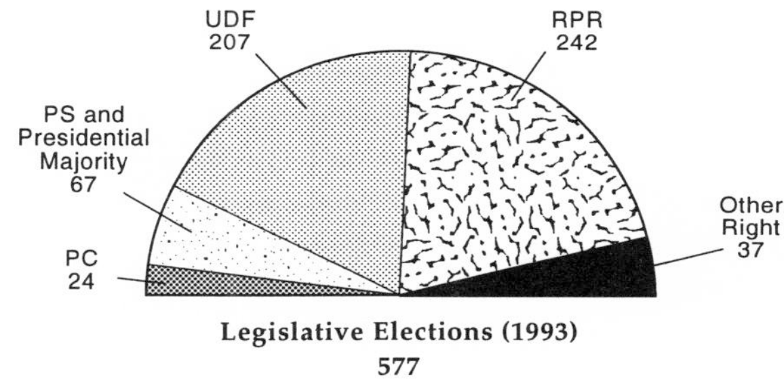

Legislative elections of 28 March 1993

PC; PS including Left-wing radicals and presidential majority; UDF; RPR; other Right.

FIG. 19. The National Assembly in 1993 and in 1988

French voters had achieved. The extremists, the Communists and the National Front, held few seats (twenty-seven and one respectively) while the slight left-wing lead of twenty-one obliged the Socialists to compromise with other political forces on major issues. Pragmatism seemed to have replaced dogmatism in French politics as voters became aware that neither the Left nor the Right had ready-made solutions to the problems facing France in the late eighties. This was an entirely new behavior that was underscored in the 1992 regional elections, when four out of ten voters voted for parties other than the four that have occupied the political scene for decades. The 1993 legislative elections confirmed this tendency, but owing to the winner-take-all majority voting system, the protest vote against the Socialists turned into a right-wing triumph. The new majority holds 80 percent of the 577 seats in the National Assembly, the Socialists have fifty-four, and a score of other parties, including the ecologists, have no seat. While undoubtedly an effective instrument for political expression the results of the elections show the limits of the voting booth as an effective system of checks and balances in the Fifth Republic.

The Luxembourg Palace: The Senate

The Senate is the second branch of Parliament, but its powers are even more limited than those of the National Assembly. Contrary to what happens in most democracies with two legislative assemblies, the higher chamber is not elected by the people but by an electoral college of leading citizens (municipal delegates, members of the *conseil général*, National Assembly deputies). In this sense, it is akin to the old assembly of *notables* (small-town personalities, mostly lawyers) that used to represent the aristocracy and was a Gaullist concession to grass-roots politics in exchange for the election of the president by the people. Half of the Senate members are representatives of communities with fewer than fifteen hundred inhabitants—which account for only one-quarter of the population of the country.

France has no vice president, and in the event of the president's resigning or dying in office it is the president of the Senate who stands in for the head of state pending a new election. In spite of this privilege the Senate has little power. In the case of a conflict with the National Assembly on a bill, the *députés* have the last word. Thus a law can be passed without the approval of the Senate, in which case the following cynical formula is used in the *Bulletin Officiel*: "The National Assembly and the Senate have deliberated, the National Assembly has adopted, and the president of the Republic promulgates."

The only power the Senate really has is obstruction of government by stalling the implementation of new laws. During the early days of the Fifth Republic it was the seat of Gaullist opposition, as its very existence was threatened by the regime. General de Gaulle's defeat in the 1969 referendum was due as much to the reform of the Senate that his project of greater power for the regions implied as to the rejection of a man who was out of tune with the desires of his contemporaries. If the decentralization plan had been adopted, the Senate would have become merely a regional consultative body, and the prime minister would have replaced the president of the Senate during a vacancy of the head of state. Politically close to the presidency in the seventies, the Senate systematically obstructed the Socialist government's legislative policy between 1981 and 1986, then favored the projects of the Right-of-center for two years before returning to obstructionist tactics when the Socialists came back to power in 1988. The landslide, Right-wing victory in the 1993 legislative elections is likely to lead to closer cooperation again between the Senate and the National Assembly.

The 320 Senators are elected for a nine-year term, one-third of the members coming up for renewal every three years. In the thirty-four years of its existence, the higher chamber has been dominated by the same majority and has had only two presidents. Alain Duhamel sums up the disrepute into which it has fallen: "As for the Senate, which the general continually wished to reform, it remains this museum of a rural, conservative France, allergic to change and even to modern society, without any prestige, any vocation, and without any real use. Maybe the general had not premeditated this cruelty: he made a eunuch of Parliament."[18]

Yet, in 1992 the senators proved they still existed when they forced the Bérégovoy government to make a major concession on the question of the constitutional amendment for the ratification of the Maastricht treaty, which paves the way for European political and monetary integration. The Senate obtained the right to veto the organic law designed to allow people from other EC countries residing in France to vote in French local elections. This was a major victory for the upper chamber, whose right to veto is strictly limited by the constitution. The Socialists, on account of their fluctuating majority in the National Assembly, could not oppose this move by the conservative Senate to reinforce its powers without jeopardizing the chances of prompt ratification of the Maastricht treaty.

---

18. Alain Duhamel, *De Gaulle-Mitterrand: La Marque et la Trace* (Paris: Flammarion, 1991), 61.

Constitutional Reform

Perhaps history will reproach President Mitterrand with not having seized the opportunity of his two terms in office to undertake major constitutional reform and set up a Sixth Republic instead of accepting the Gaullian institutional heritage lock, stock, and barrel. This is the message a number of Socialists spelled out in an article in *Le Monde* in July 1990. According to the authors, "The general loved France and mistrusted the French." The constitution thus quells political parties and prevents democratic expression. It infantilizes the French. The reign of de Gaulle corresponded to the reign of technocrats not only in business and industry but in every sphere of life—technocrats who made decisions for others.[19]

No one is more aware of the drawbacks and dangers of the current constitution than Mitterrand, but the political turnover of the 1980s was so dizzying that constitutional reform would not have been easily accepted. In an interview with Jean Lacouture, de Gaulle's biographer, in 1987, the president declared that the time was not yet ripe for major reform. The French, he said, have the habit of not answering the questions they are asked but the questions they ask themselves. "I have not yet addressed the people to modify the institutions. The French had other things in mind. They would have said: 'What is he asking us at a time when unemployment, inflation, and the economic crisis have to be settled?'"[20]

The amendment related to the Maastricht treaty was approved by the National Assembly in June 1992. Because of the balance of power in the assembly, where the Left had only a relative majority, the likelihood of major constitutional reform seemed very remote to most observers. Why then did Mitterrand propose a revision of the thirty-five-year-old constitution in November 1992?

For his political opponents the answer was obvious: the president's motives were purely tactical. Faced with the diasagreeable prospect of a second cohabitation with a right-wing premier, Mitterrand, true to his

---

19. Julien Dray, Jean-Yves Le Déaut, Jean-Yves le Drian, Marie-Noëlle Lienemann, and Jean-Luc Mélenchon, "Vite la VIème République," *Le Monde*, 12 July 1990.

20. "La pratique de la constitution," *Le Monde Dossiers et Documents: Bilan du Septennat 1981–1988*, 37.

policy of dividing to rule, proposed a series of amendments that he knows well are a bone of contention for the various parties in the Right-wing coalition. This would also divert attention before the elections from the serious difficulties facing France that the Socialists had proved incapable of solving.

While it would be naive to exclude political opportunism in the presidential proposal, it would also be unfair to suggest that these were the main motives. Mitterrand has always denounced the dangers for democracy inherent in the 1958 constitution and had promised reform before the end of his mandate.

The proposals of the consultative committee set up in November were made public in February 1993. They were quite conservative. For example, the experts proposed maintaining the "special powers" (article 16) but giving the Constitutional Council some measure of control. (Mitterrand himself, true to his convictions, favors the abolition of article 16.) Moreover, the committee failed to reach an agreement on the duration of the presidential mandate (five, six, or seven years).

However, if the reform is not likely to pave the way for a "Sixth Republic," the importance of many of the proposed amendments should not be underestimated: the powers of the executive are more clearly defined, parliament is given a more active role, magistrates have more independence, and ordinary citizens have a greater say in matters that concern them. Whether these amendments ever see the day depends on the new government because, according to the constitution, the president needs the agreement of the prime minister to launch the reform.[21] This is unlikely, though perhaps more necessary than ever considering the overwhelming neo-Gaullist majority in the 1993 National Assembly in which the opposition will find it harder than ever to exercise to the full its legislative role, as was the case in the "reign" of General de Gaulle.

Control

The Constitutional Council

France has no supreme court; it is not possible in the course of a trial to plead the unconstitutionality of a law as in the United States. In

21. See Alain Rollat, "Le jeu et la chandelle," *Le Monde,* 2 December 1992 and Thierry Bréhier, "Un exécutif mieux défini, un Parlement plus actif, un citoyen plus présent," *Le Monde,* 17 February 1993.

France, it is *before* a law is voted that its constitutionality can be contested. However, the Constitutional Council did not have any power to control laws before 1974, and it has not been asked to control nine-tenths of the laws voted since that date. Thus, in theory, a person may be condemned in court under a law that violates the constitution!

The control of the constitutionality of law falls on the Constitutional Council in France, but the council can only be petitioned by the president of the Republic, the prime minister, or, since 1974, by the president of either parliamentary assembly or a group of sixty deputies. Designed to avoid parliamentary and governmental abuse, its role is preventive. Its powers are limited to censuring all or part of a proposed law. Since the 1970s the council has played an increasingly important role in protecting individual rights. Unfortunately, a bill designed to allow ordinary citizens involved in a court case to ask the judge to verify the constitutionality of an existing law was rejected by the conservative Senate in spring 1990.

The council is composed of nine members. Three, including the president, are named by the head of state, three by the president of the National Assembly, and three by the president of the Senate. Unlike the members of the Supreme Court, appointed for life by the president of the United States, the French nominees may serve for nine years only.

Besides controlling the constitutionality of legislation and, thus, counterbalancing the excessive weight of the government in this area, the council also oversees the respect of the interior regulations of Parliament and the regularity of elections and referenda. In the case of electoral fraud, it can nullify the results and order new elections to be organized.

Some pretend that the nine *sages*, by censuring legislation, tend to reduce even more the powers of the National Assembly. On the other hand, they certainly strengthen the opposition, which is inclined to petition the Constitutional Council more than the parliamentary majority. It can thus be perceived as a *contre-pouvoir.* Nevetheless political observers generally believe that the council, on account of its impartiality, is one of the institutions that deserves the greatest esteem of French citizens. Unfortunately, the public often ignores its very existence.

14

The Rock and the River

Charles de Gaulle est un pic, François Mitterrand est un fleuve.
—Alain Duhamel

The Fifth Republic has had four presidents: Charles de Gaulle (1959–69), Georges Pompidou (1969-74), Valéry Giscard d'Estaing (1974–81), and François Mitterrand (1981–). While the contributions of Pompidou and Giscard to the modernization of France are far from negligible, the major transformations of the past thirty years are due to the two presidents who have dominated this period, Charles de Gaulle and François Mitterrand. Any understanding of the changes that have taken place in contemporary France is impossible without some knowledge of the careers, personalities, and political vision of these two contrasting Frenchmen, who embody different but complementary views of government.

Charles de Gaulle (1890–1970)

The military and political career of Charles de Gaulle, born into a patriotic bourgeois family in Lille in 1890, was marked by ups and downs. Wounded three times during World War I (1914–18) and captured by the Germans, the future *résistant* of World War II showed his determination never to submit by making five escape attempts during captivity. His military activities in the 1920s and 1930s would have been relatively ordinary were it not for the fact that he published a book vaunting the superiority of tank warfare and was nicknamed "Colonel Motor" by his fellow officers. Moreover, he enjoyed the protection of the war hero Marshall Pétain, who had been his first military superior, and who was to become the symbol of treachery when he signed the armistice with Hitler after the blitzkrieg that brought France to surrender in less than six weeks in 1940. The rapid French defeat was partly due to the fact that few had listened to Colonel Motor, the army preferring a static defense that had proved its worth in 1914–18 but was useless against a lightning air and tank strike.

President	Year	Prime minister
François Mitterrand	1993	Edouard Balladur (March 1993)
	1992	Pierre Bérégovoy (March 1992)
	1991	Edith Cresson (June 1991)
	1990	
	1989	
François Mitterrand reelected, May 1988.	1988	Michel Rocard (May 1988)
	1987	
	1986	Jacques Chirac (March 1986)
	1985	
	1984	Laurent Fabius (July 1984)
	1983	
	1982	
Election of François Mitterrand, May 1981.	1981	Pierre Mauroy (May 1981)
	1980	
	1979	
	1978	
	1977	
	1976	Raymond Barre (August 1976)
	1975	
Georges Pompidou dies, April 2, 1974. Election of Valéry Giscard d'Estaing, May 1974.	1974	Jacques Chirac (May 1974)
	1973	
	1972	Pierre Messmer (July 1972)
	1971	
	1970	
Charles de Gaulle resigns April 22, 1969. Election of Georges Pompidou, June 15, 1969.	1969	Jacques Chaban-Delmas (June 1969)
	1968	Maurice Couve de Murville (July 1968)
	1967	
	1966	
Charles de Gaulle reelected, December 1965.	1965	
	1964	
	1963	
	1962	Georges Pompidou (April 1962)
	1961	
	1960	
Election of Charles de Gaulle, December 1959.	1959	
Constitution of Fifth Republic	1958	

FIG. 20. Presidents and prime ministers of the Fifth Republic

In 1940, de Gaulle fled to London, from where he broadcast his famous message on the BBC on 18 June condemming in advance the humiliating armistice and calling on the French to resist the German occupation. It took a large dose of courage and optimism at a time when Hitler had crushed his country to proclaim that France had "lost a battle but not the war." The famous message fell largely on deaf ears, although it should not be forgotten that among the 569 parliamentarians, eighty voted against granting full powers to Marshall Pétain on 10 July and that an internal resistance movement, in which the Communists played a leading role, was formed. Only a handful of French, about three hundred in all, rallied around the dissident colonel, who was sentenced to death in his absence by the Vichy regime of his old protector.

In London, the aloof, lanky Frenchman had a job in convincing the skeptical Churchill of the representativeness of his France Libre movement, but the British minister of war had little choice. Franklin Roosevelt was harder to convince. (The American recognized only the "legal" French government of Marshall Pétain.) The two men had little in common. Roosevelt, prosaic, pragmatic president of a modern, dynamic nation, who desired to be the champion of democracy, could not appreciate the old-fashioned patriotism of this soldier from another century who was nourished on history and heroic poetry and who firmly believed he was the man of the moment. Roosevelt described de Gaulle as ambitious, egocentric, and deeply anti-American, and the General did little to dispel the misunderstanding, although he badly needed U.S. aid. The supreme humiliation came after the Allied landing in North Africa in November 1942—about which de Gaulle was not even informed—when Roosevelt as a temporary expedient chose Pétain's right-hand man, Admiral Darlan, to govern Algeria. De Gaulle was later to gain the upper hand and form the Provisional Government of Free France in Algiers in June 1944. He was again kept in the dark until the last minute about the allied landing in Normandy, but in August two million French people massed on the Champs Elysée to give a hero's welcome to the Liberator of France, the man who had resisted when all the odds were against him. Roosevelt, whose democratic scruples had kept him from recognizing the self-designated leader of France sooner, was forced to accept de Gaulle as head of the provisional government.[1]

De Gaulle's political life was no less agitated than his military engagements. He had slammed the door on a political career in 1940 when he quit the government after twelve days as under secretary in charge of defense, preferring to be an outcast in London than agreeing to a humiliating armistice. After the war, he gave himself tirelessly for sev-

---

1. See Alain-Gérard Slama, "De Gaulle et Roosevelt," *Le Point,* 14–20 May 1990, 72–75.

enteen months to the task of reconstructing a country that was economically and morally in ruin. Then he resigned as head of the provisional government because he disagreed with the constitutional proposals for the Fourth Republic based on an all-powerful Parliament and a presidency reduced to an honorary function. The general considered this would give free rein to party politics, which he vigorously denounced. Time was to prove him right. After battling in vain—in spite of some electoral victories—to impose his views with the help of the RPF (Rassemblement du peuple français), he retired to his home in the little village of Colombey-les-Deux-Eglises in 1953, leaving the Communists and the Right-of-center and the Left-of-center parties to their squabbling. This did not prevent him from thundering from time to time against certain decisions of a regime that was trying to run the country "at the rate of a problem every six months and a [new] government per problem."[2] The man of action used to find solace in writing, and his memoirs, with their rich, lyrical evocations of the ancient land of France, proposed a dream of glory and grandeur to his countrymen.

At the age of sixty-eight de Gaulle was finally to get the opportunity to make his dream come true. But drawing a pall over the last French colonies was hardly a glorious task for a man who had chanted all his life the imperial splendor of France: "It's not very funny at my age and with my background. It's a difficult task that we have to undertake and one that holds no joy for me."[3] In 1958, the intransigence of the French in Algeria, the civil strife and sedition of the military, which the Fourth Republic was unable to control, made all eyes turn to the retired General, the savior who had liberated France, who had denounced the inanity of the political parties that were at present incapable of solving the crisis. This time it was not de Gaulle who was to call the French to save the country but the French who were to call de Gaulle. Invested with full powers in spite of the protests of the Communists and the Left, the general set about imposing his conception of government based on a servile Parliament and a strong executive. It was not the role of the president "to inaugurate chrysanthemum shows," he used to say.

Painful as it was, de Gaulle's resolution of the Algerian crisis and the

---

2. Pierre Viansson-Ponté, "Charles de Gaulle," in *La grande encyclopédie Larousse*, vol. 9 (Paris: Larousse, 1974), 5306–12.

3. See Jacques Duquesne, "De Gaulle et Salan," *Le Point*, 14–20 May 1990, 80–83.

process of decolonization was achieved without too great a loss of honor, thanks to the personality of the president, who remained in office for eleven years and strove to preserve the prestige of his country on the international scene. Though France was henceforth a medium-size nation compared to the two superpowers, the United States and the USSR, it refused to be treated as a runt, and de Gaulle never failed to assert the autonomy of France—not always tactfully or judiciously—much to the exasperation of the Americans. De Gaulle pursued a foreign policy of grandeur and independence in keeping with the elevated views of nationhood that flattered his people: development of the nuclear strike force, decision to quit the NATO military command, homage to the spirit of independence of the smaller nations, and condemnation of hegemony. On the home front his *dirigiste* (planned) economic policy bore fruit, but the aging general lost touch with the youth of France, who were fed up with an anachronistic, authoritarian regime that failed to take into account their aspirations. The 1968 student riots and the ensuing social unrest took the president by surprise, and in 1969, following his defeat in a referendum designed to reform the Senate and introduce a certain measure of decentralization, he was to quit the political scene for the last time. He died on 9 November 1970. Twenty years later France celebrated the centenary of the birth of General de Gaulle under the presidency of a man who had fought the institutions of the Fifth Republic all his life.[4]

François Mitterrand

François Mitterrand, born in the town of Jarnac in the southwest of France in 1916, was de Gaulle's archrival from the days of the Fourth Republic. Despite the differences between the two presidents, their careers have a lot in common. Like de Gaulle, who was imprisoned by the Germans during World War I, Mitterrand was captured near Verdun in 1940 and made several attempts to escape from captivity. However, he did not join the Resistance immediately. He served as commissioner general for prisoners of war under the Vichy government in 1942, but by 1943 he was already on the run, so he never received the *francisque*

4. The indispensable biography of de Gaulle is Jean Lacouture, *De Gaulle*, 3 vols. (Paris: Editions du Seuil, 1985).

(an engraved medal of the Gallic ax, the emblem of the Vichy regime) that had been awarded to him for his services. In fact, after the Liberation he was decorated for his bravery in the Resistance and was actually secretary general for prisoners of war in the provisional government of General de Gaulle for one week. Both men were ambitious and had a premonition of the role they would play: "I will be king or pope," Mitterrand used to say when he was a child. Both had a very high opinion of themselves, and there is something regal in their bearing, although they are physically so different. The political careers of both men were full of ups and downs. Recalled from retirement at the age of sixty-eight, de Gaulle was finally to "reign" for ten years as president of the Republic he founded; Mitterrand, who after three unsuccessful attempts was elected president at the age of sixty-five, has already reigned twelve years. Both were well-read in history and accomplished authors. Like de Gaulle, Mitterrand has proved to be an ardent defender of smaller nations, of the Third World, and even of the French nuclear strike force. For Elie Cohen, writer and associate professor at the Institute of Political Science in Paris, the two presidents share another quality: political courage. Comparing Mitterrand's tough choice in 1983, which involved renouncing socialist economic theory, to de Gaulle's decision on French withdrawal from Algeria, Cohen says: "In both instances the leaders who had been elected by a large majority had the courage to override the interests of their voters and face unpopularity to safeguard the future of their country."[5]

The King of the French

Tempting as the comparisons are—comparisons that their respective followers vehemently refute—the two "republican monarchs" could hardly be more different. Alain Duhamel has put it nicely: "The general behaved like the king of France, François Mitterrand like the king of the French."[6] De Gaulle called upon his compatriots to live up to an uncompromising idea of France; Mitterrand strives to adjust the presidential role to the contradictory aspirations of French citizens. That is why he is so hard to pin down. Yet both in their separate ways have been marvelously in

5. Elie Cohen, "Le tournant de la rigueur," *L'Histoire* 143, April 1991, 62.
6. Duhamel, *De Gaulle-Mitterrand,* 45.

tune with the national consciousness. Psychologically, they are at the antipodes. Rocklike, General de Gaulle was "a man of thundering ruptures"; riverlike, Mitterrand is "a man of synthesis."[7]

The Politician

The president in office is a politician to the fingertips. Among the adjectives most frequently used by pundits to describe him are "Machiavellian" and "Byzantine." This is one biographer's portrait of Mitterrand:

> Eloquent, he has trouble in matching words and facial expression; a politeness verging on insolence, the more familiar he tries to be, the more distant he is; gentle, with a feminine gentleness, suave in fact, his mildness is equal only to his icy causticity; skeptical, he distrusts his passions above all. To persuade, he raises his hand with a delicate tremor, unbearably affected [*précieux*], expressive of genuine emotion and his search for the right word. Each of his speeches blends lyric sensitiveness, cold irony, amused irony, and pathetic gravity. The complexity of the man is but one step from the duplicity of the politician.[8]

According to Franz-Olivier Giesbert, writer and editor in chief of *Le Figaro*, few French politicians since Talleyrand (1754–1838), who served under five different regimes, have used dodgery and side-stepping with as much skill. The portrait is cruel: "His whole character is built on ambiguity. That is his manufacturing secret. It replaces genius. It allows him to believe one thing in the morning and to be convinced of the very opposite in the evening."[9] Less cruelly, Alain Duhamel declares that the president is "the quintessence of the politician."[10]

In the early days of the Fourth Republic, Mitterrand joined the Democratic and Socialist Union of the Resistance, which was opposed to de Gaulle. In 1947 he was appointed minister for war veterans in the Socialist government and occupied several ministerial posts during the troubled political life of the Fourth Republic, serving in turn the Popular Republi-

---

7. Alain Duhamel, "De Gaulle et Mitterrand," *Le Point*, 14 May 1990, 84–87.
8. Jean-Marie Borzeix, *Mitterrand lui-même* (Paris: Stock, 1973), 7.
9. Franz-Olivier Giesbert, *Le Président* (Paris: Editions du Seuil, 1990), 11.
10. Duhamel, *De Gaulle–Mitterrand*, 19.

can Movement coalition that was opposed to the Communists and de Gaulle; the Right of center; the Socialist-Radicals; and the Republican Front. Though he defended the idea of French Algeria—"L'Algérie, c'est la France"—the right-wing never really trusted him.

In 1958, François Mitterrand was among three out of thirteen members of his parliamentary group to oppose granting full powers to General de Gaulle. He lost his seat in the subsequent elections. Held in as much suspicion by the Left as by the Right, he applied in the early 1960s to join the United Socialist Party (PSU), led by the young Michel Rocard, and was refused on two occasions. Undaunted, he managed to found a new political group and have himself designated the official candidate of the Left to run against de Gaulle in the 1965 presidential election. His showing of 45 percent came as a surprise and gave a new momentum to the Left.

In the 1970s François Mitterrand helped construct the new Socialist party, of which he was soon to become secretary general. He was henceforth the champion of those who dreamed of overthrowing the Right-of-center coalition that had ruled the country since 1958. With legendary foresight the secretary general set about engineering the Union of the Left, the new alliance of the Socialists and Communists who had split up in 1938. This was to become the springboard for his 1981 election as president of the Republic, when he obtained an unexpected 51.7 percent of the votes.

Whatever misgivings one may have about the means Mitterrand employs to achieve his ends—his uses and abuses of political adversaries and allies alike—one cannot but admire his tenacity, foresight, and political finesse. His principal opponents, such as Jacques Chirac, leader of the neo-Gaullist party, Valéry Giscard d'Estaing, the former technocratic president of the Republic, or his sometimes ally and arch enemy Georges Marchais, the Communist party boss, lack his accumulated political experience in the Fourth and Fifth Republics and are no match for the man in the Elysée Palace. As Alain Duhamel points out, few politicians have acquired such a wide range of experience in the field over fifty years. Few are more familiar with the ballot box. From mayor to president of the Republic, François Mitterrand has been a candidate for various local or national public functions twenty-seven times.[11]

His track record in the last two decades is impressive. In the seventies

11. Duhamel, *De Gaulle–Mitterrand*, 47.

he collected the fragments of the Socialist party, rebuilt it, and engineered the virtual annihilation of the Communist party, whose alliance with the Socialists in the Union of the Left paid more electoral dividends to the Socialists, as Mitterrand had shrewdly calculated; he brought the Left to power for the first time in the history of the Fifth Republic in the aftermath of his election as president; in 1983, he approved the economic U-turn of the Socialist government and turned his back on the dogmatic brand of socialism that had brought him to power; in 1986 he "cohabited" with a Right-wing governmental majority; reelected president of the Republic in 1988 on a Left-of-center ticket, he appointed a Socialist would-be presidential candidate and long-time rival, Michel Rocard, as prime minister. The latter, a self-proclaimed, realistic administrator—a dream buster (*un briseur de rêves*)—who prides himself on his pragmatism, carried out a policy closer to Right-of-center than to traditional Left-wing philosophy. In the run-up to the 1991 regional elections Mitterrand created a sensation by dismissing the Rocard ministry and appointing Edith Cresson, who became the first woman prime minister in the history of France. While in retrospect this may have been a political faux pas, as Cresson's replacement ten months after her appointment by Pierre Bérégovoy showed, the president undeniably benefited for a short period from his spectacular nomination of a woman to the highest office in the French government at a time when a certain morosity with Rocard's austere policies was setting in. In 1993 Mitterrand, though ill, took the uncomfortable decision of accepting a second cohabitation period with a tough, triumphant Right-wing, and became the last recourse of a stricken French Left that owed its humiliating defeat in part to the president, who had sapped the very foundations of the Socialist party ten years previously.

The Fall from Grace

Without neglecting the numerous reforms undertaken since 1981 that have contributed to modernize France—decentralization, abolition of the death penalty, overhaul of corporate and penal law, and so on—it is clear that François Mitterrand's greatest political achievements have undoubtedly been to reconcile the Socialists with the free market and the nation with the Left, even if the socialism of today has little in common with its revolutionary heritage. The concessions of the Socialists to ideology during "the grace period" (1981–83)—five weeks paid-vacation (instead of four) for all, retirement at sixty, massive recruitment of functionaries, the nationalization of major industrial groups—proved ruinous for the economy and were like the fiasco of the proposed Savary educational reform, a disguised penance that opened the eyes of the Left to the limits of doctrine and paved the way for the economic realism that has helped France to maintain its leadership role in Europe. For Mitterrand's adversaries, the conversion of the Socialists to free-market principles, which the president facilitated, is a manifestation of cynical opportunism; for his supporters, it is a mark of his political genius.

Tonton

Opinion polls have recorded the changing attitudes of the French toward François Mitterrand and the president himself has taken pains to adjust his image to the expectations of his people with the aid of a brash advertising mogul, Jacques Séguela, who created the "force tranquille" slogan in 1981. This presented a Mitterrand who could appeal to a new type of French voter "respectful of order but open to change." According to Franz-Olivier Giesbert, it was Séguela who persuaded the candidate to have his prominent canines filed, to dress "Left" rather than "like a banker," to stand straight and stick out his chin "like Richard Nixon at General de Gaulle's funeral." Such a posture, he said, "would confer nobility to chimpanzees"![12]

When a political opponent suggested that he was a bit old to govern France, Mitterrand retorted that sixty was the ideal age because it was the age of a great-uncle and thus reassuring for the younger generation. The familiar name *tonton* (uncle) was to stick. Following the program of economic austerity imposed by the Left in 1983, Mitterrand's popularity rating hit an all-time low, and it was only after the Socialist defeat in the 1986 legislative elections, during the troubled cohabitation with a Right-wing prime minister, that tonton really came into his own and gained the affection of the French public. Battling to maintain his presidential prerogatives, which the opposition cabinet was intent upon paring, he proclaimed himself the guardian of the constitution and, like the monarchs of the past, became the supreme arbiter in the conflicts between the people and the administration, the wicked Right-wing government that was pawning the national assets to private interest groups and turning a deaf ear to the lamentations of students, strikers, immigrants,

12. Giesbert, *Le Président*, 69.

and the needy. He exploited the "tonton craze" (*tontonmanie*) to the full—"*Tiens bon, tonton*" ("Stick to your guns, tonton") was among the encouragements students yelled during the 1986 demonstrations—and he never missed an opportunity to humiliate, on the sly, Prime Minister Jacques Chirac, whose impulsiveness made him an easy target. Throning above the political melee like some sage, the reassuring tonton admonished the government and proffered words of comfort to the befuddled French, who had been whirled in less than a decade from a socialist paradise into an economic depression and from there into the harsh realities of capitalism. Mitterrand, outwardly at least, preached tolerance and cooperation to Left and Right alike. He thus appeared as the *grand rassembleur* (the great uniter). Among the candidates for the 1988 presidential election only the outgoing president seemed capable of uniting the quarrelsome French and putting an end to the Left-Right bickering that was beginning to exasperate voters. His campaign was based on the slogan "A United France."

It is hardly surprising that political commentators should underline the regal drift of presidential power in contemporary France. It is hard to avoid references to ancient royalty when speaking of the presidency today. Not only does the president of the French Republic bear the title Co-Prince of Andorra—the tiny principality (175 square miles) situated

FIG. 21. Mitterrand I (1981–88) and Mitterrand II (1988–95): "Congratulations again!" (*Le Monde.* Copyright © Plantu 1988.)

in the Pyrenees between France and Spain has been under the joint suzerainty of the French state and the Spanish bishop of Urgel since 1278—but many of his prerogatives are akin to the privileges of the monarchs of the past. For instance, early monarchs were elected and, like the president today, were considered to be above the political system. The king was supreme overlord, at the top of the feudal pyramid, and owed allegiance to nobody. Only the king could muster an army for the defense of the kingdom—"the right of ban"; the president is chief of the army, and only he can decide upon the use of the nuclear strike force. (This aspect of the presidential role was strikingly evident during the Persian Gulf crisis and the Desert Storm offensive, during which the prime minister kept a very low profile.) The king of France was enthroned after being annointed with holy oil in the cathedral of Reims; in 1981 the Socialist president received his consecration in the secular temple of the Pantheon before the eyes of millions of TV viewers: "Nowadays," writes historian Jacques le Goff, "the coronation in Reims only lives on in memory. But does not our Republican, secular age, deprived of the symbolic and of things sacred, yearn for a substitute to the coronation? No doubt, François Mitterrand was reminded of this as he advanced toward the Pantheon, a rose in his hand—the modern version of the *fleur-de-lis*."[13] The great kings of the past were builders who left cathedrals, castles, and palaces for posterity to admire—Chartres, the chateaux of the Loire Valley, Versailles—Mitterrand has been an untiring promoter of prestigious monuments and exciting architecture, *les grands travaux*, which are changing the face of Paris: the Grand Louvre with its pyramid, l'Arche de la Défense, l'Opéra Bastille, the TGB (*très grande bibliothèque*), the library of the future. Early monarchs were credited with healing powers—they could cure scurvy by their very touch—the president arrogates the power of curing the political and social ills of contemporary France, as his attitude during the first cohabitation episode illustrates in particular.

Because of his republican background, it is astonishing that François Mitterrand should have donned the cloak of the monarch and laid himself so open to criticism, but the constitution of the Fifth Republic probably

---

13. The rose is the emblem of the Socialist party; the fleur-de-lis of the monarchy. See Jacques le Goff, "Reims, la mémoire du sacre," *L'Histoire*, January 1987, 106–11.

left little option if presidential prerogatives were to be defended. According to Catherine Nay, "The president of the Republic has totally assumed the Gaullian heritage."[14] Moreover, Mitterrand's natural reserve and keen taste for secrecy—even his European partners were kept in the dark about his daring visit to Sarajevo in the heat of the combat in Bosnia and Herzegovina—have helped reinforce etiquette and protocol, with the result that the monarchical trappings of the presidency are stronger than ever. But no one knows better than François Mitterrand that the French expect their presidents to incarnate what France would wish to be rather than what it is. His preoccupation with the "rank" of France is very Gaullian, even if the means he uses are less spectacular.

However, this anachronistic image is incompatible with the image of modernism that Mitterrand constantly tries to incarnate at the risk of appearing ridiculous. Indeed, in the 1990s, in the immensely popular *Bébête show,* the French version of the Muppets, Mitterrand the Second has become so remote from ordinary mortals in his celestial palace of the Elysée that tonton has become *Dieu* (God), and the hero of a song, *Appele-moi Dieu* (Call me God)! Such irreverence would have been unheard of in the "reign" of de Gaulle and shows that public opinion is not duped by the role the president is playing. The cartoonist Plantu recorded the transformation of Mitterrand following the 1990 student demonstrations, when the president hastily assumed the role of mediator between the students and the government while his prime minister was away in Japan. In these perceptive drawings, the new "rap" tonton—76 years old in 1992—who has lost the veneration he enjoyed with French youth in 1986 seems to be overdoing it.

Desert Storm

Try as he might, Francois Mitterrand had never been able to reach the popularity ratings of his Fifth Republic predecessors, and, after his ten-year reign, there were signs that his popularity was waning before the Persian Gulf crisis. While his public image remained good, he was rated low on achievement, as if the role of arbiter he had chosen to play cramped his style.[15] The president's decision to engage the French forces

14. Catherine Nay, *Les sept Mitterrand* (Paris: Grasset, 1988), 103–204.

15. Olivier Duhamel and Jerôme Jaffré, *L'état de l'opinion 1990* (Paris: Editions du Seuil, 1990), 228. See also Jerôme Jaffré, "Les trois erreurs de la gauche," *Le Monde,* 10–11 June 1990.

in Iraq and the triumph of the coalition was a personal triumph for Mitterrand, who obtained a blockbuster approval rating of 85 percent in the polls, leading pundits to speak of "a second grace period."

The president's handling of the gulf crisis, one of the greatest challenges of his presidency according to a political correspondent for *Le Monde*, Jean-Marie Colombani, was yet another proof of his political skill.[16] The dilemma for François Mitterrand was to choose between a policy of maintaining France's symbolic role on the international scene as defender of the smaller nations and preserving France's rank as a military power (symbolized by the seat it holds on the Security Council of the United Nations) by supporting the position of the United States. Had the French president opted for nonalignment, he would have underlined France's sympathy with the Arab world at the same time as he encouraged the anti-Americanism so ready to flourish among politicans from Left and Right. However, this would have ruined France's credibility as a military power and denied it any say in the postwar negotiations. By opting for the second solution, with all due reserve concerning the limits of France's engagement, the president managed to maintain the "role and rank" of France, as he said himself. The happy outcome of Desert Storm for the coalition forces allowed the president to collect the dividends of his strategy from the relieved French, who approved an operation that had reinforced France's image in the Western world at little human cost. The resignation of the minister of defense and the agitation of the Communists and the Greens, who were opposed to military intervention, did not harm the presidency very much. Perhaps more serious was the damage to European military credibility, as Europe seemed to be left out of the global strategy of the Elysée Palace. Never, since World War II had the synergy between the United States and France been so perfect, the difference from de Gaulle's foreign policy based on the preeminence of nationhood been so marked. Mitterrand pulled off the tour de force of reconciling the Gaullian notion of rank with a foreign policy that owes more to pragmatism than prestige—the military power of France hardly justifies its Security Council seat—and that his neoGaullist opponents were unable to criticize because it had the assent of a population ever ready to thrill to an appeal to grandeur.

Mitterrand's triumph was short-lived. His exceptional ratings in the

16. Jean-Marie Colombani, "Le 'rang' de la France," *Le Monde*, 5 February 1991.

polls after the Persian Gulf War plummeted in late 1991 following unfounded rumors that he was envisaging a major revision of the constitution that would reduce the presidential mandate to five years. The opposition suspected he would take the opportunity of such an amendment to resign at an opportune time before the end of his mandate to pave the way for a Socialist successor. These rumors, continuing unemployment, and the perceived incoherence of Edith Cresson's policies, who was hamstrung by her own party, precipitated the plunge in Mitterrand's popularity ratings, which reached an even lower level than in 1984. The Bérégovoy cabinet came too late to have any chance of improving the image of the president. A poll taken between the two rounds of the 1993 legislative elections that were to prove disastrous for the Socialist majority showed that only 37 percent of the respondents felt Mitterrand should remain in office if the Right-wing was victorious; 55 percent believed he should resign.[17] Only time will tell if the president was right to accept a second cohabitation in unfavorable circumstances, and if this extraordinary tactician did not foul up his departure from the political scene. It might be rash to make any forecasts. Mitterrand is never so good as in adversity and his whole life has been a series of setbacks and comebacks. He is an enigmatic personality whose motives are not always very clear even to his closest friends. The more would-be biographers and analysts study the president, the more the mystery deepens. As André Laurens says, "François Mitterrand escapes his pursuers like the best characters in a novel from their author."[18]

---

17. BVA-France 2, Europe 1, Paris Match, Libération poll, 25 and 26 March 1995. See *Libération*, 29 March 1993.

18. André Laurens, "Mitterrand: intérieurs, extérieurs," *Le Monde*, 11 June 1990.

15

Politics Today

Politics is the art of preventing people from minding their own business.

—Paul Valéry

What's What?

Political terminology in the United States and France does not always cover the same ground, and words like *liberalism, conservatism,* and *socialism* need to be redefined in a French context. *Libéralisme* in contemporary France tends to be identified with the neoliberalism imported from the United States in 1984. It is classed with Reaganism and Thatcherism, and thus becomes synonymous with conservatism. Socialism, often associated with communism in the United States, has frequently been the defender of political and civil liberties in France, a position that has been the prerogative of the liberals in America. However, it would be naive to imagine that American liberalism covers the same realities as French *socialisme,* or even that American conservatism is akin to French *conservatisme.* It would be just as naive to believe that *socialisme* and *communisme* are identical in contemporary France.

Two Hundred Years of Politics in a Nutshell

Today, even the terms *left* and *right* that come from the seating arrangement in the Convention (1792–95)—the Left was known as the Mountain and the Right as the Gironde, the region of well-to-do merchants—have not quite the same symbolic value or significance that they have had for two hundred years, in spite of all the ink slung on the 1989 bicentenary celebrations. The two opposing political forces in contemporary France—the Socialists and the conservative, neo-Gaullist RPR (Rassemblement pour la République) party with its "liberal" and Right-of-center allies—have probably more in common nowadays than either has in common with the extreme Left or Right.

The traditional dichotomy served to distinguish between the moderates (Right) and the extremists (Left), who favored radical political change—execution of the king—in the Convention. The nineteenth century, one of the most complicated periods in French history, was marked by the struggle between the conservatives, who wanted to restore the monarchy, and the divided supporters of the Republic. Not until the end of the century did the latter (moderate and extremist Republicans) manage to form a united front against the conservative Right (monarchists and others, supporters of an authoritarian form of government). The anticlerical Radical leader, Georges Clemenceau, declared that the Revolution, which was the work of both moderates and extremists, formed a "bloc," that is, a unit that had to be accepted lock, stock, and barrel by all those who believed in Republicanism. The church had been the ardent supporter of the monarchists since the Revolution. The reconciliation (*le ralliement*) of Catholic voters with the moderate Republicans in the 1890s was the coup de grace for the nostalgists of the ancien régime.

During the troubled post–World War I period, the nationalistic Right was attracted by the tough totalitarian regimes in Germany, Italy, and Spain and in 1940 Republican values were trampled underfoot by the French State of Marshall Pétain in occupied France. After the Liberation all the political parties were to be Republican in spite of the ambiguous status of the French Communists. The Fourth Republic was characterized by the battle between Left and Left-of-center parties.

General de Gaulle's return to power and the 1958 constitution, which reinforced the executive to the detriment of the legislative assembly, worried the Left, who feared a return to an authoritarian regime. In the 1960s and 1970s the Christian Democratic center split with General de Gaulle, while the Socialists, Communists, and part of the Radical party, *les radicaux de gauche,* formed an electoral alliance in opposition to the Gaullist regime, which was backed by the conservative Right and Right-of-center parties.

In 1974, the Socialist candidate François Mitterrand narrowly missed becoming president of the Republic. He ran for the presidency again in 1981 and beat the outgoing president, Giscard d'Estaing, a liberal, right-wing *technocrate.* The victory of the Left in the ensuing National Assembly elections led to a revival of the extreme Right, which gained 34 seats in 1986, when the right-wing coalition obtained a narrow majority in the assembly. Mitterrand was elected for a second seven-year term in

1988, and the Socialists, abandoned by their Communist allies, won back the National Assembly, where the combined Left had only a relative majority and was thus condemned to moderate its more radical members. This, together with the limited influence of the extremists (Communists and FN) in the assembly, as well as the latent conflict between the conservative, neoliberal Right and the center—sometimes willing to side with moderate Socialist policy to spite their allies—enabled the government to conduct a social democratic approach to issues between 1988 and 1993. The landslide victory of the Right in the 1993 legislative elections, due in part to the way in which the winner-take-all voting system distorts the real representativity of political parties, led to a second cohabitation between President Mitterrand and Edouard Balladur, the new Right-wing premier.

Who's Who? The Right and Center

The French Right is represented nowadays by two mainstream conservative groups, the neo-Gaullist, Rassemblement pour la république (RPR) and a mixed bag of liberals and Christian Democrats—free marketeers with a social conscience—grouped together in a fragile confederation of parties known as the UDF (Union pour la démocratie française). The extremist National Front (FN) completes the picture.

Le Rassemblement pour la République (RPR)

Party president: Jacques Chirac.[1]
Secretary General: Alain Juppé
Representativity: with 242 seats, the RPR is the largest party represented in the National Assembly. RPR mayors run sixty cities of more than 20,000 inhabitants including seven very large cities, that is, with a population of over 100,000. Sixty senators are party members. Following the 1992 cantonal elections twenty-four of the ninety-nine *conseils généraux* (département councils) have an RPR president.

The party, founded by Géneral de Gaulle in 1947 as an election vehicle,

1. All the party presidents and secretary generals mentioned in this section are those who still held these functions in March 1993. Some of them are relatively recent appointments; other have been in office for several years.

has had several denominations, the latest being RPR. This Gaullist spin-off was created in 1976 by Jacques Chirac, former prime minister of Valéry Giscard d'Estaing from 1974 to 1976 and of François Mitterrand during the first cohabitation period.

Fidelity to General de Gaulle can hardly be called a political doctrine, and it is hard to say what distinguishes this party ideologically from the other Right-wing parties. As Alain Duhamel says, "Gaullism appears to be a form of fidelity, a cult, a tradition; at its best a style of behavior, at its worst a feathered nest; never a formal ideology."[2] In fact, the ingredients of Gaullism were patriotism, populism, and conservative strongman rule—a mixture the RPR has trouble in coping with.

During the brief Right-wing National Assembly interlude (1986–88) the finance minister, Edouard Balladur, Chirac's mentor for cohabitation, flirted with the neoliberalism propounded by his political allies of the Republican party, while the minister of the interior, Charles Pasqua, who represents the populist, authoritarian streak of the RPR, by his tough handling of questions of immigration and security strove to appeal to the far Right that is Le Pen's hunting ground. Locally, some party members were not beyond striking up electoral alliances with the FN.

The short-lived victory of the RPR in the 1986 legislative elections seemed to signify the decline of the thirty-year-reign of a party whose leader was defeated in the 1988 presidential election and which failed to obtain the majority in the 1981 and 1988 assemblies. In 1989 the revolt of the younger, mostly provincial, party members, the self-styled "innovators" against the political style and hands-on management of their elders, were signs of a deep crisis. Michel Noir, the mayor of Lyon; Michèle Barzach, former minister of health; and Alain Carignon, mayor of Grenoble figured among the most outspoken critics of the ambiguous party line on racism. Michel Noir, soon followed by Michèle Barzach, quit the party in late 1990, which was a troubled year for Jacques Chirac, whose leadership was seriously challenged by the former minister of labour, Philippe Séguin, and by Charles Pasqua. They criticized severely the party policy on European integration throughout 1991 and 1992. In July 1992, they formed an association to campaign against the Maastricht treaty. Chirac, who announced after much hesitation that he would vote yes to the referendum on the ratification of the treaty, was booed by

2. Alain Duhamel, "Les partis la recherche de leur identité," *Le Monde*, 12 May 1985.

party members at their annual symposium. However, the leader's popularity with grass roots militants remained strong and the victory of the RPR (henceforth the strongest party in France) in the 1993 National Assembly elections makes Chirac the natural right-wing candidate for the presidency unless Balladur's popularity shadows his.

In 1990, to avoid the suicidal confrontation of two right-wingers for the next presidential election scheduled to be held in 1995, the RPR signed an electoral alliance with the UDF that involves, among other things, organizing a primary between the prospective candidates of each parliamentary group. This alliance, known as l'Union pour la France (UPF), is at best a shaky union that may not be able to temper the intense rivalries between the different leaders. However, the victory of the mainstream Right-wing parties in the cantonal elections of 1992, when they conquered even some of the traditional Left-wing fiefdoms, and especially their victory in the National Assembly elections of 1993, was proof that the union could pay electoral dividends. The combined Right now holds the presidency of seventy départements out of ninety-nine (overseas départements included) and has 486 seats out of 557 in the new assembly. Will it triumph over the internal dissensions that are sure to surface again in the run-up to the 1995 presidential election?

L'Union pour la démocratie française (UDF)

Cartel president: Valéry Giscard d'Estaing.

Representativity: with a total of 207 seats in the National Assembly the UDF, should it remain united, may be able to challenge the RPR for right-wing leadership. While the political hearing of the UDF is, overall, very large—it holds 144 seats in the Senate, controls fifty-three medium-sized municipalities, and presides over forty-three of the ninety-nine *conseils géneraux*—the numerous rival tendencies within the cartel hamper united action.

The UDF was founded in February 1978 by the leaders of the CDS (Centre de démocrates sociaux), the PR (Parti républicain), and Radical party in view of the 1978 legislative elections. The aim was to provide parliamentary backing for then president Valéry Giscard d'Estaing, whose liberty of maneuver was hampered by the conservative Gaullist majority in the National Assembly. The name of the union was borrowed from the title of Giscard's book, *Démocratie française* (1976). For the former president, the UDF is essentially a vehicle for his ambition to represent the Right for the next presidential election, and to prevent Chirac from controlling the Union pour la France (UPF), which is to designate the Right-wing candidate.

The UDF represents both the Christian Democratic tradition and that of the liberal Right-wing. There have been intense rivalries between the two main components of the confederation: the middle-of-the-road CDS and the neoliberals of the PR, who suspect the former of flirting with the Socialists. A few smaller parties, among them the Right wing of the Radical party, also belong to the union, as do a few independent deputies (*adhérents directs*) who have refused affiliation to any particular party. The maverick Raymond Barre, former chairman of the EC Commission and prime minister of President Giscard d'Estaing from 1976 to 1981, is the best known of these. Under the UDF banner, he was the Right-wing's hot favorite in the first round of the 1988 presidential election, but unexpectedly scored three percentage points lower than Chirac. He thus had to withdraw for the second round. He was the only leading personality to denounce the cohabitation experiment as being contrary to the spirit of the constitution. Apparently, voters did not think so. The avuncular, plain-spoken Barre, who prides himself on his economic realism—he is a professor of economics—had been the most unpopular prime minister of the Fifth Republic in the late 1970s, when his name became synonymous with belt-tightening. Yet, many of the economic measures introduced by the Socialists, after 1983, were not far removed from what he had been recommending.

It is hard to perceive what political difference there is between the UDF and the RPR, except perhaps that the former appears more favorable to the EC. The UDF campaigned heavily in favor of the constitutional amendment to ratify the Maastricht treaty, while stressing that their support of the Socialists did not necessarily imply any agreement with them on other issues.

Le Centre de démocrates sociaux (CDS)

Party president: Pierre Méhaignerie.

Representativity: fifty-seven National Assembly deputies.

If in 1993 the UDF managed to form a single though fragile parliamentary group to counterbalance the weight of the RPR, in the 1988 assembly it was split up into several groups. The more centrally minded members of the CDS had formed their own group to recover some independence under the acronym UDC (Union du centre) headed by Pierre Méhaignerie. The latent conflict between the center and its electoral allies reached a climax prior to the European Parliament elections in 1989, when the UDC refused to back Giscard, designated by their partners in the election coalition (RPR and PR) to head the right-wing list of candidates. Instead, Pierre Méhaignery and his followers decided to draw up their own list and insolently chose the popular Simone Weil for leader. Some center deputies were tempted by the overture announced by François Mitterrand after his election in 1988, but the party was afraid of becoming the hostage of the Socialists. That is why the president of the Republic dissolved the National Assembly. The few defectors from the center who did rally to the Socialists and become ministers were all ousted or withdrew from the cabinet—two in very ambiguous circumstances following the 1992 regional ballot in which their election as regional presidents was attributed to National Front support. Thus there was some surprise when Premier Bérégovoy later reinstated Jean-Pierre Soisson as minister of agriculture. In 1993 Pierre Méhaignery became minister of justice in the Balladur cabinet.

Le Parti républicain (PR)

Party president: Gérard Longuet.

Representativity: 104 National Assembly deputies.

The heyday of the neoliberals was in 1985, when one million demonstrators—but not only liberals—marched through Versailles to oppose the Socialist project of banning state aid to private schooling. The stock market crash of 1987 that was to halt the French privatization program somewhat tempered the liberalism of the French, which had really only flourished in reaction to Socialist abuses. It would be electoral suicide in France for any party to propose complete state withdrawal from economic policy, and though the French liberals pay lip service to Milton Friedman and the Chicago School, they made it quite clear before the 1988 elections that, if elected, they would not go back on the social reforms introduced by the Left in 1981. The young Turks of the party, Alain Madelin, and François Léotard, who can scarcely disguise his presidential ambitions, or the president of the Rhône-Alpes region, Charles Millon, do not always see eye to eye with the older generation, led by Valéry Giscard d'Estaing. One PR deputy, Philippe de Villiers, founder of a "Movement for Values," became something of an embarrassment to the moderate Right in 1992 with his glib sarcasm directed at the political establishment, which resembles strangely the style of another Breton, Le Pen. De Villiers, in defiance of the party line, also campaigned against the Maastricht treaty.

Le Front National (FN)

Party leader: Jean-Marie Le Pen.

Representativity: no National Assembly deputy.[3] Represented in all Regional Councils since 1992, when they scored 13.9 percent of the votes, one percentage point less than the combined ecologist vote. Even though the FN scored 12.5 percent of the votes in the first round of the 1993 legislative elections all its candidates, including Le Pen himself, were eliminated in the second round, and it lost the one and only seat it had in the National Assembly.

Modeled on the prewar "national" Right-wing movement, this party was set up in 1972 by a group of leaders of the neofascist Ordre nouveau organization in view of the legislative elections that were to take place the following year. Their objective was to update the 1941–42 *révolution nationale* program of Philippe Pétain that aimed to put a stop to national "decadence," renewing thus an older French tradition founded on Comte de Gobineau's *Essai sur l'inégalité des races humaines* (1853–55), which proclaimed long before Hitler the superiority of the white race.[4] Historians have shown that the idea of *décadence* expressed today in the three main themes of the FN—immigration, AIDS, moral decadence[5]—was already stressed in the writings of Jules Soury and his disciple Maurice Barrès and in Edouard Drumont's *La France Juive* (1886). It

3. The importance given to Le Front National in this book may appear exaggerated considering the parliamentary representativity of the party, but no study of contemporary France can afford to ignore this latest manifestation of a particular brand of French nationalism that has been amply studied by historians, notably Zeev Sternhell, Pierre Milza, and Michel Winock. A knowledge of the postulates of the FN and of their development is necessary for an understanding of the political, social, and economic stakes of the nineties in France, because these postulates are the antithesis of the ideals of liberty, equality, and fraternity that the French continue to claim as their own.

4. The author has drawn heavily on the series of detailed articles published in *Le Monde* from 4 February through 10 February 1992.

5. See Birgitta Orfali, *L'adhésion au Front National* (Paris: Editions Kimé, 1990).

was one of the main arguments of the prefascist nationalists of the late nineteenth century in France, who were active in the Dreyfus affair, before being picked up in the thirties by l'Action française, and in the forties, by the French State of Vichy. Ideologically, the FN owes far more to this French tradition of conservative nationalism than it does to Hitler or Mussolini.

The founders of the movement were mainly Algérie française revanchists and Vichy nostalgists. Le Pen quickly became president of the new organization, thanks to his popularity with the younger members fascinated by his "prestige as a former Poujadiste deputy, his reputation as a rabble rouser, and his irreproachable antipathy for the Gaullists."[6] Rooted in the "national populist" ideological tradition that has emerged on several occasions in the past, the FN today is a sort of *syndicat des mécontents* (union of the discontented), which explains to a large extent the success it enjoys among many categories of the population who are not racist but who feel abandoned by the other political parties in a France that is undergoing profound changes. As historian Michel Winock has pointed out, Le Pen has done what none of his predecessors were able to do, that is, "unite all the protesters, traditionalists, and Catholic fundamentalists, nostalgists of l'Algérie française, neonazis, neopoujadistes, anti-Semites, nationalists, ordinary folk terrified by the social and economic upheavals, rising delinquency, urban violence."[7]

In a country that has barely adjusted to the transformations of a postindustrial society and that is being forced to undergo the economic and social upheavals of the single market (the Europe without borders of 1993) the ultranationalism of Le Pen, strongly rooted in French ideological tradition and *Poujadisme,* has a powerful appeal to those who refuse the European consensus of the major political parties. A discontented

6. Alain Rollat, "Vaincre la peur," *Le Monde,* 4 February 1992. Pierre Poujade set up a nationalistic, *corporatiste* political organization in the 1950s. It originated as an antitax crusade by conservative shopkeepers and small businesses. See Stanley Hoffmann et al., *Le Mouvement Poujade,* Cahiers de la Fondation nationale des sciences politiques (Paris: Colin, 1956). Jean-Marie Le Pen, who dreamt of "pacifying" the leftist Latin Quarter, was among the activists of the organization. He was elected to the National Assembly in 1956 at the age of twenty-eight. He was to lose his seat in 1961 and disappeared from the political scene until the early 1980s.

7. Michel Winock, "L'extrême droite en questions." See Travaux du Cercle Condorcet, Ligue des droits de l'homme. *Etudes et Documentation Internationales,* 1991. Quoted in Rollat, "Vaincre la peur."

middle class, fearful of losing the numerous corporatist privileges it has clung to for so long, which were never really threatened as long as the right-of-center parties were in power, gives a favorable hearing to the ultraconservative, nationalistic rantings of the demagogue. At the same time, in a country beset with high unemployment where the worker unions strive to maintain only the prerogatives of those who hold down a job and where the influence of the Communist party, the traditional defender of the under class, has dwindled, those excluded from the new prosperity find in Le Pen's party a sort of brotherhood and warmth that has disappeared from their urban environment.[8] These are the people moved by his passionate speeches, which evoke the patriotism of Joan of Arc—his party has appropriated the national heroine!—and the "true" values of *la France profonde* (grass-roots France), which do not seem to be very far removed from the "work, family, fatherland" with which the Vichy regime supplanted liberty, equality, and fraternity.

Le Pen's party program is designed to appeal to the different audiences he represents. Besides xeophobia for the use of the poorer French in the ZUP, as well as for all those obsessed with insecurity and delinquency, he preaches economic liberalism. This is meant to appeal to the business community and liberal professionals, tradesmen, and shopkeepers who constantly complain of governmental regulations, high taxes, and social security contributions. Criticism of the "rock-rap-tag-Coca underculture" by his lieutenant Bruno Megret stirs up anti-American feeling, while refusal of the EC is meant to preserve the interests of France in danger of being sacrificed to Eurobureaucracy. His attacks on the "political establishment" at a time when the other parties are not exactly paragons of virtue naturally appeal to all the discontented. Le Pen's attempts to gain respectabilty in other circles, such as the world of art and entertainment or the army, do not generally appear to have been very successful. Meanwhile the churches and the Catholic hierarchy have kept the FN at arm's reach despite the close links between the *intégristes* and the party that venerates Joan of Arc and makes masses in Latin a regular feature of its gatherings. After the 1988 presidential election Cardinal Lustiger, archbishop of Paris, condemned the FN very severely, comparing it to the "antichristian, neopaganism of l'Action Française" (the prewar, anti-Semitic, monarchist movement of Charles Maurras de-

8. See the remarkable investigation by Anne Tristan, *Au Front* (Paris: Gallimard, 1987).

nounced by Pope Pius XI in 1926). On March 28, 1993, the aging, but still alert abbé Pierre, defender of the under class, galvanized a conventional election night TV program when he expressed sorrow and anger for the twelve percent of voters who had been duped "by someone [Le Pen] who had published Nazi songs."

With the skill and vehemence of a TV preacher, Le Pen appeals to the emotions of his audience, crying out "I love you" in the more intense moments, and the more he is ostracized by the political establishment, the more his militants and supporters admire him.[9] Among Le Pen's followers are disappointed Gaullists and disillusioned Socialists and Communists, not to mention a collection of dissatisfied intellectuals from the universities of Lyons, Aix-en-Provence, and Montpellier: "Deprived for decades of the exaltation of the fatherland, of the blood shed for France, of good moral conduct, of virile fortitude, these French people have turned to the FN to escape from the percentages, the inflation differentials, international interdependence, and Madonna's panties," writes Pierre Servent.[10]

This incongruous gathering of skinheads and petits bourgeois, of *pieds noirs*[11] and Vichy nostalgists, would be laughable if the Front had not more sinister designs than turning its back on the new France. The authoritarian, militaristic structure of the party, the instructions given to its militants, the list of words to be avoided or used by them in public debate, leave no doubt as to the political strategy of the movement that hopes to rule the country with an iron fist one day.[12]

---

9. The National Front advises its militants to provoke the hatred of its adversaries and quotes a "Prussian proverb": "A great many enemies, a great honor." Edwy Plenel, "Les militants-soldats du Front National," *Le Monde*, 30 March 1990.

10. Pierre Servent, "Une clientèle populaire mêlée aux habitués de l'extrême droite," *Le Monde*, 25 February 1988.

11. *Pied noir* (lit. "black foot"), a name given to the citizens of Algiers because they walked barefooted. It designates the inhabitants of Algeria, of European origin, before independence.

12. The quotations from internal documents of the National Front published in *Le Monde* in March 1990 expose the military-type strategy ("order, discipline, organization") to be adopted by activists: "Politics is a combat, and our Movement is an army." Two types of words are to be avoided in debate: "those belonging to Marxist ideology and those belonging to the ideology of human rights." Thus a National Front activist should not use the term *masses* but *peoples* and should say "socioprofessional categories" instead of "classes." Likewise, the word *employers* should be used instead of *bosses*. The *proimmigrationists* are

Media Bashing

Bashing the media—which he sees as controlled by Jews—and discrediting the other political parties are among Le Pen's more visible talents. The fact is that neither the journalists, always ready to make headlines of his outrageous remarks, nor the politicians from Right and Left who seem to have no easy answers to the issues he raises—there are none—seem capable of effectively countering his attacks. The leader of the FN makes skillful use of the democratic principle of freedom of expression to ridicule Parliament and undermine democracy. It is true that the other political parties are too involved in vote-catching maneuvering and intraparty bickering to be able to present unanimous condemnation of his racist proposals, thus justifying to a large extent the withering criticism Le Pen levels at them. Having no united strategy, they react rather than act. In this way the National Front became the centerpiece in French political life in the 1980s. The position of all the other players was determined by their variable distance from Le Pen on the issues he had deliberately chosen to focus attention on.

The FN's first electoral success came in 1983 in a municipal by-election in the city of Dreux, which became the symbol of neo-Gaullist connivance with the extremists. In the following year, the Front scored 11 percent in the European Parliament election. The system of proportional representation, introduced for the 1986 legislative elections, allowed the FN to win thirty-four seats in the National Assembly, but with the return to the old majority voting system, reintroduced by the Chirac government, the party got only one seat in June 1988. The real surprise was the first round of the presidential election in March 1988, when more than four million French people voted for Le Pen.

It is often said that in France people vote with the heart in the first round and with the head in the second round. Pundits analyzed Le Pen's relatively high score in the first round—14.39 percent as against 16.55

---

to be dubbed the *foreigner party* and the antiracist organizations the *immigration lobby. Cosmopolitanism* or *globalism* will replace *universalism* and the *rights and duties of the citizen* will be used instead of *human rights.* The French term *l'établissement* should be used instead of the English term the *establishment*—commonly used in France—because the anglicism reinforces the "influence of 'the American way of life' on European culture." (Oddly, "American way of life" was not translated into French in the original!) Plenel, "Les militants-soldats du Front National."

percent for Raymond Barre (UDF) and 19,94 percent for Jacques Chirac (RPR)—as indicating agreement with his scathing criticism of the politicking of the establishment, "the Gang of Four" (Socialists, Communists, UDF, and RPR), more than approval of his xenophobic platform. In any case, it had the advantage of forcing the Right to clarify, for a time, its position vis-à-vis the FN. In the subsequent legislative elections the latter lost two million voters who had supported Le Pen two months previously. Nevertheless, 1989 municipal elections confirmed that the National Front is henceforth a party to be reckoned with. Some 230 sympathizers sit on municipal councils in medium-sized cities, and the town of Saint-Gilles (more than ten thousand inhabitants) in the south of France enjoyed the dubious distinction of having an aristocratic mayor who was a member of the FN, until he was ousted in 1992 for mismanagement of city affairs.

Many see François Mitterrand's scheming behind the introduction of proportional representation for the 1986 elections, which gave a national hearing and political respectability to the Front. According to one view the National Front was "the bomb thrown into the game of skittles" the UDF and the RPR were playing. If this is true, the president of the Republic was playing with fire. Whether contrived or not, the electoral success of the extremists served the Left by dividing the Right. The repeated flirting of the UDF deputy and boss of the Provence-Côte d'Azur region, Jean-Claude Gaudin, with Le Pen's party drew only embarrassed murmurs from the Right, while other deputies (Carignon, Barzach, Noir) were ostracized for suggesting a tougher attitude toward the FN. On the other hand, in the 1989 municipal elections, some local Right-wing alliances with the National Front actually contributed to the downfall of outgoing RPR and UDF mayors. The mainstream Right now seems to have learned the lesson, at least insofar as electoral alliances are concerned. The clear refusal of UPF candidates to negotiate with the FN for the 1992 cantonal and the 1993 legislative elections not only paid electoral dividends but was a severe blow for the FN, further disadvantaged by the majority voting system. However, its showing in the regional elections, in which proportional representation is used, offsets this relative setback. With a score of 13.9 percent—over 4 percent more than in 1986—the Front now holds 239 seats on regional councils across the country compared to 137 previously. And if Gaudin this time refused FN votes to win the presidency of the coveted Provence-Côte d'Azur region, at least one other president had less scruples, while two more, including Jean-Pierre

Soisson, successively minister in the Rocard, Cresson, and Bérégovoy cabinets, wittingly or unwittingly owed their election to FN votes.

The facade of unity presented by the National Front is deceptive. There have been rumors of a hostile takeover by a small conservative group close to the RPR and, in 1990, an open challenge to Jean-Marie Le Pen's leadership by followers of his lieutenant, Jean-Pierre Stirbois, who helped rule the party with an iron fist until his death in an auto accident in 1989. A number of high-ranking party members, including Olivier d'Ormesson, François Bachelot, and Pascal Arrighi have quit the party, as did the only National Assembly representative the Front managed to have elected in 1988, Yann Piat. She was replaced by Stirbois' widow, Marie-France Stirbois, who was elected in a by-election. Le Pen's autocratic rule, presidential ambitions, and verbal excesses exasperate Front members in search of political respectability. Not all FN supporters approve the initiatives of their leader. His pre-Gulf War visit to Saddam Hussein, from whom he obtained the liberation of a number of European hostages, was perceived as an ill-inspired attempt to recover national respectability as a serious politician and expert negotiator. The style reminded people too much of concessions made to another dictator by a regime that bowed its head in 1940. For Le Pen, an admirer of authoritarian government, Saddam Hussein had the additional charm of being an enemy of Israel, according to former FN cadre, Olivier d'Ormesson.

While the National Front proclaims its concern for "a better functioning of democracy and intends to bring new life to Parliament," an incident in the Palais Bourbon on the night of 10–11 October 1987, when it had thirty-four deputies in the National Assembly, showed its contempt for parliamentary procedure. This was the FN deputies' interference with the mechanical voting system that allows deputies present in the National Assembly to vote for absent colleagues. During a vote on a bill on drug prevention, the minister of justice proposed adding to this bill an amendment to a law on the liberty of the press that would allow people guilty of vindicating crimes against humanity to be indicted. (This was just a few days after Le Pen's declaration that the Holocaust was a mere "point of detail.") As few mainstream right-wing deputies were present at that late hour, the FN representatives, led by Le Pen, took it upon themselves to vote in their place, pushing aside those who were entitled to vote by proxy for the absent deputies and turning the voting keys in the locks.

Le Pen defended this commando operation as "a deed to defend democracy and give their say to the people."[13]

The chances of the FN governing the country one day, which previously seemed remote to observers, are no longer felt to be so following the Front's regular progression in the polls and local elections. A survey published in fall 1991 showed, paradoxically, that if a majority of people consider the FN "a danger for democracy" as well as "sectarian, racist, and not capable of governing France" 32 percent of the respondents declared they "totally agreed" or "quite agreed" with the ideas defended by Le Pen.[14] More than three million people voted for the National Front in the first round of the 1993 National Assembly elections.

The Left

The Left in France is represented chiefly by the Socialists and Communists. The left wing of the old Radical party that was so active in the Fourth Republic has only a small hearing today. Under the name Mouvement des radicaux de gauche (MRG) these radicals, who represent the Left-of-center tendency, joined the Union of the Left, which brought François Mitterrand to power in 1981. The MRG has ten senators and six deputies in the National Assembly, but only four mayors of towns with more than thirty thousand inhabitants. The extreme Left, contrary to the extreme Right, has no parliamentary representative. The presidential election is generally the only important occasion when these minority parties get to air their views. (In France, any adult can run for the presidency, if he or she can collect five hundred signatures from elected representatives (deputies, mayors, regional or departmental councillors). The tireless Arlette Laguiller, leader of Lutte ouvrière, the Worker's party, collected only 1.99 percent of the votes in 1988 and Pierre Juquin, the Communist party defector, 2.1 percent. (All the smaller parties are disadvantaged by the majority voting system used for the presidential, legislative, and cantonal elections.)

---

13. Nicolas Domenach, "Le Front National veut-il brûler le parlement?" *L'Histoire*, October 1990, 44–45.

14. SOFRES-*Le Monde*-RTL survey, 15–17 October 1991. See Olivier Biffaud, "La défiance envers M. Le Pen demeure élévée mais un Français sur trois partage ses idées," *Le Monde*, 25 October 1991.

Le Parti Socialiste (PS)

Party president: Michel Rocard

Representativity: the Socialist Party, after becoming the largest political movement in France in 1988 with 258 deputies in the National Assembly, lost more than two hundred seats in the 1993 assembly where it has only fifty-three representatives. Moreover, it holds only sixty-four seats out of a total of 320 in the Senate. After ten years in power the PS has lost the confidence of its voters. With only 17.6 percent of the votes in the second round of the legislative elections the Socialists obtained their lowest score in the history of the Fifth Republic. The regional and cantonal elections of 1992 had already revealed the extent of the damage. With a score of 17.87 percent in the regional ballot the Socialists were down twelve percentage points on their 1986 results. They even lost one of the two regional presidencies that they had won six years before. In addition to the loss of the Nord-Pas-de-Calais region, a traditional Socialist stronghold, they lost five other fiefdoms in the cantonal elections. They now have a majority in only twenty-four of the ninety-nine départements.

In 1905 Jean Jaurès managed to unite the various socialist movements in France and set up the SFIO (Séction française de l'internationale ouvrière), a revolutionary workers' party. In 1920, the socialist minority opposed the pro-Leninist majority and quit the movement under the leadership of Léon Blum. In 1969 a new Socialist party that merged various tendencies, with the exception of the Communists and the PSU (Parti socialiste unifié, led by Michel Rocard), was founded.[15] François Mitterrand was to join two years later. Mitterrand's genius as secretary general of the new party was to reconcile Socialists and Communists, provisionally at least, in the electoral cartel of the Union of the Left, which proved so profitable to the Socialists.

The Socialists' first-hand experience of power has somewhat modified their radicalism. During their first spell of government, under Premier Pierre Mauroy (1981–83), they discovered that there are no easy solutions to unemployment and the economic crisis. They learned the hard way

15. In 1960 Michel Rocard, then a student activist, helped found the PSU, which came to the fore during the 1968 student riots. In 1974, he quit this leftist organization to join the Socialist party. The PSU no longer exists.

that a Keynesian policy of reflation, sweeping nationalization of industry, and price and wage controls does not necessarily work in a world of interdependent economies. The lesson came too late to pay electoral dividends in 1986, although the Socialists had already abandoned their ideological approach to issues under the government of Laurent Fabius, Mitterrand's second prime minister (1983–86). The Right-wing government of Jacques Chirac (1986–88) made the fatal mistake of thinking that neoliberal doctrine could replace socialist doctrine, and the Socialists finally collected the dividends of their conversion to moderation in 1988. Until mid-1991 the pragmatic approach of Prime Minister Michel Rocard in the aftermath of the 1988 electoral victory seemed to indicate that the Socialists had finally abandoned ideology and would remain in power for a long time if, in their own words, they "didn't play the fool." Scarcely a year later, the record unpopularity rating of Edith Cresson, whom Mitterrand inexplicably appointed to replace Rocard in May 1991, and the disastrous results of the regional and cantonal elections, forced the president to demand the resignation of the feisty lady he had chosen to give "a fresh start" (*un nouvel élan*) to an increasingly peevish France that had succumbed to inexplicable *sinistrose* (gloom). The reassuring, but hardly inspiring Pierre Bérégovoy, ex-minister of finance and father of the policy of rigueur, was given the task of patching up the damage before the legislative elections of 1993. Jacques Delors, chairman of the European Commission, might have proved a more popular choice, but the latter seemed to have little desire to jeopardize his chances of becoming president of the Republic one day by tying his destiny to a party that is falling to pieces. Bérégovoy, despite his legendary powers of negotiation, failed to rehabilitate the reputation of the Socialists, tainted by financial scandals, incompetence at the highest level (illustrated, in particular, by the AIDS scandal that led to the contamination of hundreds of hemophiliacs), political intrigues, an inability to foresee and address the everyday preoccupations of citizens, and above all, the absence of any real project to change society.[16] In other words, the Socialists had disappointed their voters, who expected something more from them than artful management of the growth rate and inflation.

---

16. Jerôme Jaffré, "Socialistes et opinion: le divorce," *Le Monde*, 23 January 1992. Deeply affected by the Socialists' defeat in the legislative elections and an insidious press campaign, Pierre Bérégovoy committed suicide in May 1993.

Currents and Waves

The various ideological currents that have agitated the Socialist party throughout its troubled history, which it managed to downplay in the post-1981 euphoria, have surfaced again. One tendency is Socialisme et République, which remains the most Marxist element, favorable to a hands-on state control and deeply critical of "the Europe of merchants" being ushered in by the single market. It is led by former minister of defense Jean-Pierre Chevènement, whose surprise resignation in the heat of the Desert Storm operation in the Persian Gulf revealed the complexity of relations among the various Socialist currents. The leader of Socialisme et République has always believed that the interests of the United States and those of Europe have little in common and that France's future lies in forging links with the Arab countries, a policy he believed the country's participation in the Gulf War with the Americans would jeopardize.

The social-democratic "revisionist" Rocard current, which believes in free-market principles and appeals more to the middle classes, is headed by former prime minister Michel Rocard (1988–1991). The Mitterrand current is split between the *jospinistes,* the supporters of Lionel Jospin, former minister of education, and the *fabusiens,* the supporters of former premier Laurent Fabius. The Jospin current has been described as "the center of gravity" of the party, opposed to both the Marxist extreme and the "free-market" tendency that was favored by Michel Rocard. Finally, Pierre Mauroy, another former premier, heads the Action socialiste current, which is closest to the spirit of the old SFIO and is allied to the *Mitterrandistes.* A new current, the Gauche socialiste, led by Julien Dray and Jean-Luc Mélenchon, has been very vocal on racial issues and, like Chevènement's followers, was extremely critical of Rocard's economic policies. It advocates "a beautiful alliance" of Reds (Communists), Pinks (Socialists), and Greens. In 1992 this tendency proposed setting up "an indicator of human development," a qualitative measure of the progress of society based on "individual self-realization." The conversion of the PS to economic realism and the social inequalities that persist, indeed the increasing gap between the haves and have-nots in contemporary France, made many grass-roots militants feel that the leaders of the Rocard current had sold the socialist soul to the devil of capitalism. The Cresson interlude did little to allay these suspicions. The ministerial team behind Pierre Bérégovoy was dominated by the *fabusiens.*

The War of Succession

The rivalries between the various clans have been sharpened by the personal ambition of their leaders, who all have their eyes set on Mitterrand's succession. The president himself, who is said to be a master at dividing to rule, is not beyond pouring oil on the fire, and it was he who opened "the war of succession" among the *Mitterrandistes* by proposing in 1990 his favorite, Laurent Fabius, for the coveted, influential position of party leader to replace Pierre Mauroy. (Mitterrand saw the former as the best man to renovate and shake up a party that has become somewhat lethargic after a ten-year reign.) The Jospin clan, bitterly opposed to Fabius, refused this arrangement. At the Socialist congress in Rennes the same year, the dirty linen was washed in public and had a disastrous effect on the brand image of the party, and even on Mitterrand, who made a last ditch effort in favor of his protégé, despite the opposition of the majority, who scarcely appreciated this presidential meddling in the affairs of a party that has always prided itself on its independence and respect of democratic debate. The result was that Pierre Mauroy was reelected party leader, but he stood down in favor of Fabius in 1991. This public airing of their interior divisions, and the attempts of party members to undermine Madame Cresson, may account in part for the defeat of the Socialists in the regional and cantonal elections of 1992. This shock treatment had a salutary effect, because, at the Bordeaux Congress in July 1992, the Socialists finally started to get their act together for the legislative elections. Incredibly, Fabius made peace with Rocard, whom the Socialists deem their best bet for the post-Mitterrand era on account of his continuous high ratings in opinion polls that, paradoxically, were not even seriously affected by his not so popular policies as prime minister from 1988 to 1991. In typical Socialist fashion the peace was to be short-lived.

A month before the legislative elections in 1993 Rocard, sensing the coming disaster, announced what he called a political "big bang." He warned the Socialists that times had changed, that their analysis of society in terms of the class struggle was no longer pertinent, that it was high time for the party to realize that the political landscape had changed. For political commentator's Rocard's speech, which was a plea for a renovated Left embracing Communist party dissidents, ecologists, social democrats and representatives of the Center, announced the end of the Mitterrand era, the end of a form of socialism inherited from the nineteenth century, which Mitterrand himself helped destroy after using it as a stepping stone to come to power in 1981.[17] Unfortunately for Rocard, his personal unexpected defeat in the legislative elections ruined the impact of his controversial initiative, and possibly his chances of running for the presidency in 1995. This did not deter him from launching a "putsch" in April 1993 against the party leadership. As a result latent quarrels among the different currents exploded. Fabius was ousted as party leader and a provisional executive controlled by Rocard took over. Meanwhile, a new current, the so-called *quadras* (that is, *quadragénaires* or forty-year-olds), headed by Franois Hollande and Ségolène Royal emerged. They look toward Jacques Delors to build a new Socialist party.

Le Parti Communiste (PC)

Secretary general: Georges Marchais

Representativity: the PC, like the FN, was favored by the system of proportional representation in the 1986 elections and obtained thirty-five seats in the National Assembly. In 1988 the Communists obtained only twenty-seven under the majority voting system when the PC totalled 11.2 percent of the vote compared to 9.7 percent in 1986 and 16 percent in 1981. Yet, to the surprise of all they lost only three seats in the 1993 tidal wave that washed away two hundred Socialist deputies. There are fifteen Communist senators, and the party controls sixty-eight medium-sized municipalities. The port city of Le Havre is now the only town of more than 100,000 inhabitants governed by a Communist mayor. In the 1992 regional elections the PC scored 8 percent (2.32 percent lower than in 1986), and 6.94 percent in the cantonal elections, compared to 6.35 percent for the FN.

The ideology of the Communist party, which grew out of the rift in the SFIO in 1920, is based on Marxism and Leninism. Their split with the socialist minority led to the setting up of the SFIC (Section française de l'internationale communiste), a mixed bag of pacifists, anarchists, and Leninists that was gradually to become one of the most hermetic bolshevist parties in the world by the exclusion of all those who did not

17. See Jacques Julliard, "Une quatrième vie pour la gauche," *Le Nouvel Observateur*, 25 February–3 March 1993, 44–45.

toe the official party line through the strict application of the principle of "democratic centralism." In 1922 the SFIC officially became the French Communist party. Its present leader, Georges Marchais, has headed the party for twenty years.

The colorless André Lajoinie obtained only 6.76 percent of the votes in the last presidential election compared to 15.4 percent for the Communist candidate (Marchais) in 1981. The never-ending rows with the Socialist party, which they generally supported as a last resort in the National Assembly, has divided the Communists. However, by voting with the Right on the motion to censure the agricultural policy of the government in June 1992 they nearly toppled the Bérégovoy cabinet.

Pierre Juquin, who was expelled from the party, has formed a group he calls the "Renovators." A number of other members, the so-called "Rebuilders," have rallied round Claude Poperen. They react by boycotting the decision-making departments of the party. A third group of opponents, the "Remodelers," led by three of the four Communist ministers that participated in the first Socialist government in 1981—Charles Fiterman, Anicet Le Pors, and Jack Ralite—want to reform the party from the inside. The iron rule of Georges Marchais is seriously challenged, but nothing—not even the dismantling of Communism in Eastern Europe and the USSR—seems capable of shaking the unswerving Stalinist line of the French Communist party leader, who was triumphantly reelected in December 1990 thanks to the bizarre electoral process inspired by democratic centralism. The stability of the Communist vote in the 1993 legislative elections is likely to reinforce Marchais's leadership.

The Communist party predictably opposed France's participation in the Persian Gulf War, and in its pacifist zeal went so far as to forge somewhat unnatural alliances with the extreme Left. This helped to discredit the French peace movement, which proved incapable of enrolling significant support among the population at large.

The Ecology Movements

The ecology movements in France have never had widespread appeal on account of the consensus on nuclear energy and a mistaken belief that France, with its extensive farmlands and forests and relatively low population density compared to the EC average, is not seriously menaced by pollution. The divisions among the early ecologists in the seventies and the tendency of their then leader, Brice Lalonde—later minister of the environment (1988–92)—to political compromise with the Left, hampered the ecology movements, which could count on an electoral base of only half a million voters, a million in the best of cases. Chernobyl, about which the French were grossly misinformed, the pollution of the beautiful Loire and the Mediterranean, and some "incidents" in nuclear power stations, as well as dissatisfaction with the political establishment, have helped the French ecology movements to gain a new hearing. Two million people voted Green in the 1989 European Parliament election—the Greens won nine seats, one less than the National Front and two more than the French Communist party—confirming the breakthrough of their leader, Antoine Waechter, in the 1988 presidential election in France. Although the party has no seat in the National Assembly, the Greens are becoming a movement to be reckoned with in a country tired of political bickering and increasingly aware of ecological issues, where even industrialists have jumped on the Green bandwagon in answer to consumer demand for "natural" products. There are now two main ecology movements in France: Les Verts (The Greens) and Génération écologie. A third movement, *Chasse, pêche, nature et tradition* (Hunting, Fishing, Nature, and Tradition), CPNT for short, a self-styled greener than the Greens movement, which started as a revolt against EC legislation designed to ban the ancestral ring-dove shooting in the southwest of France, is difficult to classify. While there are doubtlessly nature lovers among the CPNT followers, they have had epic battles with the Greens, who have a different conception of nature that does not include shooting wild animals and bullfighting. Ten representatives of this movement were elected in the Aquitaine region, that is, one representative more than the two ecology parties. In their way, the members of the CPNT, like the ecologists, express the frustrations of people whose life-styles are affected by bureaucratic decisions that fail to take into account their aspirations for a quality of life that the calculations of the technocrats obsessed with the quantitative (economics) omit. They naturally campaigned against the Maastricht treaty.

Les Verts

Party spokesman: Antoine Waechter

Representativity: in the 1988 presidential election Waechter, who was virtually unknown, totaled 3.78 percent of the votes, that is, just half the score of the Communist candidate. The Green's break-

> through in the European Parliament elections of 1989, with a score of 10.8 percent, made them serious contenders of the FN (11.1 percent) for leadership among voters dissatisfied with the mainstream Right- and Left-wing parties. This was confirmed in the 1992 regional elections when four out of ten of French voters voted for candidates other than those of the four traditional parties (RPR, UDF, PS, and PC). However, the Greens score of 6.8 percent was slightly lower than that of Lalonde's Génération écologie, probably indicating voters preference for "neoecologist reformism" over "primary ecology dogmatism" (*dogmatisme arcéo-écologique*),[18] that is, the Green's reputation for intransigence. The two parties signed an electoral alliance before the 1993 legislative elections and, like the FN, vowed they would maintain their candidates in the second round even though the Socialists, in a last ditch effort to ward off catastrophy, announced their unilateral decision to step down for better placed ecologist candidates The ecologist coalition's intransigence was, like Le Pen's, electoral suicide in a majority voting system. Although two million people voted for the Greens in the first round they obtained no seat in the new assembly.

The Green party, faithful to its principles of participatory democracy, has no official leader, but Antoine Waechter is its leading spokesman. The party has had a troubled history. The split between Brice Lalonde, who became minister for the environment in the Rocard governement—which had discovered the charms of ecology—and the ecological diehards who were understandably reticent about losing their identity in "the Socialist supermarket"[19] led to the founding of the Green Party in 1984. While Minister Lalonde's objective was "to ecologize politics," the Green party had a far more radical standpoint, which paid electoral dividends in the 1980s. According to a poll taken in late 1989, the ecology militants "do not appreciate the Socialists and are hostile to the right-wing parties; they do not like the army nor the Communists."[20] The Greens, fiercely jealous of their independence, have not always been able to avoid taking sides in political debate as their participation in the peace marches during

18. Jean-François Kahn, "L'explosion protestataire," *L'Evènement du Jeudi*, 26 March–1 April 1992, 6–9.

19. Valérie Devillechabrolle, "Les élus de la Manche se méfient du 'Supermarché' socialiste," *Le Monde*, 18 November 1989.

20. SOFRES–*Le Monde* poll, November 1989. See Olivier Biffaud, "Des militants purs et durs," *Le Monde*, 28 November 1989.

the Persian Gulf War showed. After much hesitation they also finally came out strongly against racism and declared before the 1993 elections that they would step down in favor of a candidate from another party in the second round only if a member of the FN was in danger of winning.

Génération Ecologie (GE)

Party leader: Brice Lalonde

Representativity: in late 1990, Brice Lalonde formed his own ecological party, Génération écologie, to defend his more pragmatic conception of the role of the ecologists, and in the 1992 regional elections, when the voters showed their rejection of traditional Left and Right alike, his fledgling organization scored 7.1 percent of the votes. GE and Les verts combined collected almost 15 percent compared to 18.3 percent for the Socialist National Assembly majority.

While the Greens have laboriously developed a political organization with complicated internal statutes and a party platform, GE is largely the brainchild of one man, Brice Lalonde, who sets the tone for the movement, many of whose members are reticent about any formal type of organization. Lalonde, who declared after the regional ballot that his organization would not make alliances with any single mainstream party for the election of the presidents of the regions but would vote on an ad hoc basis, was forced to resign from his position as minister of the environment after declaring that he did not consider it was his duty to participate in "a Union of the Left strategy."

The results of the 1992 regional elections were to raise two issues: first, the possibility of an alliance between the two ecological parties, the lower score of the radical Greens making them more receptive than before to forming a united front with their reformist rivals of Génération écologie; second, the question of applying the system of proportional representation—at present used for the election of the regional council—for the 1993 legislative elections. In fact, as the cantonal elections, which were organized simultaneously with the regional elections but on the principle of "winner takes all," demonstrated, the ecologists, who totaled in all only two percent of the votes, would have no real chance of parliamentary representation unless the voting system were changed. The Socialists' refusal to change the rules of the electoral game less than a year before the legislative elections forced the two ecology movements to get their act together. The polls credited the new alliance with 15 percent or more of the vote as election date drew near. As a result, green and pink (for Génération écologie) became the favorite colors of all the political parties, including the macho FN, in their attempts to woo ecology voters. The decision taken in June 1992 to suspend the start-up of Superphénix was clearly a major concession of the Socialists to the ecology parties, because the PS was hit most by the breakthrough of the Greens and GE. The Socialists could no longer rely on the Communists, who had nothing to gain from their support. It was the refusal of the PC to cooperate that forced the PS to vote for the first Green regional president, Marie-Christine Blandin, in the Nord-Pas-de-Calais region to prevent this traditional Socialist stronghold from falling into the hands of the Right. As Lalonde pointed out, the Socialists were no longer in a position to dictate their behavior to the ecology parties because "the ladder [had] been pulled from under them."[21] The misunderstanding between the ecologists and the Socialists would prove fatal for both. This was apparently the message Rocard had tried to transmit to his party before the legislative elections when he spoke of the urgency of a political "big bang." His warning came too late to be of any use for the elections, but following the electoral shakeout, it is hard to see how either the ecologists or the Socialists can do without allies. A "big bang," that is, a new political deal, seems to be inevitable.

A New Page

The landslide victory of the Right wing in the 1993 legislative elections opens a new page in the history of the Fifth Republic. Never had an election stirred up so little enthusiasm and never had a political campaign been so calm. The gravity of the economic and social problems facing the country where one out of ten people are unemployed, and the discredit in which the political class has fallen, tempered the triumph of the victors who have only two years to prove they can govern better than their predecessors. The presidential election is scheduled to take place in 1995 and the volatile French voters will be carefully watching the new team. On account of its overwhelming majority, and because it now controls all the political decision making structures both local

21. Nicolas Domenach and Murielle Szac, "Brice Lalonde," *L'Evènement du Jeudi* 2–8 April 1992, 16.

and national, except the presidency, the Right will have no excuse if it fails to address the problem of unemployment. The prudent declarations of the new cabinet, which is a subtle blend of the various RPR and UDF tendencies, the personality of Premier Balladur, and the presence of ministers, such as Simone Weil, in charge of social affairs, seem to indicate that cohabitation with a President of the Republic who has lost his troops should give rise to less friction than during the 1986–88 period.

The Left, which was severely punished, has also two years to reunite its scattered troops. Even though many of the party bigwigs, including Rocard, lost their parliamentary seat the majority voting system, which distorts the real representativity of the political parties, should not hide the fact that in the second round the Socialists were able to rally 30 percent of the voters, and that in terms of votes rather than seats the Right collected less than 50 percent of the total votes cast. The Left, therefore, cannot simply be written off. Moreover the Right and the Left should not forget that in the first round more than 20 percent of voters voted for other parties such as the ecologists or the National Front who have no representatives in the National Assembly, nor that more than 30 percent of French voters did not bother to vote in the second round. All those deprived of political representation are likely to become more frustrated if the recession continues and social tension may increase unless the voting system is changed, or unless the mainstream parties manage to bring the dissident members of their "spiritual family" back to the fold This will be the big political challenge of the nineties for both Right and Left.

The Electoral Game

There is no obligation to vote in France unlike some countries. The legal age is eighteen and voters have to be registered at their local town hall. Before elections, the town hall mails the electoral propaganda of all parties and candidates to voters. Elections always take place on Sunday. While abstentionism is increasing, turnout is still very high for national elections compared to the United States, about 70 percent for the first round of the 1993 legislative elections.

Except for the brief interlude of the 1986 legislative elections, when the Socialists introduced proportional representation following their split with the Communists to ensure a high score for themselves and, incidentally, for Le Pen, the electoral system of the Fifth Republic has always been the two-round, winner-take-all, majority voting system. Each French département is carved up into a number of electoral districts in which the number of seats in the National Assembly is not necessarily proportional to the number of voters. (There is much political haggling in drawing up the list of districts and the opposition is constantly complaining of gerrymandering.) Deputies are thus elected in single-member constituencies, and only the candidate who obtains an absolute majority in the first round is elected. If no candidate is elected, a second ballot takes place a week later. Only candidates who score at least 12.5 percent of the votes cast in the first round may run. In the second round a relative majority suffices. The first thus amounts to a primary within each camp. Those who score poorly withdraw but will generally advise their followers to vote for one of the remaining candidates. This permits much political maneuvering or interparty arrangements between the two rounds and adds an element of suspense to French elections.

With the system of proportional representation introduced for the 1986 legislative election, each electoral district has a number of seats roughly proportional to the number of voters, and there is a complex process for alloting seats to party lists according to the number of votes cast for each party. There is no element of surprise in this system because it is *before the elections* that negotiations take place. While proportional representation gives a picture of the real representativeness of each party and allows the smaller ones to get a political hearing, the main criticism is that it gives too much power to the party bigwigs who draw up the lists and who can use their power over dependent or servile deputies to make and break coalitions. These were the intrigues that de Gaulle denounced so vehemently.

The introduction of proportional representation in 1986 did help the Socialists, because even though they lost the elections, the PS remained the largest single party in France. The right-of-center coalition that obtained the majority in the National Assembly reverted to the majority system in 1988. If this damaged the National Front and to a lesser degree the Communists, it did not have the result the Right expected, as the Socialists with their "open-arms" strategy were able to rake up a lot of the swing votes that make the difference. As the 1993 legislative elections approached, the Socialists, whose audience had dwindled in the meantime, were sorely tempted to reintroduce proportional representation. Moreover, this seemed to be a logical step considering the increasing influence of the ecology movements, deprived of representation in the

National Assembly, even if there was a risk that it would also give a boost to the PC and the FN.

In March 1992 the results of the regional election, which is the only ballot to apply integral proportional representation, gave a new impetus to the debate on the electoral system. A SOFRES simulation based on the results showed that if the system of proportional representation were used for the upcoming legislative elections, the ecologists would hold seventy-six seats.[22] In fact, owing to the maintenance of the majority voting system, the Green parties got no seat in the National Assembly although two million people had voted for them in the first round, whereas the Communists, with less than 2.5 million votes in the first round, won twenty-five seats.

Unfortunately, the shady transactions that took place after the regional ballot in 1992 to elect the twenty-two presidents of the regional councils hardly proved the virtues of proportional representation. The backdoor negotiations of the candidates of each party, striving to constitute a majority at the cost of sometimes unnatural alliances, was reminiscent of the disreputable practices that were common in the Fourth Republic but which the Fifth had managed to eradicate thanks to strong parliamentary majorities obtained by the first-past-the-post system. *Le Point* spoke of the "Fourth Republic ragoût. . . . Swaps, offers of compensation, negotiations, sinecures became the common vocabulary of all, from the PC to the RPR, from the PS to the Greens."[23] If the voting system could cause such havoc for the election of twenty-two regional presidents, what would be the result if it were applied to the election of the 577 members of the National Assembly? One thing is sure: General de Gaulle would turn in his grave!

According to *Le Point* journalist Claude Imbert, the majority system is better because "it corrects two major defects of the French people: on the one hand the ancient Gallic propensity for disagreement; on the other hand, the confiscation, indeed the appropriation by a political caste of the will of the people."[24] Most observers feel that, rather than integral proportional representation, some sort of mixed system that gives a

22. Fabrice Rousselot, "Proportionnelle, la droite crie au loup," *Libération*, 24 March 1992.

23. Christophe Barbier, Denis Jeambear, Christian Makarian, and Catherine Pégard, "Le ragoût de la IVème," *Le Point*, 30 March–3 April 1992, 36.

24. Claude Imbert, "La règle du jeu," *Le Point*, 30 March–3 April 1992, 5.

preponderance to first-past-the-post criteria would be the most suitable solution. However, the Socialists' shaky majority in the National Assembly prevented them from reintroducing proportional representation at less than a year from the legislative elections. The victorious Right is not likely to be in any haste to change a system that has served it so well.

Political Marketing

> Who can measure how much of an actor goes into the making of a politician?
>
> —Alfred de Vigny (1798–1863)

Nowadays politicians are marketed like any other product, sometimes with bizarre results such as the series of Socialist posters for the 1988 National Assembly elections that featured a svelte young athlete in the nude with a rose (the emblem of the Socialist party) in his hand and a pregnant young woman, also naked, holding a rose. The least that could be said was that the symbolism was not very clear to the general public! National campaigns are increasingly Americanized, that is, big media events with laser shows and rock music. No self-respecting candidate today is without a cohort of stars.

Whatever misgivings the politically sophisticated French may have about the excessive personalization of election campaigns or about the politicians' use of gimmicks, foreign observers still continue to be fascinated by the quality of political discussion in contemporary France. The television debate of the leading candidates offers a brilliant demonstration of the political savvy and intellectual training of the French elite. Most of the major political figures since the 1960s have been énarques, graduates of the prestigious Ecole nationale d'administration. According to Scott Sullivan, head of *Newsweek*'s European bureau, to compare the quality of the television debate between Mitterrand and Chirac in 1988 with the American duel between Reagan and Mondale "is to put on the same level a reception speech to the French Academy of Letters and a series of Laurel and Hardy sketches."[25]

25. Scott Sullivan, "Deux classes politiques, deux façons de gouverner," *Le Monde Dossiers et Documents: Les Elections Législatives 1988*. Translated by the author.

Campaign Financing

In France, as in other democracies, election campaign costs are soaring. French political parties are funded by the donations of their members, which amount to less than one fifth of the total; the contributions of the deputies, between 1 percent and 40 percent according to the party; state aid; European Parliament aid, which is particularly generous for the Greens and the FN; and numerous illegal methods! Following a series of scandals involving political favors to party backers, Parliament finally passed a law in late 1989 designed to limit the expenditure on political campaigns and draw up a code of conduct. A ceiling has been put on donations by individuals and businesses as well as on campaign expenditures, which should not exceed Fr 360,000 (about $65,000) per deputy. Parties with representatives in the National Assembly or Senate are entitled to public financing. Finally, all preelection advertising is forbidden during the three months preceding the month designated for the first round. Apparently this new legislation is not entirely equitable; nor has it put a stop to shady financing operations, as the numerous scandals involving well-known politicians from Right and Left show. A report commissioned by Premier Bérégovoy, published in July 1992, showed that there was extensive corruption, even in local government, in the areas of public procurement and planning permits for large supermarkets, which require the authorization of the local mayor. Originally designed to protect small shopkeepers from big-store competition, the so-called Royer law has given rise to endless abuse.

Politicians

All in all, French politicians, who sincerely see themselves as serving the public good, are probably no less honest than politicians elsewhere, even if scandals tend to be nipped in the bud or peter out after an initial outcry in the media and an explosion of public indignation. (People seem to be more interested in the details, the unexpected developments, the pros and cons of the controversy than in the ethical dimension of the affair. The denouement of a Watergate or an Irangate would be impossible in France. Unlike in the United States, the press is more a spectator than an actor.) Considering the generally high qualifications and meager emoluments of professional politicians—in 1990 a deputy earned a gross monthly salary of Fr 36,867 (about $7,000) per month, but the net income of the average deputy rarely exceeds Fr 20,000 (less than $4,000)[26]—one can conclude that, in the majority of cases, a political career in France is a genuine vocation that is rewarded by the prestige it procures, or used to procure before politician bashing, aided by Le Pen—"they're all rotten"—became a national sport. It is not uncommon for French politicians to accumulate responsibilities on both the local and national levels. These persons are known as *cumulards* (multiple office-holders). A draft bill presented to the National Assembly in December 1991 proposed that the accumulated earnings of an elected representative of the people from his various offices should not exceed Fr 43,000 per month.

According to a law voted in 1985 elected representatives may only exercise two mandates simultaneously, but ministerial responsibilities are not included. Thus in 1993 Alain Carignon was minister of communication, president of the Conseil général, and mayor of the city of Grenoble! The danger of the system of *cumul* is that local interests may prevail over national interests in the National Assembly, as already happens in the Senate.

The Ideological Gap

Since the early 1980s political commentators and sociologists in France have been declaring that ideology is dead, that the Left-Right political cleavage makes no sense to the "soft generation" described by Gilles Lipovetski in his book, *L'ère du vide* (*The Empty Era*).[27] If this were true, the rivers of ink already wasted on the topic should have drowned the question for good. The idea that "the Revolution is over," popularized by a group of historians for the 1989 bicentennial celebrations, which were lauded as the expression of a new consensus on the revolutionary heritage, cannot hide the fact the majority of the French still remain faithful to their "spiritual family."[28] As an illustration of this, the results of an interregional survey by l'observatoire interrégional de la politique, published in March 1991, in which respondents were asked whether they thought public or private financing was most suitable for promoting

26. Pierre Servent, "Combien gagne un député?" *Le Monde*, 22 December 1990.

27. Gilles Lipovetski, *L'Ere du Vide* (Paris: Gallimard, 1983).

28. Jacques de Montalais, "Souhaits et réalités," *Le Monde*, 30 December 1986.

economic development, showed that the regions and areas (rural, urban) that vote Left consider that the public authorities should be the primary promoters of economic development, whereas those that vote Right have more confidence in private initiative. In other words, the Right-Left split continues to divide opinion about how to manage the economy. As Jean-Claude Thoenig, research director at the Centre national de la recherche scientifique remarks, such conclusions suggest that "a great deal of modesty is in order when referring to the discourse on the changing cultural and ideological scene in France. The relationship between the economy and the public authorities (state, region, département, commune) remains a stake in the game."[29]

Guy Michelat of the Centre d'études de la vie politique française has shown with the aid of factorial analysis that attitudes and behavior toward questions that have, strictly speaking, no relationship with politics, such as opinions concerning religion, hierarchy, the death penalty, worker unions, and the family, are firmly anchored Left or Right. In other words the inherited value system is different in each case.[30] On a political level, according to historian Michel Vovelle, the maps used to describe the sociology of voters today continue to show quite clearly the confrontation between two Frances that can be traced to the revolutionary split discernible in the map depicting supporters and adversaries of the oath of allegiance to the constitution of 1791 or the one that illustrates the dechristianization of France in 1793. The historian wonders if the end of the Revolution, decreed by the specialists, means the end of "French exceptionalism" and cannot resist expressing the hope that "the political culture of the French, which comes from the particularities of its history, in which the Revolution was the founding act, will remain alive: a practice of democracy, a conception of the state—as well as the idea of a secular society that is one of the originalities of the French—and, why not, the idea that the world can be changed, as it was in 1789, are not memories that one easily abandons."[31]

It would indeed be surprising if two hundred years of history could be wiped out in a couple of decades and if the 1980s, turbulent though

29. Jean-Claude Thoenig, "Pragmatisme économique et clivage gauche-droite," *Le Monde*, 4 March 1991.

30. Guy Michelat, "La dimension gauche-droite est-elle encore d'actualité?" in *Données Sociales 1990*, 389–93.

31. Michel Vovelle, "1789–1989: Héritage et contrastes," in Verdié, *L'état de la France*, 24–26.

they were, could have sufficed to Americanize French political life.[32] In fact, one of the less desirable aspects of Americanization—indifference to political issues—is criticized by the very promoters of a less conflictual society on "the Anglo-Saxon model." Alain Duhamel, among others, deplores the depoliticization of French society today, which he attributes to a triple crisis: ethical, in the indifference of a cocooning society to "community values"; cultural, in the ideological gap ("The production of political ideas is momentarily halted due to a lack of sellers and buyers"); and institutional, in the imbalance between the executive and legislative powers, which induces "a deficit of democracy."[33] That such an advocate of political consensus and "civil society" as Alain Duhamel should be distressed by the depoliticization of France shows the contradiction of a society that yearns for consensus and yet relies on politics, by its very nature antagonistic, to furnish solutions to the challenges facing France in the nineties (racial integration, unemployment, education, social inequalities, the single market). He is not the only expert to be preoccupied, and the modish term *consensus* is even becoming suspect. Jean Baudrillard suggests that there is something "suspicious" in the present "epidemic of consensus" in the world.[34] Meanwhile that odd species, the French intellectuals, the traditional providers of ideas to the politicians, are chided for their navel-gazing,[35] and the Greens, who do not always take a clear stance on political questions, are accused of "a certain ambiguity."[36]

Even the hackneyed expression *civil society* is being questioned. According to Nicolas Tenzer, "Present-day civil society has not a single common conscience but is made up of groups of individuals, indeed even individuals, who go about their business on their own." What the term has come to mean, he says, is basically an assortment of social groups lacking a collective goal: "To promote civil society, in the abstract,

---

32. As philosopher Luc Ferry declared, "It would be truly astonishing if the terrific political investment that characterized the 1960s had given way to the era of emptiness [*l'ère du vide*] in barely a score of years." Luc Ferry, "Le temps de la culture," *Le Monde,* 30 November 1990.

33. Alain Duhamel, "La crise de la société politique." *Le Monde,* 5 June 1990.

34. Jean Baudrillard, "L'hystérésie du millenium," *Le Débat,* May-August 1990, 65–73.

35. Roger Fauroux, "Les comptes de la politique," *Le Monde,* 9 June 1990.

36. Jean-Marie Colombani, "Un poujadisme démocratique," *Le Monde,* 7 June 1990.

means that whole areas of social life (e.g., education, the media, mores) ought to be independent of politics, that is, that a part of society, considered to be nonpolitical, can and ought to organize itself exclusively on a private basis."[37] This confusion between the private and public spheres leads to "consensus by default" or the absence of public discussion of issues for which there is no a priori agreement. The author of *La société dépolitisée* extols a center with a strong political philosophy capable of putting an end to and going beyond the sterile Left-Right quarreling by introducing new themes of discussion capable of repoliticizing society and of rediscovering the noble sense of *politique,* the original meaning of which is "pertaining to citizens."

The current debate is a vivid refutation of the idea of a depoliticized France. This soul-searching nation has not renounced politics, which remains central to the French conception of society, but is groping for a new definition after two hundred years of polemic. It would, therefore, be hasty to conclude that the present disenchantment with the political scene signifies the end of French exceptionalism: "The 'end of French exceptionalism' is, first and foremost, the end of the belief in the capacity of politicians to carry out politics on their own and thus atone for the weakness, indeed the lack of courage of the people. This state of affairs is forcing politics to become discussion."[38] In other words, politics is too important a subject to be left in the hands of the professional politicians. It is the business of citizens. This means that the decline of party politics does not signify the end of political debate. No politics, no France!

37. Nicolas Tenzer, *La société dépolitisée* (Paris: Presses Universitaires de France, 1990), 73.

38. Tenzer, *La société dépolitisée,* 309.

16

The French Garden

Imagine a garden of Lenôtre,
Correct, ridiculous, and charming.

—Paul Verlaine (1844–96)

French public gardens are models of geometrical precision and arrangement. Hedges are trimmed to an inch, color schemes respected scrupulously, paths traced in a beeline. Not a blade of grass is out of place. Each shrub and flower bed contributes to the harmony of the whole. In much the same spirit, French planners, since the 1960s, have played the role of gardeners to the hexagon and have consistently striven to correct the anarchical economic development of the country, which was the result of industrialization in the nineteenth century, concentrated principally in the mining regions of the northeast and along the major highways that inevitably converged in Paris. Industrial, prosperous France was situated east of a diagonal running from Caen in the north to Grenoble. The famous formula of a top administrator, "Paris and the French desert," summed up the lopsided economic development of the hexagon in the late 1940s and 1950s.

The massive exodus from the country in the 1960s and the tumultous development of urban centers, spawned DATAR (Délégation à l'aménagement du territoire et à l'action régionale), a governmental agency that was to play the role of head gardener and whose mission was to weed out the regional disparities and promote the harmonious development of urban, industrial, and rural environments nationwide. However, in the liberal-minded 1980s, official planning, and with it, top-down, technocratic blueprints for urbanization and rural development that had given mixed results in the late 1960s and 1970s, were downplayed. The Chirac government (1986–88) even toyed with the idea of closing down DATAR.

The decentralization reform, that is, the attempt to loosen the grasp of centralized government over local authorities, paradoxically launched by a Socialist majority in 1982, is now in full stride. It has given a new

FIG. 22. The precision of a French garden

bottom-up vitality to regional and urban development at a time when a revigorated European Community is changing the map of French economic dynamism in a postindustrial society where the Glasgow-Rome axis cuts across the southwestern axis that links Madrid to Catalonia in Spain and Toulouse in the southwest of France to Nice in the southeast and cuts across northern Italy to Bavaria. The classical distinction between the prosperous north and the underdeveloped south of France is no longer quite valid, although a "fragile, rural France" persists west of a diagonal running from the Ardennes to the Pyrenees. As Pierre Maclouf points out, the uneven development of the various regions has not been eliminated but has become more complex in the framework of a united Europe.[1] DATAR expertise, if not top-down programming, is thus more necessary than ever.

Decentralization

Decentralization in France should not be confused with decentralization in the United States or other countries. As some geographers have re-

1. Pierre Maclouf, "Redistribution des cartes" in Verdié, *L'état de la France*, 148–49.

marked, "It is altogether symptomatic that in all the European countries people speak of *auto-administration locale* (self-government or Selbstverwaltung), whereas in France the equivalent notion is *décentralisation*."[2] Napoleon, pursuing the work of the French monarchy, thwarted the revolutionaries' aborted attempt to set up a truly decentralized administration, although throughout the nineteenth century the process of centralization was tempered by laws that gave increasing powers to local authorities and a certain balance of power between the *préfet* (the officer who represented central government in each of the départements) and the elected representatives of the départements and communes. Nonetheless, none of the successive reforms of local administration to date has modified the central role of the state in France, whose political, economic, and social institutions (schools, hospitals, prisons, etc.) reflect the value system of the Republic that puts a damper on private or local initiative. This means that each of the territorial divisions is seen as a fragment of the larger entity—the state—and cannot create laws as in the United States, where each individual state is entitled to its own constitution and its own laws in so far as they are not in contradiction with the federal constitution. The French constitution states that "local governments are administered freely by their elected councils under the conditions stipulated by the law," that is, the law of the state.

Nevertheless, the importance of the 1982 decentralization reform, which has considerably increased the political power of local government entities, largely confined previously to administering the decisions made in Paris, should not be underestimated. The powers of the préfet, who incarnated the authority of the state, have been transferred to the elected representatives of the people. (No doubt one of the reasons why the decentralization reform was adopted in record time—it only took six months—was the increased power it gave to local politicians. One of the aims of the reform, drawn up by "the most legendary of the Socialists' local notables, Gaston Deferre," was "to bolster the power of the Socialists' locally elected representatives.")[3] A new impetus has been given to a territorial division of recent date—*la région*—henceforth on a par with the département and the commune. Meanwhile the communes and départements have received a fresh definition of their roles that has helped

---

2. Pumain, Saint-Julien, and Ferras, *France-Europe du sud*, 60.

3. D. S. Bell and Byron Criddle, *The French Socialist Party* (New York: Oxford University Press, 1988), 184.

to dynamize local development. The regions, départements, and communes are playing an increasing role in economic development, a task that used to be that of the state.

Important as decentralization is, some observers point out that things have not changed that much. Speaking at a commemoration of a decade of decentalization in Marseille in May 1992, the sociologist Michel Crozier declared, "We used to suffer from a confusion of power [between the state and local authorities], from a lack of responsibility, from insufficient participation of citizens. We have not made much progress on these three points." He concluded by saying that for the nature of the state to change, it would have to be able to tolerate the existence of other power centers.[4]

The financial autonomy of local authorities is limited by the powers of the *Trésor,* the French Treasury. Not only are they dependent on the state (which determines local tax rates) for their financial resources, but also the local taxes are collected by the state officials of the Treasury. And it is the Treasury that also manages local government funds, funds they are obliged to deposit at this institution and for which they receive no interest! "The state continues to be the banker, teller, tax farmer, tax payer, troubleshooter, good Samaritan, writ officer, fault finder, creditor, and debtor of the mayors and presidents of the general and regional councils."[5]

Les Régions

There are twenty-two regions (plus four overseas regions), each governed by a regional council, elected by the people for six years and presided over by a president. The region is a recent development in local government in France and is a purely technocratic creation, first formulated in the 1950s. The aim was to facilitate the application of national planning directives, as numerous administrative divisions (housing, transport, education—one calculation mentioned more than eighty) straddled the boundaries of individual départements. No attempt was made to take into account the ethnic, historical, or linguistic affinities between the départements that were to merge into this larger territorial division. One of the criteria that was used was the number of telephone calls

4. Rafaël Rivais, "La décentralisation, et après?" *Le Monde,* 1 June 1992.

5. François Grosrichard, "Malfaçons au Trésor," *Le Monde,* 26 November, 1991.

Local Government Financing

The main sources of finance for the various divisions of local government in France—commune, département, *région*—are:

1. Local taxes: property tax, land tax residential tax, and the professional tax paid by businesses, which alone covers about 50 percent of local government resources. There are different rates for the département and the commune, and they also vary from one part of France to another. Each of the three administrative divisions is entitled to a certain percentage of the total amount collected.
2. Certain taxes collected by the state, for example, road tax (*la vignette*), are transferred to the local government entities.
3. State subsidies, which are particularly generous for poorer places.

The bulk of these resources goes to the départements and communes, and it has been calculated that each French person contributes less than the price of a full tank of gas to a *région.** In 1987, regional budgets accounted for barely 6 percent of total local government resources.

The problem of local finances is a crucial one. Two-thirds of the French communes have fewer than five hundred inhabitants; and 90 percent have fewer than two thousand. Thus all have meager financial resources. Yet, they are called upon to provide services that cost money. One controversial solution has been to ask users to pay for services that, as taxpayers, they deem should be free. Top-down attempts to force small municipalities to group together so as to achieve economies of scale have not been very successful. Everyone agrees that it is necessary to develop new forms of intercommunal cooperation in both the cities and rural areas. One incentive might be to give greater autonomy to local government generally and to work out new contractual relations with the state. The French have been talking about intercommunal cooperation for a hundred years, but little progress has been made in this direction—37,000 communes in 1800; 36,452 today.[†]

*Some examples of regional taxes per inhabitant in 1989: Ile-de-France: Fr 506; Alpes-Côte d'Azur: Fr 370; Nord Pas-de-Calais: Fr 239; Bretagne: Fr 254 (*Le Monde*, 6 December 1990).

†Between 1971 and 1981 fewer than 150 of the 36,000 communes merged and the recent tendency is for some of those that did to recover their autonomy. See Armand Frémont, *France: Géographie d'une société* (Paris: Flammarion 1988), 36.

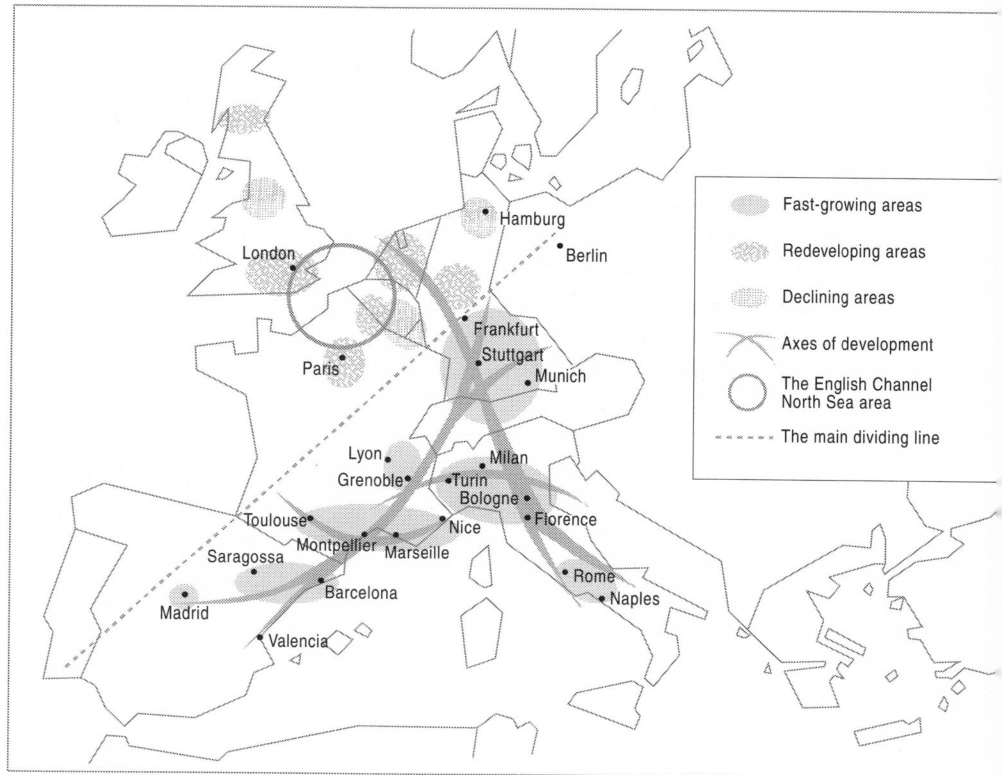

FIG. 23. The axes of European development. (From DATAR, Copyright © DATAR.)

between the major towns in the region-to-be! This may explain why many of the French do not know the name of their region, particularly when it does not bear the name of one of the ancient provinces. The creation of megaregions "of European dimensions" proposed by the Left in the late 1960s was rejected on the grounds that it threatened the unity of the state. The regions set up by the Socialist government in 1982 were modeled on the early blueprint. The first regional elections took place in 1986. Ironically, twenty of the twenty-two metropolitan regions were governed by a right-wing majority, although the Right had opposed the decentralization reform. In the 1992 election the Socialists lost to a Green candidate the presidency of one of the two regions they had managed to hold on to six years previously. This was Nord-Pas-de-

FIG. 24. The regions

Calais. The only region where they now have a majority is the poor Limousin.

The main role of the region is to encourage and organize economic development and professional training and to adapt national planning to local conditions through contracts with the state. It provides extra aids for housing, looks after transportation, and is responsible for the construction and maintenance of lycées. It also organizes educational, sports, and cultural activities on a regional basis.

In 1988, education and training, henceforth considered to be the most important resource and factor of economic expansion, accounted for almost 43 percent of regional spending. The regions are more than willing to finance local universities and institutes of higher education but naturally want to have their say in educational matters. This the state is loath to grant, seeing that it is a challenge to the very vehicle of the Republican value system.

Each region has a *préfet,* who is at the same time *commissaire de la république* of the major *département* in the region. (This means that the title préfet is now reserved for the representative of central government *in the region;* the state representative *in the département* is no longer called préfet but *commissaire de la république*!) The préfet is in charge of public security and defense.

Les Départements

The départements were set up during the French Revolution to put an end to the threat the feudal fiefs—the thirty-four provinces of the ancien régime—represented. Like the regions more recently, their boundaries were not established on the basis of economic, linguistic, or ethnic considerations but on the number of kilometers the gendarmes could travel on horseback in less than forty-eight hours from the main town in each département to quell possible rebellion. As of 1793 the préfets had a hotline to the authorities in Paris, at first via the optical telegraph invented by Claude Chappe (1763–1805).[6] Geographical designations—mostly names of rivers and mountains—replaced the old provincial names. Départements, which average sixty-one hundred square kilometers (about twenty-four hundred square miles) in size, are divided into a number of administrative subdivisions called cantons, in turn subdivided into a number of communes (townships) that can have anything from a handful of citizens in rural areas to the hundreds of thousands of large cities.

There are ninety-five metropolitan départements today (plus four overseas départements, French Guiana, Guadeloupe, Martinique, and Réunion), each governed by a general council (*conseil général*) elected for six years (50 percent of members are renewed every three years) by the people in the cantonal elections. The canton today is simply an administrative division used for electing the members of the general council, which has an elected president. In addition, each département also has a *commissaire de la République,* who represents the state. He or she oversees the conformity of the decisions of the general council with state regulations and is in charge of the police and security (Paris, Lille, and Marseille have a *préfet de police* as well).

The main role of the département today is the administration of social assistance programs (aid for families in trouble, the unemployed, the

6. Yves Lacoste, "La formation du territoire," in Cordellier, *L'état de la France 1992,* 160–61.

FIG. 25. The old provinces

poor); the organization of transport, including school busing; the construction and maintenance of collèges; the administration of public libraries; the care of mountain paths for hikers; the organization of sports, cultural, and educational activities within the département; as well as the construction and maintenance of the road network (*routes départementales*).

There have been some conflicts between the state and local authorities. The La Ciotat affair is a good example. The shipyards in this Mediterranean port near Marseille, crippled by the crisis in shipbuilding, were threatened with closure. The state, which already pours subsidies into Saint-Nazaire and Le Havre, refused to sustain the Mediterranean site, deeming that La Ciotat should abandon shipbuilding and develop new industries. The Left-wing majority in the general council of the département, whose president is himself a Socialist, did not see things in the same light. In 1991, pressured by the CGT (Confédération générale de travail), the tough pro-Communist workers' union, it conceded the shipyards for thirty years to an American-Swedish group, Lexmar. The

France's Overseas Départements and Territories

The four overseas départements, known as the DOM (*Départements d'outre-mer*), are: French Guiana (91,000 sq. km.) in equatorial South America; the islands of Guadeloupe (1,780 sq. km.) and Martinique (1,100 sq. km.) in the Carribean; and, since 1978, the island of Réunion in the Indian Ocean. These four départements enjoy the same status as any of the 95 domestic départements, and their citizens have the same rights and benefits. The Comoro island of Mayotte and St. Pierre and Miquelon (242 sq. km.) in the North Atlantic have a special status.

The overseas territories, TOM (*Territoires d'outre-mer*) are New Caledonia (19,058 sq. km.) in the Pacific Ocean; the islands of Wallis and Futuna (255 sq. km.); and French Polynesia (3,250 sq. km. for the inhabited islands). The overseas territories enjoy greater local autonomy than the overseas départements but have fewer rights and benefits.

The Southern and French Antarctic lands consist of the eastern part of the Antarctic mainland, Adélie Land (432,000 sq. km.) and the archipelagos of Crozet (300 sq. km.) and Kerguelen (7,215 sq. km) as well as the islands of St. Paul (54 sq. km.) and Amsterdam (7 sq. km.). These territories have a special status and are only inhabited by scientific and military personnel.

Both the départements and territories send delegates to the National Assembly and the Senate.

---

general council was able to do this because since 1982 the public maritime area is no longer under the control of the state but of the local authorities. La Ciotat's chances of being able to compete with the Japanese and Korean shipbuilding giants are very slight, and the state rightly believed that the venture was unrealistic, but its hands were tied by the decentralization laws. In a country where central government plays such a powerful role in the economy, La Ciotat's rebellion is a proof, even if it is a negative one, that local authorities are no longer under the heel of the state in economic matters. In the past, the préfet would have simply ordered the *conseil général* to comply with the wishes of Paris.

One of the biggest gripes with the département is that the urban centers are underrepresented and that the rural cantons have an excessive influence, considering their smaller population. The Socialists envisaged a reform of the cantonal election system that would include some measure of proportional representation to correct the present imbalance. But the mainstream Right that controls the majority of the départements clings to the two-round, first-past-the-post system.

Liberty versus Reason

The France of thirty-six thousand communes has espoused neither the spirit of geometry of the Enlightment nor the economic efficiency of the twentieth century. The map is a crumbled jigsaw puzzle that dates from another age. The phenomenon seems to be sufficiently important and persistent not to be the fruit of pure chance. Very few nations in the world have pushed to such an extreme the paradox of such a centralized state and such a large number of communes, so antiquated, so archaic very often, and nearly always so lovable. The paradox is costly and is, no doubt, largely responsible for the economic deficit of the country at a time when it is necessary to pay tribute to the tough rules of international competition. But it is also related to a value system that the majority of the French esteem irreplaceable as well. France cannot afford to forgo this cost. In the final analysis, the multiplicity of communes can be analyzed as a very tight but very solid network of local liberties won a long time ago, of solidarity constantly recomposed, of quaint enjoyment and amusements, of identification with a varied landscape. The relations between men have the fresh tang of informal companionship, with a faint tinge of craftiness and dishonesty for good measure directed at the uniformity of the urban environment and also a bit at the state, even if its legitimacy is never called in question. Liberty expressed in this way is not abstract. The speeches of the *notables*, the commemoration of the dead, the bravados of the rugby team, the accents of the sunny south, or the silence of the Normands express it in the corner of the village squares, under the linden trees or the arcades, and even in the cafés at the crossroads in the suburbs. Viewed from Paris it is grass-roots France (*la France profonde*), an incomprehensible mystery and the very first form of legitimacy.

Armand Frémont, *France: Géographie d'une société* (Paris: Flammarion, 1988), 37.

Les Communes

There are 36,394 communes in France, each with a mayor and municipal council elected by the people for six years. The French commune, the smallest administrative division, is five times smaller than the average European comparable entity.

According to the number of inhabitants the municipal council will have between nine and sixty-nine members (Paris, Lyon, and Marseille have more). There are, in all, about 700,000 local representatives in France.

French mayors have considerable power. Elected for six years by the council, they cannot be forced to resign, although they can freely delegate specific responsibilities to their aides (*adjoints*) and just as freely withdraw them. They represent the state and are in charge of the census, the updating of electoral lists, and the material organization of elections. They supervise births, deaths, and marriages and actually perform marriages. The mayor is also chief of the municipal police and is in charge of public health, order, and security in the commune. All the polls show that, of all the political representatives in France, the mayor is the most popular.

The main role of the commune is the registration of births, deaths, and marriages, urban development and intercommunal development, land stewardship (*plans d'occupation des sols*), and the granting of building permits. Local housing projects and transportation, the construction and maintenance of nursery and elementary schools, and looking after the local road network (*chemins communaux*) are among the other tasks of the municipal council.

The new powers of the communes have changed the status of the mayor, who has little in common with the local *notable* of the past except in the smallest rural communities. A self-assessment survey undertaken in 1988 shows that the mayors underscored professionalism, interest in economics and social questions, openness to new techniques, and prudence in financial matters. The political complexion of the respondents did not appear to be a very important element in this survey.[7]

Yet, politics is very much alive on a local level, and there are many cases of abuse of new mayoral prerogatives, particularly in the granting of building permits. Another issue that has stirred up considerable controversy is the question of the privatization of certain services—school canteens, transport, trash disposal, street parking lots, funeral services—hitherto considered public. Even the municipal police, whose powers are strictly preventive, are looked upon with suspicion by the national police.

In a France where issues tend to be perceived in terms of winning or losing rather than compromise and where, consequently, the abuse of power by people in positions of authority is commonplace (a mayor who refuses to register an immigrant child in the local primary school because he feels that his commune is already swamped by immigrant families), the withdrawal of the state, the traditional guarantor of equal treatment

7. CSA–*Le Monde, Le Monde Dossiers et Documents,* no. 164, March 1989.

of all citizens, is not easily accepted. People want to have a greater say in local affairs, but as participatory democracy is still in its infancy, they still rely heavily on state intervention to resolve conflict. In the case in point the minister of education ordered the mayor to respect the law on the right to free education for all.

On the other hand, some local initiatives are becoming models for national policy. For example, a municipal version of the minimum integration income existed in several cities before it was adopted by the government nationwide. In the words of one journalist, "The commune remains the testing ground for community life."[8]

A Two-Track France?

There are enormous discrepancies among regions. Thus l'Ile de France (Parisian area) produces more than a quarter of total French gross domestic product and the rural Limousin only 1 percent. The ambitious, egalitarian principles that had given birth in the 1970s to regional planning, which was designed to reduce the disparities between the poorer and wealthier regions, were largely abandoned in the 1980s, and subsidies dwindled. As a result, "Hundreds of rural cantons are dying, amid the general indifference of public officials, south of the Ardennes, in the Morvan and Creuse regions, and at the foot of the Cevennes. How many older people, having no automobile, complain that they cannot find a bus on a Sunday afternoon to get back home to their villages from Montpellier, Dijon, or Clermont-Ferrand." Meanwhile, says *Le Monde* journalist François Grosrichard, the hypertrophy of the Parisian region is getting worse and worse in spite of soaring transport costs and waste of money:

> France would be wise to do something about the situation: ministers tend to go more and more frequently and easily down to the country to deliver their political message, but all they see are the large towns between two airplanes, a squadron of bodyguards and collaborators urging them to stick to their schedule. The rural areas are growing numb, the towns are growing jealous of each other, and the strong regions are taking advantage of the decentralization laws. However,

8. Jacques-François Simon, "La nouvelle vie locale," *Le Monde Dossiers et Documents*, no. 164, March 1989.

the specter of a two-track France haunts the golden, paneled ceilings of the ministerial mansions in the Saint-Germain faubourg.[9]

Superregions

France is the only country in Europe to superimpose four levels of administration each with a deliberative assembly, a local executive, and executive services.[10] The system is not only costly but also difficult to manage. French regions in general are too small, in terms of population, and too numerous to compete successfully with other European regions in the EC. Current proposals suggest that ten or eleven would be sufficient instead of the present twenty-two. Yet any attempt to reduce their number, which has the favor of the Socialists in particular, encounters the opposition of those who fear that powerful regions may be a threat "to the unity and authority of the state." François Mitterrand himself is a staunch defender of the département. Département bosses, already disturbed by the increasing power of the regions, and the mayors of regional capitals, who have become quite powerful, are also not very keen on relinquishing their power to superregions.

There is even an increasing tendency to consider that the future lies in the development of the cities or, more precisely, networks of cities, and an interministerial commission has been set up to study the international dimension of French towns. France has only six or seven cities capable of competing with Milan, Barcelona, Geneva, Frankfurt, or Brussels. If Paris is one of the top two European capitals, Lyon, the second largest French city, ranks twentieth on the European scale. The gargantuan size of Paris has stifled the development of the smaller towns. While it is no longer possible to speak of "Paris and the French desert," the capital remains and will continue to remain unchallenged. The few large cities that have been able to emancipate themselves somewhat from the magnetism of Paris are all situated on the periphery of the hexagon. Only in the developing countries does one find such an imbalance between the capital and the other large towns. As geographer Armand

9. François Grosrichard, "Le Waterloo de l'aménagement du territoire," *Le Monde*, 16 December 1988. The Bourbon Palace and many of the ministries are in the Faubourg Saint Germain quarter in Paris.

10. Pierre Mazeaud, "Refaire la carte de la France," *Le Monde*, 1 February 1989.

Frémont shrewdly remarks, Paris, unlike large American cities, has no central business district to highlight the importance of this function. The center of Paris "expresses first and foremost the power of the state and only incidentally that of merchants, financiers, and industrialists, in keeping with the very image of France."[11]

At a symposium held in Bordeaux in April 1990 on the future of the French cities in the EC, Jean Auroux, mayor of Roanne, declared that the combined state subsidies his city received were "barely equivalent to the cost of five kilometers of highway in Ile-de-France." The medium-sized towns (30,000 to 100,000 inhabitants), "the ultimate bond with rural France," in the words of Auroux, no longer want to be left in the lurch.[12]

Acting on this in early 1992, Edith Cresson showed that regional planning had not been abandoned. In her typical outspoken style, the prime minister created a neologism and an uproar with her *délocalisation* plan that involved transferring some of the major French administrative structures—research centers, education, and defense departments—from Paris to the provinces in order to reduce the "hypertrophy of the Parisian area." The loudest complaints came from the teachers, students, and graduates of l'Ecole nationale d'administration, "exiled" to Strasbourg, and there were cries of "exodus" and "deportation" from civil servants' unions. It is true that they had not been consulted on this move to the "French desert!"

A report delivered to the prime minister in fall 1989 warned against "the fratricidal competition between the cities that is damaging to all concerned" and urged the state to use its powers of "persuasion and decision" to incite the cities to cooperate in a European perspective.[13] This illustrates the limits of decentralization in France. Even if the mode of intervention of the state has changed—contractual relations tend to replace the governmental decrees of the past—it does not turn a blind eye on local affairs and is indeed expected to regulate, arbitrate, and stimulate local initiative as the report stresses. Planning is back in a new style and the Tenth Plan (1989–93), designed to develop contracts be-

---

11. Frémont, *France, géographie d'une société*, 211–12.

12. François Grosrichard, "Entre la puissance et la convivialité," *Le Monde*, 10 May 1989.

13. François Grosrichard, "L'Etat doit réagir contre la fragilisation de certaines villes et régions," *Le Monde*, 6 September 1989.

tween the state and the regions, underscores the importance of national solidarity. Rightly or wrongly, the French are not overconfident about the capacity of their society for self-regulation, and decentralization *à la française* does not exclude a certain *dirigisme* (state control). In other words, the head gardener will continue to keep an eye on the rose beds without neglecting the kitchen garden.

PART 7

France, Inc.

How can you fall in love with a growth rate?

—1968 student slogan

17

Understanding the French Economy

Fortress France

In France, state interventionism has been one of the most characteristic features of the economy since the seventeenth century, when French industrialism already bore a marked difference from British commercialism. There was no competition, strictly speaking, since the privilege of production was granted to approved factories by the king and the *manufactures royales* represented a pure monopoly. The state intervened in other ways, too, and Jean-Baptiste Colbert, Louis XIV's finance minister, published thirty-eight regulations and 150 edicts concerning quality norms for products. The tobacco monopoly today is only one relic of the ancien régime. There was no real labor market, and the conditions for joining the various corporations and exercising a trade were strictly regulated. In this sense, the French Revolution, by abolishing royal prerogatives in the social and economic spheres, may be considered liberal in inspiration.[1] Alas, many of the corporatist privileges abolished on the night of 4 August 1789 were to creep back in the nineteenth and twentieth centuries and new ones to be created. In fact many of the "obstacles to economic expansion" denounced in a hard-hitting report thirty years ago still persist, and most of the lobbies cited are as powerful as ever: notaries, pharmacists, taxi drivers, maritime brokers, not to mention "the aristocrats of today," the *corpsards* who, thanks to their brilliant performance in a competitive examination at the age of twenty-two, are guaranteed a salary for the rest of their lives no matter what their professional competence.[2]

During the industrial revolution gunpowder and tobacco were to remain state monoplies, but interference in other industries was regarded

1. Pierre Rosanvallon, "Une idée neuve en 1789: Le marché," *L'Expansion*, 21 October 1988, 60–63.

2. Airy Routier, "Les corpsards sont partout," *L'Expansion*, 21 October 1988, 84–87.

with suspicion by liberals and socialists alike, albeit for different reasons. Indeed, the nationalization of the Western Railroad Company (Compagnie des chemins de fer de l'ouest) in 1906 was fiercely opposed by some socialists, who feared that the buyout would play into the hands of the influential bourgeoisie intent on creating a monopoly to the detriment of the working population. The Communists had similar misgivings about the nationalization of the entire railway network in 1937, when the SNCF was set up, and they were to voice the same fears about the massive nationalization program of 1981 after their split with the Socialists.[3]

The father of nationalization and modern *dirigisme* was not a socialist or a Communist but the conservative General de Gaulle, which proves, if anything, that state control of industry owes more to the French obsession with centralization than to bolshevism. If the brief Popular Front government (1936–38) had been content to nationalize the railways, armament, and part of the Banque de France, the Constitutional Assembly (1944–46) in postwar France was to carry out a whole series of nationalizations designed, in the words of de Gaulle, speaking in Paris in September 1944, "to put the general interest before individual interest."[4] He was even more explicit in Lille three weeks later:

> We want to develop together all that we possess on this land, and to do so there is no other means than what is called the planned economy (*l'économie dirigée*). We want the state to direct the economic struggle of the whole nation for the benefit of all, to improve the life of every Frenchman and every Frenchwoman.
>
> At this stage it is no longer possible to accept this concentration of private interests known as trusts [elsewhere] in the world. . . . [It is necessary for] the collectivity, that is, the state, to take in hand the great sources of the common riches, and to control certain others without banishing, of course, those powerful instruments of human endeavor that [private] initiative and fair profit are.[5]

In order to facilitate postwar construction, energy (EDF and GDF [Gaz de France]), transportation (Air France and the RATP), banking (Banque

3. Jean-Noël Jeanneney, "Les nationalisations des chemins de fer de l'ouest," *Le Monde*, 19 August 1987.

4. Quoted by Lacouture, *De Gaulle*, 2:23.

5. Lacouture, *De Gaulle*, 2:117.

de France plus the four largest deposit banks) and thirty-four insurance companies were to come under state control, while Renault (autos) was nationalized as a punishment for its collaboration with the Germans in occupied France.

Planning

French strategic planning, the work of Jean Monnet, was to be so successful because the state controlled the key sectors of the economy, which it could regulate at will. Inflation could be kept in check through price and wage controls and growth fostered thanks to joint ventures between the public and private sectors and the enormous reserves of the state-supervised banking and financial institutions. The national electricity utility EDF could thus develop nuclear energy with the blessing of the state, and the launching of the French computer industry in the 1960s was made possible by state subsidies. Thanks to planning and mass production, which the French call *Fordisme*, France, for "thirty glorious years" (1945–75), enjoyed the highest annual growth rate of all the industrialized nations, including the United States—5.8 percent on average—and foreign experts were fascinated by the achievements of the successive economic and social plans that, continuing the far from negligible modernization of the country undertaken during the Vichy regime and the Fourth Republic, helped transform France from an agricultural to an industrial society.

Not everyone agreed with *dirigisme*, which pervaded almost every aspect of economic life. Many of the smaller and medium-sized firms that are the backbone of French industry complained of state interference, of excessive taxation, and about the tightly regulated stock market that was detrimental to investment and private initiative. At the same time, they kept asking for more state assistance.

Planning worked great in a buoyant world economy, but overconfident French planners greatly underestimated the seriousness of the 1973 oil crisis. They realized too late that cumbersome regulations were a handicap in a period of economic recession, when small was beautiful and adaptability to a volatile environment was the key to corporate survival. State nursing of lame ducks to prevent layoffs and purchase industrial peace, index-linked salaries, price controls, credit restrictions, and foreign exchange regulations, were so many fetters to industrial dynamism. It was in this economic context that France had its bloodless revolution of the 1980s, a three-round political sparring match between Right and Left that was to end in a draw.

The Revolution of the 1980s

There is no better introduction to contemporary France than the vicissitudes of economic life in the last decade, which reveal a powerful urge to reconcile certain features inherited from the history of French society, business, industry, and agriculture with the challenges of an open, interdependent world economy. With what can be considered either as recklessness, or an abiding self-interest, the country has submitted the main economic theories in vogue in the twentieth century to the litmus test of experience and has revealed a capacity for adaptation and modernization that leave nations with a shorter history on the sidelines. Even if some French fortresses still resist, there has been a profound transformation in mentalities concerning the role of the state in the economy.

"The morning after François Mitterrand was reelected, the Bourse index rose two and a half points. After his first victory in 1981 shares fell so fast that trading had to be suspended."[6] This wry comment in the *Economist* in May 1988 reflected not only the confidence of investors in "Mitterrand the Second" but the change in economic thinking that had taken place in France in less than a decade. Six months previously a correspondent for the *Times* (London), writing in *Le Monde*, announced the death of Colbert, the father of French protectionism,[7] and in 1990, the "Socialist" president was hailed as a great monetarist by the *Financial Times*, which suggested that *Mitterrandisme* not Reaganism or Thatcherism might be the lesson best worth remembering from the 1980s.[8]

The strength of the French franc today, together with the rehabilitation of the corporation, of profit making, of risk taking, so uncharacteristic of the country, have indeed ushered in a new France, but it might be overoptimistic to conclude from the economic liberalism, paradoxically dictated from on high, that grass-roots France has jumped on the monetarist bandwagon or that protectionism, in the form of corporatism and resistance to change, has been definitely eradicated. It is a story of ideological conflict for a nation fraught with contradictions in which,

---

6. "The Desirable Face of Socialism," *Economist*, 14 May 1988, 27.
7. Paul Betts, "Les funérailles du colbertisme," *Le Monde*, 9 September 1987.
8. "Mitterrand the Monetarist," *Financial Times*, 20 April 1990, 20.

according to General de Gaulle, the love of privilege goes hand in hand with a yearning for equality.

Round 1: Nationalization (1981–86)

Phase 1: The "New Society" (1981–82)

In the run-up to the 1981 presidential elections, after two years of recession following the second oil crisis, Prime Minister Raymond Barre managed to apply in a hostile social context the austerity measures that the other western economies had introduced five years previously, notably a wage freeze to bridle galloping inflation. This unpopular decision precipitated the downfall of president Giscard d'Estaing and his Right-of-center government. Discontented voters, alarmed by increasing unemployment, suddenly realized that *les trente glorieuses* were definitely over. They were therefore ready to be seduced by the *programme commun* (common program) of the Left. The Socialist-Communist coalition proclaimed that, if elected, there would be no austerity. It would create a "new society," notably by nationalizing the major sectors of the economy to facilitate the implementation of a redistributive policy that private corporations were apparently incapable of guaranteeing.

That such a radical program should have appealed to a relatively pampered society can only be understood in terms of the ideological debate between Left and Right and the suspicion, more often than not justified, that the government in power is more a regal protector of the inherited privileges of its clientele than an architect of progress. France, rudely awakened from its glorious years of economic prosperity, thought its present misfortunes (declining growth rate, high unemployment, belt-tightening) were due to the mishandling of the economy by what was considered the liberal Right, which had governed for thirty years with methods that would hardly have been considered liberal elsewhere but, in keeping with French tradition, had preserved the corporations from the harsh law of competition and thus weakened their investment and export capacity.

The Socialists came to power declaring that the state would stand in to replace "the lack of private capital" and make state-owned public enterprises "the spearhead of the economy to build a new future" through state investment, research and development, and so forth. "The nationalization program," declared François Mitterrand, "is a historical event . . . an undertaking of revolutionary importance."[9] Christian Stoffaës and A. Delion summed up the triple goal of the nationalizations as follows: *antitrust* (to prevent private or semiprivate monopolies in strategic industrial sectors of vital importance to the nation from falling into the hands of foreign competitors), *anticonflict* (to improve industrial relations, notoriously conflictual in France), and *antirecession* (to boost the economy through investment, technological innovation, and employment).[10]

The main idea was that state ownership would facilitate the handling of industrial strategy, that the large, hitherto undercapitalized enterprises, once nationalized, would act as a booster to the smaller corporations, and that they would become models for industrial relations by developing worker participation in a country where employees had little say in corporate decisions that concerned them directly. The new society of the Socialists would be more egalitarian, the fruits of prosperity more evenly and more generously distributed. This in turn would fuel economic growth. It was in this utopian context that the major French manufacturing groups, with few exceptions (e.g., Michelin, the tire maker, BSN, the food conglomerate, and Peugeot, the auto manufacturer) were brought under state control. The nationalization of thirty-six private banks and the complete nationalization of banks that were only partially nationalized previously brought 75 percent of French credit under the control of the state that offered "a pledge of superior rationality," this supposedly meaning that banks were not in business for the money but were to be partners in economic development as conceived by the Socialists.[11] (This had also been the objective of de Gaulle when he nationalized the big deposit banks in 1945.)

The scarcity of private investors—1.3 million in all at the end of the 1970s—made the nationalization operation relatively easy, considering how strongly attached the country is to private property. Nine of the largest industries that accounted for 20 percent of industrial turnover and 16 percent of jobs were nationalized. The buyout cost the state (that

9. "Nationalisations: le dogme battu en brèche," in *Le Monde Dossiers et Documents: Les élections législatives du 16 mars 1986,* 14.

10. See "Nationalisations et politique industrielle," in *Les Cahiers Français,* January–February 1984. Of special relevance in this number are: Christian Stoffaës, "Les restructurations depuis 1982," 56–64, and André Delion, "Le vrai problème, adapter l'Etat," 65–70.

11. François Renard, "Le pari perdu de la nationalisation du crédit," *Le Monde,* 17 March 1992.

is, the taxpayers) Fr 43 billion, but the stockholders had little to complain about, as the shares of the firms to be nationalized were valued on average 26 percent above their market value, and nearly all the industrial enterprises were debt ridden. For some companies, nationalization was a disguised blessing. ITT raked up Fr 215 million for the sale of its French subsidiary, which was Fr 2.3 billion in the red![12]

The Grace Period

The state in France was henceforth the principal banker, investor, and producer as well as the chief employer. It controlled air, sea, and road transportation, energy, and insurance, and the government could proclaim, like Louis XIV, "l'etat c'est moi." The French themselves could hardly believe their eyes, and for six months they went on a spree while the rest of the industrialized world tightened its belt and contemplated with a mixture of envy and irony "the Socialist experiment." Alas, the nationalizations, the five weeks of paid vacation, the lowering of the retirement age, the extensive hiring of functionaries, the generous wage hikes, the huge sums of money pumped into the formerly undercapitalized corporations during the period of indulgence that was later to be dubbed the "period of grace" (l'état de grâce) strained the financial capacity of the country.

The Socialists' diagnosis of the ills of the French economy was correct, but their remedy was hardly appropriate at a time when deregulation and deflation had become the battle cries in the other industrialized countries. Above all, the government had grossly overestimated the production capacity of French industry, which was incapable of responding to the demand their reflationary policy provoked. Imports shot up in spite of state bracing of the corporations and two devaluations of the franc, which were in vain because French industrial goods were not competitive and lacked major outlets abroad. The national growth rate dropped to 1.1 percent, inflation was running at more than 9 percent, and unemployment was on the increase. The utopian dream of the "new society" was shattered. Soon *nationalisation* would become a dirty word, while the state, incapable of sufficiently funding industrial development, had to turn to private capital. The EDF had to borrow heavily on international markets at sky-high dollar rates to finance its nuclear power stations; the SNCF did likewise in order to develop the high-speed train.

12. See Giesbert, *Le président*, 186.

The government had pumped an average of 12 billion francs per year into the nationalized enterprises—far more than could have been collected from private shareholders. In spite of this, the shortage of capital continued to be crucial. Most of the corporations remained in the red, with a deficit seven times higher than before nationalization, although a few thrived (notably, CGE, Pechiney, Rhône-Poulenc, and St. Gobain). Steel and coal were in a sorry plight, and the French chemical industry dropped far behind competitors.

Phase 2: Apostasy (1983–86)

In 1983, with its back to the wall—the reserves of the Banque de France had reached a dangerously low level—the Socialist government executed an abrupt U-turn and refused a third devaluation of the French franc—the classical response to industry's lack of competitiveness abroad. A curb was put on public spending and a wage freeze introduced to halt the importation of foreign products, which accounted for 40 percent of industrial and consumer imports combined. The state-owned lame ducks—coal, steel, shipbuilding—were told that they could no longer rely on the government to subsidize their poor industrial performance. The streamlining of the work force led to painful layoffs right in the very stronghold of French worker organizations: the Renault plant in Billancourt.

Unable to cover the financial needs of state controlled companies, the state strained its ingenuity to raise private capital. The Paris Bourse had its Big Bang, and Pierre Bérégovoy, the minister of economy and finance, became the darling of financial circles. Public enterprises were allowed to issue nonvoting *certificats d'investissement* worth up to 25 percent of their capital and *titres participatifs* that lay somewhere between shares and bonds with tax breaks attached. Another project designed to allow state-owned parent companies to sell off and purchase subsidiaries never became official, and there was much murmuring on the Left about "backdoor privatization" and on the Right about "backdoor nationalization." *Restructuration* became the buzz word, while the state acted with all the unscrupulousness of a capitalist: window-dressing company accounts, forced mergers, massive layoffs. As Bruno de Thomas remarked in *Le Monde:* "There is hardly any difference in France between state capitalism and private capitalism."[13]

---

13. Bruno de Thomas, "La privatisation en marche," *Le Monde*, 1 October 1985.

Economically, the Socialist experiment was a failure, although the restructuring of French industry would pay dividends in the long run. The five weeks paid vacation, early retirement, increase of the minimum wage, important reform of labor legislation, and so on were undeniable victories for those who were lucky enough to hold down a job, but the economic policy of 1981 was to have devastating long-term effects on employment.

Politically, the Socialists' conversion to economic realism came too late to save them from electoral defeat in 1986. They learned the hard way that social progress is conditioned by a healthy economy. As Alain Vernholes pointed out, "by a trick of history" only the Left was in a position to accomplish this mental revolution. The Socialists' enduring battle for a more egalitarian society, their undeniable generosity during "the grace period," conferred a certain legitimacy to the necessary *rigueur.* Only they could "accomplish the essential reforms and have them accepted peaceably by the country." Only they could get the French to swallow the bitter pill of austerity, to accept an end to wage indexes, to recognize the role of the corporation, to consent to a low profile state, to accept the importance of France's links with the EC and the EMS (European monetary system) as well as the risk of throwing open its borders: "The opening up to foreign countries is no longer considered as a danger that threatens our autonomy, that limits our independence of decision but, on the contrary, as a stimulant that gives a pep to our creative capacity, develops trade with other countries, and cuts prices for the good of consumers and our purchasing power."[14]

Round 2: Privatization (1986–88)

In 1986, prepared by the Socialists' conversion to free-market principles, the French were ready for another experiment. The National Assembly elections brought a right-wing coalition to power on a ticket of sweeping privatization and deregulation. (By that time it was calculated that 24 percent of the French economy was in the hands of the state, compared to 18 percent before nationalization.) The program was an ambitious one that went beyond reprivatization of the companies nationalized by the Left in 1981 to include the nationalizations carried out by de Gaulle in 1945. In all, sixty-five companies in industry, banking, insurance, and communication were earmarked for privatization.

14. Alain Vernholes, "L'apprentissage du réel," *Le Monde*, 24 March 1988.

In the space of one year thirteen state-owned enterprises were sold to private investors for a total sum of Fr 120 billion. The government could well be pleased with the result, as it had realized in a short time 40 percent of the privatization program that it had planned for the duration of its mandate (1986–91) and made a handsome profit into the bargain. In addition, the privatizations increased capital holdings by 30 percent on the Parisian financial marketplace and popularized the idea of investment for millions of middle-income people not used to playing on the stock exchange. (Nevertheless, only one in ten French people holds shares today, compared to one in five in Britain and one in four in the United States.)[15]

With the same enthusiasm that they had shown for nationalization five years previously, the French became ardent supporters of a money-spinning economy. Almost four million small investors bought shares in Paribas following an intense advertising drive in the media. The sales pitch was based completely on the snob value of becoming an *actionnaire:* by buying shares you would be among the happy few to participate in the adventures of a prestigious financial institution! However, the stock market collapse of October 1987 made the inexperienced investors very wary. By November the small fry had lost on average ten percent of their initial investment in the privatized companies. As a result, the final price of Suez, another financial group, was a flop, and the government was forced to slow down its privatization program, which has been justifiably criticized.

Deregulation

The government proceeded warily in the area of deregulation, partly to make the transition to a free market as painless as possible, partly to prevent foreign companies from taking control of major sectors of the French economy. Perhaps this was also due to a lack of real conviction, or to the innate incapacity of French Right-wingers, in spite of lip service

15. In 1991, the number of direct shareholders in France was between 5.5 and 6 million, a slightly lower figure than just after the privatization program in 1987. (However the number of indirect shareholders, that is, members of investment funds, almost doubled over the same period. Sixty-eight percent of the French still have no securities. Property remains the favorite investment for most people.) SOFRES survey for the Commission des opérations de Bourse and the Banque de France. See Dominique Gallois, "Les petits actionnaires, une mine abandonnée," *Le Monde,* 27 September 1991.

French Corporations Nationalized in 1981

Saint Gobain (glass)
Usinor-Sacilor (steel)
Péchiney (aluminum)
Rhône-Poulenc and Roussel-UCLAF (chemicals and pharmaceuticals)
CGE (electrical engineering)
CII-Honeywell-Bull (computers)
Thompson-Brandt and ITT-France (high tech and electronics)
Matra (weaponry): 51 percent
Dassault (aircraft): 51 percent
Paribas and Suez (finance) and 36 major banks

Cost of operation to taxpayers: Fr 43 billion.

French Corporations Privatized in 1987

Saint Gobain (glass)
Rhône-Poulenc and Roussel-UCLAF (chemicals and pharmaceuticals)
CGE (electrical engineering)
Matra (weaponry): 20 percent
Paribas (finance)
Suez (finance)
Crédit Commercial de France (finance)
Société Générale (bank)
Crédit Agricole (bank)
UAP (insurance)
Havas (advertising)
TF1 (television)

Earnings on transaction for state: Fr 120 billion.

to liberalism, to conceive of a really deregulated society. The state continued to keep a firm grip on the "invisible hand" of Adam Smith. True, price controls, which had been one of the unmistakable marks of *dirigisme* for nearly forty years, were abolished, but this major reform had been initiated by the Socialists. Foreign exchange controls were also scheduled to be removed. However, none of the state monopolies in energy, the utilities, or transportation were threatened. The *postes et télécommunications* were not deregulated although the value-added services were henceforth open to private entrepreneurs. It is true that the Chirac government that was to remain in office only two years had had its hands full.

All in all the French had every reason to be happy with the running of the economy. The policy of a strong franc and wage austerity introduced by his predecessor in the second phase of Socialist government enabled the minister of economy and finance, Edouard Balladur, to pursue the battle against inflation. Thanks to cheaper oil and the windfall from the privatizations, he was able to grant tax breaks to corporations and individuals and ease somewhat the effects of wage restrictions. Investment was on the rise, and France, though still trailing slightly behind the other Western countries, was beginning to share in the newfound prosperity of the rich nations after the dark years of recession. The growth rate improved, and even employment was beginning to pick up again. The only black spots were the worrisome foreign trade deficit and the sacrifice of research and development to the liberal myth of state withdrawal from the economy.

"Reaganism" à la française

The Chirac government's defeat in the 1988 legislative elections following the dissolution of the National Assembly after François Mitterrand's reelection was not due to economic problems but to political blunders that the president had been quick to turn to his advantage. The tensions engendered by cohabitation as well as the unnatural alliance between conservative neo-Gaullists and the ultraliberals of the Parti républicain in the governmental coalition sharpened ideological conflict at a time when the country was anxious to downplay its "hexagonal" divisions to meet the challenges of the 1990s.

According to Alain Lipietz, the downfall of the conservative government was due to a twin refusal: the refusal of people to accept uncontrolled competition and the refusal of authority epitomized in the student demonstrations of 1986. The conservative neo-Gaullists, like the Reaganites, were not beyond pandering to the imaginary "moral majority," and a number of authoritarian decisions boded ill for a government that professed liberalism. The banning of some allegedly pornographic magazines from newstands, the project to imprison drug users, the proposed reform of the legislation governing naturalization were seen as attacks on civil liberties: "Apparently liberalism was overthrown by an unexpected adversary: youth."[16]

16. Alain Lipietz, "Les contradictions du libéralisme," in Verdié, *L'état de la France*, 320–23.

The French, with an ingrained pessimism about human nature—de Gaulle thought that the great weakness of the French was their powerlessness to believe in anything—have little faith in the British notion of fair play, and the government in office, because of the extensive constitutional powers it enjoys, is always suspected of ulterior motives.[17] The Right-wing coalition did little to allay these suspicions, and many of the concessions to corporate France made in the name of economic liberalism[18] were perceived as a return to corporatism: "The contrast is striking between the advantages accorded to the minority and the austerity imposed on the majority," wrote Christian de Brie in 1987.[19] The suppression of the wealth tax introduced by the Socialists, the tax breaks to corporations with no strings attached, the laundering of funds illegally invested abroad when the Left came to power, the concessions to the medical profession were seen as disguised favors to the indestructible lobbies at a time when the reform of labor legislation to make hiring and firing "more flexible," wage austerity, and increased social security

---

17.

> Shortly before his death [de Gaulle] told Malraux that the great weakness of the French was their powerlessness to believe in anything. They were both blessed and cursed with a corrosive intellect which cast doubt on everything and destroyed their enthusiasm for any cause for fear that it might turn out to be empty. They had too much intellect and too little instinct. Following Bergson, he claimed that it was always the weakness of intelligence to be embarrassed by reality, because the untidy inconsistencies of reality do not correspond to the expectations of intelligence. And it is here that instinct and intuition come to the rescue, recognizing the nature of the situation when the intelligence is merely bewildered by it.

See Maurice Larkin, *France since the Popular Front: Government and People, 1936–1986* (Oxford: Clarendon Press, 1988; rpt. New York: Oxford University Press, 1991), 280.

18. According to Nicola Tenzer, France, which remained a profoundly rural society for so long, deeply attached to protectionism, was opposed to economic liberalism because of insufficient modernization rather than for ideological reasons. "This explains why, today, a government that proclaims itself liberal is unable to embody politically the liberal doctrine it professes. Politically positioned on the right, it cannot really be liberal beacause of the sociological composition of its voters" (Tenzer, *La société dépolitisée*, 45).

19. Christian De Brie, "Une avalanche de bienfaits," *Le Monde Diplomatique: Le Libéralisme Contre Les Libertés*, April 1988, 68–71. The same writer has noted a similar drift in the policy of the Right-wing majority elected in 1992. See "Une cascade de liberalités pour les clients de la droite," *Le Monde Diplomatique*, September 1993.

contributions for all were an added burden for the working population. The students' refusal of "Coca-Cola lycées" and "Tapie universities" (Bernard Tapie was the very symbol of the get-rich-quick mentality) symbolized the rejection of a society based on the survival of the fittest. The government's error was to assume that the conversion of the French to free-market principles signified their willingness to sacrifice hard-won social advantages to an irresponsible liberalism.

Round 3: Neither-Nor (1988–92)

Ni . . . Ni

In his wordy and generally unread "Letter to All the French" before the 1988 Presidential election, François Mitterrand, while not hiding his preference for partnerships between the state and private corporations in the form of *sociétés mixtes*, declared that there had been enough yo-yoing and that, if reelected, he would not undertake neither nationalization nor denationalization. This policy came to be known as *ni . . . ni* (neither/nor). Michel Rocard, a pragmatic "dream buster" who was suspected of right-wing leanings and who had fallen from grace for his criticism of the unrealistic economic measures introduced by the Socialists in 1981, was appointed premier, dashing any misconceptions the left of the party might have about how best to run the economy. True to the Socialist president's conversion of late 1982 to economic realism and worship of corporate France (symbolically celebrated by a presidential visit to Silicon Valley, the very citadel of capitalism), there would be no revenge. Indeed there was no fundamental difference in the approach to the economy of Pierre Bérégovoy—who had already been minister of economy and finance from 1983 to 1986—with that of his predecessor in the Chirac government, Edouard Balladur. His policy of a healthy franc, of wage restrictions to contain inflation, of budget cuts to reduce the deficit, of tax breaks for corporations in order to facilitate industrial development could hardly be considered socialist in inspiration. Even the Left's criticism of the privatizations was a refusal less of the principle in a world where mergers and acquisitions have become a necessity than of the way in which they were carried out.

Backdoor Tactics

Yet, for historical reasons, the old guard could not refrain from state meddling in the economy as the attempt, shortly after Mitterrand's reelection, at "backdoor renationalization" of the Société générale, one of the big banks privatized by the Chirac government, was to prove. This operation, organized by Bérégovoy undoubtedly with the approval of the president, whose ingrained suspicion of capitalism had not changed, was frowned upon by Rocard, a genuine believer in the free market. The aim was to enroll major institutional investors such as the Caisse des dépôts et consignations (the major French public savings institution) and state-controlled insurance groups, noted for their political neutrality, under the Socialist banner in order to break the power of the "tough core" (stable) shareholders the previous government had co-opted to ensure that the newly privatized groups would not become the victims of hostile takeovers.[20] The scheme fell through when the CEOs of the institutions solicited to participate in the raid declined the bizarre invitation and the press got wind of the scandal.

Initial public outcry against the shady dealings ended with a knowing shrug of the shoulders when Bérégovoy announced that there would be a full, impartial inquiry. It is true that the COB (Commission des opérations de bourse) has not the same powers of investigation as the Securities and Exchange Commission in the United States. However, a report by a senatorial commission published in April 1989 revealed "pressure" by public authorities in the affair. The scandal would have seriously jeopardized the credibility of the Socialist government with the business establishment had not Bérégovoy's skill in monetary matters and the firm attitude of the minister for industry and commerce, Roger Fauroux, who dared criticize this flirting with nationalization, healed the wounds. Less than a year after the abortive attempt to renationalize the Société générale, Volvo, a private company, was authorized to acquire a 25 percent share in Renault, the corporate symbol of all the nationalizations, which the Chirac government had not dared to privatize.

Partnerships

The problem of the role of the state in the economy is a real one in France on account of the history of French capitalism and *dirigisme*. The worldwide economic war for market share that demands huge capital investments to finance new technology and corporate buyouts shows that

20. Eric Le Boucher, "La restructuration du capitalisme français 1," *Le Monde*, 19 April 1990.

Hard Core

In 1987, to guarantee a certain stability to the fragile privatized and reprivatized companies, as well as to prevent a takeover by foreign raiders, a group of core investors (*noyaux durs*) was formed by the government and obtained the privilege of a 20 percent to 50 percent holding, which was frozen. This large minority stake was reserved for a small group of institutional investors politically close to the Chirac cabinet. As *Le Monde* remarked, "The paradox of this transfer [of state ownership to private shareholders], which was meant to symbolize the triumph of liberalism, is that it was carried out in the most top-down manner possible by an all-powerful minister of state who was the sole judge of who was to become a 'core investor' and of the price at which the shares were to be sold."* The haste with which the privatizations were carried out—for obvious political reasons due to the tensions of the tenuous cohabitation—and which strained the capacity of the financial market, has also come under fire, as well as the decision to privatize completely when partial privatization might have proved more judicious and more lucrative. A parliamentary report published in late 1989 revived the privatization polemic by suggesting that the value of the companies to be privatized had been grossly underestimated by the Chirac government to the benefit of the core investors.

While the operation was undoubtedly a success, the government ran little risk insofar as the firms chosen for privatization were far from being lame ducks. With the exception of Saint-Gobain, Rhône-Poulenc, CGE, and part of Matra, a large advertising agency, Havas, and one of the three national television channels, TF1, all the reprivatized firms were thriving banks or financial institutions and not industrial companies. The decision to privatize TF1—the equivalent of the BBC in Britain—was a first in Europe and provoked bitter controversy on account of its obvious ideological implications. At the same time, fearful of industrial conflict, the authorities balked at privatizing Renault, the stronghold of French worker organizations.

*Claire Blandin, "Privatisation en apparence," *Le Monde: Bilan Economique et Social 1987*, 53.

---

the "capitalism without capital" that characterized France in the 1970s, with its narrow, tightly controlled financial market, is no longer viable in the nineties. As Eric le Boucher explained, corporate dynamism, the wave of acquisitions in the United States and Europe, obliges businesses to hedge against takeovers by relying on stable partners: "In short they need money and friends."[21] If private companies want to control their

21. Eric Le Boucher, "La restructuration du capitalisme français 2," *Le Monde*, 20 April 1990.

shareholders they cannot afford to rely solely on the stock exchange. Neither can they afford to completely ignore the state-controlled financial institutions—insurance companies, some big banks, the Caisse des dépôts, the various building societies—that still distribute two-thirds of French credit: "The state remains an unavoidable partner."

Similarly, state-controlled enterprises cannot afford to despise private capital. In 1989, if the state allocated Fr 4.1 billion to public companies, it asked them for Fr 4.8 billion back in dividends: "The budgetary choice of the government is increasingly leaving more room for private financing of the public sector which will inevitably lead to partial privatizations." The constraints of European integration are forcing the authorities in the same direction: "Whether Paris deplores it or not, Europe is liberal and favorable to privatizations." In fact, none of the nationalized companies today is financed completely by the state, and they are discovering ingenious ways of raising private funds: "Each time that a nationalized firm needed money to finance its investments or acquisitions," writes Claire Blandin, "it has been able to find it."[22]

The Color of the Capital

"Public-Private: the color of the funds," says Eric Le Boucher, "no longer counts." There seems to be national agreement on the necessity of strengthening all French corporations faced with the challenges of the 1990s, whatever their legal status, and giving the companies the solid capitalistic backing that has always been wanting. Thanks to nationalization and privatization the tightly compartmentalized French elite has exploded. The aloof state technocrats have been confronted with the gritty task of running profit-making businesses, while skilled CEOs from the private sector have been called upon by the government to outline industrial policy. There is even a brain drain of *énarques* to the private sector, lured by the new-found prestige of the corporation and high rewards. Fears of a takeover by the Right, or of a Left-wing revenge, have faded into the background, even if all the players continue to defend their positions. The restructuring of French capitalism is not yet complete, and there seems to be a variety of approaches illustrated by the numerous mergers and acquisitions, public and private, national and international,

22. Claire Blandin, "Les véritables missions de l'Etat actionnaire," *Le Monde*, 10 June 1989.

in banking, insurance, finance, and industry that show the new dynamism of the country. In 1985 there were 264 transactions of this nature, in 1989 1,377—a 30 percent increase over 1988. The French are handling these operations in their own style:

> One thing is certain in any case: France rejects the American or British model of a completely watered-down capital structure dominated by investment trusts seeking a maximum return. In 1987 Mr. Balladur had put a group of "core" investors in the midst of the privatized firms. They had two drawbacks: they were too politicized and too fragmented (each stockholder was entitled to a small percentage). But the idea of a strong and stable capital backing has become a subject of national consensus. The corporations are seeking "tough cores," public, private, or mixed, capable of defending them and, above all, of supplying long-term financing.[23]

Perhaps the color of the capital no longer mattered, but the central question of state ownership and control remained unanswered. The state might not be as quick on the draw as in the past, but the old reflexes were still there. Air France's buyout of UTA amounted to backdoor nationalization of a private airline; the Caisse des dépôts was ordered by the minister of finance to contribute Fr 1.5 billion to the undercapitalized Crédit lyonnais when it might have been just as easy to authorize the state-owned bank to raise private capital. These examples, together with the laborious negotiations between the reprivatized CGE (electrical engineering) and Framatome (nuclear generators), which Mitterrand wanted to keep public, showed that the "neither/nor" doctrine was no longer tenable. In May 1992, it was discretely abandoned for the *et . . . et* (both/and) philosophy.

Et . . . Et

Dominique Strauss-Kahn, who was to be the last Socialist minister for industry, paved the way for denationalization. According to him the state should abandon the passivity expressed in the neither/nor doctrine and behave as an active shareholder, even if its objectives are different from those of private investors. This is really the essence of the idea of

23. Le Boucher, "La restructuration du capitalisme français 2."

sociètés mixtes, of joint public-private ventures. The border between state-owned and private companies is not rigid, and the state may *both* sell *and* buy as it pleases, the main criterion being the increased competitiveness on the domestic and international market of the enterprises in question. "Why should the state be more passive than a private shareholder?" said Strauss-Kahn. "Trying to manage in the best possible way may be successful or not, but is not in itself an interventionist policy."[24]

Of course it is a national and international sport to decry French interventionism, which, on account of the history of the French economy, lends itself to brilliant exegesis. Yet, Jean-Louis Levet may well be right when he points out that the inferiority complex modern France has developed about this matter cramps its style in a world where economic battles are no longer won or lost between corporations but between states:

> Everything remains to be done. If France is not, quantitatively, more interventionist than the other developed countries and even quite less so, [its interventionism] has neither the quality nor efficiency of the interventionism of other states, not by a long shot. One could almost say, without exaggerating, that French interventionism is not applied either when or where it is necessary, and in any case it lacks the efficiency of that of its competitors. In other words, France has a complex about being an interventionist country when it should rather have a complex about the inefficiency of its interventionism.[25]

According to Strauss-Kahn, who was defending Socialist policy, corporations that are strategic "for national sovereignty" (defense industries, electronic components) and areas where "private enterprises are loath to take risks" (biotechnology and activities linked to the environment such as waste disposal) should remain under state control. While the right-wing also believe that the state should keep a majority holding in strategic sectors they do not agree at all with state ownership of industries that they believe should be privately run. One of the severest criticisms

24. See Pierre-Angel Gay, "L'Etat coordinateur industriel?" *Le Monde,* 9 June 1992.

25. Jean-Louis Levet, *Une France sans complexes* (Paris: Economica, 1990), 162.

the Right made of the sale of part of the capital of state-controlled ELF-Aquitaine (petroleum) in spring 1992 was that it was an operation that did not respond to any clear long-term industrial or financial strategy. It was just a means for the government to obtain some ready cash to finance the budget deficit, like the sale of 20 percent of the capital of Crédit Local de France in November 1991. Edouard Balladur was extremely critical of the fuzzy borders between public and private advocated by the Socialists. He wanted a clear separation between the two, and less than a year before he was to become prime minister of a right-wing parliamentary majority, condemned "the confusion of the policy of the [Socialist] government on the subject of privatization," a policy he believed "constantly hesitates between the recognition of the liberty of corporations and the maintenance of state control." Yet the ambitious privatization program of the new Balladur government that covers twenty-one businesses ranging from industrial corporations, banks, and insurance companies to SEITA Renault and Aérospatiale is not entirely liberal in inspiration. Even though a theoretically independent privatization commission has been set up to designate a group of stable shareholders and preserve "the higher interests of the state," the minister of the economy will have the last word. Moreover, part of the windfall from the sale of state-owned enterprises will be used to finance the budget deficit, though this was something Edouard Balladur criticized the Socialists for a few months before!

While the politicians discuss nationalization and privatization the people have more down to earth preoccupations nowadays and do not seem to care whether industry is state-owned or private so long as jobs are created. France, for demographic reasons, requires a higher growth rate than its neighbors if unemployment, which affected more than 10 percent of the working population in March 1993, is to be reduced. A healthy economy means more jobs, which has to be the goal of any government, Left or Right.[26]

The French Left proved that it could manage the economy as well as the Right. However, its supporters apparently expected something more than "liberal socialism," which is not really very different from "social liberalism." The task for the Left is henceforth to adapt to the necessities

26. Françoise Fressoz and Nicolas Beytout, "Edouard Balladur dénonce la confusion de l'actuelle politique de privatisation," *Les Echos*, 19 May 1992. See also Erik Izraelewicz, "La dernière mort du *ni-ni*," *Le Monde*, 25 May 1992.

of the modern world's global economy without losing its value system based on the revolutionary principles of liberty, equality, and fraternity. This means something more than having a healthy franc and modernizing industry and the services to make them more competitive in a Europe without frontiers; something more than social cushioning for those who have no share of the fruits of economic prosperity. It involves such questions as burden sharing and the use to be made of the national wealth in a country where capitalism has so often been associated with privilege and social inequalities. One of the main griefs with the Socialists was the *déficit moral* (moral deficit), their inability to propose any ideal other than that of the market after their conversion in 1982. Unless they are able to do so they are unlikely to get the chance to run the country for a long time. As for the Right, unless they give in to their old demons of pandering to their more diehard conservative supporters, or make political blunders, there seems to be no reason why they should not be able to remain in power as social liberalism will always be more acceptable in France than liberal socialism.

18

Assets and Liabilities

If the peacock weren't proud of his tail it would be a hindrance to him.

—Gilbert Cesbron (1913–79)

Industry

While the volume and value of foreign trade puts it in fourth position after Japan, the United States, and Germany, France today is an intermediate economic power. The "thirty glorious years" of industrial expansion that followed postwar reconstruction came to an end in the early 1970s, and whole sectors of French industry, many of which had been the lifeblood of certain regions since the Industrial Revolution, faced obsolescence, inflation, market contraction, and competition from abroad. Shipbuilding, steel, textiles, leather, and industrial equipment were the major victims. But even chemicals, paper, electronics, household appliances, and autos were affected. Between 1974 and 1990 France lost 1.5 million jobs in industry, that is, about 30 percent of the industrial work force.[1]

The causes of decline were numerous. The two oil crises of the 1970s, which sparked worldwide recession, were naturally decisive, but a number of peculiarly French ailments aggravated the vulnerability of manufacturing: insufficient capital investment, overtaxation of corporations to finance social cushioning, bad work habits and a lack of flexibility of the work force—industrial production decreases considerably in August because of vacations!—overfinancing of lame ducks to the detriment of investment in high tech, insufficient governmental support for small and medium-size firms that are the traditional suppliers of parts to the champion industries such as autos, insufficient investment in research

1. Christian Stoffaës, "La restructuration industrielle" in Lévy-Leboyer and Casanova, *Entre l'Etat et le marché,* 445–72.

and development, the separation between theoretical and applied research, and the maladaptation of the educational system.

While a number of these questions have not yet received full treatment, the comeback of French industry in the late 1980s and early nineties after years of stagnation shows that restructuring though painful is now bearing fruit. Although industrial investment was down in 1991 following the Persian Gulf War, it grew by 60 percent between 1985 and 1990. The improved foreign trade balance in 1992 was largely due to industrial exports. While world demand for manufactured products increased by 5.6 percent in 1991, France's exports of these products reached 6.2 percent.[2] Some sectors remain vulnerable (textiles, machinery, household and consumer goods), but other French industries are among the world's leaders and more show promise of expansion. The large manufacturing industries are aerospace, steel, pharmaceuticals, chemicals, autos, railways, glass, machinery, electrical equipment, household appliances, electronics, paper, and plastics. Usinor-Sacilor is the second largest steel manufacturer in the world after Nippon Steel; France is the fourth world producer and third exporter of autos after Japan and Germany; the French pharmaceutical industry ranks third in the world for innovation. The wave of mergers and acquisitions, national and international, that is helping to increase the competitiveness of French industry is proof of a new corporate dynamism, as are the *technopoles* (science parks) that have sprouted all over France.

Name-dropping

Since the seventeenth century France has enjoyed a unique reputation as a purveyor of luxury goods to the rich and famous. French industrialism, fostered by Colbert, Louis XIV's finance minister, was based on the exportation of value-added products—hence the quality norms and strictly regulated corporations—that ensured a high return: tapestries, furniture, silverware, perfumes. Even today many of the champion French exporters are manufacturers of luxury products: Cartier with its five thousand outlets in 127 countries; Christofle, the only really international silversmith; and the LVMH group (Louis Vuitton, Moët-Hennessy), which produces perfumes (Dior-Givenchy) and fine luggage (Vuitton) as well as champagne and brandy. Louis XV and other French

2. *Bilan Economique et Social* 1991, 55.

furniture styles are big exports and bring in more foreign currency than perfumes.

High fashion, launched by the English employee of a Parisian silk merchant in the second half of the eighteenth century, was to become the trademark of France in the twentieth century, when well-to-do Americans went wild about Parisian designer clothes and Doeuillet, Patou, Molyneux, and Balenciaga were synonymous with discreet, refined elegance between the world wars. Coco Chanel, who created the *garçonne* or boyish, feminine look, offered "golden indigence" to the rich. Her graceful flask for the famous No. 5, the first perfume to be launched by a fashion designer—in 1921—is on show in the Metropolitan Museum in New York. (France exports 40 percent of its production of cosmetics and perfumes.) The Pierre Cardin, Christian-Dior, Yves Saint-Laurent, André Courrèges, and Christian Lacroix labels are internationally coveted, and Paris continues to be a Mecca of high fashion in spite of the growing importance of other centers.

The French are justifiably proud of their gastronomy, and one of the natural advantages of a country that has a refined *art de vivre* lies in its foie gras, vast variety of cheeses, champagne, cognac, and quality wines. One-third of all the Bordeaux wines are exported, but the figure is much higher for the top *crus*—Pauillac, Médoc, Saint Julien, Margaux. Nor should the less plentiful but equally renowned wines of Burgundy (Pommard, Nuits-Saint-Georges) be forgotten. The biggest foreign consumers of French wines are the Germans, followed by the British. Sixty million bottles of Champagne are exported too, and the United States consumes more than any other country. Cognac has been exported since the seventeenth century. The leading consumers today are the Japanese, followed by the Americans. The United States has become a large market for mineral water (Perrier, Evian) as well. French cuisine is also internationally known, and baguettes and croissants can be found from Tokyo to New York. However, the French themselves remain the greatest consumers of the cheese they produce—on average fifteen kilos per person annually. Only 5 percent of *Camembert,* about which an enthusiastic connoisseur was to exclaim that "it smelled like the feet of the good Lord," is exported.

France's tradition of craft and quality goods since the seventeenth century, or perhaps the mistrust of an essentially rural nation for a throwaway society, may have hampered the development of a strong industry of everyday products. The enduring *coccotte minute* (pressure cooker), which figures on every bride's list of wedding gifts, or the ubiquitous *opinel,* the wooden-handled pocket knife that no self-respecting Frenchman would be without—four to five million are sold annually—bear the marks of solidity and ingeniousness that nostalgic consumers still associate with quality. Two of the few corporations that have successfully responded to the demands of a modern consumer society are Moulinex (electrical appliances) and Bic, which meets more than 80 percent of world demand for ballpoint pens, lighters, and razors. Of course lighting a cigarette with a Bic does not confer the same chic as flashing a Cartier. There is much the same difference as riding a vulgar jumbo jet from Paris to New York in ten hours or streaking across the Atlantic in three and a half hours in the Concorde.

In the 1970s Concorde became the symbol of the strengths and weaknesses of French business. The supersonic commercial jet was a brilliant technical achievement but a commercial disaster. It cost thirty billion francs to develop, and only sixteen planes were sold instead of the projected three hundred! Nevertheless, it announced France's entry into the realm of high technology and facilitated the development of the highly successful fly-by-wire Airbus. Above all it served as a lesson that would be remembered by the developers of Airbus, Ariane, the TGV, and the Minitel, which proved that state-inspired projects could be commercially successful. The Concorde is still flying and transported 61,000 passengers between Paris and New York in 1988, bringing in ninety-five million francs for Air France. There are even projects to develop with other international partners a new long-distance supersonic plane of the future (*avion de transport supersonique futur,* or ATSF) that would carry twice as many passengers.

Nuclear Energy

It is in the realm of peaceful applications of atomic power that the French have shown the greatest foresight or, as the ecologists would say, folly. An ambitious program to develop nuclear energy was launched in the 1970s, and today France produces 74.5 percent of its electricity with nuclear power. This has helped the country to reduce its overall dependence on imported energy, oil and gas in particular. In 1973, oil accounted for 70 percent of total energy consumption. Today the figure

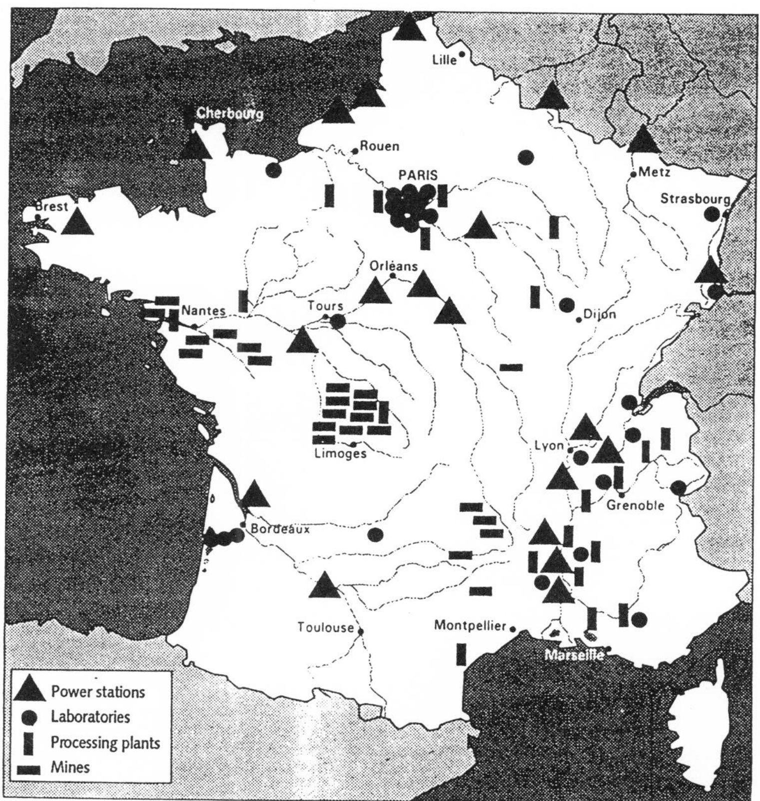

FIG. 26. L'Hexagone nucléaire. (*Le Monde Dossiers et Documents,* June 1990. Copyright © The New York Times Syndication Sales Corporation.)

is 42.4 percent. By the end of the century nuclear power is expected to cover more than 40 percent of total national energy needs.[3]

Energy independence has been one of the prime goals of the French economy since World War II because the country lacks natural resources. This explains why France joined the European Coal and Steel Community, why hydroelectric power was developed, why coal production was phased out, why efforts were undertaken to exploit oil fields in the Sahara and the Middle East, why the nuclear energy program was launched

3. *La France en chiffres,* 40–43, 49–51.

conjointly by the CEA and EDF, and why France has invested heavily in the extraction of uranium and the reprocessing of combustibles.

In the late 1960s relations between the CEA and EDF became very tense, the former favoring heavy-water (graphite-gas) reactors and the latter the light-water system developed by Westinghouse in the United States. In 1969 the government arbitrated in favor of EDF, and the CEA had little choice but to "Frenchify" the American invention. In 1981 Westinghouse signed over its patents, and the nuclear program today is an entirely French undertaking.[4] Of late, the CEA has been trying to step up diversification by developing its research in areas such as microelectronics and robotics, while maintaining control of the nuclear energy sector.

Meanwhile EDF, which has been called "a state within the state," was able to carry out its ambitious nuclear reactor program in the face of opposition from environmentalists because it is a state monopoly. EDF, a monopoly since 1946, is the largest producer of electricity in the world, which it exports to England, Switzerland, Italy, Germany, Spain, and the Benelux. It is the second largest French corporation after Renault in terms of turnover. No other French company invests more in research and development. At a time when the world is at the mercy of Middle East turmoil and oil shortages, it would be hard to deny the economic wisdom of the French nuclear program. John Harrington, U.S. secretary for energy, was one of its greatest admirers. In an interview published in *Le Monde* in October 1988, he declared:

> I am a great admirer of the French nuclear program. I have visited Superphénix and the reprocessing plant in Marcoule; I have studied your program and I think it is one of the best, if not the best, in the world. France has done what we should have done. . . . [W]e made a lot of mistakes. We did not standardize our power stations like the French; neither did we use central services such as control rooms and personnel training centers. We worked badly in reprocessing combustibles. We voted against fast-breeder reactors like Superphénix, which is a good project. There have been some problems, but it is paving the way for the future.[5]

4. Véronique Maurus, "Les quarante ans du CEA: l'énergie à l'arraché," *Le Monde*, 6–7 October 1985.

5. Véronique Maurus, "'La France a fait ce que nous aurions dû faire', nous déclare John Harrington," *Le Monde*, 19 October 1988.

In France the public has had very little say in decisions concerning nuclear energy, which are dictated from on high in the interest of the national economy. Yet EDF policy has been subjected to much criticism on economic as well as technical and environmental grounds. In its attempt to promote electric domestic heating it has made electricity cheaper for ordinary consumers than for business and industrial users. At the same time, home consumption is erratic and is concentrated essentially in four months of the year, with the result that the nuclear power stations, which are designed to produce a regular output, cannot respond to peak demand in severe winter conditions, and "the most nuclearized country in the world," a major exporter of electricity, has to import to meet demand! Moreover, the drought of 1989 and 1990, when there were numerous breakdowns, illustrated the deficiencies of the hydraulic cooling system.

A good deal of criticism is aimed at the grandiose but costly ambition of the "plutonocrats." In 1989 the deficit of EDF amounted to Fr 4 billion. The company has a debt of Fr 232 billion on which it pays Fr 27 billion in interest. Yet, banking on a world energy shortage around the year 2020, the state-controlled company has no intention of slackening the pace in spite of the present overcapacity of its nuclear network. It envisages the construction of seven new nuclear power stations by the year 2000. The utility is also engaged with the Germans and British in the European fast-breeder reactor project.

The most severe criticism has been leveled at Superphénix and at the nagging questions of security and of what to do with the radioactive waste from the power stations that are to be dismantled within the next two or three decades.

Superphénix, the only industrial fast-breeder reactor prototype in the world, has been dogged with technical problems. From its inauguration in 1985 until it was provisionally closed down in 1992 it had run only a little over two years, destroying the myth of cheap energy that was its main attraction. Moreover, the reactor, which has the capacity to produce more plutonium than it consumes, like the mythical phoenix that rose alive from its ashes, was designed at a time when there were fears of a world uranium shortage—fears that have since proved to be unfounded. Until 1992, when the Bérégovoy government decided to suspend the program pending a full inquiry—yet another!—into the security of the Creys-Malville reactor, France was injecting half a billion francs a year into Superphénix despite increasing doubts about its profitability and numerous technical problems, which EDF declared were simply the teething troubles of a new invention.

According to Dominique Finon, an economic expert at the University of Grenoble, the reluctance of the CEA and the EDF to lay off the engineers behind the project and assume the political risk of putting a damper on a costly program that is no longer justified, together with "the evangelical fervor" of the French electronuclear community, explain why they continue to defend it: "The decision-making process in our country takes place in an airtight compartment, which is an obstacle to the flexibility major programs like this require. It was the case for Concorde; it is the case for Superphénix and the Hermès space shuttle today."[6] Whatever the pros and cons of the fast-breeder reactor, it is hard to deny this assertion. The public has never been consulted on the question of nuclear energy, and the numerically insignificant Greens are not likely to get the referendum they have been calling for.[7] Criticizing, in early 1991, the way in which nuclear waste is administered, the committe for the prevention of technological hazards described the EDF-CEA group as "a self-contained assessment center with a dogmatic doctrine" and suggested it should call in foreign experts to guarantee independence.[8]

If France has so far been spared any major nuclear accident like Three Mile Island, it may be in part due to antinuclear activism that, even if it was powerless to influence energy policy, has forced the engineers and scientists to put a premium on security. Nonetheless, there have been several alerts, and there are an increasing number of what have been qualified as "minor" incidents due to aging equipment, design flaws, and human negligence. During recent controls seventeen French reactors were discovered to have faulty lids with tiny cracks due to corrosion, and in March 1993 Greenpeace demanded they be closed pending repairs. The EDF considers the Greenpeace reaction as "excessive."

One of the major problems facing the nuclear industry worldwide is

---

6. Claude Francillon, "La contestation du surgénérateur Superphénix," *Le Monde,* 23–24 September 1990. See also Dominique Finon, *Echec des surgénérateurs: une autopsie d'un grand programme* (Grenoble: Presses Universitaires de Grenoble, 1989).

7. In fact Bérégovoy's decision for a moratorium on Superphénix was essentially a political one and a major concession to the ecological parties following their success in the 1992 regional elections.

8. Roger Cans, "Les 'sages' remettent en cause la gestion des déchets nucléaires," *Le Monde,* 24–25 February 1991.

what to do with the radiated equipment and rubble from the power stations that are to be demolished. The question will be particularly acute for France around the year 2015, when the majority of the reactors constructed in the 1970s will reach the end of their life cycle. No suitable solution has yet been found anywhere, and "the most nuclearized country in the world" is likely to become the world's largest nuclear graveyard.

Aerospace

France was a pioneer in aeronautical development, and today it is the third largest world producer of aircraft after the American and Russian giants. Dassault's sophisticated fighter planes, the Mirage and the Rafale, and the successful Mystère Falcon (a small private plane); high-tech aviation gear, produced by Matra and Thompson; helicopters (Puma, Alouette—Aérospatiale is the number one world exporter of helicopters); and, above all, Airbus show the vitality of an expanding industry that accounts for higher incomes than autos or agribusiness. While the sophisticated commercial plane is not entirely French, it nevertheless weighs heavily in the trade balance. The A-320 is expected to bring in Fr 50 billion over the next ten years and the A-330, A-340 program, Fr 120 billion over the next twenty years.[9] Ariane, the satellite launcher with headquarters in Toulouse, is also a European venture but 56.6 percent of the capital is French. In July 1992, the fifty-first successful launch took place from the French launching pad in Kourou, French Guiana. Arianespace has already thirty-one more launches on order.

Small Is Beautiful

The majority of French firms are medium-sized or small. The highest-ranking corporation among the world's top fifty is Renault at thirty-first; there are only three others on the list. Fewer than 15 percent of workers are employed in enterprises with five hundred or more employees. More than half the working population is employed in those with fewer than fifty.

Medium-sized and small corporations are nowadays among the most dynamic, and the majority of industrial and service jobs created since 1988 are to be found in these smaller firms. The abolition of price controls

9. *La France en chiffres*, 66

and the greater liberty for hiring and firing given to employers have certainly helped, but the adaptability of the smaller units in times of economic turbulence has been their principal asset. In all the growth sectors, food and agribusiness, distribution, the manufacture of consumer goods, transport and telecommunications, construction and public works (where only 4 percent of the work force is employed in corporations having more than five hundred employees), the smaller concerns predominate. The most serious handicap for these enterprises is the difficulty of recruiting highly qualified personnel at a time when large firms are willing to pay fabulous salaries to attract top talent.

Handicaps

According to Roger Fauroux, former minister of industry, "France is not yet an industrial country."[10] Manufactured goods account only for 20 percent of GDP, as against 30 percent in Germany. The country is specialized only in a few areas—nuclear energy, telecommunications, aerospace, autos, railways, weaponry—but has always insisted on manufacturing everything. Some economic experts believe this lack of specialization, that is, of a strong industrial sector, is one of the main causes of the foreign trade deficit. A comparison for trade between France and Germany covering the period 1975–87 shows that in the twenty-eight industrial areas studied, Germany bested France in twenty-six. As the country lacks a strong manufacturing base it is unable to respond to the needs of high-demand foreign markets, and whenever purchasing power and consumption increase imports rise, because French industry is incapable of satisfying the demand on the home market. Manufacturers have relied on protectionism—French import quotas for non-EC member are among the most restrictive in Europe[11]—to shelter themselves from foreign competition: "By preventing the comparative advantages from showing up on the home market, by artificially maintaining fictitious export advantages, French protectionism has thus blocked the development of an efficient specialization in industry," writes Gérard Lafay, deputy

---

10. Eric le Boucher, "Une déclaration de M. Fauroux, ministre de l'industrie," *Le Monde*, 5 February 1990.

11. This does not prevent France from being one of the EC countries that imports the most. 31 percent of the domestic market demand is covered by imports. See Levet, *Une France sans complexes*, 82.

director of the CEPII (Centre d'études prospectives et d'informations internationales).[12] Owing to this absence of specialization the enormous sacrifices made by taxpayers to save uncompetitive sectors is useless and France remains "very vulnerable to fluctuations in the economic situation, particularly to exchange rate variations." By having too many irons in the fire, French manufacturing has lost market share abroad and, according to experts, France is in for a rude awakening in the single market because "French industry has not yet fully confronted on the home market the new forms of international competition."[13] However, for economist Jean-Louis Levet, the debate on the absence of specialization tends to put the cart before the horse. It is the capacity of corporations to develop their human and technical potential to the full, not specialization, that is the key to success.[14]

Other changes in mentality will be necessary too. According to former premier Edith Cresson, management structures are obsolete, and "promotions rely on diplomas and not on competence."[15] The educational system does not produce enough production engineers and technicians. Above all, not enough attention has been paid to human resources. The "thirty glorious years" had given bad habits to corporate bosses, and the old top-down structure is no longer productive. Yet, in spite of the difficulties to be resolved the fact that the French are questioning their whole approach to industry reveals a new awareness of the role of the corporation and a profound change in attitudes to industry, which used to be the theater of ideological confrontation.

The Services

France is the second largest world exporter of services after the United States. The foreign trade balance in this sector grows year by year and has helped to offset patchy industrial performance. More than 60 percent

12. Eric le Boucher, "Le déclin de l'Europe se poursuit, affirme le CEPII," *Le Monde*, 7 November 1989.

13. Eric le Boucher, "Un manque de spécialisation," *Le Monde*, 14 March 1989.

14. See Levet, *Une France sans complexes*, 155.

15. Olivier Drouin and Jeanne Villeneuve, "Edith Cresson, 'la dégradation de nos échanges est spectaculaire,'" *L'Evénement du Jeudi*, 30 November–6 December 1989.

of the total working population works in the services, and it is estimated that by the year 2000 three quarters of the work force will be employed in this area. (Experts forecast that jobs will become available in two areas in particular: data processing and noncommercial services.) Deregulation, which would abolish national frontiers in the framework of GATT, and the implementation of the EC Single Act (which has a similar goal on the European level), should present new opportunities for France on account of the intellectual potential and know-how the French have developed in public transportation, telecommunications, leisure, data processing, and finance, if they consent to the necessary investment in research and training.

As in industry there has been a wave of mergers and acquisitions, mostly in France and Europe, a noteworthy exception being the Filippachi-Hachette group's buyout of the U.S. corporations Grolier Inc. and Diamandis Communication's Inc., which has made the French company the largest magazine publishing group in the world with titles like *Woman's Day, Car and Driver,* and *Paris Match.*

Insurance and Banking

Insurance companies, the main ones state owned, which have their fingers in many pies—property, transport, and industry—have been joining forces to face the single market challenge. French banks have been forging crossborder alliances as well. Only the United States and Britain have more extensive banking networks than France; four French banks figure among the world's top ten. With its twenty-five thousand outlets, France has the largest number of banks in Europe.

Transportation

France has always played a preeminent role in transportation, and the extension of the highway network, the development of the TGV, and the new deal in air travel show the dynamism of this service sector. The two weak links are river transport and shipping.

Postes et Télécommunications

After 40 years in the red, the French P&T is making profit again in spite of its huge indebtedness. *La Poste* (the post office) is the largest banker in France, and its modernized savings department gets wealthier year by year. Indeed, French banks are worried that the financial services of the P&T, limited at present to current accounts, insurance, and savings, may be extended to include credit operations, making it a bank in its own right with its seventeen thousand post offices. The other arm of the P&T, France Télécom, is one of the world leaders in technological innovation. The laborious but successful 1990 agreement to give more commercial and administrative autonomy to the two branches of the state monopoly should enhance its chances in a deregulated Europe.

Data Processing

While the restructuring of the fragile French computer industry and the new dynamism of Bull have been affected by the worldwide shakeout in hardware—in 1992 Bull signed over 5.7 percent of its capital to IBM shortly after a previous deal with the Japanese company, NEC—France has the consolation of having the best data-processing services network in Europe. The capacity for abstraction, nurtured by the educational system, produces software wizards. The leading French specialist in sophisticated data systems is Cap Gemini Sogeti. Here again to be able to confront the American giants in a deregulated market French companies are building up alliances at home and abroad. Meanwhile, CGI Informatique is aiming to exploit the growing European market in off-the-shelf products, at present dominated by the United States. Japanese research into fifth-generation computers is using PROLOG, a computer language developed in Marseille, and the Pentagon has adopted ADA, a language the French helped to elaborate.

Tourism

Tourism is one of the big money spinners of the service industry, and in 1989, thanks to the bicentenary celebrations, France became the number one tourist destination, followed by the United States, Spain, and Italy. The cultural, gastronomic, and scenic riches of the country offset some of the drawbacks such as weak back-up services—try finding a hotel or taxi in Paris at short notice—and a lack of professionalism that is often confused with hostility to foreign visitors. Local rivalry between regions vying for the tourist trade, poor marketing, and sometimes unprofitable investments are the main handicaps. In spite of that profits from tourism reached a record Fr 57 billion in 1992.

The ACCOR hotel group as well as the luxurious Méridien hotel chain, a subsidiary of Air France, are established in many countries, although they cannot rival the giant American chains. Club Méditerranée has a worldwide network with holiday villages in thirty-eight countries. In late 1990 it signed a worldwide agreement with American Express.

Dormitory Cities in the Snow

Winter sports facilities both private and public (exploited by local villages) are highly developed in France. French resorts have an extensive network of *pistes* and a record four thousand modern ski lifts of every shape and size, the latest being the underground funicular railways in Tignes that climb two miles up the Alps. More than sixty resorts have "snow factories" with hundreds of snow cannons to make artificial snow when necessary. While the topography of the country allows for varied, exciting downhill and cross-country skiing, some criticism has been made of the tendency to develop skiing for the pros to the neglect of the holidaymakers. Most skiers are mediocre performers who do not want to "devour snow" eight hours a day. The larger resorts have made laudable efforts to develop after-ski activities, including swimming pools, film festivals, and music.

The boom in winter sports has led to the construction of mammoth resorts that have been dubbed *Sarcelles de neige*, dormitory cities in the snow. These do not always fit in very well with the environment. The policy of property development (thirty thousand new apartments per year) encouraged by the French craze for vacation homes has hampered the setting up of an adequate hotel structure to attract foreign visitors, and winter sports accounts for only a small percentage of the turnover of the tourist industry.[16] As in other areas a lack of a long-term commercial strategy, a misplaced confidence in technical prowess, a greed for quick gains, and poor marketing have prevented France from taking full advantage of its winter sports resources. The prestige of the 1992 Winter Olympics in Albertville gave an enormous boost to the Alpine resorts. It is hoped that the numerous charming village resorts in the

16. Marc Ambroise-Rendu, "Les stations de ski en panne," *Le Monde*, 16 January 1990.

Pyrenees, the Jura, and the Alps, which have resisted the temptation of mass tourism, will remain havens of powdered bliss.

Astérix and Mickey Mouse

Amusement parks are a new thing in France, where organized leisure is not as widespread as in the United States. Yet the Astérix Park in the Picardy region, inspired by the hero of the famous comic strip, received over one million visitors in 1988, the year of its inauguration. Eurodisneyland situated in Marne-la-Vallée near Paris, which was snootily described by one prominent French personality as a "cultural Chernobyl," seems to be a popular attraction for both French and other Europeans. It had registered more than 1.5 million visitors less than two months after its inauguration. The goal is 11 million visitors per year. A lot of the rhetoric about the amusement park had to do with the phobia of *américanisation* and the common confusion in people's minds between American culture and entertainment. On the other hand there has been some criticism of the particularly generous governmental support for Eurodisneyland in the form of low-interest loans, tax breaks, and administrative rule bending by the state, which barely consulted the local authorities of Marne-la-Vallée in its haste to attract Disney Corporation to set up in France.

Distribution

One of the major changes that has taken place in France in the past twenty-five years is the transformation of the channels of distribution, particularly retail outlets. The corner store, more often than not a *superette* nowadays, still exists in dwindling numbers, but its social and commercial role is no longer the same. The supermarket and hypermarkets with their bare, treeless, macadam parking lots, garish shop signs, and glitzy annexes, drain the weary masses of anonymous, resigned shoppers. The larger hypermarkets cover an area of four acres of floor space. The Carrefour store in Toulouse occupies six acres! Commercial centers grouping a variety of stores have developed in the outskirts of cities. More recently shopping malls with underground car parks, which are pale architectural and decorative copies of American consumer palaces, have sprouted in the larger towns.

The *supermarché* is more like a large-scale general store, where you can buy anything from shoes to paint, clothing, television, and groceries under the same roof. Food sales account for about half of the total sales of supermarkets, the most important being fruit and vegetables, dairy products, beverages. Bread and pastry are still mostly purchased directly at local bakeries. Meanwhile butchers, bakers, and grocers have disappeared by the thousands in country areas, and it is sometimes difficult for the older or less mobile villagers to procure basic necessities on the spot. The surroundings of most cities are spoiled by commercial eyesores: furniture shops, construction materials enterprises, and dreary depots. The urban and suburban lanscapes have more often than not been been modified for the worse. Such is the price of progress for an urban, mass consumer society that has replaced its legs with four wheels.

The first supermarket opened in 1957, twenty years after the term had come into use in the United States, but it should not be forgotten that France pioneered large shops, and the big Parisian *magasins populaires* such as the Samaritaine and the Bon Marché, which "democratized luxury" (Zola) and were to be the models for the American department store, date from the Second Empire. The Bon Marché was set up in 1852.

Large-scale distribution is a flourishing sector. Department stores, chain stores both general and specialized (hardware, home electronics, furniture, etc.), and mail-order firms have high turnover, and many are breaking into the international market. Carrefour has taken a 12 percent share in the American company Office Depot, and Auchan, which has many supermarkets in France, has opened French-style hypermarkets in the United States. Only time will tell if the Gallic strategy of the director of the group's hypermarket in Houston, Wilfrid d'Audiffret, is exportable: "We are inventing the business of the future in the United States. We are the only store where you can buy jam and a suitcase."[17]

In spite of the decline of *le petit commerce*—20 percent of self-employed shopkeepers have disappeared in less than quarter of a century—one of the benefits of the shopping shift to the city outskirts has been the rehabilitation of the old quarters of towns and the development of pedestrian precincts where one can stroll around among chic fashion boutiques, tempting delicatessen shops, and antique stores. Arts and

17. F. Ch. "L'aventure américaine d'Auchan," *Le Monde*, 4 January 1989.

crafts are developing again far from the bustle of mass consumption, and self-employment in this area has increased slightly because of the difficulty of finding a salaried job.

L'Artisanat

L'Artisanat or the trades, which include today not only the traditional professions of baker, plumber, carpenter, but also hairstyling, cosmetology, prosthetics making, and so on, has undergone profound changes. Gone are the glovemakers, the dressmakers, the shoemakers, and the milliners who were part of the charm of French towns and villages. The survivors are employed by the high-fashion firms that continue to use traditional techniques. The same goes for the cutlers that now work in luxury silverware or in the surgical instrument trade. The blacksmiths, the barrelmakers, the wheelwrights, and combmakers have almost completely disappeared.

Yet *l'artisanat* still employs two and a half million people (more than one in ten workers) and continues to be a rich source of employment. Only four professions nowadays require a licence (*patente*): hair stylists, bakers, taxi drivers, and movers. The building trade (carpenters, tilers, stonemasons, and so forth) is the most important. Bakers have withstood the onslaught of the supermarkets by diversifying into fine bakery and pastry, but butchers, particularly horse butchers, are losing ground. Twenty percent of repair and maintenance is carried out by tradespeople specialized in traditional fields like auto repairs but also in new high-tech areas such as computers and electronics. Many of the large corporations subcontract precision work to tradespeople, and it has been said with some truth that Airbus is the fruit of the skill of French *artisans.*[18]

Outlook

In France services in general are the driving forces of the economy and the fastest growing sector. However, if they are to maintain their lead in a deregulated European or world market, experts feel they will have to overcome certain handicaps such as a lower productivity rate than

---

18. Liliane Delwasse, "Métiers qui disparaissent, métiers qui apparaissent," *Le Monde*, 23 March 1990.

Customer Service

Alain Schifrès distinguishes five main types of Parisian dispute: "the steering wheel quarrel, the neighborhood quarrel, the post office window quarrel, the architecture quarrel (every new project gives rise to an outburst of hatred), and the gratuitous quarrel, which is by far the most frequent." Who in France has never witnessed a scene like the following, which illustrates a not uncommon conception of customer service? Here is an example of a completely gratuitous quarrel recorded under cover at 10:32 P.M., June 12, 1989, at a newsvendor's in the Abbesses district:

Customer: Excuse me, *madame,* I don't see *Needlework.* Hasn't it arrived?
Vendor: No, *madame.*
Customer: But, how come? I get it here every month.
Vendor: You shouldn't be touchy like that, *madame.*
Customer: But it's you who's being touchy, *madame.*
Vendor: Don't you use that tone to me, *if you please.*
Customer: Well, I never!
Vendor: Allez vous faire enculer! (The customer goes out.)
Vendor: (completely calm now to a male customer who witnessed the scene): Oh, I don't know what's wrong with people these times, they're so rude!
Customer: Paris is very touchy these days.

From Alain Schifrès, *Les Parisiens* (Paris: J.C. Lattès, 1990), 36.

their competitors, an unsteady financial basis, and often, heavier taxation than their foreign counterparts. The present trend of mergers and acquisitions, fiscal policy, and a new commercial agressiveness (in 1989 French tourist operators, whose spending on advertising in the United States used to be lower than that of the Bahamas, were the leading advertisers in the United States) suggest that France is on the right track.

Services and Service

It is a pity that the development of services has not led to the development of service. French opening hours for businesses, stores, and administrative offices (usually from 8 a.m. to 7 p.m. frequently with one- or two-hour closing for lunch), the indifference if not downright hostility of sales personnel and bureaucrats to the desires of customers and citizens, and the spread of "self-service" are frustrating. Saving on staff is one of the best investments a French business can make, and it need not fear the competition because all act alike on account of the cost (social security contributions) of hiring. However, this hardly explains the lack of attention to customers. The French do not like the overzealous salesperson, but there are limits! Only in the small, single-owner stores, the boutiques, the full-service shops will you still be greeted by "Bonjour monsieur et dame" or hear the expression "à votre service." In 1988, the ministry of tourism edited a brochure containing the Ten Commandments for people working in the trade, in which one could read that hospitality began with "knowing how to smile, to be obliging, to be patient."

But, due to French notions of status, service in France often rhymes with servility in the minds of providers of services. In China they say that if you chase a Japanese salesman out the door, he comes back in through the window. A Frenchman would never put himself to such indignity.

19

The Macadam Fields

The farmer is a man who perspires a lot to make of his son a gentleman who will be ashamed of him later.

—Adrien Decourcelle

On a sunny July afternoon in 1990, five acres of golden wheat were harvested on the macadam fields of the Champs Elysées, and thousands of Parisians flocked to see the tractors, the loaders, and the combined harvesters at work. Corn, grown in sturdy pallets, had been transported to the capital for the Great Harvest and arranged to form an open field that the machinery could roll on. This spectacular public relations operation, organized by the National Center of Young Farmers (CNJA or Centre national de jeunes agriculteurs), was designed to show the city slickers that French agriculture was alive and kicking, but it was an inadvertent reminder of the changes that have taken place in France in half a century, and of the isolation of the farming community.

The Town Mouse and the Field Mouse

Centuries of tax revolts against the wasteful state, of antagonism between the citizens and the peasantry, often armed with pikes to prove its point, were largely erased with the development of public schooling and in the camaraderie of the trenches during World War I. The rural exodus and the discovery of city life by small property owners, who often had, and still have, one leg on the farm and the other in the factory, contributed to better understanding between the two communities, even if tensions between the neorurals and the farmers sometimes revive ancient mistrust. Today, it is the city dweller who has more cause to protest against the tax burden that a costly and wasteful farm policy has engendered. The violent agricultural demonstrations, born of frustration, in the regional capitals only one month after the Great Harvest in Paris have further deformed the already ambiguous image the city dweller has of the farming community.

The middle-aged urbanite, who has a two-to-one chance of having had grandparents who worked on the farm, has always had a soft spot for the farmer and nostalgia for a way of life, the realities of which are generally ignored. "Once again," says Annie Moulin, "we are witnessing a reversal of the values connected with the farming world. The craze of city people for everything rural and the exultation of peasantness (*paysannisme*) have replaced the contempt of the 1950s."[1] The urbanites' judgment is founded on the clichés of "a lost paradise," of a healthy life in the open air, of homemade jam and natural food, of "a good address" to procure a wine or a farm chicken unobtainable in stores, of the hardy virtues of the land, of the refuge a country cousin was for their parents during the rationed years of German occupation, or again, of the "green revolution" that transformed France's backward farms into modern production units. None of these images, which the powerful if divided farming lobby is careful to promote, quite corresponds to reality. The farmer today has more in common with the city dweller than either cares to think. According to the sociologist Henri Mendras, it was the professional independence of the farmer's wife, who relinquished her role on the land to take up a job of her own in the nearby town or city, that put an end to the family farm and drew the two worlds together: "Today, the profession of farmer is separated from family life. It is the final stage of the disappearance of the peasantry, but also the main development of the past ten years."[2]

The structure of French farming is extraordinarily varied on account of the diversity of the land and a long history of agriculture. The open field of the cereal and beet plains of the north and east, the woodland and pasture of Brittany and the Massif central, or the terraced vineyards and olive orchards of the Midi—to name but the predominant patterns—naturally beget different modes of farming, rural architectures, and organizations of community life. Yet farmers today avail themselves of all the conveniences of modern life that were the privilege of city dwellers in the past, and, globally, their living standard is similar. However, there are vast differences in average earnings per farm, which depend on the size, produce, and location of the land. The powerful lobby of cereal

1. Annie Moulin, *Les paysans dans la société française,* 244.

2. Interview with Frantz Woerly. See "Les montants de la pluriactivité," *Le Monde Dossiers et Documents,* no. 153, March 1988.

and beet growers is deft at exploiting the theme of small farm misery to gain a favorable hearing for state aid to agriculture.

Harsh Reality

The restructuring of French farming, begun in the 1950s, is entering its final phase, and the process is painful for a country where 85 percent of the area is made up of farmland (60 percent) and forests (25 percent) and where the number of farms, about one million, is still very high. Historically, the large number of small properties is due to the Napoleonic law of equal inheritance, but also to the ingrained attachment of the French to the possession of land even when it is not their main source of livelihood. Gérard Départdieu, the filmstar and greatest living French actor, who owns a vineyard in his native Anjou, typifies this love of the land: "I'm too rooted in the earth to bear the city, which is a closed, dank room that makes a man claustrophobic and ill-humored. The most beautiful thing a man can have is land. What for? To walk on it, nitwit!"[3]

In spite of the trend toward larger, specialized, more profitable production units that has intensified over the past forty years, nearly one quarter of farms have less than twelve acres of land, most of which are in the hands of the older generation, and another quarter are managed on a part-time basis by tenant farmers with another job. Farms of less than thirty acres that produce a bit of everything still account for 50 percent of the total number. One out of two farmers no longer earns a living entirely from the land. Provincial France now makes its living more from industry, tourism, business, and services than from agriculture. The Basse Normandie region has the highest concentration of farmers (17.2 percent), but most regions have fewer than 15 percent of farmers in their active population.

Thirty years ago 20 percent of the working population was engaged in agriculture. The figure today is 6 percent and is likely to be halved in the nineties as the older generation disappears, leaving no successors. Increasing mechanization and productivity are wiping out the smaller units, and EC policy to reduce surpluses threatens to leave two million acres of land untilled. France, which is fifteen times smaller than the

3. Quoted in the documentary "Dépardieu Vigneron," Canal Plus, 24 March 1991.

United States, has twice as many farmers in the active population. Agriculture, which fashioned the French landscape and value system for centuries and constituted the principal wealth of the country, is fighting a losing battle against the harsh realities of a modern economy that defies logic.

The Green Revolution

Not that the farming community has anything to blush about. This nation of farmers, which was incapable of nourishing itself after the war, now has the largest herd of cattle in Europe. It is the second largest world producer of beets and produces more cereals than Canada. France produces even more wine than Italy and is top for quality. Agricultural output accounts for one-quarter of the EC total. All told, agribusiness today earns a trade surplus of more than FR 50 billion, which helps to offset the poor industrial performance of the country. (In 1990 industrial activities, with a volume of international trade six or seven times higher, had a foreign trade deficit of Fr 85.4 billion.)[4]

The desperation of farmers today is a measure of their bewilderment. Did they not root up the vines when they were told to plant Golden Delicious and then root up the apple trees to sow thirsty corn and are they not now advised to grow sunflowers instead of maize? Are they not up to their necks in debt for investing in machinery, in state-of-the-art pig and poultry farms to industrialize their production methods? Have they not used and abused all the wizardry of chemistry to boost productivity and are they not asked to accept quotas with good grace? Were they not told by the national and European technocrats to invest in France's natural resource of "green oil" and are they not now accused of polluting the land?

The very success of France's green revolution, which boosted productivity, is today a serious handicap, and agriculture is on the brink of a financial crisis. The EC's restrictions on the production of cereals, milk quotas, and price freezes hit French farming hard. Even the sheer amount of farmland is a handicap. The supply being greater than the demand, land prices have dropped, and French farmland is the cheapest in the EC, as many foreign speculators have been quick to realize. Encircled by Dutch pork, British lamb, Italian soya beans, sugar, and wine,

4. *La France en chiffres,* 88.

Spanish oils, and to crown it all, cheap beef from eastern Europe, the poor French farmer does not know what to produce.

The Mower Cow

In fact the much vaunted green revolution was less spectacular than appears at first sight, considering the natural advantages of France. Overall agricultural productivity is lower than in Britain, Germany, or the Benelux countries. The achievements of the more dynamic farmers hide the mediocre performance of the majority, who owe their survival to state cushioning, subsidies, and tax exonerations. However, one can understand the dilemma of the authorities faced with the choice of lengthening the dole queues or maintaining unprofitable hill farmers on their farm with aids such as the "bonus for the mower cow" (*prime à la vache tondeuse*). Former premier Michel Rocard stated that he preferred to spend money on keeping people on the land than paying the jobless, and probably most of his compatriots feel the same on account of their emotional attachment to the farming community.

Agribusiness

French agriculture, confronted with a rich developed world staggering under food surpluses and a starving, insolvent Third World, has serious handicaps. Although the agrofood industry is one of the major business sectors with a turnover of Fr 330 billion—the equivalent of the combined turnover of Renault and Peugeot[5]—the country has few products that can make the difference on world markets, and food processing is still largely undeveloped. Most of the farm produce exported is unprocessed and has therefore no added value. According to experts, if French farming is to be viable, it will have to use its imagination to produce novel quality products.

Another handicap is the size of processing plants. The majority of French food corporations are too small. Eighty percent of the enterprises have between 10 and 100 employees. Among the 110 top international food groups only seven are French: BSN Inc., which bought out the European subsidiaries of Nabisco in 1989; Moët-Hennessy-Louis Vuitton (cognac and champagne but also fine luggage); Perrier (mineral waters,

---

5. *La France en chiffres*, 92.

soft drinks, cheese); Pernod-Ricard, maker of the famous *pastis* and other popular appetizers as well as soft drinks; the big agricultural cooperatives SODIAAL (dairy products) and SOCOPA (the leading world meat processor); and Unilever-France, the French subsidiary of the Anglo-Dutch giant (margarine, detergents, etc.). The future of French agribusiness lies in mergers so as to attain the critical European, indeed world dimension. It lies in research, in launching new products regardless of the costs involved in advertizing, and in long-term investment to gain a larger market share.

There is no reason why France, with its extensive farming land, with its long tradition and renowned skill in wine making and culinary arts, should not be able to meet the agricultural challenges of the 1990s. Indeed, there are signs of a new awareness. New uses are being found for existing products. An illustration might be the numerous industrial applications (synthetic textiles, road covering, solvents) made possible by the processing of corncob waste that a small company located in Agen, Agrifurane, is engaged in. Agen, famous for its prunes, is the very model of a new rural France that has not been content to rest on its laurels. Biotechnology is also helping to develop new food and non-food products. For instance, a new grass to retain the snow on ski slopes and keep the pistes green in summer has been sown in the little resort of Gresse-en-Vercors near Grenoble.

The inevitable shakeout in farming will bring to the fore younger, more entrepreneurial, and, it is to be hoped, better-trained farmers. It is significant that less than half of the twelve thousand young people attending French agricultural schools reach a level equivalent to the last year of junior high, whereas in Holland, which is the model of agricultural dynamism, the required level of training is equivalent to two years of college.

Wasteland

But what about the land that people have tilled since time immemorial, clearing, draining, ploughing, sowing, irrigating, pruning? Should the mad logic of short-term profitability that has done so much damage wipe out the toil of generations that have shaped the variegated garden of France? Should the country become a vast agricultural desert with an oasis here and there, a wasteland dotted with high-tech farms and electronic cottages?

Farm policy over the past forty years has been the result of fruitful collaboration between the government and farmer organizations, when not of open connivance with the active pressure groups. It has helped modernize agriculture but at a terrible ecological and human cost, in spite of the laudable attempts of the Sixth Plan (1971–75) to encourage rural development and renovation. Quantitative criteria have dominated, and the political influence of a lobby that has a network of *notables* capable of defending its interests at all administrative and political levels as well as a capacity for mobilization that makes industrial worker unions blush, has led to a narrow, protectionist view of the role of the farmer in the community. Still, the lobby has been largely incapable of preventing the extinction of rural life. It is not only the property holders that have been affected by the agricultural crisis: local trades and stores, schools, transport, medical facilities, social activities, the whole fabric of community life has disappeared in many areas. (Some two hundred cantons are practically in a situation of economic and demographic destruction.)[6] This short-sighted protectionism has prevented the emergence of a global perception of the farmer's role in a pampered society where the quality of life has become more important than the supply of food. The majority of farmers, debt-ridden, plagued by drought and falling incomes, cannot conceive any answer to their plight other than more and more state aid. However, this can only be a palliative measure. What is needed is a new blueprint of rural development on the lines of what has been accomplished in many places with regional council assistance and is based on cooperation between communes designed to develop and integrate multiple activities (farming, industry, tourism, social development, environmental protection) and use the accumulated experience and know-how of all the local players to elaborate a new conception of rurality. Nevertheless, the complexity of the issue should not be underestimated, as José Catanzano's excellent study shows.[7] The lukewarm reception given to the former minister of agriculture's proposals for the development of organic foods and environmental protection that might open new perspectives to farming, and the violent demonstrations of 1990, 1991, and 1992, which bore the mark of despair, seemed to indicate that the farming community was not yet ready for

6. François Grosrichard, "Certaines régions en difficulté," *Le Monde Dossiers et Documents*, no. 197, March 1992, 2.

7. Catanzano, *Retour vers l'arrière pays*.

this qualitative revolution. The road block set up around Eurodisneyland on 26 June 1992 was symbolic of the refusal of farmers to give up agricultural production and take up a new profession, such as catering to the leisure needs of city dwellers and tourists; the sprawling amusement park disfigured some of the richest farmland in Europe.

Yet can the smaller farmers who are not responsible for the present situation really be blamed for not wanting to become manufacturers of organic foods and the guardians of nature for weary urbanites nostalgic about "paradise lost"? They are the victims of the policy of the Brussels and Parisian technocrats and of the connivance of the big farm lobby with the authorities. According to one expert, the overall electoral support the farming community enjoys—the spillover effect—is such that it accounts for as much as 17 percent of all the votes cast in national elections.[8]

The EC decision taken in May 1992 to phase out over three years the massive subsidies European farmers obtain in the framework of the Common Agricultural Policy angered French farmers, who made an aborted attempt to cut off Paris with roadblocks. However, when less than two months later the authorities made public the specific measures France, "in an effort of solidarity," would introduce in favor of farmers to facilitate the transition to nonsubsidized farming and to promote modernization, the government received the support of the powerful farmers' union, the FNSEA (Fédération nationale des syndicats d'exploitants agricoles). It is true that these measures were particularly generous (tax breaks, concessions on social security payments, renegotiation of farm loans at reduced interest rates, aids to modernization).

If rural community life is to survive and thrive, many farmers will have to abandon the idea of being simple producers of primary products. "Collectively," says Henri Mendras, "farmers should adopt the mentality of businessmen, and individually the mentality of providers of services." It is rural development that will ensure the growth of farming. "Local

8. "If one includes the retired farmers, farmers' wives, and all those who have a stake in agriculture, and if one considers that the number of farmers enrolled on the electoral lists is greater than that of other categories of voters, and that they have a greater rate of participation in elections," says CNRS researcher Bertrand Hervieu, it is possible to estimate "that 17 percent of voters have strong agricultural attributes." The majority of these spillover votes go to the neo-Gaullist right. Georges Chatain, "Une agriculture en voie de disparition," *Le Monde*, 29–30 September 1992.

demand is becoming increasingly important and regional development is holistic: growth in one area benefits other areas. All the available studies show that the economic development of a small region follows a movement of social developments rather than vice versa."[9] It is significant that the Great Harvest in Paris was a hymn of glory to a mode of production that is increasingly contested: "Why make a demonstration of a model that has reached its limits when agriculture has to prove that it is capable of doing more than sheaving wheat?"[10]

9. Henri Mendras, "Réinventer une politique," *Le Monde*, 29 September 1991.
10. Eric Fottorino, "Un hymne productiviste," *Le Monde*, 23 June 1990.

20

A Tough Job

The worker is a man who watches the machines working.
—André Prévot (1844–1964)

France has a working population of twenty-four million—or 43 percent of the total number of inhabitants: fifty-six million. (This figure includes the jobless and young people seeking their first job.) This percentage is lower than at the beginning of the century, when one in two people was employed outside the home. In other words, employment has not grown at the same rate as the population. The overall picture is one of decline in agriculture and in single-owner businesses such as small factories and stores, and an increase in liberal and other professional branches. Globally, white-collar workers have increased and represent 52 percent of the working population today. Blue-collar workers have decreased to 28 percent. Finally, 83 percent of the population now earns a salary. Another shift is the spectacular growth in female employment outside the home. In thirty years the figure has jumped from 35 percent to 43 percent of the working population, and although a large number of women are still confined to unskilled jobs, this is changing rapidly too. While these trends are not all that different from those in other developed countries, France, for historical and cultural reasons, has specific problems of adaptation to the new economic deal of the 1990s, as the high unemployment rate shows.

Joblessness

In the ten to fifteen years after World War II, France had practically no unemployment and in fact had to recruit huge numbers of immigrant workers in certain sectors. In 1962, with the independence of Algeria and the return of one million *pieds noirs*, joblessness began to rise. Yet, a decade later it had only reached 2.7 percent. It was after the oil crisis, from 1974 onward, that unemployment figures soared, peaking at 10.7 percent of the active population in 1985. In 1993, after nearly two decades of restructuring, in which one million jobs were lost in agriculture and another million in industry, the jobless represented 11 percent of the working population. The principal victims continue to be youth, female workers, and the poorly qualified in general.

The economic euphemism *restructuring* and the cold statistics cannot hide the hardships and psychological trauma that millions of victims of the recession, workers and their families, have suffered, although their situation may seem enviable to employees in some countries that do not have the comprehensive welfare system the French enjoy. Over and beyond the human suffering, unemployment has had far-reaching social consequences that can explain many of the changes in mores, ethics, and values of the past two decades. The concepts of work and money, educational objectives, community life, the image of worker unions, the perception of the role of corporations, and ideological postures have all been affected by the bane of joblessness, which is the high price France has had to pay for the belated modernization of its economy.

Workers' Rights

The right to work was written into the constitution in 1946 but, of course, remains largely theoretical in a capitalistic system. However, it does imply a certain number of legal and social obligations on the part of the state. One of the specificities of the French minimum integration income (RMI) is that it links the right to a minimum subsistence written into the constitution with the right to work, which puts the onus on the state to provide for the development of employment.

In fact, labor legislation got off to a late start in France, and most of the laws designed to protect workers from exploitation by unscrupulous employers were introduced in the present century. Even today after the extensive reform undertaken by the Socialists in 1982, the five hundred articles of the so-called Lois Auroux, the legality of certain procedures (for example, the firing, on the grounds of "economic motives," of a worker who has participated in a strike) is far from being clear.

Fortunately, today there is no comparison with the plight of the working population in the nineteenth century, when children eight years old worked in the mines and factories, when a normal workday was thirteen to fourteen hours, when undernourished workers toiled in unsanitary conditions and were victims of tuberculosis, when pay was minimal and wage deductions were practiced on the slightest pretext by employers. It took 150 years of social struggle to impose restriction on the employment of children, to limit work hours, to prescribe safety regulations, to develop the idea of the work contract and collective bargaining, to guarantee the rights of striking workers, to introduce paid vacations and the minimum wage, and so on. The majority of these concessions to social progress in France were won after bitter, and sometimes bloody, battles between Left and Right, which helps explain the rigidities of the labor market and why, for example, it is impossible for a schoolchild who is a minor to pick up a part-time job nowadays or why it is still illegal for most stores to open on Sundays.

The major developments in labor legislation since midcentury have been the introduction of a minimum wage in 1950; the generalization of paid vacations, which were extended to four weeks in 1965 and five weeks in 1982; the guarantee of a minimum income in the case of illness, maternity, or unemployment; equal opportunity and equal pay for men and women (1972); the numerous laws concerning further education and professional training; the lowering of the retirement age to sixty (1982); and the range of measures that have been taken since 1981 to ease the hardships of unemployment for different categories of workers.

Liberal economists suggest that many of the rights won by the workers are counterproductive and inhibit employment. They consider that the minimum wage (SMIC) is too high and thus discourages the hiring of less qualified workers, that state regulation of work hours handicaps corporate adaptability to changing demand, that shorter hours damage productivity, hence growth and jobs; that employers' social security contributions—double the U.S. figure—are too high for corporations and dissuade hiring, that early retirement programs have upset the age pyramid of corporations and deprived them of experience and know-how, that unemployment benefits are too high to encourage the jobless to seek work.

Whatever the relevance of these remarks, often inspired by a comparison with the jobless rate in the United States, which used to be almost half that in France in the late 1980s, neither the Left nor the Right has dared tamper with overall employment policy, although some concessions were made in an attempt to adapt legislation to a changing economic environment and give greater flexibility to corporations. One of the more daring moves was the suppression by the Chirac government in 1986 of the complicated procedure for laying off workers, which used to require the prior authorization of the administration and was designed to prevent abusive dismissals. Likewise, the revocation of the law that forbade industry from employing female workers at night was an obvious attempt to revamp labor legislation in a more liberal spirit. It is hard to know how far the neoliberals would have gone in this direction had they stayed in power in 1988. The right-wing majority elected in 1993 has made no secret of its intention to loosen constraints on employers, which it sees as essential to developing the job market.

Basically there have been two approaches to the problem of unemployment in France. In the late 1970s and early 1980s the main policy was to limit the working population in spite of the continuing population growth. The reduction of the retirement age from sixty-five years to sixty (a right not an obligation)—or the equivalent of 37.5 years of work—plus the possibility of "early retirement" (*préretraite*) with a reduced pension between fifty-five and sixty, helped to curb the normal increase of the working population. In 1985, for example, the 150,000 workers who availed themselves of this opportunity cut the jobless figure by the same number. Meanwhile, training programs and community service jobs for early school-leavers not entitled to the dole (and, therefore, not *officially* unemployed), delayed the arrival of young people on the regular job market, while retraining opportunities for older, laid-off workers also kept the unemployment statistics in check. Overall, between 200,000 and 300,000 people have been saved from unemployment annually since 1974 thanks to these measures.

The second approach has been to modify regulations that were designed to limit the development of temporary employment, and there has been a considerable growth in what the INSEE calls "atypical" jobs, that is, temporary work usually limited to a few months, which has put an end to job security but has the advantage of keeping people off the unemployment lines and the official unemployment statistics. Privately run temporary employment bureaus that previously were limited to the domestic help sector—the public ANPE (Agence nationale pour l'emploi) was the only authorized employment agency—mushroomed not only in the major cities but in towns all over France. Part-time jobs, not always freely chosen, have also increased in the past decade. In 1990, almost three million employees, 11.8 percent of the work force, held a part-time job.[1]

A series of measures accompanied by financial incentives for corpo-

1. *Tableaux de l'économie française* 1991–92, 64.

rations were introduced to facilitate the hiring of young people and the reemployment of older workers who had been unemployed for a long period—in 1990 the average duration was more than sixteen months.[2] The state-funded community service, part-time jobs for unemployed youth, the preprofessional training programs in industry, the development of short-term employment contracts have no doubt tempered the harshness of the recession, particularly for the younger generation, but have given rise to a dual job market that is a major cause of social inequalities.

In fact temporary jobs are often a smooth way for corporations to get around paying the minimum wage, which is frequently a deterrent to employment (an employee's salary of five thousand francs costs an employer eight thousand francs due to social security charges). Only 30 percent of the sixteen to twenty-five age group employed now has a regular job, and the unemployment rate of young people without any educational qualifications is three times higher than that of college graduates. At the other end of the scale, the over fifties, the victims of layoffs in declining industrial sectors, have practically no chance of finding permanent employment. Moreover, three-quarters of the combined unstable and part-time jobs are held by female employees. Worried by the extension of temporary work, the government decided in 1989 to exonerate small firms from all social security contributions for one year in exchange for the hiring of a first worker with a regular employment contract. This scheme has provided sixty-five thousand jobs, 40 percent of which did not exist before. Nonetheless, as long as the working population continues to increase and the growth rate remains at present levels, there is little likelihood of a return, if ever, to prerecession employment patterns.

Cushioning

To ease the hardship of the unemployed there is a complex system of welfare benefits in which the rates and duration of payment vary according to the age and previous remuneration of the beneficiaries as well as the uninterrupted number of months or years they have paid mandatory unemployment insurance, jointly financed in France by employers

2. Thierry Lacroix, "Le marché du travail dans les années 80," in *Données Sociales 1990*, 36–49.

and employees, prior to losing their job. When they have exhausted the possibilities of degressive unemployment insurance, usually limited from a few months to one year, the jobless are entitled to benefits under the state-run national solidarity plan, which tides them over for a further variable period. Yet, over one million jobless, mostly youth, women, and manual workers, who remain unemployed for long periods between two temporary jobs get no unemployment allowances. This is the main cause of poverty in France today, and it is hardly surprising that the principal beneficiaries of the minimum integration income introduced in 1989 are young singles with no financial resources. Unfortunately, those under twenty-five are not eligible for it. Obviously, these aids, which have largely preserved the victims of the recession in France from the destitution that their counterparts in some countries experienced, do not offset the loss of income due to loss of regular employment.

The New Poverty

A number of unemployed workers, having exhausted all the possibilities of institutional aid, joined the ranks of the "new paupers" (*les nouveaux pauvres*) in the 1980s and can be seen in the Paris Métro and in the streets of the larger cities. The comic artist Coluche was the first to attract the attention of public opinion to the plight of these victims of dire poverty and to set up soup kitchens, *les restaus du coeur*—not the glitzy, high-tech France of the glossy business magazines. By a strange paradox it is not the Socialist politicians who governed France for most of the 1980s but a music hall artist and a priest, l'Abbé Pierre, the spokesman of the *clochards* for nearly forty years, who represent the real social conscience of France today. The abbé, who has thundered against the new poverty and flown to the defense of the squatters evicted by the police in the Paris of uncontrolled property speculation, is a popular figure in this lay society where the insufficient collective effort in favor of the poor does not exclude individual generosity and concern for the misery of others, as the success of the highly publicized "charity business" shows. The relative inability of the politicians and labor union leaders to maintain a strong network of institutional solidarity has led to increasing privatization of aid and cooperation on the U.S. model that corresponds to a new trend in social relations generally.

Of course the welfare system is not perfect, of course there are abuses as elsewhere, and of course there are a number of bogus jobless, but the misery is undeniable. The social and psychological ravages of unemployment are more serious than the statistics show. In Bordeaux, for example, an evaluation of a city program for the integration of older unemployed workers (*programme d'insertion locale*) along the lines of the community service jobs for young people revealed that out of 1,000 eligible persons, only 250 appeared to have the physical and mental capacities necessary to act as traffic wardens at school crossings. These numbers show the difficulty of the unemployment problem in an increasingly complex society.

It is to the credit of the successive governments in France from the midseventies to have done their best to relieve the hardships induced by unemployment. According to Serge Milano, the number of poor people has actually decreased in the past decade but is more visible nowadays because it affects the younger generation of unemployed adults.[3] An estimated 50,000 young people under twenty-five can be considered as having no chance of employment in the future, 250,000 others are in dire need from time to time, and 120,000 quit school every year with no qualification. This explains the frequent explosions of violence in the ZUP, and the development of gangs, and of ghettos. Exclusion from the workplace leads to social exclusion.[4]

Part of the trouble is that the politicians have been better at relieving the jobless than developing the job market. According to experts, French spending on unemployment, which amounts to 3 percent of GDP, has not been wisely spent. Sweden, for an equivalent investment, has an unemployment rate of 2 to 3 percent, compared to 11 percent in France. In France, 75 percent of financing goes to welfare and only 25 percent to training and job integration programs. In Sweden the numbers are reversed. Another reason for the inefficiency of the French approach lies in the obsession with productivity, or rather a narrow view of the factors governing productivity, which leads, according to the political tendency of the moment, to alternating policies of keeping on too many workers or engaging in massive layoffs: "In the United States the situation is different; adaptation is heavy-handed and productivity sluggish, but geographical mobility and the capacity for job creation are far superior."[5]

3. Serge Milano, *La pauvreté absolue* (Paris: Hachette 1988).
4. Alain Lebaube, "L'explosif chômage des jeunes," *Le Monde*, 14 May 1991.
5. Elie Cohen, "Le miroir des inégalités," *Le Monde*, 1 May 1990.

The production model is another drawback. The traditional three-tier structure of French industry, with unskilled and badly paid line personnel at its base, highly qualified and highly paid management at the top, and supervisory staff in the middle, is not conducive to in-house promotions, so that when layoffs are in order the less qualified are the first victims. This production model is flexible enough in boom times but becomes rigid in times of crisis.

> The result: the million jobless, out of a total of two and a half million, who remain unemployed over a long period are the real losers of the recession, and the RMI dumping ground is the tangible sign of our collective incapacity to ensure a carefully planned adaptation to the new economic deal without a loss of [people's] professional potentiality [*qualification*].[6]

In addition to this structural explanation for the high rate of unemployment in France, the economist Philippe d'Iribarne has suggested that there might also be a cultural reason. In *Le chômage paradoxal,* he points out that "the plasticity of national cultures is not infinite" and suggests that national traits such as "codes of honor" that lead French workers to refuse jobs they esteem a professional loss of face may explain, in part, the lack of flexibility of the job market in France.[7]

It is hard to see how French unemployment policy based on cushioning of the victims could have been changed in the heat of the economic crisis. The structural drawbacks of French corporations were hidden from view during the "thirty glorious years," and France could hardly do less than strive to preserve from hardship the millions of workers who had contributed to postwar growth. Could the latter be blamed for the shortsightedness of industrial and political leaders who had neglected human resources and training in their calculations? Meanwhile, had not their own legal representatives, the worker unions, obsessed with preserving and extending the tangible rights of "the working population," been blind to the storm that was brewing? But that is another story.

---

6. Cohen, "Le miroir des inégalités."

7. Philippe D'Iribarne, *Le Chômage Paradoxal* (Paris: Presses Universitaires de France, 1990), 169.

Labor Relations

The popular joke in Paris is that transport workers no longer give strike notice but notice of the day they have decided to work. Yet, contrary to what might be imagined by foreign visitors to the capital who become the victims of sudden strikes in the Métro, airlines, trains, or taxis, labor conflicts are far from endemic in France and have actually decreased in the past decade. The number of work days lost on labor disputes in 1986 was one-third the 1976 figure. The difficulty of mobilizing troops and scarce financial resources mean that sporadic stoppages are more common than the enduring type of action practiced by British and U.S. unions, although there have been notable exceptions. The sit-ins, the go-slow strikes, the token stoppages of a few hours, "a safety valve for discontent," in the words of John Ardagh,[8] do not unduly punish workers financially but can seriously disrupt production and services. Occasionally the strikers will not even be penalized. Thus in 1988 a strike by dockers in Calais did not result in any deduction on their paychecks, as the *Beaujolais nouveau* was shipped on time to England through the port of Dunkerque! In an increasingly technological society a stoppage by a few key employees can create havoc. The repetitive airline and public transportation strikes make literal hostages of travelers, not to mention the ten-day truckers' strike in June 1992 that paralyzed traffic all over France. The practice in the public service of deducting one hour of pay for a strike of one hour's duration is hardly a deterrent. In higher education the administration may deduct a day's pay from the academic's paycheck only if the person concerned signs a paper declaring he or she was on strike. There is no other control! What is even more surprising is that strikers will sign, showing that even if unions have few members, those who do join are active. Or maybe academics are too honest?

Of course the fact that there are fewer strikes does not mean that tensions in the workplace have disappeared. It would be naive to think that Taylorism is dead. Even if conditions in the factories have changed, the neo-Taylorism of today, which offers a better organization of work, gives little relief to workers and creates new frustrations. The aspirations of workers today do not always fit in with a conception of the corporation that often continues to be founded on discipline and authority while

---

8. See John Ardagh, *France Today* (London: Penguin Books, 1990), 100. Ardagh's book is a classic on contemporary French society.

CGT, FO, CFDT, and All That

The five major national interprofessional worker organizations are all known by their acronyms, which adds to the confusion of foreigners puzzled by the numerous tendencies and subtle ideological distinctions that the French can appreciate. The oldest and largest of these unions is the CGT (Conféderation générale du travail), founded in 1895 and close to the Communist party. The present leader is Louis Viannet. The CFDT (Confédération française démocratique du travail), a lay offshoot of the minority social-Christian CFTC (Confédération française des travailleurs chrétiens), after championing *autogestion* (participative management) in the 1970s, has veered toward reformism today. It is the most progressive of all the organizations and the best if not always willing ally of the Socialists. Nicole Notat became union leader in 1992. FO (Force ouvrière), which grew out of a split in the CGT and is also of a reformist tendency, has become slightly less cooperative under its new leader Marc Blondel. The last of the big interprofessional confederations is the CGC (Confédération générale des cadres), led by Paul Marchelli. It sees managerial staff as the key to the modernization of business and is bent on defending the interests of the *cadres.*

Another limited group of unions, the *autonomes,* confine themselves to the defense of a specific profession. Thus, the police, journalists, tax officials, and airport controllers have their own organizations. The most powerful of these is the FEN (Fédération de l'éducation nationale), itself split up into several rival tendencies, which explains in part the impossibility of developing any real consensus on educational reform among the profession. The farmer unions, in particular the FNSEA (Fédération nationale des syndicats d'exploitants agricoles), also wield considerable power. Generally speaking, corporatist agitation seems to be more widespread than interprofessional solidarity these days and is yet another proof of the new, pervasive individualism in French society.

A curious, though marginal, type of labor organization exists in France. It is the in-house trade union close to the management of certain corporations. The Confédération des syndicats libres in the Peugeot auto plants is one of the best known. Until recently membership was practically mandatory.

---

demanding adaptability and adherence to the corporate culture—"forced consensus"—in lean times, designed to exploit the capacity of workers to the full. The interests of the latter need not necessarily correspond to those of the enterprise when it decides, for example, to introduce robots and lay off hundreds of employees. The demise of trade unions does not signify an end to industrial conflict in France.[9]

In fact, all the labor conflicts in recent years have fallen victim to

9. See Labbé and Perrin, *Que reste-t-il de Billancourt?*

the austerity policy at a time when to have a job is considered quite a privilege. Yet this does not excuse the anachronistic management of human resources in what pretends to be a modern technological society. Even private corporations are no models of personnel management. The Peugeot autoworkers strike in 1989 was largely a revolt against an outdated approach to staff relations. According to one worker, interviewed by *Le Monde,* the company was not beyond pressuring an employee on sick leave to return to the assembly line, even if he or she was not required to work, so that the absentee rate that determines the amount of social security payments due by the firm for work accidents did not increase.[10] As for the civil service, former premier Rocard made its modernization one of the priorities of his government. In lean budget times it is doubtful that the means will be available to carry out this reform. It is all very fine to exhort the official in a cramped tax office in the south of France to be smiling and pleasant toward the impatient public when room temperature is close to eighty degrees in the summer heat and it is not his or her day to have the one and only electric fan that has to to be shared in turns with two colleagues!

While the CGT's "betrayal" of the striking workers at the Renault factory in Cléon in December 1991,[11] and the truckers' unions acceptance of the government's conditions in June 1992—which undermined the unrealistic demands of the coordinations—are proof of a more constructive attitude of the official unions, they also highlight the fragility of French society, which results from the lack of trusted intermediaries to resolve conflict: "In reality, compared to the active role of associations, collective action by union or professional groups has never been widely developed in France," says journalist Jean-Michel Normand, writing about the truckers' strike. "Unless we resign ourselves to seeing selfish interests paralyze the slightest reform voted by Parliament and threaten united action, it is high time to become aware that the weakness of intermediary bodies represents one of the fundamental ills of French society—and the visible sign of the deterioration of the social fabric."[12]

10. Jean-Michel Normand, "Les grévistes mettent en cause l'ensemble de la politique sociale de Peugeot," *Le Monde,* 20 September 1989.

11. This conflict, decided by union hardliners, failed to obtain the support of the majority of the workers and was called off by the union delegate, who was then insulted by the strikers.

12. Jean-Michel Normand, "La déroute des corps intermédiaires," *Le Monde,* 7 July 1992.

Managerial Zapping

This was how Rocard described the feverish experimentation of new management methods by some corporations that have introduced quality circles, management by objectives, a merit system, and other boardroom toys, which actual corporate practices frequently contradict. Nevertheless, the natural mistrust of the French and the strong hold of traditional corporate culture have limited the development of these new approaches to the management of human resources. Alain d'Iribarne explained in an interview in *Le Monde* why, in his opinion, French enterprises are so reticent about introducing changes in technology and personnel management:

> Globally, French society is conservative because it strives to preserve the foundations of its social system that are rooted in its history. We are confronted with a strong urge to establish distinctions between groups of individuals, which leads, among other things, to pronounced professional and social stratifications such as the distance between workers and managers. French society only accepts changes that do not challenge it.

After underlining the lack of investment by French enterprises in management tools necessary to obtain data on working conditions, salaries, and so on, the economist went on:

> France has not a coherent approach in this matter. It is scarcely possible to borrow individualized wages from the Americans, quality circles from the Japanese, or again the corporate project from the Americans without carrying out the overall task of adapting them to our society's characteristic way of functioning.[13]

The disdainful reaction of a Peugeot worker to quality circles shows how delicate the introduction of new management techniques may be: "That too is a fine invention. Before, the acceptance of technical improvements meant a bonus. Now we do it for nothing. At least the

13. Nathalie Schneider, "'La compétitivité des entreprises passe par l'innovation sociale' nous déclare Alain d'Iribarne, économiste au CNRS," *Le Monde*, 13 April 1990.

meetings give us a break from the chronometer." Another worker commenting on merit payments declared: "It's a means of blackmail used by the *petits chefs* (foremen) because they are the ones who allot them."[14] Interestingly, many of these so-called innovations were already in use in the nineteenth century. Jean-Baptiste-André Godin, maker of the famous stove that bears his name (it has become something of a must for neorurals), was a pioneer in labor relations who rewarded workers who proposed product developments or improvements in work methods with special bonuses.

The sweeping reform of labor legislation undertaken by the Socialist minister of labor, Jean Auroux, in 1982 was designed to democratize internal corporate relations, notoriously autarkical and conflictual in France, and put them on a par with practices in other democracies. The new laws guarantee liberty of expression inside the corporation and strive to limit abusive firing, reinforce the authority of workers' representatives as well as of the committees of hygiene and safety, and introduce internal collective bargaining to negotiate salaries annually. (Formerly, these were established sector by sector on a national basis.) The very need for "expression groups," a French invention instituted by Lois Auroux in 1982, shows how antiquated labor law and working conditions used to be. Even today it is forbidden for workers on some assembly lines to talk on the job. However, many of the *groupes d'expression* are run by hierarchical superiors, which is hardly conducive to free speech.

While the new legislation has led to a growing number of in-house salary agreements in the larger firms, the widespread absence of labor organizations in the numerous enterprises that employ fewer than fifty workers limits the extension of decentralized collective bargaining procedures, and the national, sector-by-sector labor agreements on salaries, hierarchy, and so on remain important. The interprofessional worker confederations play a vital role in these discussions. A lot of employers in the smaller firms are hostile to trade unions, although legally any company with more than ten employees is entitled to have worker delegates. Fewer than 40 percent of those having between eleven and fifty employees actually do have a delegate. A report delivered to the minister of labor in 1990 suggested setting up an external representative body for employees who have no in-house structure. One recent development

14. Normand, "Les grévistes mettent en cause l'ensemble de la politique sociale de Peugeot."

was the initiative first launched in 1990 by the big private insurance group, AXA, which consists in offering a regular "union check" to encourage employees to join the labor organization of their choice, the idea being that strong trade unions, capable of making economically credible proposals to management, are healthy for a corporation. The reaction of the confederations has been mixed. The CFDT saw the experiment as a pioneering development whereas FO, true to its new hard line, declared that trade unionism was not for sale. However, by 1992 FO had accepted the system. The CGT is still opposed. France, on account of its troubled history of labor relations, is still a long way from comanagement on the Swedish model that it admires so much. Do the cantankerous French really want it anyway? Who but the French could associate "soft" and "consensus" in the disdainful tautological expression *consensus mou*?

Lazy France?

The forty-hour week was introduced in France in 1936, but there were numerous exceptions, and up to the end of the 1960s the average workweek was about forty-five hours. Following the 1968 student riots and ensuing social unrest, this figure dropped gradually to reach a little over forty hours in 1980. This helps to put in proper perspective the reduction of the legal work time to thirty-nine hours by the Socialist government in 1981, which was far from a revolution despite all the hype about the subject. Even today the picture is more complex than appears at first sight because of the flexibility of labor contracts, which allow as many as forty-five hours and even, in some sectors, forty-nine hours per week, the extra hours being paid as overtime. This is more than twice the gap that exists between legal work time and practices in industry in Germany. In fact, industrial workers in France have a longer work week than those in Belgium, Germany, or Britain.[15]

All overtime in excess of one hundred and thirty hours annually legally entitles workers to leave of absence for a corresponding number of hours. Because of the difficulty of control, many enterprises, particularly the smaller ones, offer bonuses or even covert payments to get around the law and avoid hiring extra staff, while keeping the machines or the business running as long as possible. This also largely explains the

15. Alain Lebaube, "Les abonnés des heures supplémentaires ne veulent pas décrocher," *Le Monde*, 5 October 1990.

increasing development of part-time work. A ministry of labor survey in 1986 showed that more than 45 percent of the companies used overtime. Nearly 12 percent announced workweeks of forty-two hours or more.[16]

During the spell of neoliberal government from 1986 to 1988, the French suddenly discovered that they were lazy. They could not open a newspaper or switch on their television without being chided for their sloth, which allegedly explained the lack of competitiveness of France. The exorbitant privileges of French workers—the thirty-nine hour week, the five weeks paid vacation, retirement at sixty—were set against working conditions in the United States and Japan to show just how pampered the French were. The argument had been used in the past but was usually directed against state employees. Was it to be undersood that the nationalizations had contaminated the public at large? It was strange too that the old image of the lazy Mediterranean citizen who had not been touched by the divine grace of the Protestant work ethic was used precisely when the Sun Belt was becoming a model of economic dynamism.

While industrial workers in France have a longer work week than their German or British counterparts, it is true that the total number of *annual* work hours in France (1,682) is lower than in the United States (1,912). The Japanese work 500 hours more than the French annually, but the Germans even less. French employers regularly complain about the religious feast days and public holidays the French are entitled to as well as the famous *ponts.* A *pont*—bridge—is a working day intervening between a public holiday and Saturday or between Sunday and a public holiday. This day is also taken off to help bridge the gap between two nonwork days so that in fact people get three consecutive days off. People carefully thumb the calendar each year to see how many *ponts* there are. During the month of May 1991, the French worked only nineteen days in all! Paradoxically, France, where religious practice is lower than in Italy, insists upon respecting church feasts, whereas the Italians have struck most of the feast days off the calendar. In fact if the French have three days more annual vacation than the Italians, the "hardworking" Germans have five days more than the French.

Jean-Louis Levet says that the highly publicized debate on the supposed laziness of the French, like the question of insufficient industrial investment, hides a far more fundamental issue: "It's no use working and

16. M. N., "Innovation sociale sans assurances," *Le Monde,* 5 July 1990.

Work Patterns

Work patterns in contemporary France obviously vary a great deal according to the type of business and the rank of the employees. It is only possible to outline some of the more recent developments, such as the use of flextime, which increases the higher up the hierarchy people are, the decline in absenteeism, and the slight rise in the number of those who work on weekends. Globally, the self-employed have a longer workday and work more days in the week than salaried employees. In general female workers tend to take more long weekends and days off (Wednesday, the kids' free day from school) than their male counterparts. The majority of people start work between 8 and 9 A.M. and finish between 5 and 6 P.M. About one in ten employees starts before 7 A.M. and one in twelve finishes after 8 P.M. Cafés and bars as well as bakeries will be open very early in the morning, frequently at 6 A.M.

Contrary to what happens in some countries, it is quite easy to contact professionals in certain areas such as advertising, marketing, publishing, or real estate after 7 P.M. People higher up the hierarchy seem ready enough to work late in the evenings. However, for the majority of employees the thirty-nine-hour week has meant starting the day later and finishing earlier, while the lunch break tends to be shorter than before. Most smaller stores will be closed between 12 and 2 P.M. The main preoccupation for industry is to keep the machines running longer hours without recruiting extra personnel so that the shorter work week has not been the booster to employment that it was designed to be. The present trend is to introduce greater flexibility and develop shift work to increase competitiveness—which explains, in part, the growing amount of overtime and the development of part-time jobs.

---

investing more and more if the economy doesn't know how to get the most out of people and capital: that's the basic cause of the insufficient industrial competiveness of France. . . . " In other words, the strict respect of work hours doesn't guarantee that the work will be well done.[17]

A Question of Priorities

In spite of all the chiding done with the support of figures and graphs it is doubtful if the French really developed a guilt complex about their alleged laziness. At a time when work was glorified, it would have been presumptious if not ill-mannered to pass yourself off as a busy beaver, in much the same way as it is considered rude to brag about your wealth.

17. Levet, *Une France sans complexes,* 50.

Today, the French seem to have forgotten how lazy they were a few years ago. The latest chic is to say how busy you are. People do not have a minute to spare. The message may be: "I've reached the limits of productivity. Don't ask me to do any more." More seriously, the plight of the unemployed no longer allows people with a minimum of courtesy to have a dilettantist attitude toward work, even in speech.

The French are probably no lazier than people elsewhere, but their priorities are different. They tend to keep a very strict separation between work time and leisure time, be it at school (French campuses are like ghost towns on weekends) or on the job. They do not mix their private and social life with their professional life and usually avoid mingling with the people they work with after leaving the workplace. The overall impression one gets is that they are conscientious and hardworking on the job and enjoy their work, unless they are discouraged by conditions or lack of consideration, as is too often the case. Young people, as elsewhere in Europe, dream of an enriching profession rather than the fast-track, get-rich-quick career path. The French do not seem to be ready to let working life interfere with family or personal projects. In brief, they like their independence and refuse to be shackled.

PART 8

Opening French Windows Wide

It is necessary to go abroad, to discover the world. The most frequent cause of the egocentrism of men and nations lies in their ignorance of the difficulties of others, each one tending to see only what corresponds to his immediate interest.

—Jean Monnet (1888–1979)

21

From Cognac to Europe

On 9 November 1988 the remains of Jean Monnet, the man John F. Kennedy called "the statesman of the World," were transferred to the Panthéon in Paris, the highest posthumous honor the French can bestow on a great citizen. The pomp and solemnity of the ceremony, presided over by François Mitterrand in the company of the European heads of state and flag-bearing youth from the different countries, were a fitting tribute to the "Father of Europe," born in the little town of Cognac one hundred years before.

The son of a brandy maker, Monnet was sent to England to learn the language when he was sixteen and dropped out of school before receiving the baccalauréat, thus being something of an exception in the French caste system based on the elitist education of the *grandes écoles*. It was as a traveling salesman for Jean-Gabriel Monnet cognac in the United States, Sweden, Russia, and Egypt that he got his first training in the art of international negotiation. His ability to learn from others came from dealing with his father's international clients, and his legendary patience sprang, in his own words, from the observation of the slow maturation of fine brandy: "In Cognac we know how to wait. It is the only way to make a good product."[1]

Jean Monnet was a man of many talents. During World War I he was responsible for providing the French with supplies from London, and in 1920 became deputy secretary general of the League of Nations, forerunner of the United Nations. Financial consultant to Poland and Romania in the 1920s, he helped the authorities to save the national currencies. He founded a bank in San Francisco to facilitate U.S. investment in China, became a consultant to the Chinese government in Shanghai, and was behind the financing operation for Chinese railways. Between 1939 and 1944 he acted as an adviser in London, Washington, and Algiers to Churchill, Roosevelt, and de Gaulle respectively.

1. Jean Monnet, *Mémoires* (Paris: Librairie Arthème Fayard, 1976), 50.

After World War II he was to devote most of his activity to domestic affairs in France—he was appointed first Commissioner of the modernization plan in postwar France—and in association with Robert Schuman, minister of foreign affairs, launched the European Coal and Steel Community (ECSC), which was to develop into the European Community, for which Jean Monnet was to toil tirelessly with those other great Europeans, Konrad Adenauer in Germany and Alcide de Gasperi in Italy. Few people were better qualified than Monnet for such a vast undertaking, which required foresight, tolerance, tenacity, infinite patience, and a grasp of international issues.

The Western Influence

Even if the French have not always been so enthusiastic about a united Europe as they seem to be today, historically, geographically, and intellectually France was predestined to play a leading role in spite of its traditional conservatism. Nor should the endless squabbling with the United States over Airbus, beef hormones, and agricultural subsidies hide the fact that the Common Market was made possible by generous American aid to postwar Europe. Perhaps even more important than the Marshall Plan and the NATO umbrella, which permitted the peaceful development of western European trade for half a century despite the cold war, was the "Western influence," without which France could never have played its privileged role as a cultural and economic crossroads. Just as the great discoveries of the sixteenth century had created an upheaval in the European perception of the world, the economic power and dynamism of the New World in the 1950s and 1960s became a model for the Old World to imitate in spite of the reservations the older generation had about many aspects of the American way of life.

In his homage to Jean Monnet at the Panthéon ceremony, François Mitterrand appropriately underlined the importance of the great statesman's early American experience: "In America, at eighteen years of age, right at the beginning of the century, he met men whose advance toward the West seemed boundless, a nation bent on developing rather than administering the dynamism of a changing world that made the customs of old Europe look decidedly static."[2] Creating a united, dynamic Europe was to become the obsession of his life.

2. "Les trois leçons de sa jeunesse," *Le Monde*, 10 November 1988.

The laborious elaboration of Jean Monnet's dream of a united Europe seems painstakingly slow to contemporaries, but what is three decades in the long history of the continent? The unity that Julius Caesar, Charlemagne, Napoleon, and Hitler were unable to impose by force is taking shape before our eyes thanks to a model of behavior based on negotiated settlement of differences that the "Father of Europe" was the first to enact. The 340 million people "represent the strength of a new form of democratic cooperation and integration, which demonstrably works." A millenium of mutual distrust between nations has given way to "mutual pride in centuries of cross-fertilized culture and history, a new explosion of creative genius based on cooperation as well as competition between peoples, and a joint approach to an exciting but increasingly unpredictable future."[3] The Single Act, voted in 1985, was to revitalize economic and political cooperation that had become bogged down in petty wrangling.

The Single Act

> Build a home to live together? Maybe yes, later. Meanwhile, separate bedrooms!
>
> —Claude Sarraute

The aim of the Treaty of Rome that brought the EC into being was not simply to set up a customs union but to abolish all barriers to the free movement of goods and people between the member countries. This has been far from the case. Each nation developed protective measures to shelter its native market, and this has resulted in endless red tape at border crossings for truckers in the form of disguised obstacles to the importation of goods from other member countries. Health restrictions, environmental and consumer protection regulations, anti-inflationary measures, and national quality standards have at one time or another served as an excuse to combat the free trade stipulated in the Treaty of Rome. Likewise, public employment and public procurement have been strictly national. The cost of these neoprotectionist measures to the EC has been estimated at 50 billion ECU. It is worth adding that the myriad "invisible" national regulations have also protected Europe from

3. Stanley Budd and Alun Jones, *The European Community: A Guide to the Maze* (London: Kogan Page, 1989), 27.

non-European exporters, particularly the Japanese. There is some fear that the Single Act, which is designed to ban all restrictions to free trade, may make an open Europe with clear game rules particularly vulnerable to both a Japanese and a U.S. export drive.

While France has not been the least diligent in protecting its interests, it was a French citizen, Jacques Delors, president of the European Commission—who seems to possess the unshakable resolve of Jean Monnet, if not his patience—who proposed the Single Act, which simply stated that all barriers to the free movement of goods and people should be removed by 1993. The pace at which the three hundred odd directives in areas as diverse as trucking, product safety, education, telecommunications, and the environment were adopted surprised even the most optimistic Europeans familiar with the bureaucratic rhythm of Brussels. France and Germany have been the driving forces of change, with Britain, more often than not, stamping on the brake. Ideally the EC market, with a population of 340 million, would represent a powerful economic bloc capable of competing with the United States and Asia. The main danger is that the demons of European division will break loose when national interests are at stake, when the more fragile sectors of the economy as well as jobs are threatened, and the inhabitants of social democracies begin to feel the pinch of unbridled competition. The French preoccupation with "the social dimension" of the Community shows that the Europeans are searching for a model of development that will be neither American nor Japanese. The success of the Single Act will depend on its ability to reconcile the demands of global competition with the aspirations of European men and women.

Europe, France, and the United States

In 1987, following the annual meeting between the European Commission and a U.S. delegation, a headline in *Le Monde* ran: "The EEC and the United States have excellent relations and serious differences,"[4] which just about sums up the ambiguous nature of their relationship. The sources of friction concern military questions of security, as well as monetary, agricultural, and industrial policy.

---

4. Philippe Lemaître, "La CEE et les Etats-Unis ont d'excellents rapports et de sérieuses difficultés," *Le Monde*, 16 December 1987.

European Security

America has often been tempted to let Europe fend for itself and only reluctantly entered the two world wars to protect the old continent. After World War II, when the GIs returned home, Europe was practically defenseless and the anachronistic Brussels Treaty—the future Western European Union—signed in 1948 between Britain, France, Belgium, Holland, and Luxembourg (designed to protect against agression by a nonexistent German army!) could not have withstood Soviet expansion when the cold war began and Communist agitation was spreading in Europe. The Europeans suddenly realized that they had mistaken their enemy and pleaded with the United States for help. Thus, in 1949, for the first time in the history of the United States, the country formed an alliance in times of peace when it signed the North Atlantic Treaty with twelve European countries, on the insistent request of France, in particular.

The NATO umbrella still protects Europe today, but even before the fall of the Berlin Wall and the turmoil in Eastern Europe, things had begun to change with the rapprochement between the Soviet Union and the United States, the Intermediate-range Nuclear Forces agreement (1987), which involved a reduction in intermediate-range U.S. nuclear warheads, and talks of "burden sharing" in Washington.

While Britain and Germany have been stalwart supporters of the North Atlantic Treaty Organization, relations with France have never been easy. In 1966 the country withdrew from NATO military command, and its headquarters were moved from Paris to Brussels. General de Gaulle did not want French forces obeying foreign officers. "France's determination to command its own affairs," declared the General, "is incompatible with a defense organization in which it is a subordinate." This is a typical example of French particularism that infuriates the United States. Nevertheless France is still a NATO member. Following the fall of the Berlin Wall, the United States would like to see the French play an active role in a new multinational European defense force and in this way participate again in the integrated military structure of NATO. But France, contrary to Britain, favors strengthening links with the Western European Union.

The French were among the first to discover the principles of atomic fission, and were it not for World War II, which dispersed the team of Fréderic Joliot-Curie that was working at the Collège de France, they would probably have built the first atomic heavy-water reactor. After the Liberation the CEA (Commission de l'énergie atomique) was set up with a view to guaranteeing the atomic military and industrial independence of France. The first atomic bomb was tested in 1960, and, in 1968, the country became the fifth world nuclear power. It has today a credible, if small, deterrent strike force, *la force de frappe,* comprising nuclear submarines, missiles, bombers, and a variety of launchers. What Lothar Baier has called the "nuclear phallus" is one of the country's proudest symbols, and, apart from the ecologists, all the political parties support the principle of an independent nuclear deterrent force. The Socialists, who were opposed to the *force de frappe* before they came to power in 1981, have been among its staunchest supporters. The *Rainbow Warrior* scandal in 1985 and its aftermath showed the extent of public consensus when the *raison d'état* triumphed over the principles of justice.[5] A survey taken in 1989 showed that 57 percent of the French are in favor of the nuclear force that has given France an influence in the modern world that far exceeds its economic importance.[6]

The Western European Union (WEU)

The nine-nation WEU—Germany, Italy, Spain, and Portugal are now members—the only West European parliamentary body authorized to discuss defense, is divided on the goals of the organization, at present under the operational command of NATO. France sees it essentially as a means of affirming European—maybe even French—identity in matters of security, while Britain, the only other nuclear power in Europe, sees it as a pillar of NATO. So far the Europeans have carefully avoided a clear decision on this issue, and in truth there has been more rivalry than cooperation between European countries in the area of defense, a situation that has largely benefited the U.S. weapons industry. Of the sixteen NATO allies, five different countries build fourteen different fighter planes, eight build six differnt types of warship, and four different tanks are built by four different countries! The United States sells three times more arms to NATO members than it purchases from them, and

5. The Greenpeace ship protesting French nuclear tests in the Pacific was blown up in Auckland Harbor (New Zealand) in 1985 by French secret agents. One of the crew members was killed in the explosion. A grotesque political scandal followed, but there was to be no French Watergate.

6. CSA-*Le Monde*-FR 3 (16–23 May 1989), *Le Monde,* 23 May 1989.

the Europeans feel they are getting a raw deal, as imported arms are not taxed when similar products are not manufactured in Europe: "Transatlantic [arms] trade follows a highway from the United States to Europe and a mule track in the opposite direction," declared one French industrialist.[7] When by some miracle Europeans do manage to cooperate, the United States is quick to chide. Richard Burt, the U.S. Ambassador to Bonn, commenting on the laborious agreement between France and Germany to produce an antitank helicopter, expressed dismay that the Europeans had not purchased the less expensive and more up-to-date McDonnell-Douglas Apache. He went on to declare that by acting in this way the Europeans were weakening the Western defense system.

In spite of the difficulty of erasing in half a century the griefs accumulated over centuries of embittered nationalism there have been encouraging signs of progress toward European military cooperation. Who but the wildest utopists could have imagined even thirty years ago that a French-German troop contingent under joint command would see the day? In 1992 France and Germany finalized plans for a forty-thousand-strong joint defense corps. This is intended to be the nucleus of a fully fledged European defense arm. Whether this will be with or without NATO will depend on the influence of the Atlantic lobby in Europe. (Britain and the Netherlands will not contemplate any EC defense role that cuts across the primary role of the United States in European defense.) In any case, strategists fail to see how a militarily vulnerable Europe could become a powerful economic power. Defense is one of the most sensitive issues to be faced by the EC in the coming years, and the ability of Europeans to set up a common defense force will be a test of their cohesion.

The Common Agricultural Policy

One of the most enduring conflicts between the United States and Europe is related to the question of agricultural subsidies. The EC's Common Agricultural Policy has been the principal target of the Americans.

The aim of the CAP, essentially a farm subsidy program set up in the early 1960s, was to make the European countries self-sufficient in agriculture. It has succeeded beyond the wildest dreams; Europe, formerly a net

7. Jacques Isnard, "Un pavé dans la mare transatlantique," *Le Monde*, 1 December 1988.

importer, has become not only self-sufficient but a major exporter of agricultural produce. The system is based on two principles: (1) guaranteed prices for farmers; and (2) Community preference.

Guaranteed Prices

As soon as prices drop below the ceiling fixed at the annual marathon bargaining sessions in Brussels, the agricultural products concerned are withdrawn from the market and stockpiled to maintain price levels. Originally designed to keep German corn producers in business, the system was subsequently extended to cover dairy products, beef, sugar, olive oil, tobacco, fruits and vegetables, and so on. The stockpiles are later sold at a loss on the international market. The authorized dealer who has stockpiled the products will then receive an agreed-upon sum from the EC budget to cover the difference. It has been estimated that the system contributes to 50 percent of the price fluctuations for wheat worldwide.

Producer assistance programs like the CAP are not only barriers to the liberalization of trade, they are also expensive. Stockpiling and transportation costs for surplus wheat cost the Community a thousand francs per tonne, and it is the same story for powdered milk, beef, and butter. This policy has also favored the most productive farmers, basically the bigger ones who have boosted productivity standards. It is a vicious circle: the more they produce, the more they earn, consequently the greater the cost to the EC and the less money there is left for that part of the budget designed to improve the lot of smaller farmers.

U.S. criticism of the policy of guaranteed prices practiced in Europe—justified under the Carter administration—would carry more weight if the United States did not also heavily subsidize and protect its own agriculture in ways more subtle than exportation aids (e.g., the Farm Bill and the Trade Act). As one critic has pointed out, EC aid to its farmers—four times the number of their American counterparts on one fourth the land!—is lower than or equivalent to the total amount of U.S. farm subsidies.[8]

---

8. Jacques Mallet, "L'Europe, ni forteresse ni terrain vague," *Le Monde*, 7 December 1988.

Community Preference

Community preference, which requires European countries to buy agricultural products from EC partners rather than from outside the Community, even if they can be bought cheaper on world markets, has also come under U.S. fire. The scheme involves taxing imported goods so heavily that it is cheaper for the EC buyer to purchase in Europe. Import duties are not based on the price in the country of origin but on the price (usually higher) of the product in question in the EC. This is sheer protectionism with blatant disregard for GATT regulations and has led to conflict not only with the United States but also with Canada, Australia, and New Zealand. In the Europeans' defense it should be mentioned that they impose no tariffs on feed grain products—corn gluten feed, soya, manioc—which the Americans export in huge quantities. Imports of these have increased at such an alarming rate that the EC, while being the top world exporter of agricultural products, is the second importer and has in fact a deficit in this area with the United States. There were epic battles with the United States in the 1980s over chickens, cereals, and beef, as the United States has tried to defend its farmers against Europrotectionism in a period of worrisome budget deficits. These battles have generally ended in European compromise following U.S. retaliatory measures such as the 200 percent tax Ronald Reagan threatened to slap on imports of everything from brandy to Gouda cheese in 1987.

Things came to a head in December 1990, when the GATT talks in Paris for the Uruguay Round balked on the agricultural question after four years of discussion that were far from fruitless. Although the EC made some important concessions such as imposing ceilings on the runaway subsidies (prices continued to be guaranteed but were limited by production quotas), the Europeans refused to abandon their double pricing system. Then, in 1992, the European nations decided to undertake a major reform of the CAP system, notably by phasing out over three years the system of guaranteed prices that has been the main bone of contention. If they thought this move, which provoked the anger of European farmers, would satisfy the United States, they were wrong. A short time after at the GATT talks in Geneva, the United States threatened to double the import taxes on European products if the EC did not immediately reduce aid to its soya producers. This was deemed particularly unfair at a

FIG. 27. Hopes for a break in GATT talks stalemate between Europe and the United States. (*Le Monde*, 7 December 1990. Copyright © Plantu 1990.)

time when Europe had made a major concession. Moreover, EC aid to soya farmers had in no way affected imports from other parts of the world, though countries such as Argentina and Brazil were now competing with the U.S. for market share. Apparently the United States is not very happy with the CAP reform, which, by cutting cereal prices in Europe by 29 percent, will actually make European agriculture more competitive on the home market, thus reducing imports from the Midwest. Rather than abolition of the guaranteed prices system, the United States would have preferred the Europeans to put quotas on production, which would leave market share for U.S. exporters.[9]

In a particularly virulent editorial, *Le Monde* stated:

> It is the proud America, the one that was victorious a little over a year ago in the sands of the desert, that is asking for its due: to be admired as the power of all powers entitled to depart from respect for the common rules. After the Gulf War, the United States called for a new world order, and the impression was that it would be wrapped in the stars and stripes. And here's Europe, in spite of its internal groping, becoming more united [*solide*], with greater political, monetary, commercial, and even military cohesion. . . . Cross-Atlantic

9. Philippe Lemaitre, "Les risques d'une stratégie d'affrontement," *Le Monde*, 12 June 1992.

> disputes are getting worse. European preference is appearing in the field of telecommunications and of public procurement, the equivalent of the Buy American Act. . . . that has been in use for a long time in the United States. Steel remains a thorny problem. The monetary union is a threat to the supremacy of the dollar, and the French-German defense corps has Pentagon strategists gnashing their teeth. . . . After putting a war-worn Europe back on its feet with the help of the Marshall Plan, the United States cannot resign itself to seeing a power that it fostered rising up against it.[10]

Industry and High Tech: Fortress or Drafty House?

The EC has 6 percent of the world's population and produces a quarter of the earth's wealth. With its 340 million inhabitants, it is the largest market in the world today and possesses great resources of human intelligence. It handles more than one-third of international trade, to which it has given a formidable boost. Japan apart, it is the principal supplier and export target for most countries in the world. For the sake of comparison, it is worth remembering that 13.5 percent of EC demand for industrial goods is satisfied by imports. The U.S. figure is 12.3 percent and the Japanese 4.8 percent. Incidentally, France is one of the most "open" countries in Europe. Imports cover 31 percent of its needs for industrial goods. Hence the theme of "fortress Europe" that the media in other continents have so well exploited gives a false picture of the situation.[11] Industrially, Europe is still a featherweight compared to Japan and the United States. Although Europe is strong in some key sectors—aircraft building, aerospace, nuclear energy, mass transportation equipment, telecommunications—only nineteen EC firms figure among the world's top fifty for turnover, and only three are French. While the EC computer industry has now a larger share of the European market—50 percent compared to one-third in the early 1980s—the industry is particularly vulnerable. The EC countries have to import 65 percent of the integrated circuits they use, and European firms are increasingly signing

10. Editorial, *Le Monde,* 12 June 1992.

11. According to Jean-Louis Levet, the visible quotas used by the French give the country an image of protectionism that it does not merit. Other countries, in particular the United States, use more subtle and less quantifiable types of protectionism. See *Une France sans complexes,* 82.

alliances with U.S. and Japanese corporations. Even in telecommunications the EC countries, with 6 percent of the global market share, are dwarfed by Japan (37 percent) and the United States (11 percent). If the German Bundesposte, British Telecom, and French Télécom rank respectively third, fourth, and fifth internationally, the variety of national interests is an obstacle to a united European front. Likewise, the European auto industry is divided on the strategy to be adopted toward the Japanese. Europeans also view the increasing number of bilateral agreements between the United States and Japan as a threat to European competitiveness. Finally, many firms are involved in sunset (declining) industries incapable of competing with those in newly industrialized countries, where costs are lower. France is particularly weak industrially as the country manufactures a bit of everything and imports too much of everything.

U.S. worries about European technological and business clout are based more on the potential danger a United States of Europe might represent than on the real situation today. Many psychological and political barriers will have to be removed before this happens. Nonetheless, in several high-tech areas—civil aviation, aerospace, telecommunications—Europe is moving into what used to be an American hunting ground. The Ariane space program, after a difficult start, now controls a large share of the world market for satellite launches, and Airbus, the computerized European aircraft, while hardly a threat to Boeing's supremacy, has grabbed some of the U.S. corporation's market share. One of the prime objectives of the many joint EC research programs is to break Europe's dependency on Japan and the United States for the electronic components they need to develop computers and consumer electronics. In some areas the Old World has caught up with the New; in a few fields, including high-definition television, it had a head start. Encouraging as this is overall, performance is patchy, and no one can tell what the future holds. Lacking the cohesiveness of the Japanese industrial structure and the entrepreneurial drive and power of corporate America, can a twelve-nation Europe challenge the supremacy of its two major rivals in global markets?

Ariane

Some NASA officials sneered at early attempts by Aerospace, the European consortium, to get its space program off the ground in the early

1980s, when Ariane rockets were dogged with technical problems. Ariane was a French initiative before becoming European in 1980, when Aerospace, composed of thirty-six major European industrial groups and thirteen banks, was set up. The launching site is in Kouru in French Guiana. The very successful commercial program has enabled the thirteen-nation consortium (not all are members of the EC) to grab 50 percent of the world market for satellite launching.

The next generation of Ariane 5 rockets will be capable of putting astronauts into space by 1995, and the Europeans are going ahead with Columbus, a manned module that is to be used for scientific experiments in space. This will be hooked up to the future American space station. Nevertheless, there are now talks of abandoning Hermès, the European shuttle that was to be operational by 1998.

The French like to think of Ariane as their own, and the Aérospatiale plant in Toulouse has become one of their showcases. The success of the space program is all the more remarkable since it has been achieved with a budget of eleven billion francs—less than one-sixth of NASA's.

Airbus

Airbus Industrie is also situated in Toulouse, the high-tech city of the southwest sun belt. In 1970, a European consortium associating France, Germany, Britain, and Spain—not then an EC member—was formed to produce medium-range aircraft, the A-300 and the A-310. These compete with the Boeing 737, and there were mild protests from the American corporation about unfair competition as the consortium was receiving government funding. Nevertheless, in 1979 the Civil Aircraft Agreement was signed by both the Europeans and the Americans. Both sides were delighted with this arrangement, the consortium because the United States abolished its 8 percent import duty on foreign planes, and the Americans because of articles 4 and 6 in the GATT agreement, which made it illegal to "blackmail" clients by proposing sales of weaponry, flying rights, or industrial subsidies as an incentive to purchase, and it forbade the sale of aircraft below cost—a range of tactics the U.S. suspected the Europeans were using. In the early 1980s Airbus Industrie was not selling many planes; then, in 1983, the Europeans launched the sleek-bodied, fly-by-wire A-320. This sophisticated, medium-range aircraft with a capacity of 150 passengers, which competes with the Boeing 737 and the Boeing 757, was an immediate success. "It is the first computerized plane in the world in which every gesture of the pilot is checked by some 120 calculators before being executed in the best possible way. The aircraft is constantly maintained in ideal flying conditions."[12]

By 1986, more than four hundred A-320s were on order worldwide. The consortium turned down McDonnel-Douglas's proposal to collaborate in the production of the MD-11 and announced its intention of producing the A-330 and A-340, which would compete directly with that model and with the Boeing 747 and 767 models. U.S. retaliation was direct and clumsy, but at the GATT meeting in Geneva they were unable to prove that the European practices were causing a prejudice to their aircraft builders. Envoys were then sent from Washington and met with a very cool reception. This overreaction actually stirred up what was perhaps the first demonstration of "Europatriotism." The Americans had slighted one of the proudest symbols of European prestige and cooperation.

U.S. behavior in this matter was considered unfair. After all Boeing and McDonnel-Douglas dominated the world aircraft market, and the Americans had sold far more planes to European companies than vice versa. In addition, American parts account for 30 percent of the value of Airbus, and the European consortium provides work for hundreds of subcontractors in the United States. Even the knotty problem of government funding for Airbus—in fact a repayable loan—which supposedly allows the Europeans to cut prices, is matched by the huge NASA and military contracts, to the tune of $20 billion, that enable Boeing to finance research and development.[13] In July 1992 a European-American agreement was finally signed in Washington that (hopefully) puts an end to the trans-Atlantic feud after tweny years of haggling. The Europeans agreed to limit the repayable loans they have been advancing to Airbus Industrie. These loans, which formerly covered 75 percent of the development costs, will henceforth be limited to 25 percent. Meanwhile, the United States is committed to limiting its indirect subsidies to U.S. aircraft builders in the form of research or space and military programs. This means a ceiling of 3 percent of the turnover in the aircraft sector and a ceiling of 4 percent on the turnover of aircraft builders.

One of the criticisms aimed at Airbus is that it may be too sophis-

---

12. Alain Faujas, "Le petit Airbus qui fait peur aux américains," *Le Monde*, 15 February 1988.

13. Alain Faujas, "Europe 1—Etats-Unis 0," *Le Monde*, 31 March 1987.

ticated for pilots to fly. Following the tragic crash of an A-320 near Strasbourg in 1991, the third Airbus accident, engineers have made a number of modifications to reduce the risk of human error that has apparently been responsible for all the accidents so far.

U.S. fears of competition from the European plane have proved to be justified to a certain extent: Airbus has shown itself to be a serious competitor. Five years ago the consortium had five times less orders than Boeing. In 1989, they received half as many as their rival with a total of 405 planes ordered. The A-320 is still the best seller followed by the A-330, yet to be built. In 1991 Airbus Industrie doubled its profits and has started to repay part of the loans it obtained from the European governments. The CEO of the consortium recently declared that the governments would no longer be giving subsidies but receiving royalties. In 1992 United Airlines's order of fifty Airbus planes was a shock for U.S. aircraft builders. In February 1993 the first Airbus A-321 rolled off the assembly line of the Airbus plant in Germany. This larger version of the A-320 is a direct competitor of the Boeing 757. It is financed entirely by Airbus Industries. Boeing, with 60 percent of the market in civil aircraft, is still the world leader. Airbus (15 to 20 percent) and McDonnel-Douglas share the rest.

Telecommunications

The world market in telecommunications has been estimated at 500 billion ECU, and the industry, with an annual growth rate of 7 percent, is, together with computers, one of the hottest sectors in world trade. In Europe, competing national economies and competing national corporations means that eight different digital switching systems have been developed! In Japan there are two and in the United States three. This handicaps a united commercial drive using a single standard. Aware that they must get their act together, the EC countries took a bold historical step in 1990 by opening national monopolies—utilities, autos, air transport, and telecommunications—to deregulation. But, as Eric Le Boucher points out,

> In telecommunications, the liberalization movement has not been accompanied by any genuine offensive by European P&T to set up swiftly an efficient trans-European telecommunication and data-processing network using a universal standard. Cooperation is limited

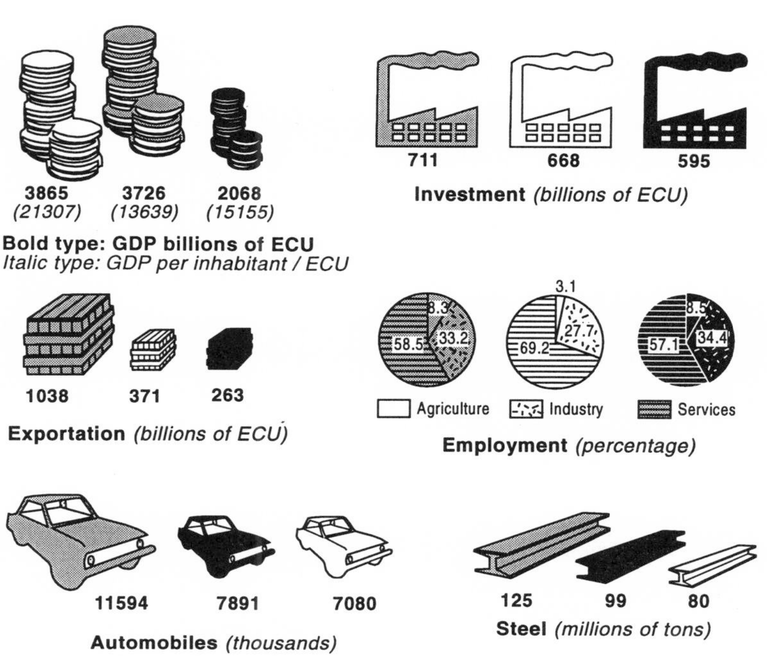

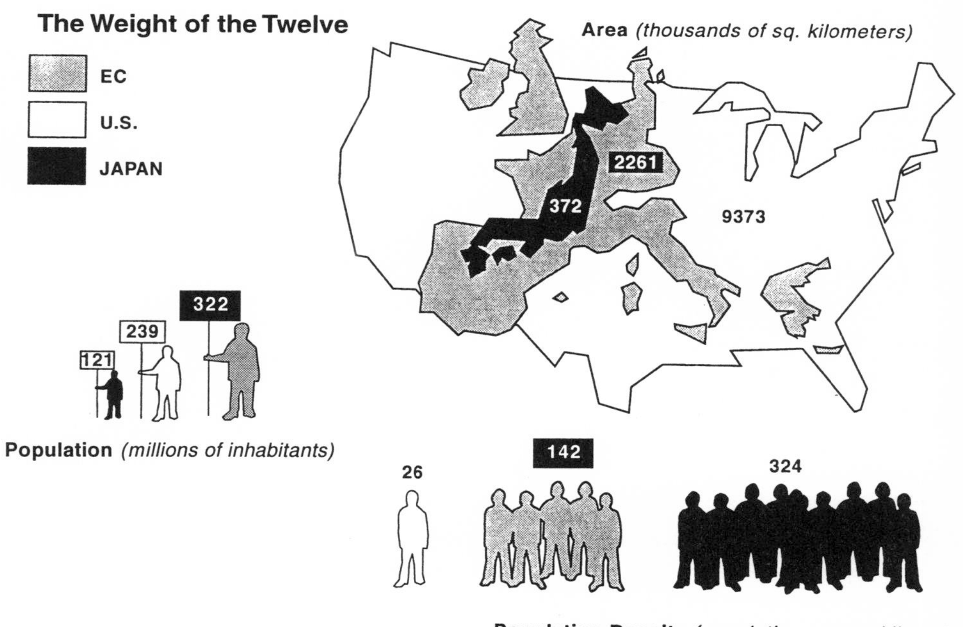

FIG. 28. Japan, the United States, and Europe. (From *Le Monde: Bilan Economique et Social 1988*. Copyright © The New York Times Syndication Sales Corporation.)

> to a few French-German linkups, whereas consumers, instead of some price cuts, badly need such a service covering the twelve member countries. Will we have to wait till the Japanese and the Americans set one up?[14]

Yet that France with its long tradition of protectionism should have decided to vote this directive, limited as it is—the mention of Community preference is designed to curb the penetration of IBM and ATT and certain exceptions for national monopolies have been written into the contract—is a sign of the evolution that has taken place in the mentality of the French with regard to free competition.

HDTV

The former French premier, Rocard, has estimated the global market for high-definition television (HDTV) to be worth $400 billion, and Ariane is launching several direct broadcasting satellites that already allow Europeans to switch on to a myriad of channels from other countries. The standard for broadband transmission, developed in Europe, that goes by the barbarous name of D 2 MAC has the capacity for the more than one thousand lines the television of tomorrow requires. The Japanese, who have developed their own standard, and the Europeans both have their sights set on the U.S. market. The big advantage of the system developed by the latter is that it is progressive: it can be adapted to existing TV receivers. The French corporation, Thompson, has mass produced a transitional version of HDTV that was put on the market in 1990 and is leading the world race to produce a high-definition camera capable of recording more than one thousand lines per frame. The United States, which both the Japanese and the Europeans thought was out of the race for HDTV, created a surprise in 1991 when it revealed that it was working on an even more sophisticated digital system (the EC system uses analog pictures) for high-definition television. Nevertheless, the Europeans believe that while digital pictures are the future—they have been working on the subject for years—digital HDTV will not be available to the general public before a decade. As it is necessary to sell televisions

14. Eric le Boucher, "Trois concessions à l'Europe," *Le Monde*, 15 December 1989.

in the meantime, they have no intention of renouncing the European standard, D 2 MAC.[15]

TV Programs

According to the Institute for Audiovisual and Telecommunications Development, Europe has a deficit of $1.8 billion with the United States in the field of audiovisual production, that is, movies, video, and television.[16] This is not because European viewers prefer American films and shows but rather because there is no real European industry able to cater to the different national tastes: sports in Italy and Germany, films in France, and serials in England. A 1989 poll showed that in each of the countries surveyed national television productions got higher ratings than imported ones.[17] Nevertheless, in this area supply determines demand and pan-European programs being in short supply and expensive to produce, it is tempting for channel directors to buy American.

The 1989 EC directive dubbed Television without Frontiers, designed to set up an audiovisual common market in television, videos, and movies, provoked the typical U.S. rhetoric: "A government has no right to filter what TV viewers want," declared Jack Valenti, president of the American Motion Picture Association,[18] and Bert Cohen, vice president of Worldvision said, "Setting up a quota is a form of censorship."[19] The French, at that time, were among the most vehement in demanding a restriction of imported television programs.

While there is some justification for the U.S. reaction, the fact is that the United States sees any attempt by the Europeans in any area as hurting its economy and, with their hard-nosed business approach, Americans fail to understand the cultural implications. They see Community preference as anti-American, whereas it is merely meant to allow

15. Jean-François Lacan, "La stratégie européenne pour la télévision haute définition devrait être réorientée," *Le Monde,* 12 February 1991.

16. Michel Colonna d'Istria, "Les échanges entre l'Europe et les Etats-Unis," *Le Monde,* 12 October 1989.

17. See *Lettre européenne des programmes,* no. 25, October 1989.

18. Annick Cojean, "Les Etats-Unis accentuent leur pression sur l'audio-visuel européen," *Le Monde,* 11 November 1989. Translated from the French by the author.

19. Annick Cojean, "Un entretien avec le principal distributeur américain," *Le Monde,* 12 October 1989.

the EC countries to build up a viable audiovisual industry emphasizing European music, theater, life-styles, and values. In addition, as Jacques Lang, the former French minister of culural affairs, has pointed out, U.S. television shows less than 5 percent of Europe's productions. Dubbing and subtitles being excluded, the American market remains very closed to foreign movies and shows. It is impossible for national producers in the EC to achieve the economies of scale that make the imported programs cheaper. A large part of the cost of producing a program in the United States is offset by the sheer size of the home market audience and the volume of advertising revenues. Thus these products can be sold in Europe at a price far below their real cost. However, with rising production costs in the United States and smaller audiences owing to the increased number of channels, American producers are now trying to develop coproductions with the Europeans to cut down on costs.[20]

Coproductions could be a solution for all, but prejudices are not easy to remove, as the International Market for Television Programs in Cannes in April 1989 showed: "A lot of Euro-American coproductions have failed," said one American, "because European producers did not listen to us, did not understand our needs." He added: "They don't know what we want nor how to work with us." Mel Harris, the president of Paramount Television, suggested that European directors should go to the United States to learn their job, and, he quipped, "to teach the wolf in Little Red Riding Hood to gobble up grandmother before the break for the commercial." The comment of the French reporters in *Le Monde* was "America is ready to set up production elsewhere but only if it can keep the structure, the style, the rhythm, and, of course, the language."[21]

The EC has backed down on mandatory quotas, for which the French clamored, but has recommended higher levels of European programming on television channels. If the EC countries are to build a real audiovisual common market and competitively sell their programs in other parts of the world, they will first have to solve a number of internal difficulties such as the thorny question of cooperation between public and private stations and crossborder advertising. With the leap from the present

---

20. Yves Mamou, "A la télévision la qualité ne paie pas," *Le Monde*, 17 April 1992.

21. Annick Cojean and Pierre-Angel Gay, "Américains et Européens rivalisent de protectionnisme," *Le Monde*, 25 April 1989. Translated from the French by the author.

250,000 hours of programming in Europe to 400,000–450,000 hours in the foreseeable future, and with the challenge of HDTV, the EC countries want to be sure that they will have their say in the television of tomorrow. It is easy to be critical of their muddling, which amuses their single-minded competitors, but business considerations, however important, cannot be the only criteria when a decision has to be taken by twelve different nationalities on a subject with such far-reaching cultural implications as the media.

Friction with the United States sometimes hides the extent of cooperation between the Old World and the New; the political rhetoric is designed mainly for home consumption in Europe or America. For instance, in 1989, Richard Ullman, professor of international relations at Princeton University, revealed one of the best-kept military secrets when he announced that the United States and France had been exchanging information on nuclear arms technology for nearly twenty years although France had quit NATO in 1966. More recently, in the Persian Gulf crisis the French gave the U.S. confidential information about the sophisticated weaponry it had delivered to Iraq before Saddam Hussein revealed the real nature of his ambitions. By its engagement in the Desert Storm operation France proved that it was a staunch ally of the United States.

In the commercial field neither continent has any interest in reinforcing protectionism because each needs the other's market for its continued prosperity. The same goes for Japan. As Jean Monnet said: "To resolve a difficulty the first thing to do is to draw up a general appraisal of the situation on a piece of paper. Then it is necessary to get men to work together. Have them sit around a table to discuss the problem. Show them that over and above their disagreements or across national boundaries they have a common interest."[22]

Conclusion

The destiny of France is henceforth inexorably linked to that of Europe (was it ever otherwise?). The physical frontiers of the hexagon the country battled for centuries to establish and consolidate have been thrown wide open to yesterday's enemies, but the hordes who invade France nowadays are armed with briefcases. The peaceful coexistence of Western

22. Quoted in *Jean Monnet: Père de l'Europe* (Paris: Association des amis de Jean Monnet).

European countries for less than half a century has sufficed to wipe out a thousand years of hostility. The shrinking of time and space made possible by modern telecommunication and high-speed communication networks has reduced the old continent to a Eurovillage. Businessmen, vacationers, researchers, journalists, students, and senior citizens feel "at home" in any of the twelve countries because over and beyond the difference of language each country shares something of the others in the nature of its rural and urban landscapes and the quality of life. France, in this respect, is a microcosm of Europe.

One of the strongest symbols of frontierless Europe today is Eurorail, which makes cheap cross-border travel available to youngsters for whom the continent has become a second homeland:

> These young Europeans are closer to each other than their parents or their grandparents were. They were born in a Europe where not war but rather community is the subject of conversation; they have forged their own links across national boundaries by chance vacation encounters, pen pals, and study-abroad language programs. These close relations seem natural to them. Their open attitude to the old continent shows that they are highly sensitive to what European regions and life-styles have in common.[23]

The statistics there are prove the existence of the Euro-movement. More than 50 percent of French foreign trade is with its European partners; four out of ten foreigners living in France are from the neighboring countries, and 46 percent of the French abroad reside in Europe. Moreover, 4.5 of the 6 million French vacationers who go abroad annually spend their vacations in Europe.[24]

The EC has been a powerful incentive to change in France, the spoiled child of mother nature, which has often in the past been tempted to withdraw behind the protective borders of the hexagon to cultivate its own garden. But the France of Renaud's song that "has not changed from all eternity" cannot halt the Euro-movement, nourished on "centuries of cross-fertilized culture and history." The Europeans have rediscovered their common heritage and the shared ideals that gave birth to Gothic cathedrals, Renaissance castles, humanism, the Enlightenment,

23. Pumain, Saint-Julien, and Ferras, *France-Europe du sud*, 48.
24. Frémont, *France*, 239.

and the Rights of Man, a concept of democracy that knows no frontiers. These are the real riches of Europe to which France has made an important contribution. In turn it has benefited from its proximity to the European breeding ground of scientific and technological innovation that today as in the past runs from the North Sea to the plain of the river Po in northern Italy, "the old Europe of merchants and navigators."[25]

25. Frémont, *France,* 239.

Appendix: Landmarks in the Construction of Europe

1951 Signing of the Treaty of Paris establishing the European Coal and Steel Community (ECSC).

The origin of the European Community (EC), with its twelve present member countries, was the plan proposed by the French foreign minister, Robert Schuman, for setting up a common European authority to regulate coal and steel production. The raison d'être of this project, conceived by Jean Monnet, was to prevent further bloodshed in Europe. France had endured three German invasions in the space of seventy-five years, and the powerful German steel industry had been almost entirely devoted to the production of weapons. The cold war that developed between the United States and the Soviet Union following World War II required the rearming of Germany, to which France was understandably opposed. The founders of the ECSC saw it as a first step to setting up a federated Europe they deemed essential for the preservation of peace. Six countries—Germany, France, Italy, Holland, Belgium and Luxembourg—signed the Treaty of Paris. The members pledged to cooperate in the building of a European steel and coal industry in lieu of the competing national enterprises. This economic pact was meant to dissipate the fear of an industrially powerful Germany, which had caused so much bloodshed in the recent past.

The ECSC made a major contribution to European unity, even if the declining industries of steel and coal created new problems. Trade between the member countries developed, and the organization helped regulate their economic growth. The ECSC borrowed capital in the United States and Switzerland and was thus in a position to grant loans for the modernization of industry. By producing steel and mining coal Europe saved precious dollars on the purchase of U.S. steel and coal, but costs of production were higher, and energy was often more expensive. However, the successful restructuring of the European steel industry following the 1973 oil crisis was one of the ECSC's major achievements, and the social measures that accompanied the shutdowns were often exemplary. The ECSC paid half the retraining costs of laid-off workers and granted subsidies to the regions hit by the crisis, thus funding more than 100,000 new jobs. It also introduced substantial long-term unemployment benefits and guaranteed the salaries of workers willing to change jobs. Without the ECSC things would have been far worse, particularly in France.

1957 Signing in Rome of treaties establishing the European Economic Community (EC) and the European Atomic Energy Community (EAEC), designed to develop peaceful use of nuclear power in Europe.

Encouraged by the success of the ECSC, the six member countries decided to extend their cooperation. The aims of the EC were to facilitate the free movement of goods and people within Europe and ultimately to abolish national borders. To this effect, a progressive lowering of import duties between member countries was initiated in 1958, and these tariffs disappeared entirely ten years later.

The 1960s were marked by the birth of "green Europe" and the Common Agricultural Policy, General de Gaulle's adamant rejection of Britain's application for membership, and his refusal to accept independent European parliamentary control of EC expenditure. De Gaulle did not share Jean Monnet's views on political integration and was bitterly opposed to any form of supranational structure. For the same reason, France, while remaining a member of NATO, was to quit the organization's unified military command in 1964, close down all NATO facilities in France, and develop the independent French nuclear *force de frappe.*

1973 Accession of Ireland, Denmark, and the United Kingdom to the EC.

1979 The European monetary system (EMS) comes into operation.

The world recession and the monetary instability of the 1970s hit the EC badly. "The EMS is designed to bring convergence between the economic performance of the member states and cooperation between monetary authorities; exchange rate stability is ensured through the exchange rate mechanism (ERM). Currencies are prevented from diverging from one another by an agreed percentage. This is ensured by coordinated market intervention." The ERM has contributed to reduce inflation by forcing countries to limit price increases so as to avoid devaluation of their currency. For instance, in 1991 the gap between the inflation rate in West Germany and France had never been so narrow. Britain's decision to join the EMS in October 1990 paves the way for a common European currency.

If a united Europe is to become a genuine economic power, a common European currency is essential. The ECU (European currency unit), which is the weighted value of the various EC currencies, is designed to fulfill this role sooner or later. (Loans are increasingly based on the ECU, and companies use it as an alternative hedge for interest and exchange rates.) If the EC goes ahead with plans for closer monetary union, the trade surplus of the EC would automatically make the ECU a reserve currency and possibly end the reign of the dollar as well as the speculative operations on national currencies that are a threat to European unity. It should also help to harmonize interest rates and facilitate the circulation of capital within the Community.

1979 First direct elections to the European Parliament.

1981 Greece accedes to the EC.

1984 Second direct elections to the European Parliament.

1985 Commitment to the Single Act.

1986 Portugal and Spain accede to the EC.

1989 Third direct elections to the European Parliament.

The 1980s brought a new vitality to the EC. Margaret Thatcher's incessant haggling over the amount of Britain's contribution to the Community budget had the salutary effect of forcing the other members to take a hard look at the ruinous Common Agricultural Policy, while the Single Act gave a fresh impetus to European cooperation. This stipulated the conditions necessary to create an entirely free market: removal of physical, technical, and legal barriers to the free movement of goods and people; reduction of fiscal disparities together with approximation of value added tax rates; freedom of people to work where they like, "mutual recognition of qualifications and the right of establishment and residence; removal of discriminatory and protective national public procurement and supply policies; freeing of all capital movements within the community."

1992 The EC undertakes a major reform of the CAP. The system of guaranteed prices is to be phased out by 1995. Politically, the major event is the ratification by the member countries of the Maastricht treaty, designed in its own words "to create an even closer union among the peoples of Europe." The treaty sets out a series of goals for economic, monetary, political, and social union. It also proposes to give greater power to the European Parliament. If ratified, the treaty would involve an eventual move towards a European central bank and a single European currency. It sets procedures for joint action by European states in foreign policy and envisages the adoption of a common EC defense policy.

1993 With the final ratification of the Maastricht treaty, the European Community becomes the European Union.

The brochure *Europe at a Glance,* produced by the UK Offices of the Commission of the European Communities and the European Parliament, provides an excellent introduction to the EC. The quotations are from this brochure.

Index

Principal page references are in **bold** type. Pages that refer to figures are in italics. References to foreign countries and cities emphasize similarities with and/or differences from developments in France. French cities are indexed under Towns, French regions under Regions, and French corporations under Corporations. Writers, researchers, and journalists quoted in the footnotes are not indexed.